Master Dogen's

Shobogenzo

Gudo Nishijima was born in Yokohama, Japan in November 1919, and graduated from the Law Department of Tokyo University in September 1946.

In October 1940 he first met Master Kodo Sawaki, whose teaching he received until Master Kodo's death in December 1965. During this time, he combined the daily practice of Zazen and study of Shobogenzo with a career at the Japanese Ministry of Finance and at a securities financing company. In December 1973 he became a priest under the late Master Renpo Niwa, and in December 1977 he received the transmission of Dharma from the same Master (who subsequently became the abbot of Eihei-ji temple). Shortly thereafter he became a consultant to the Ida Ryogokudo company, and in 1987 established the Ida Ryogokudo Zazen Dojo in Ichikawa City near Tokyo. Now in his seventies, he continues to give instruction in Zazen, and lectures on Master Dogen's works, in Japanese and in English, at various locations in Tokyo and Osaka and at Tokei-in temple in Shizuoka prefecture.

Gudo Nishijima's other publications in English include "How to Practice Zazen" (with Joe Langdon) and "To Meet the Real Dragon" (with Jeffrey Bailey). He has recently published a Japanese translation of Master Nāgārjuna's Mūlamadhyamakakārikā, and is presently at work on an English translation.

Chodo Cross was born in Birmingham, England, in December 1959. He went to Japan in January 1982, following graduation from Sheffield University, met Nishijima Roshi in June 1982, and received the Buddhist precepts in May of the following year. In December 1994 he returned to England in order to train to be a teacher of the F. M. Alexander Technique. In September 1998, having ceased work on the present translation and qualified as an Alexander teacher, he received the transmission of Dharma from Nishijima Roshi. He is currently leading a small group of Alexander colleagues in Zazen practice and welcomes inquiries from anyone interested in participating in Zazen retreats in England.

Master Dogen's

Shobogenzo

Book 4

Translated

by

Gudo Wafu Nishijima

Chodo Cross

Windbell
PUBLICATIONS

Windbell Publications Ltd.
London

4-505 Kamishakujii 3-19
Nerima-ku
Tokyo 177-0044, Japan

Distributed in Europe by Wisdom Books,
402 Hoe Street, London E17 9AA
Tel: 0181-520-5588. Fax: 0181-520-0932

Distributed in the USA by Windbell Publications,
PO Box 578, Woods Hole, MA 02543-0578

Printed and bound by Biddles Limited,
Guildford, Surrey.

ISBN 0 9523002 4 9

Contents

Acknowledgments

This translation and its publication have been made possible by the benevolence of the following sponsors:

The Japan Foundation

Mr. Hideo Ida, President of Ida Ryogokudo Co., Ltd.

Mr. Tadashi Nakamae,
President of Nakamae International Economic Research

We should like to thank Michael Luetchford and Jeremy Pearson for their efforts in publishing this book. Our thanks also go to Yoko Luetchford for her work on checking the kanji, and to Emma Gibson for her invaluable help with proofreading.

Preface

Shobogenzo was written by Master Dogen in the thirteenth century. I think that reading Shobogenzo is the best way to come to an exact understanding of Buddhist theory, because Master Dogen was outstanding in his ability to understand and explain Buddhism rationally.

Of course, Master Dogen did not depart from traditional Buddhist thought. But at the same time, his thought as expressed in Shobogenzo follows his own unique method of presentation. If we understand what this method is, Shobogenzo is not so difficult to read. But unless we understand his method of thinking, it is completely impossible for us to understand what Master Dogen is trying to say in Shobogenzo.

Buddhists revere Buddha, Dharma and Samgha. Buddha means Gautama Buddha. Samgha means those people who pursue Gautama Buddha's truth. Dharma means reality. Master Dogen's unique method of thought is his way to explain what Dharma is.

Basically, he looks at a problem from two sides, and then tries to synthesize the two viewpoints into a middle way. This method has similarities with dialectic method in western philosophy, particularly as used by Hegel and Marx.

Hegel's dialectic, however, is based on belief in spirit, and Marx's dialectic is based on belief in matter. Master Dogen, through the Buddhist dialectic, wants to lead us away from thoughts based on belief in spirit and matter.

Master Dogen recognized the existence of something which is different from thought; that is, reality in action. Action is completely different from intellectual thought and completely different from the perceptions of our senses. So Master Dogen's method of thinking is based on action, and because of that, it has some unique characteristics.

First, Master Dogen recognized that things we usually separate in our minds are, in action, one reality. To express this oneness of subject and object Master Dogen says, for example, *"If a human being, even for a single moment, manifests the Buddha's posture in the three forms of conduct, while [that person] sits up straight in samādhi, the entire world of Dharma assumes the Buddha's posture and the whole of space becomes the state of realization."* This sentence, taken from the chapter *Bendowa,* is not illogical, but it reflects a new kind of logic.

Secondly, Master Dogen recognized that in action, the only time that really exists is the moment of the present, and the only place that really exists is this place. So the present moment and this place—the here and now—are very important concepts in Master Dogen's philosophy of action.

The philosophy of action is not unique to Master Dogen; this idea was also the center of Gautama Buddha's thought. All the Buddhist patriarchs of ancient India and China relied upon this theory and realized Buddhism itself. They also recognized the oneness of reality, the importance of the present moment, and the importance of this place.

But explanations of reality are only explanations. In Shobogenzo, after he had explained a problem on the basis of action, Master Dogen wanted to point the reader into the realm of action itself. To do this, he sometimes used poems, he sometimes used old Buddhist stories that suggest reality, and he sometimes used symbolic expressions.

So the chapters of Shobogenzo usually follow a four-phased pattern. First Master Dogen picks up and outlines a Buddhist idea. In the second phase, he examines the idea very objectively or concretely, in order to defeat idealistic or intellectual interpretations of it. In the third phase, Master Dogen's expression becomes even more concrete, practical and realistic, relying on the philosophy of action. And in the fourth phase, Master Dogen tries to suggest reality with words. Ultimately, these trials are only trials. But we can feel something that can be called reality in his sincere trials, when we reach the end of each chapter.

I think this four-phased pattern is related with the *Four Noble Truths* preached by Gautama Buddha in his first lecture. By realizing Master Dogen's method of thinking, we can come to realize the true meaning of Gautama Buddha's *Four Noble Truths.* This is why we persevere in studying Shobogenzo.

Gudo Wafu Nishijima

Ida Zazen Dojo
Tokyo
February 1994

Notes on the Translation

Aim

In this book, as in Books 1, 2, and 3, the primary aim of the translation has been to stay faithful to the original Japanese text and let Master Dogen speak for himself, confining interpretation and explanation as far as possible to the footnotes.

Source text

The source text for chapters 73 to 95 is contained in volumes 10 to 12 of Nishijima Roshi's 12-volume *Gendaigo-yaku-shobogenzo (Shobogenzo in Modern Japanese). Gendaigo-yaku-shobogenzo* contains Master Dogen's original text, notes on the text, and the text rendered into modern Japanese. Reference numbers enclosed in brackets in the left margin of this translation refer to corresponding page numbers in *Gendaigo-yaku-shobogenzo,* and much of the material reproduced in the footnotes comes from *Gendaigo-yaku-shobogenzo.*

Gendaigo-yaku-shobogenzo is based upon the 95-chapter edition of Shobogenzo, which was arranged in chronological order by Master Hangyo Kozen, sometime between 1688 and 1703. The 95-chapter edition is the most comprehensive single edition, including important chapters such as *Bendowa* and *Hokke-ten-hokke* which do not appear in other editions. Furthermore, it was the first edition to be printed with woodblocks, in the Bunka era (1804–1818), and so the content was fixed at that time. The original woodblocks are still preserved at Eihei-ji, the temple in Fukui prefecture which Master Dogen founded.

Sanskrit terms

As a rule, Sanskrit words such as *samādhi* (the balanced state), *prajñā* (real wisdom), and *bhikṣu* (monk), which Master Dogen reproduces phonetically with Chinese characters, 三昧 (ZANMAI), 般若 (HANNYA), and 比丘 (BIKU), have been retained in Sanskrit form.

In addition, some Chinese characters representing the meaning of Sanskrit terms which will already be familiar to readers (or which will become familiar in the course of reading Shobogenzo) have been returned to Sanskrit. Examples are 法 (HO; "reality," "law," "method," "things and phenomena"), usually translated as "Dharma" or "dharmas"; 如来 (NYORAI; "Thus-Come"), always translated as *"Tathāgata"*; and 声聞 (SHOMON; "voice-hearer"), usually translated as *"śrāvaka."*

The glossary provided in the appendix contains the Sanskrit terms appearing in this book not included in the Sanskrit glossaries in Books 1, 2 and 3.

Chinese proper nouns

In general Chinese proper nouns have been romanized according to their Japanese pronunciation—as Master Dogen would have pronounced them for a Japanese audience. Thus, we have let the romanization of all names of Chinese masters follow the Japanese pronunciation, while also adding an appendix showing the Chinese romanization of Chinese masters' names.

Chinese text

Master Dogen wrote Shobogenzo in Japanese, that is to say, using a combination of Chinese characters (squared ideograms usually consisting of many strokes) and the Japanese phonetic alphabet which is more abbreviated. Chinese of course is written in Chinese characters only. Therefore when Master Dogen quotes a passage, or borrows a phrase, from a Chinese text—as he very often does—it is readily apparent to the eye as a string of Chinese ideograms uninterrupted by Japanese squiggles. We have attempted to mirror this effect, to some degree, by using italics for such passages and phrases.

Meaning of 正法眼蔵 (SHOBOGENZO), "The Right-Dharma-Eye Treasury"

正 (SHO) means "right" or "true."

法 (HO), "Law," represents the Sanskrit *"Dharma,"* which means reality.

眼 (GEN) "eye," represents direct experience.

正法眼 (SHOBOGEN), "the right-Dharma-eye," therefore describes the right or true experience of reality.

蔵 (ZO), "storehouse" or "treasury," suggests something that contains and preserves the right experience of reality. Thus, Nishijima Roshi has interpreted the words 正法眼蔵 (SHOBOGENZO), "the right-Dharma-eye treasury," as an expression of the practice of just sitting in Zazen.

Nishijima Roshi's right-Dharma-eye is, for me, evidenced nowhere more clearly than in his introduction to one of the chapters of this book, chapter 50, Shoho-jisso. Any virtue that this translation has stems entirely from the profoundly philosophical mind, the imperturbable balance, and the irrepressible optimism and energy of Nishijima Roshi.

Chodo Cross
5, Chiltern Close,
Aylesbury, England
February 1997

Shobogenzo

Chapters 73 to 95

開経偈

無上甚深微妙法

百千萬劫難遭遇

我今見聞得受持

願解如来真実義

KAIKYOGE

MUJO-JINSHIN-MIMYO-HO

HYAKU-SEN-MAN-GO-NAN-SOGU

GA-KON-KENMON-TOKU-JUJI

GAN-GE-NYORAI-SHINJITSU-GI

Verse for Opening the Sutras

The supreme, profound, subtle and fine Dharma,

In hundred thousand myriad kalpas is hard to meet.

Now that I see and hear it and am able to receive and retain it,

I desire to understand the real meaning of the Tathāgata's teaching.

[73]

三十七品菩提分法

SANJUSHICHI-BON-BODAI-BUNPO

Thirty-seven Elements of Bodhi

***Sanjushichi-bon** means "thirty-seven kinds." **Bodai** represents the Sanskrit bodhi, which means "the truth," and **bunpo** means "elements" or "methods." So **sanjushichi-bon-bodai-bunpo** means "thirty-seven elements of the truth." There are two fundamental schools of Buddhism; Hīnayāna (Small Vehicle) and Mahāyāna (Great Vehicle). The thirty-seven methods are usually said to belong to Hīnayāna Buddhism, because they are discussed in the Abhidharma-mahāvibhāṣa-śāstra, which is one of the primary sutras of Hīnayāna Buddhism. In Japan, and especially among Mahāyāna Buddhist masters, it was very rare for Buddhist monks to discuss these teachings. But Master Dogen has his own views on Mahāyāna and Hīnayāna. According to him, there exists only the Buddhism that Gautama Buddha taught. He thought that any distinctions between Mahāyāna and Hīnayāna are reflections of the different ages and cultures in which the two schools of Buddhism were taught, and he refused to discriminate between the two Buddhist streams. In this chapter Master Dogen explains the thirty-seven elements of the truth with no division into Hīnayāna or Mahāyāna, but based upon the practice of Zazen.*

[3] **The reality[1] of eternal Buddhas is present;** it is, namely, the teaching, practice, and experience of *the thirty-seven elements of bodhi*.[2] The entanglement of ascending and descending through their classification is just the entangled state of reality, which we call *the buddhas* and which we call *the patriarchs*.

[4] *The Four Abodes of Mindfulness*[3]

---

1. 公案 (KOAN). See chap. 3, *Genjo-koan*.

2. 三十七品菩提分法 (SANJUSHICHI-BON-BODAI-BUNPO), from the Sanskrit *saptatriṃśad-bodhipakṣa-dharma*. The original meaning of *pakṣa* is wing, side, or flank, so that *bodhipakṣa-dharma* means "dharmas that are as wings to bodhi"; i.e. dharmas (matters or practices) that are constituent parts of bodhi (the balanced state of truth which is *perfectly realized by the practice-and-experience of sitting in Zazen*—see *Fukan-zazengi*). In the Chinese translation of the Lotus Sutra (LS 3.290), the thirty-seven elements are rendered as 三十七品助道法 (SANJUSHICHI-BON-JODO-HO), lit. "thirty-seven kinds of dharmas that aid the truth" (LSW: "thirty-seven kinds of aids to the Way").

3. 四念住 (SHI-NEN-JU). The source text contains a note in small characters (added possibly by Master Dogen, probably by a later editor) that the four are also called 四念処 (SHI-NEN-JO), which also means the four abodes of mindfulness. In Theravada Buddhism today, they are

The first is the reflection that the body is not pure. The second is the reflection that feeling is suffering. The third is the reflection that mind is without constancy. The fourth is the reflection that dharmas are without self.

[5] *The reflection that the body is not pure:* The individual bag of skin reflected as a body in the present is *the whole Universe in ten directions;*[4] because it is *the real body,*[5] it is *the reflection that the body is not pure* springing up on the road of vivid action. If not for springing up, reflection would be impossible. It would be as if the body did not exist. Action itself would be impossible. The act of preaching would be impossible. The act of reflection would be impossible. But in fact the realization of realized reflection is already present: remember, it is the realized state of vivid springing up. What has been called "realized reflection" is everyday actions; sweeping the ground and sweeping the floor. Because we sweep the ground unaware *what number moon*[6] it is, and sweep the ground and sweep the floor aware that *this is just the second moon,*[7] the whole earth is as it is. Reflection on the body is the body's reflection: it is not that, by means of the body's reflection, something else reflects. Reflection itself, in the very moment of it, is the superlative having arrived. When body-reflection is realized, mental reflection is not at all worth groping for and is not realized. Thus, [body-reflection] is diamond-samādhi[8] and śūraṃgama-samādhi,[9] both of which are the reflection that the body is not pure. In general, the principle of seeing the bright star in the middle of the night is expressed as *the reflection that the body is not pure.* It is not a question of relative purity and impurity. The actual body is not pure. This real body is not pure. In learning in practice like this, when demons become buddha, they utilize

---

usually called the four foundations of mindfulness. In Sanskrit, the four are: 1) *kāya-smṛtyupasthāna,* the body as an abode of mindfulness; 2) *vedanā-smṛtyupasthāna,* feelings as an abode of mindfulness; 3) *citta-smṛtyupasthāna,* mind as an abode of mindfulness; and 4) *dharma-smṛtyupasthāna,* dharmas (real things and phenomena) as an abode of mindfulness. The Sanskrit *smṛti* means "calling to mind," "consciousness of," or "mindfulness," and *upasthāna* means "approaching," or "abode." See Glossary.

4. 尽十方界 (JIN-JUPPO-KAI).

5. 真実体 (SHINJITSU-TAI). Master Chosa Keishin said 尽十方界真実人体 (JIN-JUPPO-KAI-SHINJITSU-NIN-TAI); "*The whole Universe in the ten directions is the real human body.*" See chap. 50, *Shoho-jisso,* para. [222].

6. 第幾月 (DAI-IKU-GETSU), words of Master Ungan Donjo, quoted in *Keitoku-dento-roku,* chap. 14: *While the Master [Ungan] is sweeping, Isan says, "What a terribly hard worker!" The Master says, "You should know that there is one who does not work so hard." Isan says, "In that case, the second moon is present." The Master stands the broom on end, and asks, "What number moon is this?" Isan bows and leaves. Hearing of this, Gensa says, "That was just the second moon."*

7. 正是第二月 (SHO-ZE-DAI-NI-GETSU), the words of Master Gensa Shibi. Ibid. 第二月 (DAI-NI-GETSU), "the second moon," suggests divided consciousness.

8. 金剛定 (KONGO-JO), from the Sanskrit *vajra-samādhi,* means samādhi as a state of great stability.

9. 首楞厳定 (SHURYOGON-JO) means samādhi as a state of valiant onward progress. See Glossary, and also chap. 74, *Tenborin,* note 9.

the demon to defeat the demon and to become buddha. When buddhas become buddha, they utilize buddha to aim at buddha and to become buddha. When human beings become buddha, they utilize the human being to regulate the human being and to become buddha. We should investigate the truth that a way through exists in the utilization itself. It is like the method of washing a robe, for example: water is dirtied by the robe and the robe is permeated by the water. Whether we use this water and carry on washing or change this water and carry on washing, we are still using water, and still washing the robe. In washing it once and washing it a second time, if it does not look clean, do not linger in idle vacillation! When all the water is used up, we carry on with other water; [even] when the robe is clean, we carry on washing the robe.[10C] For water, we use many sorts of water: all sorts are suitable for washing a robe. We can investigate the truth that when water is impure, we know that there may be fish.[11C] As for robes, all sorts of robes need washing. Through effort like this, the reality of washing the robe is realized; and at the same time, we see what purity is. The point here is that to permeate the robe with water is not necessarily the original aim, and to dirty the water with the robe is not the original aim: it is in using dirty water to wash the robe that the original aim of washing the robe exists. There are also methods of washing the robe and of washing things, by using fire, wind, soil, water, and space. And there are methods of washing and cleaning earth, water, fire, wind, and space by using earth, water, fire, wind, and space. The point of the present *reflection that the body is not pure* is also like this. On this basis, the totality of *body*, the totality of *reflection*, and the totality of *not being pure*, are just the kaṣāya to which a mother gives birth.[12] If a kaṣāya is not the kaṣāya to which a mother gives birth, Buddhist patriarchs never use it—how could Śāṇavāsa be the only one? We should carefully apply our minds to this truth, learning it in practice and perfectly realizing it.

[10] *The reflection that feeling is suffering:* Suffering *is* feeling. It is neither one's own nor from outside; it is not tangible, neither is it intangible. It is the feeling of the living body, the suffering of the living body. It means sweet ripe

---

10. 水尽更用水なり。衣浄更浣衣なり。 (SUI-JIN-KO-YO-SUI *nari.* E-JO-KO-KAN-E*nari.*) This is in the style of a quotation from a Chinese text, with only the copulas なり *(nari)* written in phonetic Japanese characters. However, as no source has been traced, it is not clear whether these sentences are 1) a quotation from a Chinese source, 2) Master Dogen's own expression, 3) a combination of both the above. The many such instances of Chinese text in this chapter are indicated with [C]. Those Chinese expressions which are thought to be either Master Dogen's own expression or his variation of an original Chinese phrase are indicated with [D]. Italics have been used only when it is certain that Master Dogen is quoting directly from a Chinese source.

11. 水濁知有魚 (SUI-DAKU-CHI-U-GYO); that is to say, fish can only live in water that is tainted by the presence of something for them to eat. Source not traced—see note 10.

12. 嬢生袈裟 (JOSHO-GESA), "the kaṣāya born of a mother," alludes to the legend that Master Śāṇavāsa, the third patriarch in India, was born wearing the kaṣāya. See chap. 12, *Kesa-kudoku*, para. [74].

melons being replaced by bitter[13] gourds, which is bitter to the skin, flesh, bones, and marrow, and bitter to the conscious mind, the unconscious mind, and so on. [This reflection] is mystical power, and practice-and-experience, which are one step ascendant[14]—mystical power that springs out from the entire stem and springs out from the whole root. Thus, *"It has been said that living beings suffer; at the same time, there are suffering living beings."*[15] Living beings are beyond self and beyond others; *at the same time, there are suffering living beings:* in the end it is impossible to deceive others. Though sweet melons are totally sweet right through to their stems and bitter gourds are totally bitter right to the whole of their roots, suffering is not easily groped. We should ask ourselves: What is suffering?

[11] *The reflection that mind is without constancy:* The eternal Buddha Sokei says, *"That without constancy is the Buddha-nature."*[16] So non-constancy, though [variously] understood by various beings, is always the Buddha-nature. Great Master Yoka Shinkaku says, *"Actions are non-constancy; all is empty. Just this is the Tathāgata's great and round realization."*[17] The present *reflection that the mind is non-constancy* is itself the Tathāgata's great and round realization, and it is the great and roundly realized Tathāgata. Mind, even if it intends not to reflect, follows the external world completely; therefore, where there is mind there is also reflection. In general, arrival at the supreme truth of bodhi, realization of the supreme right and balanced truth, is just *non-constancy*, and is *reflection of the mind.* The mind is not necessarily constant: because it goes far beyond the four lines[18] and transcends the hundred negations,[19] fences, walls, tiles, and pebbles, and stones large and small, are *the mind* itself, are *non-constancy* itself, and are *reflection* itself.

[12] *The reflection that dharmas are without self:* The long has a long Dharma-body, and the short has a short Dharma-body. Because they are a realized state of vigorous activity, they are without self. A dog is the Buddha-nature as being without, and a dog is the Buddha-nature as existence.[20] All living beings are

---

13. 苦 (KU, *nigai*), "bitter," is also the character for "suffering."

14. 一上の神通 (ICHIJO *no* JINZU), i.e. a mystical power that has sprung up from the intellectual sphere into the area of reality. Words of Master Isan Reiyu quoted in *Shinji-shobogenzo,* pt. 1, no. 61. See also chap. 25, *Jinzu,* para. [186].

15. Words of Master Kyosei Dofu, quoted in *Rento-eyo,* chap. 24.

16. See chap. 22, *Bussho,* para. [38].

17. Quoted from *Shodoka* by Master Yoka Genkaku. "Great and round realization" is 大円覚 (DAI-EN-GAKU), or in other words, the great and whole state of truth. 覚 (KAKU) can mean 1) to perceive, to be aware, to realize, et cetera; 2) a reflection or objective truth that has been realized—as in the Eight Truths of a Great Human Being; see chap. 95, *Hachi-dainingaku;* 3) the state of Buddhist truth or realization—as in the phrase 無上正等覚 (MUJO-SHOTO-KAKU), "the supreme right and balanced state of truth" representing the Sanskrit *anuttara-samyak-saṃbodhi.*

18. 四句 (SHI-KU) means the four lines of a Buddhist verse, or *gāthā.*

19. 百非 (HYAPPI) means the hundreds of negations of Buddhist philosophy.

20. Refers to Master Joshu Jushin's two responses to the question "Does a dog have the

without the Buddha-nature.[21] All instances of Buddha-nature are without living beings.[22] All buddhas are without living beings. All buddhas are without buddhas. All instances of the Buddha-nature are without the Buddha-nature. All living beings are without living beings. Because it is like this, we learn all dharmas being without all dharmas as *the reflection that dharmas are without self.* Remember, it is a springing free from the whole body of self-entanglement.

[14] Śākyamuni Buddha says, *"All buddhas and bodhisattvas will rest in this teaching for ever, regarding it as a sacred womb."*

So all buddhas and bodhisattvas have regarded these four abodes of mindfulness as a sacred womb. Remember, they are the sacred womb of [bodhisattvas of] balanced awareness[23] and the sacred womb of [bodhisattvas of] fine awareness.[24] [The Buddha] has spoken of *all buddhas and bodhisattvas,* and so [the four abodes] may not stop at fine awareness. Even buddhas regard them as a sacred womb. And bodhisattvas who have sprung free from states prior to balanced awareness or beyond subtle awareness also regard these four abodes of mindfulness as a sacred womb. Truly, the skin, flesh, bones, and marrow of the buddhas and the patriarchs are nothing other than the four abodes of mindfulness.[25]

[15] *The Four Kinds of Right Restraint*[26] *(Also called the four kinds of right exertion)*

The first is to prevent bad that has not yet occurred. The second is to cause to be extinguished bad that has already occurred. The third is to cause to occur good that has

---

Buddha-nature?" In the first instance he said 無 (MU); "It is without," and in the second instance he said 有 (U); "It exists." See chap. 22, *Bussho,* para. [82] and para. [85].

21. 一切衆生無仏性 (ISSAI-SHUJO MU BUSSHO), words of Master Isan Reiyu discussed in detail in chap. 22, *Bussho,* para. [66]. Master Dogen's teaching in that chapter is that all living beings, without anything covering them, are just the Buddha-nature itself.

22. An instance of the Buddha-nature is nothing other than an instance of the Buddha-nature.

23. 等覚 (TOKAKU), or "the balanced state of truth" (see note 17), is the fifty-first of the fifty-two stages through which a bodhisattva is supposed to pass on the road to buddhahood.

24. 妙覚 (MYOKAKU), elsewhere translated as "the fine state of truth," is the fifty-second and last stage of a bodhisattva before becoming buddha.

25. 念 (NEN) in this context suggests mindfulness in Zazen and our daily life. The Sanskrit *smṛti* (Pali: *sati*) is defined by MW as "remembrance, thinking of or upon, calling to mind." The rendering "mindfulness," which is now generally used by Buddhist teachers in the west for *smṛti* and *sati,* is credited to T.W. Rhys Davids in his translations for the Pali Text Society. In Nishijima Roshi's interpretation, "mindfulness" in Zazen means the consciousness of reality, which is centered on keeping the spine straight.

26. 四正断 (SHI-SHO-DAN), from the Sanskrit *catvāri samyakprahāṇāṇi.* The note in small characters says that they are also called 四正勤 (SHI-SHO-GON). The Sanskrit *samyak* (in compounds for *samyañc*) means correct, true, right, and *prahāṇa* means 1) ceasing, giving up, or 2) exertion. See Glossary.

not yet occurred. The fourth is to promote the good that has already occurred.

[16] *To prevent bad that has not yet occurred:* What is called bad does not always have established forms and grades; the term has been established land by land and sphere by sphere. Nevertheless, prevention of that which has not yet occurred is called the Buddha-Dharma, and we have received its authentic transmission. They say that in the understanding of non-Buddhists the primeval self is seen as fundamental, but in the Buddha-Dharma we should not be like that. Now, let us inquire, at the time when *bad has not yet occurred,* where is it? To say that it will exist in the future is to be forever a non-Buddhist of nihilism.[27] To say that the future becomes the present is not an insistence of the Buddha-Dharma: the three times would have to be confused. If the three times were confused, all dharmas would be confused. If all dharmas were confused, real form would be confused. If real form were confused, buddhas alone, together with buddhas, would be confused. For this reason, we do not say that the future will, in future, become the present. Let us inquire further: what thing does "bad that has not yet occurred" describe? Who has known it or seen it? For it to be known and seen, there must be a time of its non-occurrence and a time of something other than its non-occurrence. In that case, it could not be called something that had not yet occurred. It would have to be called something that has already vanished. Without studying under non-Buddhists or śrāvakas and others of the small vehicle, we should learn in practice *the prevention of bad that has not yet occurred.* All the bad in the Universe is called "bad that has not yet occurred," and it is bad that does not appear. Non-appearance means *yesterday preaching an established rule, today preaching an exception to the rule.*[28]

† *To cause to be extinguished bad that has already occurred: Already occurring* means totally happening. Totally happening means half-happening. Half-happening means what is happening here and now. What is happening here and now is obstructed by happening itself; it has sprung free from the brains of happening. Causing this [bad] to be extinguished describes Devadatta's living body entering hell,[C] and Devadatta's living body attaining affirmation;[29C]

---

27. 断滅見 (DANMETSUKEN), lit. "view of extinction," representing the Sanskrit *uccheda-dṛṣṭi,* expresses the standpoint of materialistic determinism. See also chap. 89, *Shinjin-inga.*

28. In other words, 不生 (FUSHO), "non-appearance," describes the state at the moment of the present. The expression 昨日説定法、今日説不定法 (SAKUJITSU-SETSU-JOHO, KONNICHI-SETSU-FUJOHO), "yesterday preaching an established rule, today preaching an exception to the rule," also appears in chap. 4, *Ikka-no-myoju,* para. [101], but the original source has not been traced.

† In the original text, the first two kinds of restraint are included in one paragraph.

29. Devadatta, one of the Buddha's cousins, is said to have fallen into hell because he committed the five worst sins. Nevertheless, in the 12th chapter of the Lotus Sutra (*Devadatta*), the Buddha says, *"Devadatta also, in future, after countless ages have passed, will be able to become a buddha."* (LS 2.208.)

it describes a living body entering a donkey's womb,[C] and a living body becoming buddha.[30C] Grasping this principle, we should learn in practice what *causing extinction* means. Extinction means springing free from extinction and getting clear of it.

[19] *To cause to occur good that has not yet occurred* is satisfaction with the features we had before our parents were born, is clarification prior to the sprouting of creation, and is understanding preceding Majestic Sound.

[20] *To promote the good that has already occurred:* Remember, this does not speak of causing to occur the good that has already occurred; it is about promoting [good]. It is [the Buddha], having seen for himself the bright star, going on to make others see the bright star;[C] it is eyes becoming the bright star;[C] it is *confusion being followed by thirty years of not lacking for salt and vinegar.*[31] For example: because we are promoting [good], [good] is already happening, and so *the ravine being deep, the dipper's handle is long,*[32] and *only because we had it did he come.*[33]

[21] *The Four Bases of Mystical Ability*[34]

The first is volition as a base of mystical ability, the second is mind as a base of mystical ability, the third is forward progression as a base of mystical ability, and the fourth is thinking as a base of mystical ability.

[21] *Volition as a base of mystical ability* is the body-mind *aiming to become Buddha,*[35] it is *looking forward to the pleasure of a nap,*[36] and it is *why I bow to you.*[37] In sum, volition as a mystical basis is utterly beyond the purposes of a body

---

30. *Hoku-hiyu-kyo,* chap. 1, contains the story of Śakra-devānām-indra entering the womb of a donkey, then taking refuge in the Buddha, returning to his or her original form, and entering the first stage of Buddhahood.

31. Master Baso Do-itsu, expressing satisfaction with his life as a monk, said, "*In the thirty years that followed confusion, I have never lacked for salt and vinegar.*" See *Keitoku-dento-roku,* chap. 9.

32. 谿深杓柄長 (KEI-SHIN-SHAKU-HEI-CHO). See *Shinji-shobogenzo,* pt. 2, no. 83, and chap. 39, *Dotoku,* para. [201]. "To promote" is 増長 (ZO-CHO), lit. "increase-long."

33. 只為有所以来 (SHI-I-U-SHO-I-RAI) are the words of Master Yakusan Igen quoted in *Keitoku-dento-roku,* chap. 14. Master Yakusan's intention was that Master Bodhidharma did not introduce something new into China: he revealed to his Chinese disciples the Dharma that was already there.

34. 四神足 (SHI-JIN-SOKU), lit. "four mystical feet," from the Sanskrit *catur-ṛddhipāda,* are four faculties forming the basis for the kind of mystical power described in chap. 25, *Jinzu* and chap. 80, *Tashintsu.* In Sanskrit they are: 1) *chanda,* 2) *citta,* 3) *vīrya,* and 4) *mīmāṃsā.* The Sanskrit *ṛiddhi* means mystical power and *pāda* means a foot or a fourth part of something (the foot of a quadruped being one out of four). See Glossary.

35. 図作仏 (TO-SA-BUTSU). Master Baso's words, quoted for example in chap. 27, *Zazenshin,* para. [11].

36. 図睡快 (TO-SUI-KAI). Words of Master Sekito Kisen, quoted in chap. 64, *Kajo,* para. [101].

37. 因我礼儞 (IN-GA-RAI-JI) is the 3rd line of a poem by Master Tendo Nyojo, also quoted in chap. 64, *Kajo,* para. [108].

and mind; it is *birds flying in the boundless sky*, and *fish swimming in water that is clear to the bottom.*[38]

[22] *Mind as a base of mystical ability* is fences, walls, tiles, and pebbles; it is mountains, rivers, and the Earth; it is individual instances of the triple world; it is the completely red bamboo and wood of a chair.[39] Because all [mind] is able to be utilized, the mind of Buddhist patriarchs can exist, the mind of the common and the sacred can exist, the mind of grass and trees can exist, and the mind of fantastic apparitions can exist. All mind is mind as a base of the mystical.

[23] *Forward progression*[40] *as a base of mystical ability* is *being on top of a hundred foot pole and stepping straight ahead.* Where is the top of a hundred foot pole? They say that we cannot find it without going straight ahead. A step straight ahead is not to be denied, but *this place is the place where something ineffable exists*—explain it as going forward or explain it as going back.[41] Just in the moment of *forward progression as a base of the mystical,* the whole Universe in ten directions, following from that mystical base, arrives.[C] Following from that mystical base, it has arrived.[C]

[24] *Thinking as a base of mystical ability is all the Buddhist patriarchs, their karmic consciousness*[42] *unclear, having nothing upon which they can originally rely.*[43] There is thinking by the body, there is thinking by the mind, there is thinking by consciousness, there is thinking by straw sandals, and there is thinking by the self which precedes the Kalpa of Emptiness.

† These are also called the four bases of freewill. They are a state without hesitation. Śākyamuni Buddha says, *"Not yet moving and yet having arrived is*

---

38. Alludes to a verse by Master Wanshi Shokaku quoted in chap. 27, *Zazenshin,* para. [34].

39. The master's ceremonial chair, used for precepts ceremonies etc., is bright red.

40. 進 (SHIN, *susu[mu]*) lit. means to advance, progress, move forward. Here it represents the compound 精進 (SHOJIN), "diligence, effort, fortitude," which in turn represents the Sanskrit *vīrya.*

41. Alludes to a conversation between Master Rinzai Gigen and Master Chinshu Fuke recorded in *Shinji-shobogenzo,* pt. 1, no. 96: *Fuke and Rinzai go to a patron's house for a midday meal. [Rinzai] asks, "A hair swallows the vast ocean and a mustard seed includes Mt. Sumeru. Should we see this as 'the mystical powers and wondrous function' or should we see this as 'reality as it is?'" The Master [Fuke] duly overturns the dinner table. [Rin]zai says, "Very coarse person!" The Master [Fuke] says, "This concrete place is where it is—explain it as coarse or explain it as fine."* Master Chinshu Fuke (a successor of Master Banzan Hoshaku, died c. 860) is sometimes identified as the original fat laughing monk featured in Happy Buddha statues. See also chap. 22, *Bussho,* para. [45], and chap. 56, *Senmen,* para. [124].

42. 業識 (GOSSHIKI), "karmic consciousness," means consciousness as the result of past behavior, that is, concrete consciousness in the present.

43. Master Isan Reiyu said, *"All living beings, having only karmic consciousness, are unclear and have nothing upon which they can originally rely."* See *Shinji-shobogenzo,* pt. 2, no. 30.

† There is no paragraph break here in the original text.

called the base of freewill." In conclusion, then, sharpness is like the point of a needle, and squareness is like the side of a chisel.

[25] *The Five Root-forces*[44]

The first is belief as a root, the second is diligence as a root, the third is mindfulness as a root, the fourth is balance as a root, and the fifth is wisdom as a root.

[25] *Belief as a root,* remember, is beyond self, beyond others, beyond our own intention, beyond our own contrivance, beyond outside influence, and beyond independently-established criteria; thus *it has been transmitted intimately between east and west.*[45] Belief demonstrated with the whole body[C] is called belief. It follows inevitably from the condition of Buddhahood, *following circumstances completely*[46] and following itself completely.[47CD] Unless the condition of buddhahood is present, the belief is not realized. For this reason it is said that *"The great ocean of the Buddha-Dharma is entered by belief itself."*[48] In sum, the place where the belief is realized is the place where Buddhist patriarchs are realized.

[27] *Diligence as a root* is to have been concentrating on just sitting;[C] it is to rest without being able to rest;[C] it is to have got rest and still to be getting rest;[C] it is *a terribly hard worker;*[49] it is *one who does not work so hard;*[50] it is a terribly hard not-hard-working first and second moon.[51CD] Śākyamuni Buddha says, *"I have constantly practiced diligence, and for this reason I have already realized anuttara-samyak-saṃbodhi."*[52] This *constant practicing* is head-to-tail rightness, through the whole past, present, and future. *"I constantly practice diligence"* says *"I have already realized bodhi."* Because *"I have already realized the supreme truth of bodhi," "I constantly practice diligence."* How else could it be *constant practice?* How else could *"I have already realized"* it? Commentary-teachers and sutra-teachers cannot see or hear this teaching; how much less could they have learned it in practice.

---

44. 五根 (GOKON), from the Sanskrit *pañcendriyāṇi.* In Sanskrit they are: 1) *śraddhendriya,* 2) *vīryendriya,* 3) *smṛtindriya,* 4) *samādhindriya,* and 5) *prajñendriya.* The Sanskrit *indriya* has the connotation of inherent strength or force. See Book 3, Glossary.

45. *Sandokai* by Master Sekito Kisen begins with the words, *"The mind of the Great Saint of India, / Has been transmitted intimately between east and west."*

46. 随佗去 (ZUITAKO) is a traditional expression of a compliant attitude to all challenges posed by the outside world. The phrase is used, for example, by Master Daizui Hoshin (732–824) in *Shinji-shobogenzo,* pt. 1, no. 24. See note 141.

47. 随自去 (ZUIJIKO), suggesting independence, is Master Dogen's variation.

48. Quotation from *Daichido-ron,* the Chinese translation of the Mahā-prajña-pāramitā-upadeśa-śāstra.

49. 太区区生 (TAI-KU-KU-SHO), words of Master Isan Reiyu; see note 6.

50. 不区区者 (FU-KU-KU-SHA), words of Master Ungan Donjo. Ibid.

51. 太区不区一月二月 (TAI-KU-FU-KU-ICHIGETSU-NIGETSU), suggests the state of real activity which is not always black and white.

52. Lotus Sutra, *Ju-gaku-mugaku-nin-ki.* LS 2.128-30.

[28] *Mindfulness as a root* is a withered tree as a mass of red flesh.[53] We call a mass of red flesh "a withered tree," and a withered tree is *mindfulness as a root.* We ourselves who are groping for the mark are mindfulness. There is mindfulness that exists in moments of owning one's body,[54] and there is mindfulness that exists in moments of having no mind.[55] There is conscious mindfulness,[56] and there is mindfulness in which there is no body.[57] The very life-root of all the people on Earth is *mindfulness as a root.* The very life-root of all the buddhas in the ten directions is *mindfulness as a root.* There can be many people in one state of mindfulness and many states of mindfulness in one person. At the same time, there are people who have mindfulness and there are people who do not have mindfulness. People do not always have mindfulness, and mindfulness is not necessarily connected with people. Even so, through the skillful maintenance of this *mindfulness as a root,* the virtue of perfect realization exists.

[29] *Balance as a root* is keeping one's eyebrows to oneself[CD] or *lifting up an eyebrow.*[58] Thus, it is [both] *not being unclear about cause and effect* and *not falling subject to cause and effect*[59]—and consequently entering the womb of a donkey or entering the womb of a horse.[60] It is like a rock enveloping a jewel: we cannot call it completely rock or completely jewel. It is like the ground bearing mountains: we cannot call it totally ground or totally mountains. At the same time, it springs out from the brain, and springs in.

[30] *Wisdom as a root* is *not knowing of the existence of the buddhas of the three times,* but *knowing the existence of cats and white oxen.*[61] We should not say "Why is it

---

53. 枯木の赤肉団 (KOBOKU *no* SHAKU-NIKU-DAN). 枯木 (KOBOKU), "withered tree," suggests a person sitting in the state of detachment—a temple's Zazen Hall was sometimes called 枯木堂 (KOBOKUDO) "the Withered Tree Hall." 団 (DAN), "mass" or "group," sometimes expresses not only aggregation but also integration—as for example in the compound 団結 (DANKETSU) which means "unity" or "solidarity."

54. 有身 (USHIN), "owning one's body" or "being in the body," means having consciousness of one's real physical presence.

55. 無心 (MUSHIN), "having no mind," means being free of self-consciousness.

56. 有心の念 (USHIN *no* NEN), or "mindfulness in which there is mind," suggests for example consciousness of oneself in Zazen.

57. 無身の念 (MUSHIN *no* NEN), or "mindfulness in which there is no body," suggests the balanced state of seemingly effortless action.

58. 策起眉毛 (SAKKI-BIMO) alludes to the story of the meeting between Master Piṇḍola and King Prasenajit. It is a symbol of positive behavior. See, for example, chap. 59, *Baike,* para. [217].

59. 不昧因果 (FUMAI-INGA), "not being unclear about cause and effect," and 不落因果 (FURAKU-INGA), "not falling subject to cause and effect," express dialectically opposite views about causation. See the story of Master Hyakujo and the wild fox in chap. 76, *Dai-shugyo.*

60. Entering the womb of a donkey or horse represents the process of *saṃsāra,* the cyclical passage through successive states that we undergo even as Buddhists.

61. Master Nansen Fugan said, "*I do not know about the existence of the buddhas of the three times, but I know the existence of cats and white oxen.*" (*Shinji-shobogenzo,* pt. 3, no. 93.) According to

so?"[C] It is beyond expression. In the nostrils exist in-breath and out-breath.[C] In a fist exist fingertips.[C] A donkey maintains and relies upon a donkey, a well meets with a well,[62] and, in conclusion, a root succeeds to a root.

[31] *The Five Powers*[63]

The first is belief as a power, the second is diligence as a power, the third is mindfulness as a power, the fourth is balance as a power, and the fifth is wisdom as a power.

[32] *Belief as a power* is being duped by ourselves and having no place of escape;[C] it is being called by others and having to turn the head;[C] it is *from birth to old age, being just this;*[64] it is tumbling over seven times and carrying on regardless;[C] it is falling down eight times and gathering oneself together.[C] Thus, belief is like a crystal.[C] The transmission of Dharma and the transmission of the robe are called *"belief."* It is the transmission of buddhas and the transmission of patriarchs.

[33] *Diligence as a power* is *explaining what cannot be practiced and practicing what cannot be explained.*[65] That being so, being able to explain one inch is nothing more than[66] being able to explain one inch, and being able to practice one

---

Kenzei-ki (Kenzei's Record, a biography of Master Dogen written by the 13th abbot of Eihei-ji temple, Master Kenzei), Master Eisai said these words to Master Dogen in response to a question about the Buddha-nature.

62. In *Shinji-shobogenzo,* pt. 2, no. 25, a conversation describes the mutual relation between subject and object as represented by a donkey looking into a well and the well looking at the donkey. Master Dogen extends the imagery of the story to suggest that in the state of wisdom, all things are as they are. The story is quoted in the notes to chap. 10, *Shoaku-makusa,* para. [11].

63. 五力 (GORIKI), from the Sanskrit *pañca-balāni,* are the five elements of the previous list viewed as actual powers rather than root-faculties. In Sanskrit they are: 1) *śraddhā-bala,* 2) *vīrya-bala,* 3) *smṛti-bala,* 4) *samādhi-bala,* and 5) *prajñā-bala.* The Sanskrit *bala* means power, might, vigor. See Book 2, Glossary.

64. Words of Master Baso quoted in *Shinji-shobogenzo,* pt. 1, no. 4, and chap. 77, *Koku,* para. [139]. A similar phrase is spoken by Master Sekito Kisen in *Shinji-shobogenzo,* pt. 3, no. 100: *Master Goei Rei-moku visits Sekito's order and asks: "If [you say] a word [that] is fitting, then I will stay; otherwise, I will leave." Sekito does not take any notice. The Master [Rei-moku] swings his sleeves and sets off. He gets out as far as the three gates. [Sekito] calls: "Ācārya!" The Master turns his head. Sekito says: "From birth to death it is just this! What is the use of you turning your head and changing your mind?" At this, the Master becomes amenable to realization.*

65. Words of Master Tozan Ryokai, recorded in *Shinji-shobogenzo,* pt. 1, no. 77: *Master Daiji Kanchu preaches to the assembly, "Being able to explain one jo* [ten *shaku*] *is inferior to practicing one shaku* [ten *sun*]. *Being able to explain one shaku is inferior to practicing one sun* [about an inch]." *Tozan says, "I explain what I am unable to practice and practice what I am unable to explain."* See also chap. 30, *Gyoji,* para. [159].

66. 不如 (FUNYO). These characters (read in Japanese as *gotoku nara zu*) usually mean "is not like," "does not equal," or "is inferior to" (as in Master Kanchu's words in the preceding note). But sometimes 不如 (read in Japanese as *shika zu*) means "at best." Master Dogen's intention here has been interpreted on the basis of the second usage. See also discussion in chap. 43, *Kuge,*

word is nothing more than being able to practice one word.[C] Getting power in exertion itself[67C] is *diligence as a power.*

[34] *Mindfulness as a power* is a *great brute, pulling a person's nostrils.*[68] Thus, it is nostrils pulling a person,[CD] it is to throw away a jewel and get back a jewel,[69CD] and it is to throw away a tile and get back a tile.[CD] Further, failure to throw it away means thirty strokes.[70C] Even if used by all people in the world, it will never be eroded.[C]

[35] *Balance as a power* is *like a child getting its mother,*[71] or like a mother getting her child.[CD] Or it is like the child getting the child itself,[CD] or like the mother getting the mother herself.[CD] But it is neither the swapping of a head and a face[C] nor the buying of gold with gold.[C] It is just a song growing gradually louder.[C]

[36] *Wisdom as a power* is of deep and long years,[C] and is like a ferry coming to a crossing.[C] For this reason, it was described in ancient times as *"like a crossing getting a ferry."*[72] The point is that a crossing is inevitably just the fact of the ferry.[CD] A crossing not being hindered by a crossing is called a ferry. Spring ice naturally melts ice itself.[C]

[37] *Seven Limbs of the Balanced State of Truth*[73]

The first is deciding among teachings as a limb of the truth, the second is diligence

---

of 不如三界見於三界 (SANGAI *no* SANGAI *o genzuru ni shika zu*), *"It is best to see the triple world as the triple world."*

67. 力裏得力 (RIKI-RI TOKU-RI). 力 (RIKI, *chikara*) includes the meaning of 1) power or ability, and 2) exertion or effort.

68. Alludes to a story recorded in *Shinji-shobogenzo,* pt. 3, no. 49 and discussed at length in chap. 77, *Koku,* in which Master Shakkyo Ezo yanks the nose of Master Seido Chizo in order to explain the meaning of space.

69. 抛玉引玉 (HO-GYOKU-IN-GYOKU), lit. "to throw away a jewel and pull in a jewel," is Master Dogen's variation of the expression 抛甎引玉 (HO-SEN-IN-GYOKU), "to throw away a tile and pull in a jewel," which appears in *Keitoku-dento-roku,* chap. 10: *Joshu says, "Tonight I have given the answer. Anyone who understands the question should come forward." A monk steps forward and prostrates himself. Joshu [not impressed] says, "Just before I threw away a tile to pull in a jewel, but instead I have drawn out a lump of clay."* See also chap. 27, *Zazenshin,* para. [20]. Master Dogen's idea of mindfulness is a condition in which things are as they are.

70. If during the course of Buddhist training mindfulness arises, we should not attach to it.

71. 如子得其母 (NYO-SHI-TOKU-GO-BO), from Lotus Sutra, *Yaku-o-bosatsu-honji.* See LS 3.200.

72. 如渡得船 (NYO-TO-TOKU-SEN). Ibid.

73. 七等覚支 (SHICHI-TOKAKUSHI), also called simply 七覚支 (SHICHI-KAKUSHI), or "the seven limbs of bodhi," from the Sanskrit *sapta bodhyaṅgāni.* See Book 2, Glossary. They are: 1) *dharmapravicaya-sambodhyaṅga,* 2) *vīrya-sambodhyaṅga,* 3) *prīti-sambodhyaṅga,* 4) *praśrabdhi-sambodhyaṅga,* 5) *upekṣā-sambodhyaṅga,* 6) *samādhi-sambodhyaṅga,* and 7) *smṛti-sambodhyaṅga.* The Sanskrit prefix *sam,* which expresses conjunction, union, integration, et cetera, is here represented by 等 (TO), which lit. means equality, equivalence, balance. 覚 (KAKU) represents the Sanskrit bodhi (see note 17). 支 (SHI), "branch," represents the Sanskrit *aṅga,* which means a limb of the body.

as a limb of the truth, the third is joy as a limb of the truth, the fourth is elimination as a limb of the truth, the fifth is detachment as a limb of the truth, the sixth is balance as a limb of the truth, and the seventh is mindfulness as a limb of the truth.

[38] *Deciding among teachings as a limb of the truth is "If there is a thousandth or a hundredth of a gap, the separation is as great as that between heaven and earth."*[74] Thus, to arrive at the truth is neither difficult nor easy: all that is necessary is to decide for oneself.[75CD]

[38] *Diligence as a limb of the truth* is never having plundered a market.[76C] Both in buying oneself and in expending oneself, there is a definite price, and there is recognition of worth. Though we seem to suppress ourselves and to promote others, a blow through the whole body does not break us.[C] While we have not yet ceased expending the self on a word of total transformation,[77] we meet a trader who buys the self as a totally transformed mind.[78] *Donkey business is unfinished, but some horse business comes in.*[79]

[39] *Joy as a limb of the truth* is the sincerity of a granny's mind when blood is dripping.[C] The thousand hands and eyes of Great Compassion![C80] Leave them as they are, immensely busy.[C] Plum flowers are peeping from the December[81] snow.[C] In the scenery of coming spring a great master is cold.[C] Even so, he is full of life and belly laughter.[C]

[40] *Elimination*[82] *as a limb of the truth* is, when being in oneself, not getting

---

74. Quoted from *Shinjinmei*, by the third patriarch in China, Kanchi Sosan. The poem begins: 至道無難、唯嫌揀択。但莫憎愛、洞然明白。毫釐有差、天地懸隔。 *(Shido-munan, yui-ken-kenjaku. Tada-zo-ai nakere ba, tonen to shi te meihaku nari. Gori mo sa are ba, tenchi harukani heda taru.) "To arrive at the truth is not difficult: just avoid preference. / Just when there is no hate and love, [all] will be revealed. / [But] if there is a thousandth or a hundredth of a gap, the separation will be as great as that between heaven and earth."* These opening lines point us back to the simple state of just acting and caution against irresolution or indecision.

75. 至道不難易、唯要自揀択。 *(Shido fu nan-i, yui-yo-ji-kenjaku).* This is Master Dogen's variation on the opening line of *Shinjinmei.*

76. Alludes to Master Gensa's words *"It is forbidden for anyone to plunder a market."* See *Shinji-shobogenzo*, pt. 1. no. 38.

77. 一転語 (ICHITENGO), "word(s) of transformation" or "a turning word," is a traditional phrase; it appears for example in the story of Master Hyakujo and the wild fox quoted in chap. 76, *Dai-shugyo.*

78. 一転心 (ICHITENSHIN) is Master Dogen's variation.

79. Master Chokei Eryo asks Master Reiun Shigon, *"Just what is the Great Intent of the Buddha-Dharma?"* Master Reiun says, *"Donkey business being unfinished, but horse business coming in."* See *Shinji-shobogenzo*, pt. 2, no. 56.

80. 大悲 (DAIHI), "Great Compassion," represents the Sanskrit *Mahākaruṇā*, another name of Bodhisattva Avalokiteśvara. See chap. 36, *Kannon.*

81. 臘 (RO) means the 12th lunar month, which was probably the coldest month. In Tokyo today plum flowers usually first bloom around the beginning of February, which is the coldest month in the modern calendar.

82. 除 (JO, *nozo[ku]*), means to clear away, be rid of, exclude, eliminate. However, it

involved with oneself, and when being in the outside world, not getting involved with the outside world. It is me having got it, you not having got it.[C] It is ardently expressing ourself and going among alien beings.[C]

[41] *Detachment as a limb of the truth* is *"Though I have brought it, others do not accept it."*[83] It is Chinese, even when barefoot, walking like Chinese.[C] It is Persians from the southern seas wanting to get ivory.[C]

[41] *Balance as a limb of the truth* is, before the moment, preserving the eye that precedes the moment;[84C] it is blowing our own noses;[C] and it is grasping our own rope and leading ourselves.[C] Having said that, it is also being able to graze a castrated water buffalo.[85C]

[42] *Mindfulness as a limb of the truth* is outdoor pillars walking in the sky.[C] Thus, it is the mouth being like an acorn and the eyes being like eyebrows[C] and at the same time it is to burn sandalwood in a sandalwood forest,[C] and it is the roar of a lion in a lion's den.[86C]

[43] *The Eight Branches of the Right Path*[87]

The first is right view as a branch of the path, the second is right thinking as a branch of the path, the third is right speech as a branch of the path, the fourth is right action as a branch of the path, the fifth is right livelihood as a branch of the path, the sixth is right effort as a branch of the path, the seventh is right mindfulness as a branch of the path, and the eighth is right balance as a branch of the path.

[44] *Right view as a branch of the path* is the inside of the eyes containing the body.[C] At the same time, even prior to the body we must have the eye that is prior to the body.[88C] Though the view has been grandly realized in the past, it is realized now as the real Universe and is experienced immediately. In sum, those who do not put the body into the eyes are not Buddhist patriarchs.

---

represents the Sanskrit *praśrabdhi* (Pali: *passaddhi*). The Pali Text Society's Pali-English Dictionary defines *passaddhi* as "calmness, tranquillity, repose, serenity," and in its list of the seven *sambojjahnga* (Sanskrit: *sambodhyaṅga*) it gives passadhi as "tranquillity." *Bukkyo-jiten* gives 除覚支 (JO KAKUSHI), "cutting rough or heavy states to get a light, sharp, peaceful and serene state," as one translation of the Sanskrit *praśrabdhi-sambodhyaṅga*. See Glossary.

83. From a verse by Master Tozan Ryokai recorded in *Rento-eyo*, chap. 30.

84. 機先の眼 (KISEN *[no]* GAN), "eyes that precede the moment," suggests intuition.

85. Alludes to the words of Master Enchi Dai-an. See chap. 64, *Kajo*, para. [110].

86. 師子吼 (SHISHIKU), "the roar of a lion," is a symbol of the Buddha's preaching.

87. 八正道支 (HASSHO-DOSHI), from the Sanskrit *āryāṣṭāṅga-mārga*, that is, the eightfold noble path preached by the Buddha in his first preaching after realizing the truth. A note in small characters says that they are also called 八聖道 (HASSHODO), "the noble eightfold path." In Sanskrit they are: 1) *samyag-dṛṣṭi*, 2) *samyag-saṃkalpa*, 3) *samyag-vāc*, 4) *samyak-karmānta*, 5) *samyag-ājīva*, 6) *samyag-vyāyāma*, 7) *samyak-smṛti*, and 8) *samyak-samādhi*. See Glossary.

88. 身先眼 (SHINSEN *[no]* GEN), or "the eye that precedes the body," suggests the ability to regulate our physical actions even before we are conscious of them. See also note 84.

[44] *Right thinking*[89] *as a branch of the path:* When [we] establish this thinking, the buddhas of the ten directions all appear.[90C] So the manifestation of the ten directions, and the manifestation of the buddhas, are just the time of the establishment of this concrete thinking.[91] When we establish this concrete thinking we are beyond self and transcending the external world; at the same time, in the very moment of the present, on thinking concrete facts we go straight to Vārāṇasī.[92C] The place where the thinking exists is Vārāṇasī. An eternal Buddha[93] says, *"I am thinking the concrete state of not thinking." How can the state of not thinking be thought? "It is different from thinking."* This is right consideration, right thinking.[94] To break a zafu is right thinking.

[45] *Right speech as a branch of the path* is the mute self not being mute.[C] Mutes among [ordinary] people have never been able to express the truth. People in the mute state are not mutes: they do not aspire to be saints,[C] and do not add something spiritual onto themselves.[C] [Right speech] is mastery of the state in which the mouth is hung on the wall;[C] it is mastery of the state in which all mouths are hung on all walls;[C] it is all mouths being hung on all walls.[95C]

---

89. 正思惟 (SHO-SHI-I). 思 (SHI, *omo[u]*), covers a range of mental activities, perhaps even wider than the English word "think," including wishing and hoping. On the one hand 惟 (i, *omonmi[ru]*) means to ponder, reflect on, think over, and so the compound 思惟 (SHI-I) has a somewhat general and reflective feeling. On the other hand, the Sanskrit *saṃkalpa*, which 思惟 (SHI-I) represents, seems to carry some sense of definite purpose; see Glossary.

90. 作是思惟時、十方仏皆現なり。 *(Kono shi-i o nasu toki, juppo-butsu kai gen nari).* This looks very much like a quotation from a sutra, although the source has not been traced.

91. "Establishment of this concrete thinking" is 作是思惟 (SA ZE SHI-I). In a sutra these characters (read as *kono shi-i o nasu*) would simply mean "to have this thought," or "making this my thought"—see, for example, LS 3.36. But Master Dogen uses the characters here to suggest that "right thinking" is the state in Zazen, a state that is different from ordinary thinking, and that this state should be our standard.

92. 思惟是事已、即趣波羅奈なり *(ze-ji o shi-i seba, sunawachi Harana ni omomuku nari).* Again this is in the style of a quotation from a sutra, but no source has been traced. In the year he attained the truth, the Buddha is said to have spent his first rainy season retreat at a deer-park near Vārāṇasī. *The Verse for Laying out the Patra* recited at mealtimes begins: *Bussho-ka-pi-ra, Jo-do-ma-ka-da, Seppo-ha-ra-na...* "The Buddha was born in Kapilavastu, realized the truth in Magadha, preached the Dharma in Vārāṇasī..." So Vārāṇasī symbolizes a place where the Buddha-Dharma is being preached.

93. 思量個不思量底、不思量底如何思量、非思量 *(shiryo-ko-fushiryo-tei, fushiryo-tei ikan ga shiryo, hi-shiryo)*, the famous words of Master Yakusan Igen which Master Dogen used to express the secret of Zazen (see chap. 27, *Zazenshin*, chap. 58, *Zazengi*, et cetera). 思量 (SHIRYO) as a compound generally means the same as 思惟 (SHI-I): thinking or consideration. At the same time, 量 (RYO, *haka[ru]*), which means to measure, fathom, or calculate, has a more concrete feeling than 惟 (I, *omonmi[ru]*).

94. これ正思量、正思惟なり *(kore* SHO-SHIRYO, SHO-SHI-I *nari*). The apposition seems to confirm that Master Dogen saw the two phrases as equivalent terms.

95. Suggests the situation in the Zazen Hall. The following poem is no. 18 in a collection of 125 verses by Master Dogen recorded at the end of *Eihei-koroku*: *"The innate subtle wisdom is*

[46] *Right action as a branch of the path* is to leave family life[96] and to practice the truth, it is to go into the mountains and to gain experience. Śākyamuni Buddha says, *"The thirty-seven elements are the actions of a monk."* The actions of a monk[97] are beyond the great vehicle and beyond the small vehicle. There are buddha-monks, bodhisattva-monks, śrāvaka-monks, and so on. None has succeeded to the right action of the Buddha-Dharma, and none has received the authentic transmission of the great truth of the Buddha-Dharma, without leaving family life. Notwithstanding scant pursuit of the truth by lay people as *upāsaka* and *upāsikā*,[98] there is no past example of one arriving at the truth. When we arrive at the truth, we inevitably leave family life. How can people who are not able to leave family life succeed to the position of a buddha? Nevertheless, for the last two or three hundred years in the great kingdom of Sung, people calling themselves priests of the Zen Sect have habitually said, "Pursuit of the truth by a layman[99] and pursuit of the truth by one who has left family life[100] are just the same." They are a tribe of people who have become dogs, for the sole purpose of making the filth and urine[101] of lay people into their food and drink. Sometimes they say to kings and their ministers, "The mind in conducting the myriad affairs of state[102] is just the mind of patriarchs and buddhas, other than which there is no mind at all." Kings and ministers, never having discerned right preaching and right Dharma, delightedly bestow on them gifts such as the titles of master.[103] The monks who speak such words are Devadattas. In order that they might feed upon tears and spit, they produce childish and demented talk like this. They are deplorable. They are not the kindred of the Seven Buddhas. They are demons and animals. They are like this because they have never known learning the truth with body and mind, they do not learn in practice, they do not know leaving family life with body and mind, they are ignorant of rule by kings and ministers, and they have never seen the great truth of the Buddhist

---

itself true reality. / Why should we rely on Confucian commentaries and Buddhist texts? / Sitting upon the quiet floor, I hung my mouth on the wall. / Awareness of sound arrived at this place and took away my vacancy."

96. 出家 (SHUKKE) is lit. "to leave home," or "to get out of a family"—that is, to become a monk (using the term "monk" to include both men and women). See chap. 83, *Shukke,* and chap. 86, *Shukke-kudoku.*

97. 僧 (SO) means 1) saṃgha, and 2) monk.

98. 近事男女 (GONJI NANNYO), represents the Sanskrit *upāsaka* (layman) and *upāsikā* (laywoman). *Upāsaka* originally meant "servant" or "follower." See Book 1, Glossary.

99. 在家 (ZAIKE), lit. "one who resides at home," or "one who resides in a family."

100. 出家 (SHUKKE), i.e. a monk.

101. 屎尿 (SHINYO), filth and urine, are used as concrete symbols of fame and profit that are surplus to the real needs of a monk.

102. 万機の心 (BANKI *no* SHIN). 機 (KI) is as in the compound 機微 (KIBI), which means niceties, subtleties, intricacies.

103. That is, the titles "Zen Master So-and-So," or "Great Master So-and-So."

patriarchs even in a dream. Layman Vimalakīrti[104] met the time when the Buddha manifested himself in the world, but there was much Dharma that he left unexpressed and not a little learning that he failed to attain. Layman Ho-on[105] practiced in a succession of patriarchs' orders, but he was not admitted into the inner sanctum of Yakusan and he could not equal Kozei.[106] He merely poached a reputation for learning in practice: the reality of learning in practice was not present in him. Others such as Ri Fuma[107] and Yo Bunko[108] each felt that they had experienced satisfaction, but they never tasted dairy-cake, much less tasted picture-cake. How much less could they have eaten the gruel and rice[109] of a Buddhist patriarch? They never possessed the pātra. It is pitiful that their whole life as a bag of skin was in vain. I universally recommend celestial beings, human beings, dragon beings, and all living beings, throughout the ten directions, longingly to venerate the distant Dharma of the Tathāgata, and without delay to leave family life and practice the truth, and thus to succeed to the position of buddha and the position of a patriarch. Do not listen to the inadequate words of "Zen Masters" and the like. Because they do not know the body and do not know the mind, they speak such words. That is to say, utterly lacking compassion for living beings, having no desire to preserve the Buddha-Dharma, and solely wishing to feed upon the urine and filth of lay people, they have become evil hounds, and those dogs with human faces and dogs with human skin speak such words. Do not sit with them and do not speak with them. Do not abide with them. Their living bodies have already fallen into the state of animals. If monks had urine and filth in abundance, they would say that monks were superior. Because the urine and filth of monks are not enough for these animals, they speak such words. Among the writings of the more than five thousand scrolls,[110] we find neither evidence that, nor any principle that, the lay mind and the mind that leaves family life are the same. There is no such trace in more than two thousand years. The Buddhist patriarchs of

---

104. The subject of the Vimalakīrti Sutra (Sanskrit: *Vimalakīrti-nīrdeśa*). See for example chap. 6, *Soku-shin-ze-butsu*, para. [129]; chap. 32, *Juki*, para. [56].

105. Layman Ho-on (died 808), first practiced in the order of Master Sekito Kisen and eventually became a successor of Master Baso Do-itsu. Quoted in chap. 25, *Jinzu*, para. [194]. See also *Shinji-shobogenzo*, pt. 1, nos. 5, 88, and 99.

106. Master Baso.

107. Ri Fuma (died 1038). First practiced in the order of Master Koku-on Unso and became his successor. Later maintained a close association with Master Jimyo So-en. He compiled *Tensho-koto-roku*, one of the sequels to *Keitoku-dento-roku*.

108. Also known as Layman Yo-oku, a disciple of Master Ko-e.

109. In temples in China at that time, "gruel and rice" meant breakfast and the midday meal.

110. 五千余軸 (GOSEN-YO-JIKU), "five thousand and more scrolls," suggests the whole treasury of the sutras. *Kaigen-shakkyo-roku*, compiled in 730 by the monk Chisho (658–740), listed 5,048 fascicles of Buddhist sutras.

fifty generations, and of forty ages and more,[111] have never said so. Even to become a bhikṣu who breaks the precepts or who has no precepts, and who is without Dharma and without wisdom, may be better than possessing wisdom and keeping the precepts as a lay person. The reason is that a monk's action is wisdom itself, realization itself, the truth itself, and the Dharma itself. Although lay people may have good roots[112] and virtues appropriate to their station, in the good roots and virtues of the body-mind they are scant. During the whole life of the teaching, no-one at all has attained the truth as a lay person. This is because lay life has never been a good place for learning the Buddha's truth, and because the obstacles it presents are many. When we look into the bodies and minds of those who insist that a mind for state affairs and the mind of the ancestral masters are the same, they are never bodies and minds of the Buddha-Dharma: they may not have received the transmission of the Buddhist patriarchs' skin, flesh, bones, and marrow. It is pitiful that, even while meeting the Buddha's right Dharma, they have become animals. Because this is the way it is, the eternal Buddha of Sokei left his parent at once and went in search of a master. This is right action. Before he heard the Diamond Sutra and established the mind, he lived in a family as a woodcutter. When he heard the Diamond Sutra and was influenced by the lingering fragrance[113] of the Buddha-Dharma, he threw down his heavy burden and left family life. Remember, when the body-mind possesses the Buddha-Dharma it is impossible to remain in lay life. This has been so for all the Buddhist patriarchs. We can say that people who assert that it is unnecessary to leave family life commit a sin even heavier than the deadly sins,[114] and they are even more wicked than Devadatta. Knowing them to be worse than the group of six bhikṣus, the group of six nuns, the group of eighteen bhikṣus, and so on, do not converse with them. A lifetime is not long; there is no time to be spent conversing with such demons and animals. Furthermore, this human body, received as a result of the seeds of seeing and hearing the Buddha-Dharma in past ages, is like a tool of the Universe: it is neither to be made into a demon nor to be aligned with demons. Remembering the profound benevolence of the Buddhist patriarchs, and preserving the goodness

---

111. Fifty generations suggests the fifty generations from Master Mahākāśyapa to Master Tendo Nyojo. Forty ages suggests the ages of the Seven Buddhas and the thirty-three patriarchs from Master Mahākāśyapa to Master Daikan Eno.

112. 善根 (ZENKON), or "the roots of good," representing the meaning of the Sanskrit *kuśala-mūla,* means right conduct as the root of happiness.

113. 薫 (KUN) means 1) the fragrance which remains after incense has been burnt, and by extension 2) the lingering effect of Buddhist practice under a true teacher. See also notes on 薫禅 (KUNZEN), "assuming the fragrance of dhyāna," in chap. 27, *Zazenshin,* para. [28], and on 薫修 (KUNJU), "instilling [of true wisdom] in chap. 40, *Gabyo,* para. [211].

114. 造逆 (ZOGYAKU). 造 (ZO) means to commit and 逆 (GYAKU) stands for 五逆罪 (GOGYAKUZAI), "the five deadly sins"; namely, to kill one's father, to kill one's mother, to kill an arhat, to shed the Buddha's blood, and to cause a schism in the Saṃgha.

of the milk of Dharma, do not listen to the howling of the evil hounds, and neither sit with nor eat with the evil hounds. When the founding patriarch of the Suzan mountains, the eternal Buddha, left the Buddha's kingdom of India far behind him and came from the west to the remote country of China, the right Dharma of the Buddhist patriarchs was transmitted in his person. If he had not left family life and attained the truth, such a thing would not have been possible. Before the ancestral Master came from the west, living beings, human and celestial, in the eastern lands, had never seen or heard the right Dharma. So remember, the authentic transmission of the right Dharma is solely [due to] the merit of leaving family life. When the Great Master Śākyamuni graciously relinquished his father's throne, he declined the succession not because the position of a king has no value but because he wished to succeed to the most valuable position of all: the position of a buddha. The position of a buddha is just the position of one who has left family life; it is a position to which all the gods and human beings of the triple world bow their heads in reverence.[115] It is a seat not shared by King Brahma or by King Śakra. How much less could it be a seat shared by the human kings and dragon kings of lower worlds? It is the position of the supreme, right, and balanced truth. The position itself is able to preach Dharma to save the living, and to radiate brightness and manifest auspicious phenomena. All actions in this position of one who has left family life are right action itself, they are actions to which the many buddhas and the Seven Buddhas have long been attached, and they are not perfectly realized except by buddhas alone, together with buddhas. People who have yet to leave family life should pay homage to and provide for those who have already left family life, they should bow down their heads in respect, and they should serve offerings by sacrificing body and life. Śākyamuni Buddha says, *"To leave family life and receive the precepts is to be the seed of Buddha. It is to be a person who has already attained salvation."* So remember, salvation means leaving family life. Those who have not left family life are in a depressed state. We should feel sad for them. In general, it is impossible to enumerate the instances on which, during his lifetime of preaching, the Buddha has praised the merit of leaving family life; Śākyamuni preaches it whole-heartedly, and all the buddhas certify it. People who have left family life, even if they break the precepts and neglect training, can attain the truth. No lay person has ever attained the truth. When emperors do prostrations to monks and nuns, monks and nuns do not return the prostration. When gods do prostrations to people who have left family life, the bhikṣus and bhikṣuṇīs never return the prostration. This is because the merit of leaving family life is pre-eminent. If they received the prostrations of bhikṣus and bhikṣuṇīs who have left family

---

115. 頂戴恭敬 (CHODAI-KUGYO). 頂戴 (CHODAI) lit. means humbly to receive some venerated object, such as the kaṣāya, upon the head (see chap. 12, *Kesa-kudoku*). Here it suggests bowing at a buddha's feet.

life, the palaces, radiance, and good fortune of gods in heaven would collapse at once, and so [the custom] is like this. In sum, since the Buddha-Dharma spread to the east, while attainment of the truth by people who have left family life has been as [prevalent as] rice, flax, bamboo, and reeds, no-one has attained the truth as a lay person. Once the Buddha-Dharma has reached a person's eyes and ears, they urgently endeavor to leave family life. Clearly, the state of a lay person is not a place where the Buddha-Dharma abides. Those who say, on the contrary, that the body and mind in conducting state affairs is just the body-mind of the Buddhist patriarchs, have never seen and heard the Buddha-Dharma, they are sinners in darkest hell, they are stupid people who do not even see and hear their own words, and they are enemies of the nation. The reason they would like to establish the principle that a mind for state affairs and the mind of the Buddhist patriarchs are the same is that emperors—because the Buddha-Dharma is pre-eminent—are delighted at such an assertion. We should remember that the Buddha-Dharma is pre-eminent. It may happen that a mind in conducting state affairs is the same as the mind of the Buddhist patriarchs; however, in the rare instance when the body-mind of the Buddhist patriarchs has become a body-mind conducting state affairs, it can never be the body and mind of conducting state affairs. "Zen Masters" and the like who say that a mind for state affairs and the mind of Buddhist patriarchs are the same, are totally ignorant of how a mind actually works and how it is. How much less could they see, even in a dream, the mind of the Buddhist patriarchs? As a universal principle, [I recommend] King Brahma, King Śakra, human kings, dragon kings, demon kings, and every other kind of king: do not attach to the direct and indirect results of conduct in the triple world, but soon leave home, receive the precepts, and practice the truth of the buddhas and the patriarchs, and this will be a cause of Buddhahood for vast eons. Do you not see that if old man Vimalakīrti had left family life, we would be able to meet with one more excellent than Vimalakīrti: that is, Vimalakīrti Bhikṣu. Today we are barely able to meet [bhikṣus] like Subhūti,[116] Śāriputra,[117] Mañjuśrī, and Maitreya,[118] but we never meet half a Vimalakīrti. How much less could we meet three, four, or five Vimalakīrtis? Without meeting or knowing three, four, or five Vimalakīrtis, we can never meet, know, or maintain and rely upon the state

116. 空生 (KUSHO), lit. "born of emptiness," is a Chinese epithet of Subhūti, who, among the ten great disciples of the Buddha, was said to be foremost in understanding of śūnyatā (the state that is like emptiness).

117. Also one of the ten great disciples. The list in full is Śāriputra, Maudgalyāyana, Mahākāśyapa, Aniruddha, Subhūti, Pūrṇa, Kātyāyana, Upāli, Rāhula, and Ānanda. Subhūti and Śāriputra are cited as examples of monks who lived at the time of the historical Buddha.

118. Mañjuśrī and Maitreya are legendary bodhisattva-monks who appear in the Buddha's retinue in Mahāyāna sutras such as the Lotus Sutra.

of, a Vimalakīrti.[119] Never having maintained and relied upon the state of a Vimalakīrti we do not meet Vimalakīrti as Buddha. If we do not meet Vimalakīrti as Buddha, then Vimalakīrti as Mañjuśrī, Vimalakīrti as Maitreya, Vimalakīrti as Subhūti,[120] Vimalakīrti as Śāriputra, and so on, can never be. How much less could there be Vimalakīrti as mountains, rivers, and the Earth, or Vimalakīrti as grass, trees, tiles, and pebbles; wind, rain, water, and fire; past, present, and future; and so on. The reason that such brightness and virtues are not visible in Vimalakīrti is that he did not leave family life. If Vimalakīrti had left family life, such virtues would be present in him. "Zen Masters" and the like at the time of the Tang and Sung dynasties, never having arrived at this principle, have randomly cited Vimalakīrti, considering that what he did was right and saying that what he said was right. These cronies, pitifully, do not know the spoken teaching and are blind to the Buddha-Dharma. Furthermore, many of them have gone so far as to consider and to say that the words of Vimalakīrti and of Śākyamuni are equal. Again, these have never known, or considered, the Buddha-Dharma, the patriarchs' truth, or even Vimalakīrti himself. They say that Vimalakīrti's silence in addressing bodhisattvas[121] is the same as the Tathāgata's use of silence to teach people. This is to be grossly ignorant of the Buddha-Dharma. We can say that they have no capacity for learning the truth. The speech of the Tathāgata is, of course, different from that of others, and his silence also can never be like that of other types. That being so, the total silence of the Tathāgata and the total silence of Vimalakīrti do not deserve even to be compared. When we examine the ability of the cronies who have conceived that, although the spoken teachings were different, the silences might have been alike, they do not deserve even to be seen as people in the vicinity of Buddha. It is sad that they have never experienced sounds and forms. How much less could they have experienced the brightness that springs from within sound and form? They do not even know that they should learn the silence in silence, and they do not even hear that it exists. In general, even among various types there are differences in movement and stillness; how could we say that Śākyamuni and miscellaneous types are the same, or discuss them as dissimilar? People who do not learn in practice in the inner sanctum of a Buddhist patriarch engage in such discussion. There again, many wrong people think, "Spoken teaching and active demeanor are insubstantial matters. The silent and unmoving state is the true reality." Expressions like this also are not the Buddha-Dharma. They are the speculations of people who have heard sutras and

---

119. See also the discussion of three or four concrete moons and one conceptual moon in chap. 42, *Tsuki*, para. [10].

120. 善現 (ZENGEN), lit. "Well Manifest" or "Healthy in Appearance," approximates the meaning of the Sanskrit *subhūti*, which means well-being or welfare.

121. The Vimalakīrti Sutra relates how Vimalakīrti attempted to refute monks in the Buddha's order based on the viewpoint of śūnyatā.

teachings of Brahmadeva, Īśvara,[122] and the like. How could the Buddha-Dharma be caught by movement and stillness? In the Buddhist state of truth is there movement and stillness, or is there no movement and stillness? Do we contact movement and stillness, or are we contacted by movement and stillness? Painstakingly research it in practice. Practitioners of later ages who are present now, do not let up. When we look at the great kingdom of Sung today, people who have learned in practice the great truth of the Buddhist patriarchs appear to have become extinct; there are not [even] two or three of them. There are only people who believe that Vimalakīrti, being right, had total silence, and that we today who are not totally silent are inferior to Vimalakīrti. They utterly lack the vigorous road of the Buddha-Dharma. Likewise, there are only people who think that Vimalakīrti's total silence is just the same as the World-Honored One's total silence. They utterly lack the light of clear discrimination. We can say that people who think and speak like this have no experience at all of learning in practice to see and hear the Buddha-Dharma. Do not think that, just because they are people of the great kingdom of Sung, they must be of the Buddha-Dharma. The reason may be easy to clarify: right action is the action of a monk. It is beyond the knowledge of commentary-teachers and sutra-teachers. The action of a monk means effort inside the Cloud Hall, prostrations inside the Buddha Hall, washing the face inside the washroom,[123] and so on. It means joining hands and bowing, burning incense and boiling water. This is right action. It is not only to replace a tail with a head;[124] it is to replace a head with a head; it is to replace the mind with the mind; it is to replace buddha with buddha; and it is to replace the truth with the truth.[125] This is just *right action as a branch of the path.* If appreciation of the Buddha-Dharma is faulty, the eyebrows and whiskers fall down and out, and the face falls apart.

[62] *Right livelihood as a branch of the path* is early-morning gruel and noon rice,[126C] is to stay in a temple's grounds and to let the soul play,[127C] and is to

---

122. 自在天 (JIZAITEN), "God of Freedom," or "Almighty," represents the Sanskrit *Īśvara,* which is an epithet of Śiva, the god of destruction and regeneration in the Hindu triad of Brahmā (creator), Śiva, and Viṣṇu (preserver). "Sutras and teachings of Brahmadeva, Īśvara, and the like" suggests Indian idealism. See Book 1, Glossary.

123. 後架 (KOKA), lit. "rear stand." See chap. 56, *Senmen.*

124. 以頭換尾 (I-TO-KAN-BI), "replacing a tail with a head," here suggests bringing one's attention back down to practical matters—for example, remembering the importance of eating and digesting meals. Elsewhere in Shobogenzo 以頭換尾 (I-TO-KAN-BI) represents impractical or nonsensical behavior; see for example chap. 66, *Shunju,* para. [127].

125. 以道換道 (I-DO-KAN-DO), "replacing the truth with the truth," suggests the value system of a true Buddhist monk—one who pursues the balanced state of action just for its own sake.

126. A monk's meals.

127. 弄精魂 (ROZEIKON), "letting the soul play" or "playing with the soul," is explained in chap. 68, *Udonge,* para. [167] as follows: *Playing with the soul means just sitting and dropping off body and mind. Becoming a buddha and becoming a patriarch is called playing with the soul. Putting*

demonstrate it directly upon the round wooden chair.[128c] The less than twenty members of Old Joshu's order are the realization of right livelihood; the less than ten members of Yakusan's order are the life-blood of right livelihood; and the seven or eight members of Fun-yo's[129] order are the constant on which right livelihood hangs—because they are divorced from all forms of wrong livelihood. Śākyamuni Buddha says, *"Śrāvakas have never attained right livelihood."* So the teaching, practice, and experience of a śrāvaka are never right livelihood. The flotsam of recent times, however, have said that we should not distinguish between śrāvakas and bodhisattvas. Contending that we should rely upon the dignified forms and the precepts of each of the two, they judge the dignified forms and behavior which are the rule for a bodhisattva of the Great Vehicle, by the rules of a śrāvaka of the small vehicle. Śākyamuni Buddha says, *"A śrāvaka's keeping of the precepts is a bodhisattva's violation of the precepts."* So the śrāvaka-precepts that śrāvakas have considered to be keeping of the precepts, when viewed against the bodhisattva-precepts, are all violations of the precepts. The other [practices]—balance and wisdom[130]—are also like this. Though such [precepts] as *Do not kill living things* are apparently the same in form for a śrāvaka and for a bodhisattva, there is necessarily a difference between them which is beyond the separation between heaven and earth. How much less could the principles authentically transmitted from buddha to buddha and from patriarch to patriarch be the same as those of śrāvakas? There is not only right livelihood, but also pure livelihood. In conclusion, just to learn in practice from a Buddhist patriarch may be right livelihood. Do not rely upon the views and opinions of commentary-teachers and the like. Because *they have never attained right livelihood,* they are not truly living their own lives.

[65] *Right effort as a branch of the path* is action that gouges out a whole body, and it is the fashioning of a human face in the gouging out of the whole body.[131c] It is to ride upside down around the Buddha Hall, doing one lap, two laps, three, four, and five laps,[c] so that nine times nine comes to eighty-two.[c] It is repeatedly to repay [the benevolence of] others, thousands and tens of thousands of times; it is to turn the head in any direction of the cross, vertically or horizontally;[c] it is to change the face vertically or horizontally,

---

on clothes and eating meals is called playing with the soul.

128. 曲木座 (KYOKU-BOKU-ZA), "the round wooden chair," means the chair used in a temple for formal preaching.

129. Master Funyo Zensho (947–1024), successor of Master Shuzan Shonen, and the fourth-generation descendant of Master Rinzai.

130. Refers to 三学 (SANGAKU), "the three practices," from the Sanskrit *tisraḥ śikṣāḥ:* precepts *(śīla),* balance *(samādhi),* and wisdom *(prajñā).* See Book 1, Glossary.

131. In other words, right effort is effort that makes us more truly human in the process of Buddhist training. Cf. words of Master Tendo Nyojo in chap. 63, *Ganzei,* para. [88]: *"Gouging out Bodhidharma's Eye, I make it into a mud ball and work it into a person."*

in any direction of the cross;[C] it is to enter the [master's] room and to go to the Dharma Hall.[C] It expresses *having met*[132] *at Boshu-tei pavilion, having met on Useki-rei peak, having met in front of the Monks' Hall;*[133] and having met inside the Buddha Hall[CD]—there being two mirrors and three kinds of reflection.[134]

[66] *Right mindfulness as a branch of the path* is the eighty or ninety percent realization of the state of being duped by ourselves. To learn that wisdom occurs following from mindfulness is *leaving the father and running away.*[135C] To learn that wisdom occurs within mindfulness itself is to be fettered in the extreme.[C] To say that being without mindfulness is right mindfulness is non-Buddhism. Neither should we see the animating soul of earth, water, fire, and wind as mindfulness. Upset states of mind, will, and consciousness are not called mindfulness. *You having got my skin, flesh, bones, and marrow*[136] is just *right mindfulness as a branch of the path.*

[67] *Right balance as a branch of the path* is to get free of Buddhist patriarchs, and to get free of right balance. It is others being well able to discuss.[C] It is to make nose-holes[137] by cutting out the top of the head.[C] It is the twirling of an uḍumbara flower inside the right-Dharma-eye treasury.[C] It is the presence inside the uḍumbara flower of a hundred thousand faces of Mahākāśyapa breaking into a smile.[C] Having used [this] state of vigorous activity for a long time, a wooden dipper is broken.[138] Thus, [right balance] is six years of floundering in the wilderness[139] and a night in which a flower opens.[140C] It is,

---

132. 相見了 (SOKEN-RYO), or "having met each other." 相 (SO), which expresses a mutual or reciprocal relation, here suggests union of subject and object.

133. *Seppo addresses the assembly, "I have met you at Boshu-tei pavilion, I have met you on Useki-rei peak, and I have met you in front of the Monks' Hall." Hofuku asks Gako, "Let us forget for a while the front of the Monks' Hall. What about the meetings at Boshu-tei pavilion and Useki-rei peak?" Gako runs back to the abbot's quarters. Hofuku lowers his head and goes into the Monks' Hall.* See *Shinji-shobogenzo,* pt. 3, no. 91; see also chap. 36, *Komyo,* para. [139].

134. "Two mirrors" suggests subject and object, their combination resulting in the undivided reality of the present moment. Right effort occurs in balanced consciousness of what is happening both inside and outside, here and now.

135. 捨父逃逝 (SHA-FU-TOZEI), picked up from the parable in Lotus Sutra, *Shinge.* See LS 1.224.

136. Words of Master Bodhidharma expressing oneness between himself and each of four disciples. See chap. 46, *Katto,* para. [90].

137. 鼻孔 (BIKU), "nose-holes," i.e. nostrils, are a symbol of liveliness. Right balance is a lively state realized by ceasing the more sophisticated mental activities that take us away from the here and now.

138. 木杓破 (BOKU-SHAKU-HA), "a wooden dipper is broken," means that a Buddhist practitioner has become completely free from miscellaneous restrictive conditions.

139. 落艸六年 (RAKUSO-ROKUNEN), lit. "falling [among] weeds six years," alludes to the Buddha's six years of ascetic practice in pursuit of the truth.

140. 花開一夜 (KAKAI-ICHIYA), "a flower opening one night," suggests the Buddha's experience of balance, on the night of his enlightenment, when he just sat in the lotus posture.

[when] *the holocaust at the end of a kalpa is blazing and the great-thousand world is being totally destroyed, just to follow circumstances.*[141]

[69] These thirty-seven elements of bodhi are the very eyes and nostrils, the skin, flesh, bones, and marrow, and the hands, feet, and real features, of the Buddhist Patriarch. We have been learning in practice, as the thirty-seven elements of bodhi, the Buddhist Patriarch's whole person. At the same time, they are the realization of 1,369 realities,[142] [each of] which is a constituent element of bodhi. We should sit them away and we should get free of them.

Shobogenzo Sanjushichi-bon-bodai-bunpo

Preached to the assembly at Kippo temple in Etsu-u,[143] on the 24th day of the 2nd lunar month in the 2nd year of Kangen.[144]

141. *A monk asks Master Daizui Hoshin, "[They say that] when the holocaust at the end of a kalpa is blazing, the great-thousandfold world will be totally destroyed. I wonder whether or not this place will be destroyed." The Master says, "It will be destroyed." The monk says, "If that is so, should we just follow circumstances?" The Master says, "We just follow circumstances."* (*Goto-egen*, chap. 4; see also Shobogenzo, chap. 37, *Shinjin-gakudo*, para. [152].)

142. 一千三百六十九品の公案現成 (ISSEN-SAN BYAKU-ROKUJU-KU-BON *no* KOAN-GENJO). The number 1,369 is 37 multiplied by 37—suggesting that the whole that comprises 37 elements is present in each constituent element.

143. Present-day Fukui Prefecture.

144. 1244.

[74]

転法輪

TENBORIN

Turning the Dharma Wheel

Ten *means "turn,"* ***ho*** *means "Dharma," or the Buddha's teaching, and* ***rin*** *means "wheel"—in Sanskrit "cakra." In ancient India a cakra was a wheel with pointed spokes, used as a weapon. The Buddha's preaching was likened to the turning of a cakra, and thus* ***tenborin****, or the turning of the Dharma wheel, refers to the preaching of Buddhism. In this chapter Master Dogen explains the true meaning of preaching Buddhism. Before his explanation, he quotes the words of several masters on what happens when someone "realizes the truth and returns to the origin," in order to illustrate the value of Buddhist scriptures written in China. Some people have insisted that only scriptures written in India qualify as being genuine "Buddhist scriptures," and therefore the scriptures that were written in China do not expound true Buddhism. But Master Dogen takes a wider view: he says that any scripture quoted by a true Buddhist master is a true Buddhist scripture, even if it was written outside of India. He insists that when a true Buddhist master quotes a scripture, that act confirms the scripture as a true Buddhist teaching. From this, Master Dogen explains that the preaching of Buddhism can be done in all places and at all times, and these preachings thus have universal validity. At the same time, he asserts that to preach true Buddhism is to practice Zazen throughout one's life.*

[71] **My late Master Tendo, the eternal Buddha,** in formal preaching in the Dharma Hall, quotes: *"The World-Honored One said, 'When a person exhibits the truth and returns to the origin, space in the ten directions totally disappears.'"* The Master comments: *"This is just the preaching of the World-Honored One, but everyone has been unable to avoid producing odd interpretations of it. Tendo is not like that. When a person exhibits the truth and returns to the origin, a beggar boy breaks his food bowl."*[1]

[72] Master Ho-en[2] of Goso-zan mountain said, *"When a person exhibits the truth and returns to the origin, space in the ten directions is jostling."*[3]

---

1. *Nyojo-osho-goroku,* pt. 2.

2. Master Goso Ho-en (died 1104), successor of Master Haku-un Shutan.

3. *Ho-en-zenji-goroku,* pt 1. 築著磕著 (CHIKUJAKU-GATSUJAKU), "jostling," is an onomatopoeic expression for the crunching of stones or gravel. It suggests a condition in which miscellaneous concrete things are jostling against each other, rather than an idealistic notion of harmony.

[73] Master Bussho Hotai[4] said, *"When a person exhibits the truth and returns to the origin, space in the ten directions is just space in the ten directions"*[5]

[73] Zen Master Engo Kokugon[6] of Kassan mountain said, *"When a person exhibits the truth and returns to the origin, space in the ten directions puts on flowers over brocade."*[7]

[73] Daibutsu[8] says, *"When a person exhibits the truth and returns to the origin, space in the ten directions exhibits the truth and returns to the origin."*

[74] The expression quoted now, that *"When a person exhibits the truth and returns to the origin, space in the ten directions totally disappears,"* is an expression in the Śūraṃgama Sūtra.[9] This same phrase has been discussed by several Buddhist patriarchs. Consequently, this phrase is truly the bones and marrow of Buddhist patriarchs, and the eyes of Buddhist patriarchs. My intention in saying so is as follows: Some insist that the ten-fascicle version of the Śūraṃgama Sūtra is a forged sutra[10] while others insist that it is not a forged sutra. The two arguments have persisted from the distant past until today. There is the older translation[11] and there is the new translation;[12] the version that is

---

4. Master Bussho Hotai (dates unknown), successor of Master Engo Kokugon.

5. *Katai-futo-roku,* chap. 26.

6. Master Engo Kokugon (1063–1135), successor of Master Goso Ho-en, and editor of *Hekigan-roku (Blue Cliff Record).* See also Shobogenzo, chap. 66, *Shunju,* and chap. 89, *Shinjin-inga.*

7. *Engo-koroku,* chap. 8.

8. Master Dogen. Daibutsu-ji was the original name of the temple now known as Eihei-ji, which Master Dogen founded 1244. However, this chapter was preached at Kippo temple.

9. 首楞厳経 (SHURYOGON-KYO). The long title of the Chinese scripture in question is 大仏頂如来密因修証了義諸菩薩万行首楞厳経 (DAIBUCCHO NYORAI MITSU-IN-SHUSHO RYOGI SHOBOSATSU MANGYO SHURYOGON KYO), or "Śūraṃgama-sūtra of the Great-Buddha-Head Tathāgata's Understanding of the Myriad Ways in which Bodhisattvas Secretly Rely Upon Practice-and-Experience." This work, completed in 705, purported to be a translation of the Śūraṃgama-samādhi-nirdeśa, although its authenticity was doubted and it is no longer extant. The title of the original Sanskrit sutra means "Description of the Samādhi (state of balance in Zazen) called Śūraṃgama ('heroic march')." Addressed to the bodhisattva Dṛdhamati, it praises samādhi as a state of valiant onward progress. See Book 1, Glossary.

10. 偽経 (GIKYO), "forged sutras," describes Chinese sutras that falsely purported to be translations of Sanskrit sutras.

11. 旧訳 (KUYAKU), "older translation(s)," probably indicates Kumārajīva's translation. According to JEBD many Chinese translations of the Śūraṃgama-samādhi-nirdeśa were produced, but only Kumārajīva's version is extant. In general, 旧訳 (KUYAKU), "older translations," categorizes those Buddhist scriptures that were translated into Chinese between the time of Kumārajīva (344–413) and Genjo (600–664). Translations done before Kumārajīva's time are called 古訳 (KOYAKU), "ancient translations." Included in the latter category are translations by the Indian monk Lokakṣema who came to China in 147 and is said to have translated the Śūraṃgama-samādhi-nirdeśa in around 185.

12. 新訳 (SHIN-YAKU), "new translation(s)," generally means translations done by the Chinese monk Hsuan-tsang (Jap: Genjo) who, in 629, set off to India via Central Asia and Afghanistan in order to obtain original Sanskrit texts. After returning in 645 with the

doubted is [not these but] a translation produced during the Shinryu era.[13] However, Master Goso [Ho]en, Master Bussho [Hot]tai, and my late Master Tendo, the eternal Buddha, have each quoted the above phrase already. So this phrase has already been turned in the Dharma wheel of Buddhist patriarchs; it is the Buddhist Patriarch's Dharma wheel turning. Thus, this phrase has already turned Buddhist patriarchs and this phrase has already preached Buddhist patriarchs. By reason of being preached by Buddhist patriarchs and preaching Buddhist patriarchs, even if a sutra is forged, once Buddhist patriarchs have preached and quoted it, it is truly a sutra of buddhas and a sutra of patriarchs, and it is the intimately-experienced Dharma wheel of the Buddhist Patriarch. Even tiles and pebbles, even yellow leaves, even an uḍumbara flower, and even a robe of golden brocade,[14] are, once picked up by Buddhist patriarchs, the Buddha's Dharma wheel and the Buddha's right-Dharma-eye treasury. Remember, when living beings transcend their realization of the right state of truth, they are Buddhist patriarchs, they are the teachers and students of Buddhist patriarchs, and they are the skin, flesh, bones, and marrow of Buddhist patriarchs. They no longer see as their brothers the living beings who were formerly their brothers, for Buddhist patriarchs are their brothers. In the same way, even if every sentence of the ten fascicles is forged, the present phrase is a transcendent phrase, a phrase of buddhas and a phrase of patriarchs—one that should never be classed with other sentences and other phrases. Although this phrase is a transcendent phrase, we should not imagine that every sentence in the whole volume is, in essence and form, a saying of the Buddha or the words of a patriarch; we should not see [every sentence] as the eye of learning in practice. There are many reasons not to compare the present phrase and other phrases; I would like to take up one among them. What has been called "turning the Dharma wheel" is the behavior of Buddhist patriarchs. No Buddhist patriarch has ever gone without turning the Dharma wheel. In the real situation of turning the Dharma wheel [Buddhist patriarchs] use sound and form to get rid of sound and form; or they turn the Dharma wheel springing free of sound and form; or they turn the Dharma wheel scooping out the Eye; or they turn the Dharma wheel holding up a fist. This, at a place where nostrils are grasped or at a place where space is

---

manuscripts of six hundred and fifty-seven texts, he produced over thirteen hundred fascicles of scriptures in Chinese and completed *Daito-saiiki-ki*, an extensive record of his travels.

13. Refers to *Daibuccho-nyorai-mitsu-in-shusho-ryogi-shobosatsu-mangyo-shuryogon-kyo*, the translation of the Śūraṃgama Sūtra that Hanshi Mittai is said to have completed in the 1st year of the Shinryu Era, 705. See note 9.

14. The words "uḍumbara flower," and "robe of golden brocade" allude to the story of the transmission between the Buddha and Master Mahākāśyapa. The story, which is quoted many times in Shobogenzo, comes from *Daibonten-o-monbutsu-ketsugi-kyo (Sutra of Questions and Answers between Mahābrahman and the Buddha)*, which is also suspected of being a forged sutra.

grasped,[15] is the Dharma wheel naturally turning itself. To grasp the present phrase is, here and now, just to grasp the bright star, to grasp a nose, to grasp peach blossoms, or to grasp space: they are one. [To grasp the present phrase] is to grasp the Buddhist Patriarch and to grasp the Dharma wheel: they are one. This principle is definitely the turning of the Dharma wheel. Turning the Dharma wheel means striving to learn in practice throughout a life without leaving the temple grounds; it means requesting the benevolence of the teaching and pursuing the truth upon long platforms.

Shobogenzo Tenborin

Preached to the assembly at Kippo temple in Etsu-u on the 27th day of the 2nd lunar month in the 2nd year of Kangen.[16]

---

15. Alludes to a story about Master Seido Chizo, who grasped air when asked to explain space, and Master Shakkyo Ezo, who grasped Master Seido Chizo's nose. See chap. 77, *Koku*.

16. 1244.

[75]

自証三昧

JISHO-ZANMAI

Samādhi as Experience of the Self

Ji means "self," sho means "to experience," and ***zanmai*** *means "samādhi," or "the balanced state." So* ***jisho-zanmai*** *means samādhi, as the state of self-experience. In this chapter Master Dogen explains the meaning of* ***jisho-zanmai****, criticizing the wrong understanding of Master Dai-e Soko and his disciples. They understood* ***jisho-zanmai*** *as meaning an intellectual state referred to as "enlightenment," a state that they made their utmost efforts to attain. Master Dogen did not agree with this belief. In this chapter he strongly criticizes Master Dai-e Soko and explains the true meaning of* ***jisho-zanmai.***

[79] **What the buddhas and the patriarchs** have authentically transmitted, from all the buddhas and the Seven Buddhas, is samādhi as the state of experiencing the self. It is what is called *sometimes to follow a good counselor, sometimes to follow the sutras.*[1] This state is just the eyes of the Buddhist patriarchs. For this reason, the eternal Buddha Sokei asks a monk, *"Do you rely upon practice and experience, or not?"* The monk says, *"It is not that there is no practice-and-experience, but to taint it is impossible."*[2] So remember, untainted practice-and-experience is the Buddhist patriarchs themselves, and is the Buddhist patriarchs' samādhi as a thunderclap, wind, and rolling thunder.

[80] Just in the moment of *following a good counselor,*[3] sometimes we see half of each other's face, sometimes we see half of each other's body, sometimes we see the whole of each other's face, and sometimes we see the whole of each other's body. There are instances of meeting in each other half of the self, and

---

1. 或従知識、或従経巻 (WAKU-JU-CHISHIKI, WAKU-JU-KYOGAN) is a commonly recurring phrase in Shobogenzo: see, for example, chap. 10, *Shoaku-makusa,* para. [6]; chap. 20, *Kokyo,* para. [129]; chap. 32, *Juki,* para. [35]; chap. 52, *Bukkyo,* para. [21], et cetera.

2. This conversation between the Sixth Patriarch (Master Daikan Eno) and Master Nangaku Ejo is recorded in *Shinji-shobogenzo,* pt. 2, no. 1. See also Shobogenzo chap. 7, *Senjo,* chap. 29, *Inmo,* and chap. 62, *Hensan.*

3. 知識 (CHISHIKI) stands for 善知識 (ZENCHISHIKI), from the Sanskrit *kalyāṇa-mitra,* which means a good friend, a friend in virtue; that is, a teacher who exemplifies the Zazen life and helps and inspires others to live the Zazen life.

there are instances of meeting in each other half of the external world.[4] We experience in each other the state in which the head of a god is covered with hair, and we experience in each other the state in which the face of a demon is topped by horns. We have the experience of following circumstances[5] while going among alien types, and we go on changing while living among like beings. In these situations we do not know how many thousand myriad times we throw away the body for the sake of Dharma. And we do not know for how many koṭis of hundred kalpas we seek Dharma for the sake of our own body. This is the vigorous activity of *following a good counselor;* and it is the actual condition of exploring the self and suiting the self. At the time of mutual realization in the wink of an eye, [this condition] possesses a smiling face; and on the occasion of prostration to attainment of the marrow, it cuts off an arm. In sum, from the time before and after the Seven Buddhas to beyond the time of the Sixth Patriarch the *good counselors* who have met themselves are not one and not two. And the *good counselors* who have met the external world are neither of the past nor of the present. In the moment of *following the sutras,* when we investigate the skin, flesh, bones, and marrow of the self and get free of the skin, flesh, bones, and marrow of the self, peach blossoms are seen protruding from the eyes themselves, and the sound of bamboo is heard thundering from the ears themselves.

[82] In general, when we follow and practice *the sutras*, *the sutras* truly come forth. The meaning of *"the sutras"* is the whole Universe in ten directions, mountains, rivers, and the Earth, grass and trees, self and others; it is eating meals and putting on clothes, instantaneous movements and demeanors. When we pursue the truth following these texts, each of which is a sutra, countless thousand-myriad volumes of totally unprecedented sutras manifest themselves in reality and exist before us. They have lines of characters of affirmation that are conspicuous as they are; and their verses of characters of negation are unmistakably clear. When, becoming able to meet them, we muster the body-mind to learn in practice—therein using up long eons or making use of long eons—the destination that is thorough understanding[6] inevitably exists. When we let go of body and mind in order to learn in practice—therein gouging out eternity[7] or soaring beyond eternity—we

---

4. 他 (TA) means the other or others, that which is outside, that which is external to the self, the external world.

5. 随他来 (ZUITARAI), a variation of the traditional phrase 随他去 (ZUITAKO), "following circumstances completely." In these phrases 来 (RAI), lit. "coming" or "having come," suggests an experience that has continued to the present and 去 (KO), lit, "going" or "having gone," is emphatic. 他 (TA) is as in the preceding note.

6. 通利 (TSURI) means to be thoroughly versed in the sutras. See chap. 52, *Bukkyo.*

7. 朕兆 (CHINCHO), lit. means "the first slight showing of a sign." The expression also appears in chap. 14, *Sansuigyo,* chap. 38, *Muchu-setsumu,* para. [173], and chap. 63, *Ganzei,* para. [80], where it is suggests the genesis of the Universe ("the sprouting of creation"). Here it

inevitably realize the virtue of receiving and retaining [sutras]. The Sanskrit texts of India translated into Chinese books of Dharma now number not even five thousand fascicles.[8] Among these there are [sutras of] the three vehicles, the five vehicles, the nine parts, and the twelve parts;[9] and they are all sutras that we should follow and practice. Even if we intended to avoid following them, it would be impossible. Thus they have sometimes become the Eye[10] and have sometimes become *my marrow*.[11] They are horns on the head being right and a tail being right.[12] We receive this state from others and we impart this state to others; at the same time, it is just the lively springing out of eyes themselves, which gets free of self and others, and it is just the transmission of *my marrow* itself, which is liberated from self and others. Because eyes and *my marrow* are beyond self and beyond others, Buddhist patriarchs have authentically transmitted them from the past to the past, and Buddhist patriarchs pass them on from the present to the present. There are sutras as staffs that preach the length and preach the breadth,[13] naturally breaking "emptiness" and breaking "existence." There are sutras as fly-whisks[14] that cleanse snow and cleanse frost. There are one order and two orders of sutras as Zazen. There are sutras as kaṣāyas with ten scrolls per volume. These are guarded and maintained by the Buddhist patriarchs. Following sutras like these we perform practice-and-experience, and attain the truth. Causing to exist sometimes god faces and human faces, and sometimes sun faces and moon faces, the effort of *following the sutras* is realized. At the same time, all instances of following good counselors and of following the sutras are just to follow the self. A sutra is naturally a sutra of the self, and a good counselor is naturally a good counselor of the self. That being so, thorough exploration of good counselors[15] is thorough exploration of the self. To take up the hundred weeds is to take up the self. To take up the ten thousand trees is to take up the self. We learn in practice that the self is inevitably efforts like these. In this learning in practice, we get rid of the self, and we experience the self as exact accordance.[16] For this reason, in the great truth of the Buddhist

---

suggests the time since the genesis of the Universe, that is, eternity.

8. 半万軸 (HANMAN-JIKU), lit. "half a myriad scrolls." Cf. chap. 73, note 110.

9. See chap. 24, *Bukkyo*.

10. 眼睛 (GANZEI), that is, the view of Gautama Buddha. See chap. 62, *Ganzei*.

11. 吾随 (GOZUI), that is, the practical state of Master Bodhidharma. See chap. 46, *Katto*.

12. 頭角正なり、尾条正なり (ZUKAKU-SHO *nari*, BIJO-SHO *nari*), a variation of the familiar expression 頭正尾正 (ZUSHIN-BISHIN), lit. "head-right, tail-right," i.e., "head to tail rightnesss," or "the state that is right from beginning to end."

13. 横説縦説 (OSETSU-JUSETSU), lit. "vertically preach and horizontally preach," means to preach without restriction in any direction.

14. 払子 (HOSSU), a ceremonial fly whisk.

15. 遍参知識 (HENSAN CHISHIKI) refers to the custom of monks in China of traveling around to visit different teachers. See chap. 62, *Hensan*.

16. 自己を証契する (JIKO *o* SHOKAI *suru*). 証契 (SHOKAI) means to experience the state

patriarchs, there are concrete tools for experiencing the self and realizing the self, [but] if we are not Buddhist patriarchs as rightful successors we do not receive their authentic transmission. There are concrete tools that have been received from rightful successor to rightful successor, [but] if we are other than the bones and marrow of the Buddhist patriarchs we do not receive their authentic transmission.

[87] Because we learn in practice like this, during the transmission and reception to and from others, the transmission exists as *"You have got my marrow"*; and *"I transmit the right-Dharma-eye treasury that I possess to Mahākāśyapa."* Preaching is not necessarily connected with self and others. Preaching for others is just preaching for the self. It is listening and preaching in which self and self experience the same state.[17] One ear is listening and one ear is preaching, one tongue is preaching and one tongue is listening; and so on for eyes, ears, nose, tongue, body, and mind; for the sense organs, their consciousness, and their objects. Going further, there is experience and there is practice with one body and one mind: it is the ears themselves listening-and-preaching and the tongue itself listening-and-preaching. Yesterday we were preaching to others an exception to the rule, but today we are preaching to ourselves an established rule.[18] In this way the faces of the sun line up one after another and the faces of the moon line up one after another. To preach Dharma and to practice Dharma for the benefit of others is to hear Dharma, to clarify Dharma, and to experience Dharma in our [whole] life at each moment.[19] Even in this present life if we are sincere in preaching Dharma to others, our own attainment of Dharma is made easy. Or if we help and encourage other people to listen to Dharma, our own learning of Dharma receives good sustenance. We receive sustenance in our body, and we receive sustenance in our mind. If we hinder others in listening to Dharma, our own listening to Dharma is hindered. To preach Dharma and to listen to Dharma with our [whole] body at each moment in our [whole] life at each moment is to hear Dharma in every age, and is to listen again in the present age to Dharma that was authentically transmitted to us in the past. We are born in

---

which is exactly the same as the state of Gautama Buddha (see for example chap. 16, *Shisho*, chap. 48, *Sesshin-sessho*).

17. In other words, the subjective self that receives stimuli through the senses, and the objective self that preaches or manifests itself in the external world, become one undivided whole.

18. Master Dogen's variation of the Chinese expression 昨日説定法、今日説不定法 (SAKUJITSU-SETSU-JOHO, KONNICHI-SETSU-FUJOHO), "yesterday preaching an established rule, today preaching an exception to the rule." See chap. 73, *Sanjushichi-bon-bodai-bunpo*, para. [16], footnote 28.

19. 生生 (SHO-SHO). 生 (SHO) means life, birth, or appearance. 生生 (SHO-SHO), "life-life," or "whole life at each moment," appears several times in this paragraph, along with the words 身身 (SHIN-SHIN), "body-body," or "whole body at each moment."

Dharma, and we die in Dharma, and so, having received the authentic transmission of the Dharma while in the whole Universe in ten directions, we listen to it in our [whole] life at each moment and practice it with our [whole] body at each moment. Because we can realize our [whole] life at each moment in Dharma and make our [whole] body at each moment into Dharma, we bring together both single molecules and the universal order and let them experience Dharma. That being so, having heard a word in the east, we should preach it to a person on coming to the west. This is to use one self to make effort in listening and preaching as one act, and it is to practice-and-experience the eastern self and the western self as one self. In any event, we should be glad to, should hope to, and should resolve to bring the Buddha-Dharma and the patriarchs' truth close to our own body-mind, and to practice them. We should extend the practice from an hour to a day and from a year to a lifetime. We should let the Buddha-Dharma play as our soul. This is called not passing any life in vain. Do not think, on the contrary, that because we are not yet clear we should not preach for other people. If we expect clarification, we will not achieve it even in countless kalpas. Even if we have clarified human buddhas, we should further clarify celestial buddhas. Even if we have clarified the mind of mountains, we should further clarify the mind of waters. Even if we have clarified dharmas arisen from causes and conditions,[20] we should further clarify dharmas that are beyond causes and conditions. Even if we have clarified the outer limits of a Buddhist patriarch, we should further clarify the ascendant state of a Buddhist patriarch. To intend to complete the clarification of these things in one generation, and thereafter to act for the benefit of others, is not diligent effort, is not to be a stout fellow, and is not learning in practice. In sum, as students of the truth of the Buddhist patriarchs, from the time we learn in practice one method or one standard, we let our will to teach others rise to pierce the heavens. We thereby get free of self and others. Going further, if we exhaustively explore the self, we will already have exhaustively explored the external world. And if we exhaustively explore the external world, we will already have exhaustively explored the self. Unless received from a master, this Buddhist standard cannot be realized in bodily experience, even by the innately intelligent.[21] If the innately intelligent never meet a master, they do not know that which is beyond innate intelligence, and do not know that which is neither innate nor intelligence. Even if they are innately intelligent, they cannot thereby know the great truth of the Buddhist patriarchs. After they learn it, they can know it. To realize the self in bodily experience and to realize the external world in bodily experience is the great truth of the Buddhist patriarchs. We should just utilize our own beginner's state of learning in practice in order to experience communion with the beginner's state of

20. 因縁生法 (INNEN-SHOHO) means real entities that arise from direct or indirect causes.
21. 生知 (SHOCHI), "the innately intelligent," are discussed in chap. 26, *Daigo,* para. [217].

learning in practice of the external world. From the stage of the beginner onwards, to continue experiencing together both the self and the external world is to be in touch with the ultimate state of communion. As we work on the self, so we should promote the work of the external world.[22]

[92] However, hearing the words *"experience of the self," "realization of the self,"* and so on, crude people think that we need not receive the transmission from a teacher, but should study by ourselves. This is a great mistake. Those who wrongly conceive the thoughts and discriminations of subjective understanding, and who have no transmission from a master, are non-Buddhists of Indian naturalism. How could people who cannot discern this be people of the Buddha's truth? [There are those,] moreover, [who] when they hear the words *"experience of the self,"* because they suppose it to be an accumulation of the five skandhas,[23] equate it with Hīnayāna self-discipline.[24] Many people who do not know the difference between the great vehicle and the small vehicle experience themselves as the descendants of Buddhist patriarchs, but what person of clear eyes could be deceived by them?

[93] In the great Sung era of Shoko[25] there is a certain Soko,[26] "the Zen Master Dai-e of Kinzan mountain." Originally he is a student of sutras and commentaries. While traveling from district to district, he becomes a follower of Zen Master Ri[27] of Senshu and studies Unmon's[28] discussions of the ancients[29] together with Seccho's eulogies[30] and discussions of the ancients. This is the beginning of his learning in practice. Not understanding the ways of Unmon,

---

22. By enjoying Zazen, for example, we make our circumstances vigorous.

23. 五蘊 (GO-UN), viz. *rūpa*, matter; *vedana*, feeling; *saṃjñā*, thought; *saṃskāra*, mental conformation; and *vijñāna*, consciousness. See chap. 70, *Hotsu-bodaishin*, para. [216], note 44.

24. 自調 (JICHO). *Daichido-ron* notes the following threefold division of the noble eightfold path: 1) "self-discipline/keeping of precepts"; right speech, right action, right livelihood; 2) "self-purification/zen practice"; right mindfulness, right balance; 3) "self-control/wisdom"; right view, right thinking, right effort.

25. 1131–1162.

26. Master Dai-e Soko (1088–1163), nominally a successor of Master Engo Kokugon. He is regarded as the originator of "koan Zen." His works included *Dai-e-shobogenzo (Dai-e's Right-Dharma-Eye Treasury).* His posthumous title is Zen Master Fugaku.

27. Master Myokyo Shori (dates unknown).

28. Master Unmon Bun-en (864–949), successor of Master Seppo Gison; regarded as the founder of the Unmon Sect, but see chap. 49, *Butsudo.*

29. 拈古 (NENKO) means comments on the words and deeds of past masters.

30. 頌古 (JUKO), verses praising the words and deeds of past masters. Master Seccho Juken (980–1052; successor of Master Chimon Koso in the Unmon lineage) selected a hundred stories from *Keitoku-dento-roku*, adding comments or eulogies to each. This work later formed the basis for the popular commentary *Hekigan-roku (Blue Cliff Record)* by Master Engo Kokugon (1063–1135).

he eventually practices in the order of Master Tozan [Do]bi,[31] but [Do]bi in the end does not grant [that Soko entered] his inner sanctum. Master [Do]bi is a Dharma-child of Master Fuyo;[32] we should never rank him with idle people seated in a back row. Zen Master [So]ko continues his learning in practice for rather a long time, but he is unable to grope for [Do]bi's skin, flesh, bones, and marrow; still less does he know even of the existence of eyes inside atoms. On one occasion, as soon as he hears that in the truth of the Buddhist patriarchs there is a method [to request] the certificate of succession by burning incense on the elbow,[33] Soko eagerly requests the certificate of succession from Master [Do]bi. But Master [Do]bi does not allow it. Finally, he says, *"If you want to succeed to the Dharma, do not be hasty.[34] Just be diligent here and now. The Buddhist patriarchs' transmission is not given at random. I do not begrudge you the transmission; it is simply that you are not yet equipped with eyes."*

Then Soko says, *"Originally endowed with right eyes, I am experiencing the self[35] and realizing the self. How can you not give me the transmission?"*

Master [Do]bi smiles and leaves it there.

Later, [Soko] practices in the order of Master Tando [Bun]jun.[36] One day, Tando asks Soko, *"Why are you missing half your nose today?"*

Soko says, *"I am a disciple in the order of Hobo."*[37]

Tando says, *"Unreliable Zen priest."*[38]

---

31. Master Tozan Dobi (dates unknown), successor of Master Fuyo Dokai.

32. Master Fuyo Dokai (1043–1118), successor of Master Tosu Gisei, and the 45th patriarch in Master Dogen's lineage. See, for example, chap. 14, *Sansuigyo*, chap. 15, *Busso*, and chap. 64, *Kajo*.

33. 臂香 (BIKO), burning incense on the elbow or on the arm, was apparently an ancient custom performed when praying to gods or Buddha, or as an ascetic practice. In later ages, incense was burned not directly on the skin but in a censer suspended by a hook from the arm.

34. Up to here the sentences of this paragraph are constructed using *hiragana*, the Japanese phonetic alphabet, indicating that Master Dogen was paraphrasing from the Chinese. From here the paragraph contains sentences of Chinese characters only, with *hiragana* used only for two short linking phrases (not italicized).

35. 自証 (JISHO). In the chapter title 自 (JI), "the self," is the object of 証 (SHO), "to experience." In Soko's usage, however, 自 (JI) may have been meant as an adverb "by myself," and 証 (SHO) may have been meant to indicate the experience of so-called enlightenment, so that 自証 (JISHO *[su]*) meant "I am realizing enlightenment by myself."

36. Master Tando Bunjun (1060–1115), a successor of Master Shinjo Kokumon. Also quoted in Chap. 66, *Shunju*.

37. Hobo was the name of the mountain on which Master Tando had his order, and so it is another name for Master Tando himself. Soko did not accept responsibility for his own state.

38. 杜撰禅和 (ZUSAN *[no]* ZEN NA). 杜撰 (ZUSAN) means 1) lit. "edited by To Moku" (a notoriously unreliable editor), and by extension 2) "unreliable." 和 (NA) stands for 和尚 (OSHO), which in turn represents the Sanskrit *upādhyāya*, teacher or preceptor. 和尚 (OSHO) is used as an honorific term for a senior monk.

While [So]ko is reading a sutra, Tando asks, *"What sutra are you reading?"*

Soko says, *"The Diamond Sutra."*

Tando says, *"This Dharma is even and balanced, without high and low.*[39] *Why is Ungo-zan mountain high and Hobo-zan mountain low?"*

Soko says, *"This Dharma is even and balanced, without high and low."*

Tando says, *"You have managed to become a real archpriest."*[40]

On another day, while Tando is watching the ten [hell] kings[41] being cleansed, he asks the veteran monk Soko, *"What is the name of this eunuch?"*

[So]ko says, *"His name is Ryo."*[42]

Tando rubs his head and says, *"Why is it that, though my name is Ryo, I am without one of those hoods?"*

[So]ko says, *"The hood is missing, but the nostrils are very alike."*

Tando says, *"Unreliable Zen priest."*

Tando one day asks Soko, *"Veteran monk Ko. You are able to understand at once the principles of my here-and-now Zen. If I let you explain it, you are able to explain it. If I let you experience it, you are able to experience it. If I let you conduct eulogies of the ancients, discussions of the ancients, informal talks,*[43] *general preaching,*[44] *and requests for the benefit of instruction,*[45] *you are able to conduct them. But there is just one thing that is not yet present in you. Do you know what it is, or not?"*

---

39. 是法平等無有高下 (ZE-HO-BYODO, MU-U-KOGE) is a direct quotation from the Diamond Sutra.

40. "Archpriest" is 座主奴 (ZASU-NU). 座主 (ZASU) means the master of a temple of a lineage of intellectual study, and at the same time, in writings of the Rinzai Sect such as *Hekigan-roku (Blue Cliff Record),* the title is used ironically to describe a Zazen practitioner who understands Buddhism only intellectually. 奴 (NU, *yatsu*) means "slave," "manservant," or "fellow." It denotes lack of respect.

41. 十王 (JU-O), ten kings mentioned in the *Ju-o-kyo (Ten Kings Sutra).* Colorful guardian images.

42. Ryo was Master Tando's name before he became a monk. Master Tando probably seemed more common than Soko expected a Buddhist master to be, and so Soko saw a similarity between Master Tando and the vulgar image of a hell king.

43. 小参 (SHOSAN), lit. "small participation," means unscheduled informal instruction or questions and answers, usually done in the master's quarters. Examples of 小参 (SHOSAN) are the preaching of Master Gensa Shibi quoted in chap. 50, *Shoho-jisso,* para. [240], and that of Master Tendo Nyojo quoted at the beginning of chap. 79, *Ango.*

44. 普説 (FUSETSU) lit. "general preaching," means informal preaching or general day-to-day lectures, not necessarily in the Dharma Hall and not necessarily scheduled in advance. 普説 (FUSETSU) is less conversational than 小参 (SHOSAN) but not as formal as 上堂 (JODO), "formal preaching in the Dharma Hall." An example of 普説 (FUSETSU) is Master Tendo's recital of the cuckoo poem in chap. 50, *Shoho-jisso,* para. [234].

45. 請益 (SHIN-EKI), means a formal request for personal instruction. An example is Master Tozan's request to Master Ungan to impart to him the Eye in chap. 63, *Ganzei,* para. [83].

So[ko] says, *"What thing is not yet present?"*

Tando says, *"You lack only this one kind of understanding: Aha!*[46] *If you are without this one kind of understanding, when I preach to you in my quarters then you have Zen, but as soon as you leave my quarters you have lost it completely. When you are fully awake and thinking then you have Zen, but as soon as you fall asleep you have lost it completely. If you are like that, how can you deal with life and death?"*

So[ko] says, *"That is just Soko's doubt."*

Several years later, Tando falls sick. Soko asks, *"A hundred years after the Master, whom should Soko rely upon in order to complete the great matter?"*

Tando entrusts him as follows: *"There is a man called Gon of Ha.*[47] *I myself am not acquainted with him. Nevertheless, I am sure that if you meet him, you will be able to accomplish the [great] matter. Once you have met him, do not visit another. Practice [Za]zen when born again in a later age."*[48]

[98] When we examine this story, [it is clear that] Tando does not sanction Soko at all. Soko tries again and again to become enlightened, but in the end he lacks one thing, and he neither supplies the one thing nor gets free of the one thing. Previously, Master [Do]bi has refused Soko the certificate of succession, and urged him by saying, *"You have something which is not yet mature."* We must credit Master [Do]bi with clarity in seeing a person's makings. *That which is just Soko's doubt* he does not penetrate, does not get free of, does not break open, and does not doubt as the great doubt. He has no state hindered by doubt. Heedlessly to have requested the certificate of succession is a rash attitude in learning in practice, an extreme lack of will to the truth, and an utmost lack of veneration of the ancients.[49] We must say that he is without profound insight, and without the makings of the truth. He is an extreme case of negligence in practice. Through greed for fame and love of profit, he wants to break into the inner sanctum of the Buddhist patriarchs. It is pitiful that he is ignorant of the Buddhist patriarchs' words. He does not understand that veneration of the ancients is just experience of the self, and he neither hears nor learns that to scour the bequeathed teachings of myriad generations[50] is realization of the self. As a result, he has wrongness like this

46. 囮 (KA) is an exclamation made on realizing a truth.

47. 勤巴子 (GON HASU) is a nickname of Master Engo Kokugon (1063–1135), successor of Master Goso Ho-en, and editor of *Hekigan-roku (Blue Cliff Record).* 巴子 (HASU) is lit. "a son of Ha country."

48. The information in this paragraph is contained in the book *Dai-e-fugaku-zenji-shumon-buko (The War Chest of the School of Zen Master Dai-e Fugaku)*, which was edited by Master Soko's disciple Doken.

49. 稽古 (KEIKO) lit. "consideration of the past," or "emulation of the ancients," means daily practice based on reverence of traditional standards. See also chap. 7, *Senjo,* para. [144].

50. 万代を渉猟する (BANDAI *o* SHORYO *suru*). 万代 (BANDAI) means "ten thousand generations," i.e. many past generations of Buddhist ancestors. 渉 (SHO) lit. means to traverse water

and he has self-delusion like this. Because he is like this, in the lineage of Zen Master Soko there is not one true nose-ring,[51] or even half of one, but there are many whose basis is unreal. Failure to understand the Buddha-Dharma and failure to not understand the Buddha-Dharma is like this. Monks of the present must painstakingly learn in practice. Do not be negligent and proud.

[100] *Soko, according to Tando's assignment, after Tando's passing joins the order of Zen Master Engo at Tennei temple in the capital. Engo one day ascends the seat of formal preaching.[52] Soko experiences a mystical realization, and he reports his realization to Engo. [En]go says, "Not yet. Although the disciple's state is like that, you have never clarified the great Dharma." On another day, in formal preaching in the Dharma Hall, Engo quotes Master Goso Ho-en's words[53] on phrases of existence and phrases of non-existence.[54] Soko, on hearing these words, attains the state of great peace and joy in the Dharma. Again he expresses his understanding to Engo. Engo laughs and says, "I wonder whether I deceived you?"[55]*

[101] This is the story of how Zen Master Soko latterly practices under Engo. In Engo's order he is assigned the post of chief-clerk,[56] but no definite attainment is visible in him either before or after that time. In his own informal preaching and formal preaching,[57] he does not describe attainment. Remember, although chroniclers have said that he realized a mystical realization and have recorded that he attained the state of great peace and joy in the Dharma, he experienced no such thing. Do not think him important. He is a student of learning in practice, nothing more. Zen Master Engo is an eternal Buddha, and the most venerable person throughout the ten directions. Not since Obaku[58] has there been a venerable patriarch like Engo. He is an eternal Buddha who might be rare even in other worlds, but there are few

---

and 猟 (RYO) means to hunt, but as a compound 渉猟 (SHORYO) is often used in a literary context, meaning "to read extensively" or "to scour written sources."

51. 巴鼻 (HABI) alludes to the ring used to lead a water buffalo by the nose. It means a person of self-control.

52. 陞坐 (SHINZO), lit. "ascending the seat," is synonymous with 上堂 (JODO), lit. "going up to the [Dharma] Hall."

53. Master Goso Ho-en (died 1104), successor of Master Haku-un Shutan. Quoted in chap. 74, *Tenborin.*

54. 有句無句 (UKU MUKU) is a reference to the four-phased system elucidated by Master Nāgārjuna, whereby the philosopher considers phrases of 1) existence, 2) non-existence, 3) both, 4) neither. See, for example, chap. 81, *O-saku-sendaba*, para. [237].

55. These two stories are recorded in *Dai-e-zenji-tomei (Inscriptions on the Stupa of Zen Master Dai-e).*

56. 書記 (SHOKI), one of six assistant officers in a large Buddhist temple: 首座 (SHUSO), head monk; 書記 (SHOKI), clerk assisting the head monk, 蔵主 (ZOSU), librarian; 知客 (SHIKA), guest supervisor; 知殿 (CHIDEN), supervisor of the Buddha Hall; and 知浴 (CHIYOKU), bath supervisor.

57. 普説陞坐 (FUSETSU-SHINZO). See notes 44 and 52.

58. Master Obaku Ki-un (died between 855 and 859), successor of Master Hyakujo Ekai.

people or gods who know it; the sahā kingdom is a pitiful place. Now, when we refer to the Dharma-preaching of the eternal Buddha Engo and examine the veteran monk Soko, it is apparent that [Soko] has never had wisdom that could match the Master's, he has never had the same wisdom as the Master, and much less has he ever realized, even in a dream, wisdom that surpassed the Master's. So remember, Zen Master Soko is not equal to his Master's virtue reduced by half. He merely relates to others lines from the Flower Adornment, Śūraṃgama, and other sutras, reciting them from memory; he has never had the bones and marrow of a Buddhist patriarch. In Soko's thoughts, the viewpoint retained by great and small hermits[59]—those merely led by the spirits that inhabit grass and trees—is the Buddha-Dharma. If he imagined this [viewpoint] to be the Buddha-Dharma, clearly, he has never mastered the great truth of the Buddhist patriarchs. After Engo he does not travel to other districts and does not visit other good counselors, but randomly leads monks in practice as the master of a big temple. The words he has left behind never reach the periphery of the great Dharma. Nevertheless, those who do not know think that Zen Master Soko is not abashed even next to the ancients. Those who see and who know have decisively concluded that he is not enlightened. In the end, not having clarified the great Dharma, he is only babbling in vain. It is thus evident that Master [Do]bi of Tozan mountain, being clear in his insight into the future, was certainly not wrong. Students of Zen Master Soko, even those of later ages, have never stopped resenting Master [Do]bi. But Master [Do]bi only refuses to sanction [Soko]. Master [Bun]jun's refusals are more severe than [the refusal] of [Do]bi, who finds fault with [Soko] during each encounter. Yet [Soko's students] do not resent Master [Bun]jun. As how stupid should we see the people of the present and the past who have hated [Master Dobi]? In general, although many in the great kingdom of Sung call themselves the descendants of the Buddhist Patriarch, few have studied the truth, and so there are few who teach the truth. This point is also evidenced by the above episode. It was like this even in the Shoko era.[60] The present is incomparably worse than that age. Now people have become the leaders of monks without knowing what the great truth of the Buddhist patriarchs might even be like. Remember, in the authentic transmission of the certificate of succession from buddha to buddha and from patriarch to patriarch, in India in the west and in China in the east, the lineage from Seigen-zan mountain[61] is the authentic transmission.

---

59. 大小の隠倫 (DAISHO *no* INRIN). The Chinese called hermits who concealed themselves in towns 大隠 (DAI-IN), "great hermits," and hermits who lived in the forests and mountains 小隠 (SHO-IN), "small hermits."

60. 1131–1162.

61. Master Daikan Eno, the sixth patriarch in China, had three disciples who Master Dogen esteemed very highly: Master Nanyo Echu, Master Nangaku Ejo, and Master Seigen Gyoshi. Master Nangaku Ejo's successor was Master Baso Do-itsu, who is revered especially highly in

From the lineage of Seigen-zan mountain, the authentic transmission naturally passed to Tozan, without ever being known by others of the ten directions. All those who know it are the descendants of Tozan, and they impart themselves to monks through voice and word. Throughout his life Zen Master Soko has never understood the phrases *"experience of the self"* and *"realization of the self."* How much less could he have penetrated other realities? And how much less could any later student following Zen Veteran Soko have understood the words *"experience of the self"?* In conclusion, expressions of the self and expressions of the external world expressed by Buddhist patriarchs inevitably include a Buddhist patriarch's body-mind and a Buddhist patriarch's eyes. Because they are a Buddhist patriarch's bones and marrow, they are beyond ordinary people's attainment of the skin.

Shobogenzo Jisho-zanmai

Preached to the assembly at Kippo temple in Etsu-u on the 29th day of the 2nd lunar month in the 2nd year of Kangen.[62]

---

the Rinzai Sect. Master Seigen Gyoshi's line of succession passed to Master Sekito Kisen, then to Master Yakusan Igen, to Master Ungan Donjo, and to Master Tozan Ryokai. Master Dogen himself belongs to this lineage.

62. 1244.

[76]

大修行

DAI-SHUGYO

Great Practice

***D**ai means "great," and **shugyo** means "practice." So **dai-shugyo** means "great practice." There is a famous Chinese story about Master Hyakujo Ekai and a wild fox; the story concerns the relation between Buddhist practice and the law of cause and effect. This relation is explained in two ways, each totally at odds with the other. The first explanation says that someone of great practice "does not fall into cause and effect"; in other words, it denies the influence of cause and effect upon someone of great practice. The other explanation says "do not be unclear about cause and effect"; in other words, it affirms the influence of cause and effect upon someone of great practice. But Master Dogen considered the difference between these two explanations to be only a matter of intellectual thought, and that the situation in reality had no such dichotomy. He explained that someone of great practice transcends both the negation and the affirmation of the law of cause and effect, by acting here and now in the real world.*

[107] ***When Zen Master Daichi**[1] of Hyakujo-zan mountain in Koshu[2] (successor of Baso, called Ekai in his lifetime) gives informal instruction, an old man is generally present. He always listens to the Dharma along with the monks, and when the assembly retires, the old man also retires. Then unexpectedly one day he does not leave. The Master eventually asks him, "What person is this, standing before me?"*

The old man answers, "I am not a person. In the past age of Kāśyapa Buddha,[3] I used to live [as master] on this mountain.[4] Once a practitioner asked me, 'Do even people in the state of great practice fall into cause and effect, or not?' I answered, 'They do not fall into cause and effect.'[5] Since then I have fallen into the body of a wild fox for five hundred lives. Now I beg you, Master, to say for me a word of transformation.[6] I long to be rid

1. Master Hyakujo Ekai (749–814), successor of Master Baso Do-itsu. Zen Master Daichi is his posthumous title. The small text may have been added by a later editor.

2. A district in Kiangsi province in southeast China.

3. Kāśyapa Buddha is the sixth of the Seven Ancient Buddhas. So the time of Kāśyapa Buddha means the eternal past.

4. 住山 (JUSAN), lit. "to be in residence on a mountain," means to be a temple master.

5. 不落因果 (FURAKU-INGA), i.e. not falling subject to karmic retribution.

6. 一転語 (ICHITENGO) means a word that, when spoken and heard just at the right time and place, has the power to serve as a turning point in one's life. See also chap. 61, *Kenbutsu*, para. [26].

of the body of a wild fox." Then he asks, "Do even people in the state of great practice fall into cause and effect, or not?"

The Master says, "Do not be unclear about cause and effect."[7]

At these words the old man immediately realizes the great realization. He does prostrations and says, "I am already rid of the body of a wild fox, and would like to remain on the mountain behind this temple. Dare I ask the Master to perform for me a monk's funeral ceremony."

The Master orders the supervising monk[8] *to strike the block*[9] *and to tell the assembly, "After the meal, we will see off a deceased monk."*

All the monks discuss this among themselves, saying, "The whole community is at ease and there is no sick person in the Nirvāṇa Hall.[10] *What is the reason for this?"*

After the meal, the Master is seen leading the monks to the foot of a rock on the mountain behind the temple, and picking out a dead fox with a stick. They cremate it according to the formal method. In the evening the Master gives formal preaching in the Dharma Hall and discusses the preceding episode.

Obaku[11] *then asks, "The man in the past gave a mistaken answer as a word of transformation, and fell into the body of a wild fox for five hundred lives. If he had not made any mistake at any moment, what would he have become?"*

The Master says, "Step up here. I will tell you."

Obaku finally steps up and gives the Master a slap. The Master claps his hands and laughs, and says, "You have just expressed that a foreigner's[12] *beard is red, but it is also a fact that a red-beard is a foreigner."*[13]

[110] The koan[14] realized just now is *great practice* itself. As the old man says, *Hyakujo mountain in Koshu* exists in the past age of Kāśyapa Buddha, and

---

7. 不昧因果 (FUMAI-INGA), i.e. believing without ambiguity in the law of cause and effect. The phrases 不落因果 (FURAKU-INGA), "not falling into cause and effect," 不昧因果 (FUMAI-INGA), "not being unclear about cause and effect," are used throughout Shobogenzo as paradigms of opposing views on causation. See in particular chap. 84, *Sanji-no-go;* chap. 89, *Shinjin-inga*; and chap. 90, *Shizen-biku.*

8. 維那 (INO), supervisor of monks in the Zazen Hall; one of the six main officers.

9. 白椎 (BYAKU-TSUI) means to beat the top of an octagonal wooden pillar with a small wooden block in order to call the monks together.

10. 涅槃堂 (NEHANDO), a name for the temple infirmary.

11. Master Obaku Ki-un (died between 855 and 859), successor of Master Hyakujo.

12. 胡 (KO) originally indicated a person from a region to the northwest of China—broadly corresponding to modern-day Kazakhstan and Russia.

13. *Tensho-koto-roku,* chap. 8, and *Shinji-shobogenzo,* pt. 2, no. 2. Also quoted in Shobogenzo, chap. 89, *Shinjin-inga.*

14. 公案 (KOAN), short for 公府案牘 (KOFU AN TOKU), was originally the name given to a board on which a new official Chinese law was displayed. In Buddhism it came to mean 1) the concrete manifestation of Dharma, that is reality or the Universe itself—as in chap. 3, *Genjo-koan;* and 2) a story which manifests the universal principles of the Buddha-Dharma.

Hyakujo mountain in Koshu exists in the present age of Śākyamuni Buddha. This is a real *word of transformation*. Even so, the Hyakujo mountain of *the past age of Kāśyapa Buddha* and the Hyakujo mountain of the present age of Śākyamuni Buddha are not one. Neither are they different. They are not three and three before, and not three and three after.[15] The Hyakujo mountain of the past has not become the Hyakujo mountain of the present. The present Hyakujo mountain was not formerly the Hyakujo mountain of Kāśyapa Buddha's time. Even so: there is the [old man's] pronouncement[16] that *"I used to live on this mountain"*; the [old man's] teaching for the practitioner is akin to the teaching of the present Hyakujo for the old man; and the question which *once a practitioner asked* is akin to the question that the old man asks now. *When doing one thing, it is impossible to do another; if we neglect the first move, we will be floored at the second.*[17] The practitioner of the past asks, *"Do even people in the state of great practice on the Hyakujo mountain of the past fall into cause and effect, or not?"* This question should certainly not be understood easily or in haste. The reason [I say so] is that for the first time since the Buddha-Dharma spread east during the Later Han era of Eihei,[18] and since the ancestral Master came from the west during the Liang era of Futsu,[19] due to the words of the old wild fox, we hear the question of the practitioner of the past. It had never existed previously. So we can say that it is rarely heard. When we have groped for and grasped *great practice*, it is just great *cause-and-effect*[20] itself. Because this cause-and-effect is always the round fulfillment of causes and the complete fulfillment of effects, it has never accommodated discussion of falling or not falling and has never accommodated words of being unclear or not being unclear. If *"They do not fall into cause and effect"* is a mistake, *"Do not be unclear about cause and effect"* might also be a mistake. Even when mistakes are put in their place as mistakes, there is falling into the body of a wild fox, and there is getting free of the body of a wild fox. There is also a principle whereby *"They do not fall into cause and effect,"* though a mistake in the age of Kāśyapa Buddha is not a mistake in the age of Śākyamuni Buddha. Though

15. 前三三後三三 (ZEN SANSAN, GO SANSAN), "three and three before, three and three after," suggests for example the differences in the mountain in different seasons: white in winter, green in spring, blue in summer, yellow and red in autumn, et cetera. The real Hyakujo mountain here and now is beyond any accumulation of past impressions. See also chap. 42, *Tsuki,* para. [3], and *Shinji-shobogenzo,* pt. 2, no. 27.

16. 公案 (KOAN) in this case may be interpreted as "something to be pondered on."

17. These words of Master Kenpo, quoted from chap. 23 of *Rento-eyo,* may be seen as a conclusion to the foregoing discussion of relations between the primary consideration—reality here and now—and secondary matters such as what happened in the past.

18. 58–75. This is said to have been the time when the first Sanskrit sutras were translated into Chinese.

19. 520–526.

20. 因果 (INGA), "cause-and-effect," expresses in Shobogenzo not only the law of causation but also reality itself as cause-and-effect in momentary operation.

in the present age of Śākyamuni Buddha *"Do not be unclear about cause and effect"* gets rid of the body of a wild fox, in the age of Kāśyapa Buddha a different principle may be realized. In the old man's words *"Since then I have fallen into the body of a wild fox for five hundred lives,"* what is this *falling into the body of a wild fox*? It is not that a wild fox which existed already lures in the former Hyakujo. And it is impossible for the former Hyakujo originally to be a wild fox. The assertion that the soul of the former Hyakujo leaves him and forces itself into the skin of a wild fox is non-Buddhism; and a wild fox cannot come up and suddenly swallow the former Hyakujo. If we say that the former Hyakujo subsequently changes into a wild fox, he must first get rid of the body of the former Hyakujo, so that he may then fall into the body of a wild fox. A [master of] Hyakujo mountain can never be replaced by the body of a wild fox! How could *cause-and-effect* be like that? *Cause-and-effect* is neither inherent[21] nor initiated:[22] *cause-and-effect* never idly waits for a person. Even if the response *"They do not fall into cause and effect,"* is wrong, [the respondent] may not always fall into the body of a wild fox. If falling into the body of a wild fox were the inevitable karmic result of mistakenly answering a practitioner's question, then the Rinzais and Tokuzans of recent times, together with their followers, would have fallen into how many thousands and tens of thousands of wild foxes? Aside from them, the unreliable old veterans of the last two or three hundred years would be countless wild foxes. Yet none are heard to have fallen into wild foxes. So many [wild foxes] would be more than enough to see and hear. You may say that they have not made [such a] mistake, but in fact there have been very many outlandish and confused answers much worse than *"They do not fall into cause and effect."* Those who cannot even be placed on the periphery of the Buddha-Dharma are indeed many. We should know them with the Eye of learning in practice—unless equipped with the Eye, we cannot tell them apart. In conclusion, we should never say that as a result of answering badly [a person] becomes the body of a wild fox, or that as a result of answering well [a person] does not become the body of a wild fox. This story does not say what the state is like after getting rid of the body of a wild fox, but presumably, wrapped in a bag of skin, there might be a pearl.

[115] Contrary to this view, people who have never seen and heard the Buddha-Dharma say: "When we have completely got free of a wild fox, we return to the essential ocean of original enlightenment.[23] As a result of delu-

---

21. 本有 (HON-U), lit. "originally existing." Cf. note 23, 本覚 (HONGAKU).

22. 始起 (SHIKI). Cf. note 23, 始覚 (SHIKAKU).

23. 本覚 (HONGAKU). 本 (HON) means "original" or "inherent." 覚 (KAKU) is the Chinese character used to represent the Sanskrit *bodhi,* which means a buddha's state of intuitive wisdom, or enlightenment. In the Tendai sect the concepts 本覚 (HONGAKU), "inherent enlightenment," and 始覚 (SHIKAKU), "initiated enlightenment," represent opposing views of the Buddha-nature. It is said that this opposition set up a conflict in Master Dogen's mind during his

sion, we fall into the life of a wild fox for a while, but when we realize the great enlightenment we discard the body of a wild fox and return to the original essence." This is the non-Buddhist theory of returning to the original self; it is not the Buddha-Dharma at all. If we say that a wild fox is not the original essence and that there is no original enlightenment in a wild fox, that is not the Buddha-Dharma. If we say that when we realize the great enlightenment we have departed from and discarded the body of a wild fox, then it would not be the wild fox's great enlightenment, and we would make the wild fox serve no purpose. We should never say so.[24] [The story] says that by virtue of a word of transformation from the present Hyakujo, the wild fox which the past Hyakujo has been for five hundred lives suddenly gets free of a wild fox. We should clarify this principle. If we assert that, "When a bystander speaks a word of transformation, a bystander frees others from the body of a wild fox," then the mountains, the rivers, and the Earth have been speaking countless words of transformation since the past, and those many words of transformation have been repeated again and again. But in the past [the old man] has not got free of the body of a wild fox. He gets free of the body of a wild fox under a word of transformation from the present Hyakujo. This [assertion] casts deadly doubt upon the ancestor.[25] And if we assert that, "The mountains, rivers and the Earth have never spoken words of transformation," then the present Hyakujo might ultimately lack the means to open his mouth.[26] Furthermore, many past masters through the ages have vied to assert that the expressions *not falling into* and *not being unclear about* [cause and effect] are equally valid. But if they have never attained bodily experience of *not falling into* and *not being unclear about* [cause and effect] within the stream of those very words, they consequently neither experience the skin, flesh, bones, and marrow of falling into the body of a wild fox, nor experience the skin, flesh, bones, and marrow of getting rid of the body of a wild fox. If the head is not right, the tail is never right. In the old man's words *"Since then I have fallen into the body of a wild fox for five hundred lives,"* just what is the subject that falls and just what is the object that is fallen into? In the very moment of falling into the body of a wild fox, what form and grades does the Universe that has continued from the past have in the present? Why should the series of words *do not fall into cause and effect* result in

---

teenage years as a monk in the Tendai Sect. The conflict was finally resolved when Master Tendo Nyojo recommended Master Dogen to "just sit."

24. Master Dogen also affirms the state of a wild fox—as he says in chap. 3, *Genjo-koan,* for example, buddhas are those who have realized delusion.

25. "The ancestor" (the present Master Hyakujo) is a buddha; his words are the voice of nature. If they think that his words have some special mystical power to transform, then they are casting aspersions on Master Hyakujo's real state as a buddha.

26. In other words, if the state of natural balance did not have in itself the power to effect change, then Master Hyakujo would be powerless. Hyakujo's action was conscious human intervention, and at the same time it was natural.

five hundred repetitions? As for the one pelt of skin that is now *at the foot of a rock on the mountain behind the temple,* from what concrete place should we think that it has been able to come? To say *"They do not fall into cause and effect"* is to fall into the body of a wild fox, and to hear *"Do not be unclear about cause and effect"* is to get free of the body of a wild fox. Even though there are instances of falling in and getting free, they are just the *cause-and-effect* of the wild fox.[27] Nevertheless, since ancient times people have said: "Because *they do not fall into cause and effect* is an expression which seems to refute cause and effect, [the speaker] falls down." This assertion is without reason; it is the assertion of people who are in the dark. Even if the former Hyakujo has occasion to say *"They do not fall into cause and effect,"* he has the state in which it is impossible for the *great practice* to delude others, and it is impossible for him to refute cause and effect. Alternatively it is said: "The meaning of *do not be unclear about cause and effect,* in other words, not being ignorant of cause and effect, is that because *great practice* is transcendent *cause-and-effect* itself, it gets rid of the body of a wild fox." Truly, this is eighty or ninety percent realization of the eyes of learning in practice. At the same time:

> *In the Time of Kāśyapa Buddha,*
> *[We] have lived on this mountain.*
> *In the Time of Śākyamuni Buddha,*
> *[We] are living on this mountain.*
> *Former body and present body,*
> *The faces of the sun and the faces of the moon,*
> *Shut out the ghost of a wild fox,*
> *And manifest the ghost of a wild fox.*

How could a wild fox know its life for five hundred lives? When someone says that a wild fox knows five hundred lives by using a wild fox's intelligence, then the wild-fox-intelligence has not yet completely known the facts of one life, and a life has not yet rammed into a wild fox's skin. When a wild fox unfailingly knows its falling down, in each of five hundred lives, then reality is realized.[28] It does not completely know the whole of one life: there are instances of knowing and there are instances of not knowing. Given that body and knowing do not arise and pass together, it is impossible to count five hundred lives. If it is impossible to count [five hundred lives], the words *"five hundred lives"* might be a fabrication. If someone says that [a wild fox] knows by using intelligence other than a wild fox's intelligence, then it is not the knowing of a wild fox. What person could know these [five hundred lives] on a wild fox's behalf? Without any road of clear understanding through knowing and not knowing, we cannot speak of *falling into the body of a*

---

27. 野狐の因果 (YAKO *no* INGA) means not only "the karma of the wild fox," but the reality of the wild fox, the fox's real life.

28. 公案現成する (KOAN-GENJO *suru*). See notes 14 and 16.

wild fox, and if there is no falling into the body of a wild fox, there can be no *getting free of the body of a wild fox*. If there is neither falling in nor getting free, there can be no *former Hyakujo*. If there is no former Hyakujo, there can be no *present Hyakujo*—which cannot be conceded at random. We should research in detail like this. Utilizing this reasoning, we should test and defeat all the fallacies that have been heard again and again throughout the Liang, Chen, Sui, Tang, and Sung dynasties.[29] The old non-man, moreover, says to the present Hyakujo, *"Please perform for me the funeral ceremony for a deceased monk."* These words should not be like that. Since Hyakujo's time countless good counselors have not doubted, or been surprised at, these words. The point is this: how could a dead fox be a deceased monk, without having taken the precepts, without experience of summer retreats,[30] without the dignified forms, and without the principles of a monk? If any such being may undergo at random the funeral ceremony for a deceased monk, all dead people who have never left family life, whoever they are, would have to be accorded the rites of a deceased monk. A dead upāsaka or upāsikā,[31] if a request were forthcoming, would have to be accorded the rites of a deceased monk, as was the dead fox. When we look for such an example, there is none and we hear of none. No such ceremony has been authentically transmitted in Buddhism; even if we wanted to perform it, we would not be able to do so. The words [quoted] now that *Hyakujo cremates it according to the formal method* are not beyond doubt; it is possible that they are a mistake. Remember, there are set procedures for all the rites of a deceased monk, from efforts on entering the Nirvāṇa Hall to pursuit of the truth on arriving at the Bodhi Garden,[32] and they are not done at random. Even if a dead wild fox from the foot of a rock claims to be the former Hyakujo, how could the conduct of a full monk[33] be present in it? How could it have the bones and marrow of the Buddhist patriarchs? Who will testify that it is the former Hyakujo? Do not despise and belittle the Dharma-standards of the Buddhist patriarchs by idly accepting the transmogrification of the ghost of a wild fox as true. As the descendants of Buddhist patriarchs, attach weight to the Dharma-standards of the Buddhist patriarchs. Never follow a request as Hyakujo does. It is hard to meet even one matter or one method; do not be influenced by secular vulgarity, and do not be led by human sentiment. In this country of Japan, the forms of buddhas and the forms of patriarchs have been hard

---

29. That is, since Master Bodhidharma's coming from India during the Liang dynasty until the time of Master Dogen's preaching during the Sung dynasty.

30. 夏臘なし (GERO *nashi*), lit. "without summer year-ends"; in other words, without years as a monk. Traditionally, the years a person has been a monk are counted by the number of summer retreats passed.

31. Buddhist lay man or lay woman.

32. 菩提園 (BODAI-EN), "the Bodhi Garden," means the temple cemetery.

33. 大僧 (DAISO) means a full monk as opposed to a novice.

indeed to meet and hard indeed to hear. Now that, on rare occasions, we are able to hear them and able to see them, we should revere them more profoundly than the pearl in the topknot.[34] Unhappy people are not profound in religious conviction. It is pitiful. It is generally because they have never recognized the relative weight of things, and because they are without the wisdom of five hundred years and without the wisdom of a thousand years. Nevertheless, we should urge ourselves on and encourage others. Having been able to receive an authentic tradition from the Buddhist patriarchs—even if it is only one prostration and even if it is only one instance of upright sitting—we should profoundly feel great happiness and should rejoice in the great good fortune of having met what is difficult to meet. People who lack this mind, even if they meet the appearance in the world of a thousand buddhas, will not possess a single virtue, and will not be able to obtain a single benefit. They will just be non-Buddhists who idly attach themselves to the Buddha-Dharma. They may seem, in their mouths, to be learning the Buddha-Dharma, but real evidence of preaching the Buddha-Dharma can never be present in their mouths. In sum, if some person who has yet to become a monk—be it a king or a minister, be it Brahmadeva or Śakra-devānām-indra—comes asking for the rites of a deceased monk, never allow it. Tell them to come back when they have left family life, received the precepts, and become a full monk. People who are attached to conduct and its rewards in the triple world and who do not aspire to a noble position as one of the Three Treasures may come bringing a thousand dead skin bags to defile and to breach the rites of a deceased monk, but it would only be a most severe violation, and it would not produce any merit. If they wish to establish favorable relations with the merit of the Buddha-Dharma, they should promptly leave family life and receive the precepts, in accordance with the Buddha-Dharma, and become full monks.

[124] *In the evening the present Hyakujo gives formal preaching in the Dharma Hall and discusses the preceding episode.* The principle of this discussion is extremely dubious. What kind of discussion might they have? He seems to say that the old man, having already completed the process of five hundred lives, gets rid of his former body. Should the five hundred lives mentioned now be counted as in the human world? Should they be counted as in the state of a wild fox? Should they be counted as in the Buddha's truth? Furthermore, how could the eyes of an old wild fox glimpse Hyakujo? Those who are glimpsed by a wild fox may be the ghosts of wild foxes. Those who are glimpsed by Hyakujo are Buddhist patriarchs.[35] For this reason, Zen Master

34. Alludes to an analogy in Lotus Sutra, *Anraku-gyo: "It is like the king releasing from his topknot / The bright pearl, and giving it. / This Sutra is honored / As supreme among all sutras..."* See LS 2.276.

35. Suggests affirmation of Master Hyakujo—in chap. 61, *Kenbutsu,* Master Dogen says that only a buddha can see a buddha.

Koboku Hojo[36] eulogizes [Hyakujo] as follows:

> *Hyakujo has intimately experienced meetings with a wild fox;*
> *Questioned[37] by it, he is greatly ruffled.[38]*
> *Now I dare ask all you practitioners,*
> *Have you completely spat out a fox's drivel[39] or not?*

Thus, *a wild fox* is the Eye of *Hyakujo's intimate experience. To have spat out a fox's drivel,* even in a half measure, is to be sticking out the wide and long tongue[40] and speaking for others a word of transformation. At the very moment of so doing, we get free of the body of a wild fox, get free of the body of Hyakujo, get free of the body of an old non-man, and get free of the body of the whole Universe.

126] Obaku then asks, *"The man in the past gave a mistaken answer as a word of transformation, and fell into the body of a wild fox for five hundred lives. If he had not made any mistake at any moment, what would he have become?"* This question is the realization of the words of the Buddhist patriarchs. Among the venerable patriarchs in the lineage from Nangaku[41] there is none like Obaku, either before him or after him. Nevertheless, the old man never says "I answered the practitioner mistakenly," and Hyakujo never says "He had answered mistakenly." Why does Obaku now casually say *"The man in the past gave a mistaken answer as a word of transformation"*? If he says [Hyakujo] might be saying that the cause was the mistake, then Obaku has not grasped the great intent of Hyakujo. It is as if Obaku has never investigated the mistaken answers, and the answers beyond mistakes, that Buddhist patriarchs express. We should learn in practice that in this particular episode the past Hyakujo does not mention a mistaken answer and the present Hyakujo does not mention a mistaken answer. Rather, using five hundred skins of wild foxes, each three inches thick, [the past Hyakujo] *has experienced life on this mountain,*[42] and for the benefit of practitioners he expresses it. Because the skin of a wild fox has pointed hairs in the liberated state, the present Hyakujo exists as one

---

36. Master Koboku Hojo (died 1150), a successor of Master Fuyo Dokai.

37. 参請 (SANSHO) means to visit a master and ask for the teaching.

38. Because the question *"Do even people in the state of great practice fall into cause and effect?"* is impossible to answer with words alone.

39. 涎 (ZEN, *yodare*), as in the English "drivel," includes both the meaning of saliva and of something with no value; nonsense.

40. 広長舌 (KOCHO-ZETSU), the wide and long tongue, is one of the 32 distinguishing marks of the Buddha. See also chap. 9, *Keisei-sanshiki,* para. [210].

41. 南嶽下の尊宿 (NANGAKU-KA *no* SONSHUKU) means the lineage through Master Nangaku Ejo (677–744) to Master Baso Do-itsu (704–788) to Master Hyakujo Ekai (749–814) to Master Obaku Ki-un (died c. 855). Master Obaku was succeeded by Master Rinzai Gigen (died 867), the founder of the Rinzai Sect.

42. 曹住此山 (SO-JU-SHI-ZAN), translated in the story as "I used to live [as master] on this mountain." See note 4.

stinking skin bag, which, when we fathom it, is half a wild fox skin in the process of getting free. There is falling down and getting free which is *at every moment is beyond mistakes,*[43] and there is *cause-and-effect* which at every moment speaks words for others. They are the evident *great practice* itself. If Obaku were now to come and ask *"If he had not made any mistake at any moment, what would he have become?"* I would say, "He would still have fallen down into the body of a wild fox." If Obaku asked, *"Why is it so?"* I would say further, "You ghost of a wild fox!" Even then, it would not be a matter of mistakes or no mistakes. Do not concede that Obaku's question is a proper question! If Obaku asked again, *"What would he have become?"* I would say, "Are you able to grope the skin of the face, or not?" I would say further, "Have you got free of the body of a wild fox yet, or not?" I would say further, "Would you reply to that practitioner *'They do not fall into cause and effect'* or not?" But Hyakujo's words *"Step up here and I will tell you"* already include the expression "What will [he] become is just this!" Obaku steps up, having forgotten the past and oblivious of the future. His giving Hyakujo a slap is countless transmogrifications of a wild fox. *Hyakujo claps his hands and laughs, and says, "You have just expressed that a foreigner's beard is red, but it is also a fact that a red-beard is a foreigner."* This expression is not the boldness of spirit that belongs to one hundred percent perfection;[44] it is barely *eighty or ninety percent of realization.*[45] As a rule, even when we acknowledge eighty or ninety percent realization there is not yet eighty or ninety percent realization, and when we acknowledge one hundred percent perfection there is nothing left of eighty or ninety percent realization. That being so, I would like to say:

Hyakujo's expression pervades all directions,
Yet he still has not left the wild fox's den.
Obaku's heels are touching the ground,
Yet he seems to be stuck on the path of a praying mantis.[46]
In a slap and a clap,
There is one, not two.
Red-beards are foreigners and foreigners' beards are red.

---

43. 転転不錯 (TENTEN-FUSAKU), translated in the story as "If he had not made any mistake at any moment..."

44. 十成の志気 (JUJO *no* SHIIKI): an ironic expression; perfection does not exist in reality. Cf. *Fukan-zazengi;* 衝天の志気 (SHOTEN *no* SHIIKI), "the zeal that pierces the sky."

45. 八九成 (HAKKUJO), words spoken by Master Dogo Enchi in praise of an expression by Master Ungan Donjo. See chap. 33, *Kannon,* note 29, and *Shinji-shobogenzo,* pt. 2, no. 5.

46. The path of a praying mantis suggests a hesitant attitude—Master Dogen praised Master Obaku's practical standpoint ("heels touching the ground"), but he wondered whether Master Obaku might still be worrying about the making of mistakes.

Shobogenzo Dai-shugyo

Preached to the assembly at old Kippo temple in Etsu-u on the 9th day of the 3rd lunar month in the 2nd year of Kangen.[47]

47. 1244.

[77]

虚空

KOKU

Space

***Ko** means "vacant" or "void," and **ku** means "air," "space," or "emptiness." So **koku** means "space." Space and time have been fundamental concepts in philosophy since ancient times and in science too; even in ancient India people frequently discussed the nature of space and time. And this tradition influenced Buddhism, so the nature of space and time became a very important subject in Buddhism in India. The topic also passed to Buddhism in China, and so there are many stories of Chinese Buddhist masters discussing space and time. In this chapter Master Dogen discusses space. He first quotes a discussion about space between Master Shakkyo Ezo and Master Seido Chizo. Then he gives his own explanation, quoting a poem by Master Tendo Nyojo, a discussion between Master Baso Do-itsu and a monk called Seizan Ryo, and the words of Master Vasumitra.*

[131] **Because *"this place is where something ineffable exists,"*[1]** it is through the realization of these words that Buddhist patriarchs are caused to be. And because the realization of these words of Buddhist patriarchs passes naturally from rightful successor to rightful successor, the skin, flesh, bones, and marrow, realized as *a whole body,*[2] are *hanging in space.*[3] This space is beyond such categories as the twenty kinds of space.[4] In general, how could

1. 這裏是什麼処在 *(shari[wa] ko[re] shimo [no] shozai [zo]),* is in the form of a question: "This concrete place here and now is what location?" i.e. "This is where?" However, the phrase is generally used as a statement. See, for example, the conversation between Masters Rinzai and Fuke in *Shinji-shobogenzo*, pt. 1, no. 96. The story is recorded in notes to Shobogenzo, chap. 56, *Senmen*, para. [124], and chap. 73, *Sanjushichi-bon-bodai-bunpo*, para. [23].

2. 渾身せる (KONSHIN *seru*), or "integrated into a body," alludes to the first line of Master Tendo Nyojo's windbell poem. See para. [138].

3. 掛虚空 (KA-KOKU), "hanging in space," also alludes to the windbell in the poem. It describes the true state of all things in the Universe as entities existing in space.

4. 二十空 (NIJUKKU), "twenty kinds of space" or "twenty kinds of emptiness," are enumerated in *Dai-hannya-kyo* (the Chinese version of the Mahā-prajñā-pāramitā-sūtra) as 1) 内空 (NAIKU), "inner space"; 2) 外空 (GAIKU), "external space"; 3) 内外空 (NAIGAIKU), "the space inside and outside"; 4) 空空 (KUKU), "space as space"; 5) 大空 (DAIKU), "universal space," et cetera. The twenty are generally cited in connection with the doctrine of *śūnyatā;* viz. 諸法皆空 (SHOHO-KAI-KU), "all things and phenomena are totally empty." Thus the Sutra explains that 1) the six sense organs are transient, devoid of self, and therefore empty: this is "internal

space be limited to only twenty kinds of space? There are eighty-four thousand kinds of space, and there may be countless more besides.

[133] *Zen Master Shakkyo Ezo*[5] *of Bushu*[6] *asks Zen Master Seido Chizo*[7] *"Do you understand how to grasp space?"*

Seido says, "I understand how to grasp it."

The Master says, "How do you grasp it?"

Seido clutches at space with his hand.

The Master says, "You do not understand how to grasp space."

Seido says, "How do you grasp it, brother?"[8]

The Master grabs Seido's nostrils and pulls them.

Groaning with pain, Seido says, "It is very brutal to yank a person's nostrils, but I have directly been able to get free."

The Master says, "Directly grabbing hold like this, you should have got it from the beginning."[9]

[134] Shakkyo's words *"Do you understand how to grasp space?"* ask "Are you too *the thoroughly-realized body as hands and eyes?"*[10] Seido says *"I understand how to grasp it."* Space is one unadulterated mass, which, once touched is then tainted.[11C] Since being tainted, *space has fallen to the ground.*[12] Shakkyo's words *"How do you grasp it?"* mean "Even if you call it 'as it is,'[13] you have changed it

---

śūnyatā"; 2) the six sense objects are transient, devoid of self, and therefore empty: this is "external śūnyatā"; 3) the sense organs and their objects are transient, devoid of self, and therefore empty: this is "internal and external śūnyatā"; 4) non-attachment to the emptiness of all internal and external entities is "the emptiness of śūnyatā itself"; 5) the total emptiness of the universe in the ten directions is "universal śūnyatā"; et cetera. See also *Shodoka*: 二十空門元不著 (NIJUKKU-MON GEN JAKU SEZU), "We are originally without attachment to the twenty aspects of śūnyatā."

5. Master Shakkyo Ezo (dates unknown), successor of Master Baso Do-itsu. He was formerly a hunter. It is said that he became a monk when he came upon Master Baso's hut while hunting a deer.

6. A district of Jiangxi province in southeast China.

7. Master Seido Chizo (735–814), also a successor of Master Baso Do-itsu. Entered Master Baso's order when eight years old, and received the complete (250) precepts aged 25.

8. 師兄 (SUHIN), lit. "master-elder brother," a term of respect for a senior monk.

9. *Keitoku-dento-roku*, chap. 6, and *Shinji-shobogenzo*, pt. 3, no. 49.

10. 通身是手眼 (TSUSHIN-ZE-SHUGEN). Words of Master Dogo Enchi; see chap. 33, *Kannon*.

11. A Chinese expression for which no source has been traced, hence marked C. The sentence suggests mild criticism of Seido for tainting space with intellectual understanding.

12. 虚空落地 (KOKU RAKUCHI), "space falls to the ground," means abstract space collapses. The words appear in the preaching of Master Joshu Jushin; see chap. 35, *Hakujushi*, para. [113]. Having chided Master Seido for tainting space, Master Dogen recognizes the practical necessity of sometimes tainting space with human intellectual understanding.

13. 如如 (NYO-NYO). 如 (NYO) means "as is" or "what is as it is"; i.e. reality.

already."[C] And although it is like this, in changing with it the thus-gone[14] exists.[C] *Seido clutches at space with his hand:* this is merely understanding of how to ride a tiger's head; it is not yet understanding of how to grab the tiger's tail.[C] Shakkyo says, *"You do not understand how to grasp space."* Not only has Seido failed to understand how to grasp it; he has never realized space even in a dream.[C] And although he is like this, [Shakkyo] does not want to describe for him that which is profound and eternal.[C] Seido's words *"How do you grasp it, brother?"* mean "Say a word or half yourself, venerable elder! Do not rely so totally on me."[C] Shakkyo grabs Seido's nostrils and pulls them. Now, let us learn in practice that Shakkyo has put his body into Seido's nostrils. From the other side, realization is present of the words that "nostrils pull in Shakkyo." And although it is like this, space is a unity, and it is jostling.[15C] Seido groans with pain and says, *"It is very brutal to yank a person's nostrils, but I have directly been able to get free."* Previously he has thought about meeting another, but suddenly he has been able to meet himself. At the same time, to taint the self is not permissible:[16C] the self must be practiced.

[136] Shakkyo says, *"Directly grabbing hold like this, you should have got it from the beginning."* I do not deny that *grabbing hold by the state like this has got it from the beginning.* However, because there is neither grasping in which Shakkyo and Shakkyo each extend a hand together, nor grasping in which space and space each extend a hand together, [Shakkyo] is not yet relying upon his own exertion. In general, the Universe has no gaps to accommodate "space," but this particular story has long been resounding through space like thunder. Since the time of Shakkyo and Seido, though the practitioners who have called themselves masters of the five sects[17] are many, those who have seen, heard, or fathomed space are few. Before and after Shakkyo and Seido, several individuals have aspired to play with space, but few have put their hands on it. Shakkyo has attained some grasp of space. Seido does not glimpse space. Daibutsu[18] would like to tell Shakkyo the following: "Before, when you grabbed Seido's nostrils, if you wanted to grasp space, you should have grabbed the nostrils of yourself, Shakkyo, and you should have understood how to grasp the fingertips with the fingertips." Even so, Shakkyo does know a bit about the dignified behavior of grasping space. Even a good

---

14. 如去 (NYOKO) means "the thus-gone" or "reality passing"—in this compound 如 (NYO) can be understood as an adverb, "thus," or as a noun, "reality." Either way, 如去 (NYOKO) expresses momentary reality. Similarly 如来 (NYORAI), which represents the Sanskrit *tathāgata,* can be understood as "thus-come" or as "arrived at reality."

15. Alludes to words of Master Goso Ho-en. See chap. 74, *Tenborin,* para. [72].

16. 染汙自己即不得 *(jiko [o] zenna [seba] sunawa[chi] futoku)* alludes to Master Nangaku Ejo's famous words "Practice-and-experience is not nonexistent, but to taint it is not permissible." *Shinji-shobogenzo,* pt. 2, no. 1. See also Shobogenzo, chap. 7, *Senjo,* and chap. 29, *Inmo.*

17. 五家 (GOKE): the Hogen, Igyo, Soto, Unmon, and Rinzai sects. See chap. 49, *Butsudo.*

18. Master Dogen. See note 33.

player at grasping space needs to research the interior and exterior of space, needs to research the deadening and vitalization of space, and needs to know the lightness and weight of space. We should maintain and rely upon [the teaching] that the effort in pursuit of the truth, the establishment of the mind, the practice-and-experience, and the assertions and questions of buddhas and of patriarchs are just the grasping of space.

[138] My late Master, Tendo Nyojo, the eternal Buddha, says: *"The whole body like a mouth, hanging in space."*[19]

Clearly, the whole body of space[20] is suspended in space.

[139] *Archpriest Ryo*[21] *of Seizan mountain in Koshu once goes to practice in Baso's order.*[22] *The Patriarch [Baso] asks him, "What sutra do you lecture on?"*

The master replies, "The Heart Sutra."[23]

The Patriarch says, "With what do you lecture?"

The master says, "I lecture with mind."[24]

The Patriarch says, "[They say] mind is like a leading actor, the will is like a supporting actor, and the six kinds of consciousness are the accompanying cast: how are these able to lecture on the Sutra?"

The master says, "If mind is unable to give the lecture, space is hardly able to give the lecture, is it?"

The Patriarch says, "Space itself is indeed able to give the lecture."

The master swings his sleeves[25] *and retires.*

The Patriarch calls to him, "Archpriest!"

The master turns his head.

The Patriarch says, "From birth to old age, it is just this."

---

19. 渾身似口掛虚空 *(konshin kuchi [ni] ni[te] koku [ni] ka[ku])*. This is the first line of the windbell poem quoted in chap. 2, *Maka-hannya-haramitsu*, para. [78]: *"Whole body like a mouth, hanging in space; / Not asking if the wind is east, west, south, or north, /For all others equally, it chatters prajñā: / Chin Ten Ton Ryan Chin Ten Ton."*

20. 虚空の渾身 (KOKU *no* KONSHIN), "the whole body of space," or "the whole body as space."

21. Archpriest Seizan Ryo (dates unknown). 座主 (ZA-SHU), "archpriest," is a title for the master of a temple belonging to sect in which Zazen is not practiced. So the title is sometimes used with irony to criticize a practitioner's state as too intellectual. See, for example, chap. 75, *Jisho-zanmai*, para. [93].

22. Master Baso Do-itsu (704–788), successor of Master Nangaku Ejo.

23. 心経 (SHINGYO), that is the The Heart Sutra of Mahā-prajña-parāmitā, the short sutra that represents the heart of the six hundred volumes of the Mahā-prajña-parāmitā-śāstra. See chap. 2, *Maka-hannya-haramitsu*.

24. 心 (SHIN)—as in 心経 (SHINGYO)—means the mind or the heart.

25. A gesture of mild contempt—as also used by the old woman who wouldn't sell her rice cakes to Master Tokuzan. See chap. 18, *Shin-fukatoku*.

At this the master gains insight. Eventually he conceals himself on Seizan mountain and nothing more is heard of him.[26]

[140] Thus, every Buddhist patriarch is a sutra-lecturer. And sutra-lecturing is inevitably in space. Without space, it is impossible to lecture on even a single sutra. Whether lectures are delivered on the mind as a sutra[27] or delivered on the body as a sutra, they are always delivered through the medium of space. Thinking is realized, and not thinking is realized, through the medium of space. The development of tutored wisdom and the development of untutored wisdom, the development of innate intelligence and the development of learned intelligence: each is in space. The act of becoming a buddha and the act of becoming a patriarch, likewise, must be in space.

[141] The seventh patriarch, the Venerable Vasumitra,[28] says: *"The mind*[29]*is the same as the concrete world of space, and it reveals the reality that is coterminous with space. When we are able to experience space, there is no right and nothing wrong."*[30]

The mutual encounter and mutual realization in the moment of the present between a person facing a wall and the wall facing the person; the mind as fences and walls; and the mind as a withered tree: these are just *the concrete world of space*. To those who can be saved by this body, [buddhas] manifest at once this body and preach for them the Dharma;[31C] this is *to reveal the reality that is coterminous with space*. To those who can be saved by another body, [buddhas] manifest at once another body and preach for them the Dharma;[C] this is *to reveal the reality which is coterminous withspace*. Being used by the twelve hours,[C] and being in control of the twelve hours,[C] are both *the time when we are able to experience space*. A big stone being big and a small stone being small[32C] is *no right and nothing wrong*. We solely investigate for the present, as the right-Dharma-eye treasury and the fine mind of nirvāṇa, space like this.

26. *Keitoku-dento-roku,* chap. 8, and *Shinji-shobogenzo,* pt. 1, no. 4.

27. 心経 (SHINGYO). See note 23.

28. Born at the end of the first century A.D. in Gandhāra in northern India. Became the successor of the sixth patriarch in India, Master Mishaka (see chap. 15, *Busso*). Legend says that in his youth, before becoming the disciple of Master Mishaka, Master Vasumitra would wander aimlessly around the town drinking from a flask of liquor.

29. 心 (SHIN) here means not "mind" in general but "the [Buddha] mind"; i.e., the mind in the balanced state of action.

30. *Keitoku-dento-roku,* chap. 1.

31. Alludes to Lotus Sutra, *Kanzeon-bosatsu-fumon.* See LS 3.252.

32. See also chap. 62, *Hensan* [66]: "Thorough exploration is a big stone being big and a small stone being small."

Shobogenzo Koku

Preached to the assembly at Daibutsu-ji temple[33] in Etsu-u on the 6th day of the 3rd lunar month in the 3rd year of Kangen.[34]

33. 大仏寺 (DAIBUTSU-JI), lit. "temple of the Great Buddha." This was the first chapter of Shobogenzo preached at Daibutsu-ji, which Master Dogen founded in 1244. In 1246 he changed the name of the temple to 永平寺 (EIHEI-JI), "temple of Eternal Peace."

34. 1245.

[78]

HATSU-U

鉢盂

The Pātra

***Hatsu** is a phonetic rendering of the Sanskrit pātra, and **u** means bowl or bowls. In India, Buddhist monks ate their meals from a large bowl called a pātra, and the tradition was passed to Buddhist monks in China. In this chapter, Master Dogen explains the importance of the pātra, which has traditionally been highly revered as a symbol of Buddhist life.*

[145] **From upward of the Seven Buddhas** the authentic transmission has passed to the Seven Buddhas; from inside the Seven Buddhas the authentic transmission has passed to the Seven Buddhas; from the totality of the Seven Buddhas the authentic transmission has passed to the totality of the Seven Buddhas; and from the Seven Buddhas the authentic transmission has passed down the twenty-eight generations. The twenty-eighth ancestral master, the founding Patriarch Bodhidharma, enters China himself and passes the authentic transmission to the second patriarch, Great Master Taiso Shoshu Fugaku;[1] and, transmitted through six generations, [the transmission] reaches Sokei.[2] The total fifty-one transmissions[3] of east and west are just the right-Dharma-eye treasury and the fine mind of nirvāṇa, and the kaṣāya and the pātra. Past buddhas have maintained each as the authentic transmission of past buddhas. In this way, [each] has been authentically transmitted from buddha to buddha and from patriarch to patriarch. At the same time, the skins and flesh, the bones and marrow, the fists, and the eyes who learn the state of Buddhist patriarchs in practice, have each their own expression: some learn in practice that the pātra is the body-mind of Buddhist patriarchs; some learn in practice that the pātra is the food bowl of Buddhist patriarchs; some learn in practice that the pātra is the eyes of Buddhist patriarchs; some learn in practice that the pātra is the brightness of Buddhist patriarchs; some learn in practice that the pātra is the real substance of Buddhist patriarchs; some learn in practice that the pātra is the

1. Master Taiso Eka, the second patriarch in China. Great Master Shoshu Fugaku is his posthumous title.

2. That is, Master Daikan Eno on Sokei-zan mountain, the sixth patriarch in China.

3. From Master Mahākāśyapa to Master Dogen.

Buddhist patriarchs' right-Dharma-eye treasury and fine mind of nirvāṇa; some learn in practice that the pātra is a place in which Buddhist patriarchs transform themselves; and some learn in practice that Buddhist patriarchs are the rim and base of the pātra. The principle of learning in practice of each such group has its own standing as an expression of the truth. At the same time, there is learning in practice in a further ascendant state.

[147] My late Master Tendo, the eternal Buddha, on the day he takes up residence on Tendo, in the 1st year of the great Sung era of Hogyo,[4] says in formal preaching in the Dharma Hall, *"I remember the following: A monk asks Hyakujo,[5] 'What is a miracle?' Hyakujo says, 'Sitting alone on Great and Mighty Peak.'[6] Monks, do not be disturbed. Let the fellow kill himself by sitting[7] for a while. If someone today were suddenly to ask, 'Venerable [Nyo]jo, what is a miracle?' I would only say to them, 'What miracle could there be?' Finally, what else? The pātra of Joji[8] having passed to Tendo, I eat meals."[9]*

[149] Remember, a miracle should be done for a miraculous person, and for a miracle a miraculous tool should be used. Such are miraculous moments. Thus, the place where miracles have been realized is the miraculous pātra. Therefore to call upon the four quarter kings[10] to guard [the pātra] and upon dragon kings[11] to protect [the pātra] is a profound standard of the Buddha's truth. And for this reason we offer up [the pātra] to Buddhist patriarchs, and [the pātra] is entrusted down to us through Buddhist patriarchs. People who do not learn in practice in the inner sanctum of Buddhist patriarchs say, "The Buddha's kaṣāya is silk, is cotton, is made from fabric of transformed thread." They say, "The Buddha's pātra is stone, is tile, is iron." They speak like this because they are not yet equipped with eyes of learning in practice. The Buddha's kaṣāya is the Buddha's kaṣāya. There must never be any view about silk or cotton. Views about silk, cotton and so on, are outmoded views. The Buddha's pātra is the Buddha's pātra. We must never call it stone

---

4. 1225.

5. Master Hyakujo Ekai (749–814), successor of Master Baso Do-itsu.

6. 大雄峰 (DAIYU-HO) means Hyakujo-zan mountain, the site of Master Hyakujo's temple.

7. 坐殺 (ZASATSU), lit. "to kill [oneself] by sitting," means to keep on practicing Zazen, even when it is difficult to sit.

8. Master Tendo Nyojo was the abbot of Joji Temple when he received the invitation to become the master of Tendo Temple.

9. Also quoted in chap. 64, *Kajo*, para. [102].

10. 四天王 (SHI-TENNO), lit. "the four heaven kings," from the Sanskrit *catvāro mahā-rājikāḥ*, are four gods under the God Indra who inhabit the lowest of the six heavens in the world of desire, each guarding one quarter of the compass surrounding Mount Sumeru. See also chap. 70, *Hotsu-bodaishin*, para. [207].

11. 龍王 (RYU-O), represents the Sanskrit *nāga-rāja*, a mythical serpent-like being that guards Buddhism. In ceremonies such as that at the beginning of the summer retreat, dragons are called upon to protect the Dharma. See chap. 79, *Ango*, para. [175].

and tile, and never call it iron and wood. In general, the Buddha's pātra is not man-made,[12] it is beyond arising and passing, it neither leaves nor comes, it is without merits and faults, it does not embrace new and old, and it is not connected with past and present. The robes and bowls of Buddhist patriarchs, even if created through the collection of clouds and water, are beyond the restrictions and hindrances[13] of clouds and water. Even if created through the collection of grass and trees, they are beyond the restrictions and hindrances of grass and trees. The point is this: water, being composed of real dharmas, is water, and clouds, being composed of real dharmas, are clouds. Being composed of clouds, they are clouds. Being composed of water, it is water. With regard to the pātra: *only of real dharmas is the pātra composed;*[14] only of the pātra are real dharmas composed; only of integrated mind is the pātra composed; only of space is the pātra composed; and only of the pātra is the pātra composed. The pātra is restricted by the pātra and tainted by the pātra. The pātra that monks[15] today have received and retained is just the pātra offered up by the four quarter kings.[16] If not offered up by the four quarter kings, the pātra could not be manifest before us here and now.[17] The pātra that has now been authentically transmitted through all directions by Buddhist patriarchs who have received the Buddha's right-Dharma-eye treasury is the pātra in the state that is liberated from past and present. That being so, the pātra here and now has broken with a glance outmoded views of it held by men of iron, it is not influenced by evaluation of it as a piece of timber, and it has transcended the sound and form of tiles and pebbles—while not restricting lively appreciation of it as a rock or a jewel. Do not call it a bit of tile, and do not call it a chunk of wood. We have realized it in experience like this.

---

12. 造作 (ZOSA), lit. "made by building," from the Sanskrit *saṃskṛta*. See Book 1, Glossary, and also chap. 44, *Kobusshin*, para. [65].

13. 羅籠 (RARO), silk nets and bamboo cages used in China to catch birds and fish. The same characters appear in *Fukan-zazengi*.

14. 但以衆法合成鉢盂 *(tada shuho [o] mot[te] hatsu-u [o] gojo [su]).* This sentence borrows its structure from a line in *Yuima-gyo:* 但以衆法合成此身 *(tada shuho [o] mot[te] ko[no] mi [o] gojo [su]),* "Only of real dharmas is this body composed." Master Dogen discusses the line at length in chap. 31, *Kai-in-zanmai.*

15. 雲水 (UNSUI), lit. "clouds and water," in this case means those who live the free and homeless life; monks.

16. That is, the pātra offered by the four quarter kings to the Buddha.

17. The pātra is more than an ordinary bowl; in addition to its practical function, it has traditional value and meaning.

Shobogenzo Hatsu-u

Preached to the assembly at Daibutsu temple in Etsu-u on the 12th day of the 3rd lunar month in the 3rd year of Kangen.[18]

18. 1245.

[79]

安居

ANGO

The Retreat

***An** means "peaceful" and **go** means "reside." The word **ango** refers to the ninety-day summer retreat. In India, the rainy season lasts for about three months in the summer. Buddhists in ancient India used this time for intensive practice of Zazen, and this period was called varsika in Sanskrit. The tradition was passed to China, and when Master Dogen went to China he experienced the concentrated practice of Zazen for three months in the summer. He felt it his mission to introduce this tradition to Japan.*

[153] **My late Master, Tendo Nyojo,** the eternal Buddha, says in informal preaching[1] at the beginning of a summer retreat,

> *Stacking our bones upright on the flat earth,*
> *[We each] dig a cave in space.*
> *Directly we pass through the gate of dualism,*
> *And grasp hold of a black lacquered tub.*[2]

This being so, *[Those who] have got this ring through the nose,*[3] *Still inevitably eat meals and stretch out the legs to sleep, And have been at just this place for thirty years.*[4] Because we are like this already, we waste no time in putting tools in place. One such tool is the ninety-day summer retreat. It is the brains and the real features of the buddhas and the patriarchs, and it has been directly experienced by their skin, flesh, bones, and marrow. Picking up the eyeballs and the brains of Buddhist patriarchs, we have made them into the days and months of the ninety-day summer retreat. One summer retreat is just another name for buddhas and patriarchs. The summer retreat, start to finish, is Buddhist patriarchs themselves. Beyond this there is no additional inch of

---

1. 小参 (SHOSAN), preaching given not necessarily in the Dharma Hall, but, for example, in the Master's quarters or in a dormitory. Different from 上堂 (JODO), formal preaching in the Dharma Hall.
2. In other words, we act in the present moment.
3. 巴鼻子 (HA-BI-SU), a ring used to lead, for example, a water buffalo by the nose. A symbol of self-control.
4. The words in italics are in the style of a short verse, in Chinese characters only.

soil and no great Earth. A real summer retreat[5] is neither new nor old, it is beyond coming and beyond going. Its dimensions are the dimensions of a fist, and its characteristics are the characteristics of a ring through the nose. At the same time, because we begin the summer retreat, it comes, having blocked out space, and no *ten directions* are left over. And because we finish the retreat, it goes, tearing the whole earth asunder, and *no inch of soil* remains. For this reason, when the reality of the start of the summer retreat is realized, it seems to come; and when the restrictions of the end of the summer retreat are broken, it seems to go. Even though it is like this, the fact is only that some adherents to the state of direct experience are each coming into contact with the start and the finish. For thousands of miles there is not an inch of grass![6] Give me back the money I paid for the ninety days of meals!

[156] Master Oryu Shishin[7] says, *"Having trod the way of a mountain monk for thirty-odd years, I see ninety days as a summer. To add a day is impossible. To subtract a day is impossible."*[8]

So the insight glimpsed by the eyes of thirty-odd years as a wayfarer is simply that ninety days make one summer retreat. If we consider adding a day, the ninety days will come back vying with each other.[9] If we consider subtracting a day, the ninety days come back vying with each other.[10] We must never spring free from the cave of ninety days. [The real meaning of] this *springing free* is, using the cave of ninety days as hands and feet, to engage only in springing itself. *To see ninety days as a summer* is a tool of our lineage;[11] at the same time, because the Buddhist Patriarch did not personally decide it by himself, [the tradition] has been authentically received by buddhas and by patriarchs, rightful successor to rightful successor, until today. Therefore, to meet a summer retreat is to meet the buddhas and the patriarchs. To meet a summer retreat is to realize buddha[12] and to realize the state of a patriarch. The summer retreat has long since become a Buddhist patriarch. In this *"Ninety days makes a summer,"* though the measurement of time is a cerebral measurement, it is beyond only one kalpa or ten kalpas, and beyond only a hundred thousand countless kalpas. Other times are used up by the hun-

5. Lit. "one doorsill of a summer retreat." "Doorsill" is used as a counter. At the same time, it suggests the summer retreat as a concrete fact.

6. In reality there is nothing to lead us astray.

7. Master Oryu Goshin (1043–1114), successor of Master Oryu Soshin. He called himself 死心 (SHISHIN), "Dead Mind," and this is the name given in the original text.

8. Paraphrased from chap. 28 of *Zoku-dento-roku.*

9. To be the extra day.

10. To avoid being subtracted.

11. 我個裏 (WAGA KO RI), lit. "my concrete place." Master Tendo Nyojo used these words to describe his Buddhist order.

12. 見仏 (KENBUTSU), lit. "to meet Buddha," means to realize the state of buddha. See chap. 61, *Kenbutsu.*

dreds of thousands of countless kalpas. The ninety days command the use of the hundreds of thousands of countless kalpas; therefore, though the hundreds of thousands of countless kalpas realize buddha when they meet the ninety days, the ninety days are not always connected with kalpas. This being so, we should learn in practice that *"Ninety days makes a summer"* is just a measurement of the Eye. The retreat as body-and-mind is also like this. The fact that the summer retreat commands the use of the state of vigorous activity, and the fact that the summer retreat has sprung free from the state of vigorous activity, have their origins[13] and have their bases;[14] even so, [the summer retreat] has not come here from another place and another time, and it does not originate from just this place and just this time. When we grasp their origins the ninety days come at once. When we grope for their basis the ninety days come at once. The common and the sacred have seen these [ninety days] as their caves and as their very lives, but [the ninety days] have far transcended the states of the common and the sacred. [The ninety days] are beyond thinking discrimination, they are beyond non-thinking discrimination, and they are not confined to the state beyond thinking and non-thinking.

[160] *The World-Honored One preached the Dharma to an assembly in the country of Magadha.*[15] *Then, wanting to begin a ninety-day summer retreat,*[16] *he said to Ānanda,*[17] *"To the great disciples, and to gods and human beings of the four classes,*[18] *I am constantly preaching the Dharma, but they do not have reverence or admiration for it. I shall now go inside the Indra-ṣaila-guhā*[19] *chambers, and practice a ninety-day summer sitting. If someone should appear and ask to hear the Dharma, you should preach the following to them in my place: 'All dharmas are beyond appearance. All dharmas are beyond disappearance.'" Having spoken, he closed the chambers and sat.*[20] Since then 2,194 years have already passed. (It is now the 3rd year of the Japanese era of Kangen.[21])

---

13. For example, the Buddha's order.

14. For example, Buddhist tradition.

15. An ancient state in central India stretching along the southern bank of the Ganges, with its capital at Rājagṛha. It was in Magadha that the Buddha realized the truth and first turned the Dharma wheel.

16. "Ninety-day summer retreat" is 白夏 (BYAKU-GE), lit. "white summer." 白 (BYAKU), "white," can be interpreted as suggesting 1) the bright and sunny situation of summer, 2) the purity of effort during the retreat, or 3) the character for a hundred, 百, minus the character for one, 一, representing the number ninety in one character instead of the usual two, 九十, or 九旬.

17. The Buddha's disciple and half-brother, who later succeeded Master Mahākāśyapa and became the second patriarch in India.

18. Monks, nuns, lay men, lay women.

19. 因沙臼 (INSAKYU), represents the sound of the Sanskrit *Indra-ṣaila-guhā*, lit. "Indra's Stone Hideaway." This was one of five temples on Vulture Peak.

20. Sentences similar to the preceding sentences can be found in *Shobutsu-yoshu-kyo (The Sutra of the Collected Essential Teachings of the Buddhas)*, pt. 1.

21. 1245. The sentence in parenthesis is represented in small characters in the source text.

Descendants who do not enter the inner sanctum have often seen [the Buddha's] closing himself away in the chambers in Magadha as evidence of his preaching without words. Wrong groups today solely think as follows: *"The Buddha's intention in closing the chambers and doing a summer sitting is that to rely upon preaching with words is not completely real, but is an expedient means. The ultimate truth is the cutting of speech and the disappearance of the intellectual function. For this reason, to be without words and without intellect may fit the ultimate truth. To have words and to have images in the mind is different from the truth. For this reason, during the ninety-day summer sitting in closed chambers, [the Buddha] cut himself off from human traces."* The assertions of these people have insulted the World-Honored One's Buddhist intention. If we discuss the cutting of speech and the disappearance of the intellectual function, all livelihoods and industries are the cutting of speech and the disappearance of the intellectual function—*"the cutting of speech"* meaning all speech, and *"the disappearance of the intellectual function"* meaning all intellectual functions.[22] Furthermore, this story is not originally for the purpose of venerating the state without words. The thoroughly-realized body solely [drags through] mud and [stays in] the water, and goes into weeds, never shirking to preach the Dharma and to save people, and never shirking to turn the Dharma and to salvage things. If people who call themselves [the Buddha's] descendants say, *"The ninety-day summer sitting is the absence of verbal preaching,"* I would like to tell them, *"Give the ninety-day summer sitting back to me!"* [The Buddha] directs Ānanda to preach on his behalf, saying, *"You should preach the following in my place: 'All dharmas are beyond appearance. All dharmas are beyond disappearance.'"* We should not vacantly pass over this behavior of the Buddha. In sum, how could we see his closing the chambers and practicing a summer sitting as being without words and not preaching? Suppose, for the present, that at this time Ānanda were to address the World-Honored One as follows: *"How should I preach that 'All dharmas are beyond appearance, and all dharmas are beyond disappearance'? Even if I preach like this, what must I do?"* So saying, he would listen to the World-Honored One's words. In general, the present instance of the Buddha's behavior is itself the philosophy of supreme meaning,[23] and the philosophy of the supreme state of being without,[24] which preach the Dharma and turn the Dharma. We should never see it as evidence of preaching without words. If we see it as preaching without words, the situation may be described as *"It is pitiful that the three-foot Dragon Spring Sword, is idly*

---

22. Master Dogen did not deny the value of transcending speech and transcending intellectual thinking, but he criticized the relative interpretation of the wrong groups.

23. 第一義諦 (DAI-ICHI-GI-TAI), lit. "the philosophy which is number one in meaning," or "the consummate philosophy." This phrase appears elsewhere in Shobogenzo.

24. 第一無諦 (DAI-ICHI-MU-TAI), lit. "the philosophy which is number one in absence." This phrase is Master Dogen's variation.

hanging on the wall of the To household as a weaving shuttle."[25] In conclusion, the ninety-day summer sitting is the eternal turning of the Dharma wheel, and it is eternal Buddhist patriarchs themselves. In the present story, there are the words *"Then, wanting to begin a ninety-day summer [retreat]..."* Remember, that which is unavoidably practiced is ninety days of sitting in a summer retreat. Those who shirk it are non-Buddhists. In general, while the World-Honored One is in the world, he sometimes practices the ninety-day retreat in Trāyastriṃśa heaven, and he sometimes practices the retreat together with five hundred bhikṣus within quiet chambers on Mount Gṛdhrakūṭa.[26] Through the five lands of India, without discussing a [particular] place, when the time comes they retire for the ninety-day summer retreat, and the ninety-day retreat is practiced. It is practiced by the Buddhist patriarchs of the present as the single most important matter. It is the supreme truth of practice-and-experience. Though the winter retreat is mentioned in the Pure Net Sutra,[27] its method has not been transmitted. Only the method of the ninety-day summer retreat has been transmitted, and the authentic transmission is immediately present in its fifty-first generation.[28]

[165] Shingi says,[29] *"Itinerant practitioners who wish to go to a dwelling place to begin the summer retreat should arrive half a month in advance. It is important that the service of tea, and personal salutations,*[30] *should not be rushed."*

"Half a month in advance" means in the last ten days of the 3rd lunar month. So we should arrive during the 3rd lunar month. From the 1st day of the 4th lunar month onwards, bhikṣus do not go out. The doors of reception rooms for [monks of] many districts, and of temples' lodging facilities, are all closed. Thus, from the 1st day of the 4th lunar month, all monks will be securely installed[31] in the temple building, or will have moved into a hut.[32]

---

25. Quoted from a verse by Master Bussho Hotai recorded in *Katai-futo-roku (Katai Era Universal Record of the Lamp)*, chap. 28. The original story appears in the book *Ji-rui-zen-shu (Collection of Matters and Examples, Part One)*. A man called To-in from the Shin district fished out from Rai-taku lake what he thought to be the shuttle of a loom. He carried it home and hung it on his wall. Then one day, during a thunderstorm, it turned into a dragon and ascended to the sky, for it was in fact the precious Dragon-Spring Sword.

26. Vulture Peak.

27. In Sanskrit, the *Brahmajāla-sūtra*, a precepts sutra for monks and nuns listing the ten serious prohibitions and forty-eight less serious precepts. Translated into Chinese by Kumārajīva during the latter Shin era (384–417).

28. Master Dogen is the 51st patriarch, counting from Master Mahākāśyapa as the first.

29. *Zen-en-shingi (Pure Criteria for Zen Monasteries)*, chap. 2. The editing of *Zen-en-shingi* was completed by Master Choro Sosaku in 1103. It was based on Master Hyakujo's *Ko-shingi (Old Pure Criteria)*.

30. 人事 (NINJI), which essentially means doing prostrations, is explained in chap. 55, *Darani*.

31. "Securely installed" is 安居せり (ANGO *seri*), as in the chapter title, but here used as a verb.

32. A hut in the temple grounds.

(In other cases it is traditional to be securely installed in the house of a lay person.) This is the behavior of Buddhist patriarchs, which we should venerate and should practice. Every fist and nostril, taking residence in a temple, will have hung his or her staff at the place of the retreat. Nevertheless, demons say, *"The viewpoint of the Great Vehicle may be the essential thing. The summer retreat is a convention of the śrāvaka. We should not necessarily practice it."* People who speak like this have never seen or heard the Buddha-Dharma. The truth of anuttara-samyak-saṃbodhi is just the ninety days of sitting in the summer retreat. Even if there are pinnacles of the Great Vehicle and of the Small Vehicle,[33] they are the branches, leaves, flowers, and fruits of the ninety-day retreat. Preparations are first performed after breakfast on the 3rd day of the 4th lunar month. Beforehand, however, from the 1st day of the 4th lunar month, the supervising monk[34] prepares boards showing the number of years since participants received the precepts. After breakfast on the 3rd day of the 4th lunar month, [the supervising monk] hangs the years-since-precepts boards in front of the common quarters;[35] that is, outside the window which is to the left of the front entrance.[36] The dormitory windows are all latticed. [The supervising monk] hangs these [boards] after breakfast and puts them away after the bell at the end of practice.[37] [The supervising monk] hangs them from the 3rd to the 5th, the time for putting them away and the time for hanging them up remaining the same. There is a convention for writing the board. It is written not according to [the rank of] main officer[38] or assistant officer,[39] but just according to years since taking the precepts. Those who have been assistant officers or main officers at other temples are each written as Head Monk, as Prior [and so on]. For those who have served in several posts, the most important post held should be written.

---

33. For example, the teaching of the establishment of the will to the truth may be seen as an ultimate teaching of the great vehicle, and the teaching of the 12 dhūta, or hard practices, may be seen as an ultimate teaching of the small vehicle.

34. 堂司 (DOSU) also called 維那 (INO), the supervisor of monks in the Zazen Hall, and one of the six main officers.

35. 衆寮 (SHURYO), or monks' dormitories.

36. 下間 (GEKAN), lit. "the lower interval." The custom in China is to express the right side as upper and the left side as lower. "Interval" refers to the spaces between the outer pillars supporting the roof of the building. So "the lower interval" means the section of the front wall between the left side of the entrance and the first pillar on the left.

37. 放参鐘 (HO-SAN-SHO), lit. "release from practice bell," means the bell at the end of the last sitting of the day.

38. The six main temple officers, 六知事 (ROKU CHIJI), are 1) 都寺 (TSUSU), chief officer, head of the temple office, treasurer; 2) 監寺 (KANSU) prior; 3) 副寺 (FUSU), assistant prior; 4) 堂司 (DOSU) or 維那 (INO), supervisor of monks in the Zazen Hall, rector; 5) 典座 (TENZO), chief cook; and 6) 真歳 (SHISSUI), work leader, officer in charge of buildings and fields.

39. The six assistant officers, 六頭首 (ROKU CHOSHU) are 首座 (SHUSO), head monk (lit. "chief seat"); 書記 (SHOKI), clerk assisting the head monk; 蔵主 (ZOSU), librarian; 知客 (SHIKA), guest supervisor; 知殿 (CHIDEN), supervisor of the Buddha Hall; and 知浴 (CHIYOKU), bath supervisor.

Someone who has been the abbot of a temple is written as So-and-So Seido.[40] If a person has served as the abbot of a small temple but this is not known by the monks, that person will often hide the fact and not use the title. There are also examples of a Seido, if a member of the Master's order, not bearing the title Seido but being written as Ācārya[41] So-and-So.[42] There are many excellent examples of [such veteran monks] reposing in the attendant monks' quarters.[43] There are also past precedents of [such veteran monks themselves] serving as attendants for [the Master's] robes and pātra, or serving as attendants for the burning of incense. Any other post is [assigned to a veteran monk] according to the Master's instruction. If a disciple of another master has come to [a retreat at] a big temple, even if [that disciple] has served as the abbot of a small temple, it is a reliable example, and a fragrant trace, for [that disciple] to ask only for [a title] such as Head Monk, Clerk, Chief Officer, or Prior. The vihāra[44] will laugh at someone using a title earned while serving in a minor post in a small temple. A person of good sense who has been an abbot, but only of a small temple, will hide the fact and not use the title.

69] The form of the board is as follows:

So-and-So Mountain Temple in So-and-So district of So-and-So country is having a summer retreat this summer. Years passed since taking the precepts, for the whole saṃgha, are as follows.

The Venerable Kauṇḍinya[45]
Abbot

Received the precepts in the 1st year of Kenpo:[46]

Ācārya So-and-So	Librarian So-and-So
Ācārya So-and-So	Ācārya So-and-So

Received the precepts in the 2nd year of Kenpo:

Seido So-and-So	Supervising Monk So-and-So

---

40. 西堂 (SEIDO), lit. "West Hall," is a title for a retired master or a guest master—"Veteran Master." The title derives from a traditional temple layout in which guest rooms are located to the west.

41. 上座 (JOZA), lit. "senior seat," represents the Sanskrit *ācārya,* a term of respect for a teacher. See Book 1, Glossary.

42. For example, a retired senior monk who is living in the order where the retreat is taking place does not use the title Seido during the retreat.

43. 衣鉢侍者寮 (E-HATSU JISHA-RYO), lit. "quarters for those who attend to [the master's] robes and pātra"; in other words, "the acolytes' quarters."

44. 叢林 (SORIN), lit. "flourishing forest," representing the Sanskrit *piṇḍavana.* See Glossary.

45. Ajñāta-Kauṇḍinya, a disciple of the Buddha, and one of the five practitioners to whom the Buddha gave his first preaching after realizing the truth. He is mentioned in Lotus Sutra, *Hoben (Expedient Means).* See LS 1.74.

46. 1213.

Head Monk So-and-So	Guest-Supervisor So-and-So
Ācārya So-and-So	Bath-Manager So-and-So

Received the precepts in the 1st year of Genryaku:[47]

Work Leader So-and-So	Attendant Monk So-and-So
Head Monk So-and-So	Head Monk So-and-So
Donations Chief[48] So-and-So	Ācārya So-and-So
Chief Cook So-and-So	Infirmary Chief[49] So-and-So

Received the precepts in the 3rd year of Kenryaku:

Clerk So-and-So	Ācārya So-and-So
Seido So-and-So	Head Monk So-and-So
Ācārya So-and-So	Ācārya So-and-So

The preceding[50] is presented with respect. If there are any mistakes, please point them out. Written with respect.

The 3rd day of the 4th lunar month in so-and-so year; Supervising Bhikṣu So-and-So. Written with respect.

[172] We write like this. We write on white paper, and write in the standard noncursive style.[51] We do not use the cursive style, the ancient squared style,[52] and so on. To hang [the boards], we attach tapes of about the width of two grains of rice to the top of the paper boards, which we then hang. [They hang] straight down, like bamboo blinds. After the end of practice on the 5th day of the 4th lunar month, they are put away for the last time. The 8th day of the 4th lunar month is the Buddha's birthday celebration.

[172] After the midday meal on the 13th day of the 4th lunar month, monks of the common quarters, in their own dormitory, have tea and cakes and recite sutras. The dormitory chief[53] conducts matters. The provision of hot water and the burning of incense are all the responsibility of the dormitory chief. The dormitory chief is positioned at the back of the common quarters. The dormitory head monk is positioned to the left of the dormitory's sacred

47. 1184. The names of the eras are chosen at random, not in chronological order.

48. 化主 (KESHU), responsible for visiting the houses of supporters and collecting donations.

49. 堂主 (DOSHU), lit. "hall chief." In this case, "hall" means the temple infirmary.

50. Lit. "the right." The original is written from right to left.

51. 真書 (SHINSHO), lit. "true writing," a noncursive style (therefore easier to read) that was the standard style in Master Dogen's time. It is almost the same as the standard block style *(kaisho)* used for printed characters today.

52. 隷書 (REISHO) is derived from the *tensho* style which is used today for seals. It is midway between the *tensho* and *kaisho* styles.

53. 寮主 (RYOSHU), a monk elected from among the monks of the common quarters as their representative. In charge of inspecting the monks' clothes and pātra, preparing books, charcoal, hot water, and so on.

monk image.[54] But it is the dormitory chief who steps forward to burn incense and to conduct the ceremony. The head monks, main officers, and so on, do not attend this reciting of sutras; only the monks of the dormitory perform it. After breakfast on the 15th, the supervising monk, having prepared in advance one board showing years since precepts, hangs it on the east wall which is the front of the Monks' Hall.[55] [The supervising monk] hangs it above the front hall, that is, in the interval [between the pillars] to the south of the front entrance.[56]

173] Shingi says, *"The supervising monk puts up in advance the years-since-precepts board, and serves before it offerings of incense and flowers (putting it up in front of the Monks Hall)."*[57]

174] After the midday meal on the 14th day of the fourth lunar month, a mindful recitation board[58] is hung in front of the Monks' Hall. Mindful recitation boards are also hung in front of the other temple buildings. In the evening, a main officer prepares the Local Deities Hall[59] with incense and flowers, setting them before the shrine tablet. The monks gather together to perform the mindful recitation. The method of the mindful recitation is as follows. After all the monks have assembled, first the abbot burns incense. Next the main officers and assistant officers burn incense. [The method] is similar to the method of burning incense during the bathing of the Buddha.[60] Next, the supervising monk steps up from his or her place and goes to the front, first bows with joined hands[61] to the abbot, then bows with joined hands to the Local Deities Hall, and then facing north, that is, facing the Local Deities Hall, [the supervising monk] conducts the mindful recitation.

175] The words are as follows:

---

54. 聖僧 (SHOSO) Usually an image of the Buddha, of Mañjuśrī Bodhisattva, or of the Happy Buddha, placed in the Zazen Hall, the monks' dormitories, and other buildings of the temple.

55. The entrance to the Monks Hall (Zazen Hall) is on the east.

56. "The front hall" is 前架 (ZENKA), lit. "front stand," usually called the *gaitan*, or *zentan*. The main officers and other monks who have daily duties outside the Zazen Hall sit here so as to be able to come and go more freely.

57. The words in parenthesis are in small characters in the source text.

58. A board notifying the monks of the forthcoming recitation of the names of the Ten Buddhas.

59. 土地堂 (TOCHIDO), lit. "Lands Hall," a small hall located next to the Dharma (Lecture) Hall and containing a shrine to the gods of local lands and to guardian gods of the Dharma.

60. 浴仏 (YOKUBUTSU), also called *ko-tan-e* (celebration of the descent and birth), *bussho-e* (celebration of the Buddha's birth), and *kan-butsu-e* (celebration of sprinkling the Buddha). Performed on April 8th to celebrate the Buddha's birthday. The Buddha's image is sprinkled with perfumed water or sweet tea.

61. 問訊 (MONJIN), lit. means "to ask [how someone is]," but concretely it means to either bow with the palms of the hands together (*gassho monjin*) or with the left hand curled round the thumb and the right hand covering the back of the left hand (*shashu monjin*).

We secretly reflect that a fragrant wind is fanning the countryside, and the God of Summer[62] *is governing all directions. It is the morning on which the Dharma-King forbids travel. This is the day on which Śākyamuni's disciples preserve their life. I have gathered together the assembly so that we may pay sincere respects to the sacred shrine, and recite the vast names of myriad virtue, directing the merit to the true rulers of all the temple buildings. Our prayer is that, with their protection, we will be able to accomplish the retreat. I respectfully request the venerable assembly to recite,*

> *Perfectly pure Dharma body,*[63] *Vairocana Buddha,*[64]
> *Roundly satisfied physical body,*[65] *Vairocana Buddha.*
> *The body of thousands of hundred-koṭis of transformations,*
> *Śākyamuni Buddha.*
> *The One who will descend and be born in future,*
> *the Venerable Buddha Maitreya,*[66]
> *All buddhas in the ten directions in the Three Times.*
> *Great Saint Mañjuśrī Bodhisattva.*
> *Great Saint Universal Virtue Bodhisattva.*[67]
> *Great Compassionate Regarder of the Sounds of the World*[68] *Bodhisattva.*
> *Many venerable bodhisattva-mahāsattvas.*
> *The mahā-prajña-parāmitā.*[69]

The merit of the mindful recitation we totally direct to the dragons and gods of the land who protect and preserve the right Dharma. Bowing, we pray that divine brightness will help us manifest gainful achievements, and that the state of pure joy will flourish and eternally confer unselfish happiness. Once again, I request the venerable assembly to recite, "All buddhas in the ten directions in the Three Times. Many venerable bodhisattva-mahāsattvas. The mahā-prajña-parāmitā."[70]

---

62. 炎帝 (ENTEI), lit. "the Emperor of Flames," or the Sun.

63. 法身 (HOSSHIN), from the Sanskrit *dharmakāya*. See Book 1, Glossary.

64. The Sun Buddha.

65. 報身 (HOSHIN), from the Sanskrit *sambhogakāya*. *Sambhoga* means eating, enjoyment, use, employment, sensual pleasure, joy. So *sambhogakāya* suggests the concrete physical body. See Book 2, Glossary.

66. It is said that Maitreya Buddha will descend from heaven to save all those left unsaved by Śākyamuni Buddha.

67. Mañjuśrī and Universal Virtue (from the Sanskrit *Samantabhadra*) are legendary bodhisattvas referred to throughout the Lotus Sutra (see chap. 17, *Hokke-ten-hokke*). Their images often attend that of the Buddha. Mañjuśrī is a symbol of wisdom and Universal Virtue is a symbol of balance.

68. Bodhisattva Avalokiteśvara, a symbol of life, also praised in the Lotus Sutra. See chap. 33, *Kannon*.

69. See chap. 2, *Maka-hannya-haramitsu*. This traditional ten-line recitation is called *Jubutsu-myo (Names of the Ten Buddhas).*

70. 十方三世一切諸仏、諸尊菩薩摩訶薩、摩訶般若波羅蜜。 These words are recited after a Buddhist lecture in Japan. The characters would normally be read as *Juppo sanze issai shobutsu, Sho-son-bosatsu-makasatsu, Maka-hannya-haramitsu*. But the traditional recitation is *Ji-ho-san-*

178] Then, when the drum sounds, the monks go at once to their seats for cakes and tea in the Cloud Hall.[71] The cakes and tea are the responsibility of the Kitchen Hall officers.[72] The monks go to the Hall, they walk around the Hall in order, and when they get to their own places,[73] they face the front[74] and sit. One of the main officers conducts the Dharma-functions, that is, he or she performs the burning of incense and so on. Shingi says, *"Originally, the chief officer should conduct matters, but if necessary, the supervising monk takes [the chief officer's] place."* Before the mindful recitation a notice should be copied and presented to the head monk. A main officer, wearing the kaṣāya and carrying the prostration cloth, greets the head monk and presents the notice to the head monk, having in some cases performed two offers to spread the cloth and three prostrations.[75] The head monk returns the prostrations. [These prostrations] should be the same as the prostrations of the main officer. The notice is carried [to the head monk] in a box, in which a wrapping cloth has been spread, by a novice. The head monk welcomes and sees off the main officer.

79] The form of the notice:

> The Kitchen Hall officers, this evening
> Will serve tea and cakes in the Cloud Hall, especially for
> The Head Monk
> And all the monks. We humbly inform you of this
> celebration of the start of the retreat, and we respectfully hope
> That all the monks will kindly bestow upon us,
> Their illuminating presence.
>
> The 14th day of the 4th lunar month in the 3rd year of Kangen,
> The bhikṣus of the Kitchen Hall, So-and-So and the others,
> Expressed with respect.

---

shi-i-shi-fu, Shi-son-bu-sa-mo-ko-sa, Mo-ko-ho-ja-ho-ro-mi.

71. Another name for the Monk's (Zazen) Hall.

72. The chief officer, prior, and assistant prior (the three highest-ranking main officers). In the traditional temple layout the Kitchen Hall (or Administration Hall), the kitchen itself, and the offices of the chief officer, prior, and assistant prior are located under one roof (on the other side of the Buddha Hall from the Zazen Hall).

73. 被位 (HI-I), lit. "the covered place"—that is, the place covered by the monk's own mat.

74. They sit facing away from the wall or screen that they usually face in Zazen.

75. 両展三拝 (RYOTEN SANPAI), lit. "two spreads, three prostrations." The intention of the officer is to do three sets of three prostrations with the prostration cloth spread. But as the officer prepares to open the prostration cloth, the head monk signals with a short sweeping motion of the right hand that such a formal prostration is not necessary. This process is repeated. Finally the officer does just one set of three prostrations without spreading the prostration cloth. From here 両展三拝 (RYOTEN SANPAI) is translated as "two offers and three prostrations."

[180] The name of the senior main officer is written. After presenting the notice to the head monk, [the main officer] asks the novice to paste up [the notice] in front of the Cloud Hall; it is pasted to the left[76] of the Hall's front entrance. On the outside wall to the south[77] of the front entrance there is a board on which the notice is pasted—this board is lacquered. There is an envelope. The envelope is aligned with the right edge[78] of the board and fastened with a bamboo peg. So the envelope too is pasted up on one side. This board is made according to a formal method. The writing is in characters about half-an-inch[79] square; they are not written large. The writing on the front of the envelope is as follows:

An invitation to the Head Monk and all the monks The bhikṣus of the Kitchen Hall, So-and-So and the others, Enclosed with respect.

After the tea and cakes, the board is put away.

[182] Before breakfast on the 15th, the main officers, the assistant officers, and [the abbot's] disciples and Dharma-relatives,[80] first go into the abbot's quarters to perform personal salutations. If, on the previous day, the abbot has waived personal salutations, they should not visit the abbot's quarters at all. "To have waived personal salutations" means to have pasted on the east side of the entrance to the abbot's quarters a notice on which the abbot has written either a verse or some Dharma-words. Sometimes [the notice] is pasted up in front of the Cloud Hall as well.

[182] After ascending the seat of formal preaching on the 15th, the abbot comes down from the Dharma-seat[81] and stands in front of the steps. [The abbot] stands on the north end of the prostration mat,[82] facing south. The main officers approach and perform two offers and three bows. After the first offer they say, *"Now that we are in retreat and forbidden to travel, we are able to serve [you] towel and flask. We hope that, with the assistance and protection of the Master's Dharma-power, there will be no difficulties."* After the next offer, they

76. 下間 (GEKAN). See note 36.

77. The front of the Zazen Hall faces east, so to the south of the entrance means to the left of the entrance.

78. Lit. "the beginning." As Chinese characters are written from top to bottom and from right to left, "the beginning" suggests either the top or the right side of the board. The next line suggests that the envelope was pasted to the side of the board.

79. Five *bu;* that is, half of one *sun.* One *sun* is 1.2 inches.

80. 法眷 (HOKEN), for example, monks who are disciples of the master's master.

81. 法座 (HOZA), the lecture platform for formal preaching in the Lecture Hall.

82. 拝席 (HAISEKI), lit. "prostration seat." A rectangular straw mat.

express the compliments of the season and do three informal prostrations.[83] The master recites the following: *"It is now our great good fortune to be able to practice the retreat together. I also hope, So-and-So and So-and-So, that we will be helped by each other's Dharma-power, and that there will not be any difficulties."* The head monk and all the monks follow the same procedure. At this time, the head monk, all the monks, the main officers, and so on, all do prostrations facing north. Only the abbot, standing in front of the stairs of the Dharma-seat, faces south.[84] The abbot's prostration cloth is spread upon the prostration mat. [So] next the head monk and all the monks bow before the abbot, performing two offers and three prostrations. At this time, the disciples, attendant monks, and Dharma-relatives [of the abbot], and śramaṇeras,[85] *stand to one side; they should not blindly follow the other monks in performing personal salutations.* "Standing to one side" means standing alongside the east wall of the Dharma Hall. If strips of paper [showing the names] of sponsors are hanging along the eastern wall, [these monks] should stand by the Dharma-drum,[86] or they should stand by the west wall. When the monks have finished their prostrations, the main officers return first, to the Kitchen Hall, and stand at the place of precedence.[87] Then the head monk leads the monks to the Kitchen Hall for personal salutations; that is to say, [the monks] exchange three informal prostrations with the main officers. During this time, the disciples, attendant monks, Dharma-relatives, and so on, prostrate themselves to the abbot in the Dharma Hall. The Dharma-relatives should perform two offers and three prostrations, and the abbot returns the prostrations. The disciples and attendant monks each do nine prostrations; there is no return prostration. The śramaṇeras do nine prostrations, or sometimes twelve prostrations, which the abbot receives only by joining hands. Next, the head monk goes in front of the Monks' Hall and, to the right of the entrance,[88] level with the southern end of the main officers' [Zazen] platforms, [that is,] in front of the Cloud Hall and facing south, [the head monk] stands before the monks. The monks, facing north, make three informal prostrations to the head monk. The head monk leads the monks into the Hall and, in order of years since receiving the precepts, they go around the Hall and

---

83. 触礼 (SOKUREI), lit. "touching bow." In this case, the folded prostration cloth is placed on the ground, and only the forehead touches the prostration cloth.

84. It is a Buddhist tradition that the master faces south on formal occasions. The Buddha Hall and Lecture Hall are usually built facing south. It was the custom in China for an emperor or king to sit facing south.

85. Novices serving as the abbot's assistants.

86. That is, in the corner of the Dharma Hall.

87. The place of precedence is the northern end of the Kitchen Hall, from which the main officers would be facing south. See Note 84.

88. 上間 (JOKAN), lit. "upper interval," means the interval between the entrance and the first pillar on the right (north).

stand still at their own place.[89] The main officers enter the Hall and before the sacred monk[90] they perform three prostrations with the prostration cloth fully spread, then stand up. Next they perform three informal prostrations before the head monk. All the monks return these prostrations. The main officers do one circuit of, and then leave, the [main] Hall and remain standing at their own place[91] with hands held in *shashu*.[92] The abbot enters the Hall and before the sacred monk burns incense, performs three prostrations with the prostration cloth spread, and stands up. During this time, the disciples stand out of the way behind the sacred monk,[93] and the Dharma-relatives follow the other monks. Next the abbot performs three informal prostrations to the head monk; that is, the abbot simply remains standing at his own place and performs the informal prostrations facing west. The head monk and all the monks return these prostrations, as before. The abbot goes round the hall and leaves. The head monk, leaving through the south side of the front entrance,[94] sees the abbot off. After the abbot has left the hall, all monks from the head monk down[95] perform three prostrations and say, *"We are fortunate at this time to be practicing the retreat together. I am afraid that my behavior of body, speech, and mind[96] will not be good, and I beg for compassion."* This prostration is three prostrations with the prostration cloth spread. After this, the head monk, his assistant, the librarian and the other [department heads] each return to their own quarters. Monks in the common quarters,[97] from the dormitory chief and dormitory head monk down, perform three informal prostrations to each other. The words of salutation are the same as in the ceremony in the Hall. The abbot thereupon begins the round of the quarters, starting from the Kitchen Hall. The monks join the procession in order, escort [the abbot] as far as the abbot's quarters, and then the monks withdraw. That is to say, the abbot first goes to the Kitchen Hall. After finishing personal salutations with the main officers, the abbot leaves [the Kitchen Hall] and performs the round of the quarters, at which time the main officers are walking behind [the abbot]. Walking after the main officers are people

---

89. For the retreat, the monks' seats in the Zazen Hall are arranged according to years since receiving the precepts.

90. An image, usually of Bodhisattva Mañjuśrī. Located in the center of the Zazen Hall, it faces the main entrance, and has a prostration mat in front of it.

91. The officers' places are not in the Main Hall but in the *zentan,* or Front Hall.

92. Fingers of left hand curled into a fist around the thumb, and held in front of the chest. Palm of right hand on back of left hand.

93. They take care not to receive the prostration of their own master.

94. The master leaves the hall through the north side of the entrance.

95. That is, all monks excluding the master, the main officers, and the master's disciples, attendants, and Dharma-relatives.

96. 三業 (SANGYO), lit. "three behaviors," that is behavior of body, speech, and mind.

97. That is, monks who are staying in the 衆寮 (SHURYO), or "common quarters," as opposed to monks who are staying in the Zazen Hall.

staying near the eastern corridor.[98] At this time, the abbot does not enter the infirmary, but goes down from the eastern corridor to the west, passing the Temple Gate and continuing on the round of the quarters, whereupon people staying in quarters near the Temple Gate join the procession. From the south, [the abbot] goes around the western corridor and the various quarters. At this time, while walking through the west side, [the abbot] is heading north. And from this time, retired old people,[99] retired officers,[100] retired assistant officers,[101] centenarians,[102] and veteran monks in private quarters,[103] as well as the cleaning chief,[104] and so on, will have joined the procession. The supervising monk, the head monk, and so on walk behind them. Next in line walk the monks in the common quarters. For the round of the quarters, we join the procession according to the convenience of [the location of our] quarters. This is called "the monks' escort." Thus, ascending the western stairs to the abbot's quarters, the abbot remains on the abbot's balcony[105] at the front of the abbot's quarters, and stands facing south with hands in *shashu*. All the monks, from the main officers down, bow to the abbot with joined hands, facing north. This bow should be especially deep. The abbot returns the bow. The monks withdraw. My late Master would not lead the monks to the abbot's quarters; when he reached the Dharma Hall he would stand in front of the steps to the Dharma-seat, facing south with hands in *shashu*. The monks would bow with joined hands and withdraw. This is an ancient form. After this, monks perform personal salutations as each pleases. "Personal salutations" means doing prostrations to each other. For example, people from the same home district—even several tens of them—perhaps in the Illuminated Hall[106] or perhaps at a convenient place in a corridor, do prostrations to each other and congratulate each other on sharing the

---

98. A Buddhist temple was traditionally built on the southern slope of a mountain. To the west are the Monks' (Zazen) Hall, the Toilet, the Washroom, and monks' common quarters. By the east corridor are the Kitchen Hall, the main officers' quarters, the novices hall, and monks' common quarters. In the middle are (from top to bottom) the abbot's quarters, the Dharma (Lecture) Hall, the Buddha Hall, and the Main Gate. (The seven main temple buildings have initial capitals in the text. See Book 1, Appendices, Temple Layout.)

99. 安老 (ANRO), lit. "peaceful old-age"; people who have established the will to the truth in their old age and have therefore come to live at the temple.

100. 勤旧 (GONKYU), lit. "served formerly," usually describes a monk who has formerly held the post of a main officer.

101. 前資 (ZENSHI), lit. "former assistant," is a title reserved for a monk who has served as an assistant officer for more than 3 years.

102. 頤堂 (IDO), lit. "the hall of centenarians."

103. 単寮 (TANRYO), lit. "single quarters."

104. 浄頭 (CHINJU), the monk in charge of cleaning the toilet.

105. Lit. "the position/throne for the abbot on the main building." "The main building" means the abbot's quarters. "The position" is probably a kind of balcony or podium.

106. 照堂 (SHODO) is located behind the Zazen Hall. When the master is busy, the senior monk uses this room to instruct other monks.

summer retreat. Here too the words of salutation follow the method used in the Hall. There are also personal words conceived in the present. Sometimes there are masters who have brought their disciples. In this case the disciples must inevitably do prostrations to their own master, performing nine prostrations. The Dharma-relatives' prostration to the abbot is two offers and three prostrations; or sometimes they simply do three prostrations with the prostration cloth spread. The prostration of any Dharma-relatives among the monks should be the same. There are inevitably prostrations to the younger and elder brothers[107] of one's master. All those who sleep next to each other and sit next to each other do prostrations to each other. There are prostrations between all those who are mutually acquainted or who have practiced together in the past. Veterans staying in private quarters, and the head monk, head monk's assistant, librarian, guest supervisor, bath manager, and so on, should visit each other's quarters and perform prostrations of congratulation. Veterans staying in private quarters, and the chief officer, the prior, the supervising monk, the chief cook, the work leader, veteran masters, nun-masters, lay people of the truth, and so on, also should visit each other's quarters or visit each other's seats[108] to perform prostrations of congratulation. When we go to visit someone's quarters but the entrance is densely crowded and there is not enough room to enter the quarters, we write a card and peg it up on the entrance. We write the card on white paper an inch or so wide and about two inches long. The form of the writing is as follows:

So-un, Esho, and others[109]
Prostrations of congratulation

Another form:

So-and-So
Performs a bow of congratulation

Another form:

So-and-So
Prostrations of congratulation

---

107. That is, the master's fellow disciples in the order of his master. The master's elder brother means a monk who took the precepts before the master took them. The master's younger brother means a monk who took the precepts after the master took them.

108. In the Zazen Hall.

109. So-un and Esho are examples of visitors' names.

Another form:

So-and-So
Performs humble prostrations

191] There are many forms for the writing, but the general outline is like this. So a large number of these cards can be seen beside the entrances. We do not peg them on the left of the entrance, but peg them on the right of the entrance. These cards are taken down after the midday meal by the person in charge of the quarters. On this day[110] the bamboo blinds of entrances to all halls and quarters, big and small, are left open. There is a custom that the abbot, the Kitchen Hall officers, and the head monk, one after another, serve tea and cakes. However, on a remote island or deep in the mountains, we should dispense with it. It is simply [further] instances of prostration. Veteran monks who have retired from a temple, and those established as head monks,[111] each, in their own quarters, serve tea and cakes especially for the main officers and assistant officers. Having thus inaugurated the summer retreat, we make effort in pursuit of the truth.[112] Even if we have pursued and realized many practices, if we have never done a summer retreat we are not descendants of the Buddhist patriarchs and we are not Buddhist patriarchs. Jetavana Park[113] and Vulture Peak, by virtue of the summer retreat, are totally realized. The practice-place of a summer retreat is the mind-seal of the Buddhist Patriarch, and is the existence in the world of all the buddhas.

92] *At the end of the summer retreat, on the 13th day of the 7th lunar month, the service of tea and cakes and the reciting of sutras in the common quarters is again the responsibility of the dormitory chief for that month.*

Mindful recitation on the evening of the 14th, and formal preaching in the Dharma Hall, personal salutations, the round of the quarters, and the service of tea and cakes on the following day, are all the same as at the beginning of the retreat. Only the wording of the notices is different. The notice of the Kitchen Hall officers' service of tea says:

---

110. The 15th of the 4th lunar month.

111. Suggests head monks established as dormitory head monks for the duration of the retreat.

112. 功夫弁道 (KUFU BENDO). Master Dogen frequently uses this expression to represent the practice of Zazen itself.

113. 孤独園 (KODOKU-ON), lit. "Solitary Garden," refers to Jetavana Park (or "Prince Jeta's Park"). A rich lay follower of the Buddha, Anāthapiṇḍana, offered to provide for the Buddha's order a place for the retreat in Sāvatthi (110 km north-east of present-day Lucknow). The Buddha stipulated that the retreat should be situated in a solitary place. Anāthapiṇḍana thereupon purchased the park from Prince Jeta, a son of King Prasenajit of Kośala. It is said that the Buddha practiced eighteen summer retreats in succession at Jetavana Park.

"The Kitchen Hall officers, this evening, / Will serve tea and cakes in the Cloud Hall, / Especially for the head monk and all the monks. / We humbly announce this celebration of the end of the retreat, / And we respectfully hope / That all the monks will kindly bestow upon us your illuminating presence. / The bhikṣus of the Kitchen Hall, So-and-So, Expressed with respect."[114]

The words for the mindful recitation at the Local Deities Hall are as follows:

"We sincerely reflect that a golden wind is fanning the countryside, and the God of Autumn[115] *is governing all directions. It is the time when the King of Realization dissolves the retreat. This is the day of completion of the Dharma-year. For ninety days there have been no difficulties and all the monks are at peace. We recite the vast names of the buddhas, and respectfully thank the true rulers of all the temple buildings. I respectfully request the assembly to recite..."*[116]

After this is the same as the mindful recitation at the beginning of the retreat.

[194] After the formal preaching in the Dharma Hall, the main officers say the following words of thanks: *"We humbly rejoice that the Dharma-year is complete and there have not been any difficulties. This is likely due to the protection of the Master's Dharma-power. As humble sentient beings, we are unable to contain our extreme gratitude."*

The abbot's words of thanks are as follows: *"Now the Dharma-year is complete, and we all thank Chief Officer and Head Monk So-and-So for sharing the benefit of their Dharma-power. I cannot contain my extreme gratitude."*

The monks of the Hall,[117] from the head monk down, and the monks of the dormitories, from the dormitory chief down, say the following words of thanks: *"For the ninety days of the summer retreat we have relied upon each other. My behavior of body, speech, and mind*[118] *have not been good, and I have disturbed the assembly. Humbly I beg for compassion."*

The main officers and the assistant officers make the following announcement: *"Brothers in the assembly who are going to travel on should wait until after the service of tea, and then you may [leave] as you please."* (If there is some exigency, this limitation does not apply.)

[195] This custom[119] is more fundamental than the ages before and after King

114. *Zen-en-shingi,* chap. 2.

115. 白帝 (HAKUTEI), lit. "the white emperor." In China, each of the four directions was represented with a color. West was white. Autumn was seen as the season of the sun's setting (in the west) and so white suggests autumn.

116. *Zen-en-shingi,* chap. 2.

117. Monks staying in the Zazen Hall.

118. 三業 (SANGYO), lit. "the three behaviors."

119. The summer retreat.

Majestic Sound. Buddhist patriarchs attach importance to only this. Non-Buddhists and heavenly demons never disturb only this. Throughout the three countries,[120] not a single descendant of the Buddhist Patriarch ever fails to practice it, but non-Buddhists never learn it. It is the Buddhist Patriarch's one great[121] original hope. Therefore, from the morning of attainment of the truth until the evening of nirvāṇa, he proclaims only the meaning of the retreat. Although there are differences among the five schools of monks in India, they are all the same in guarding and retaining the ninety-day summer retreat, which they practice-and-experience without fail. Not one of the nine sects of monks in China violates the summer retreat. Those who have never in their life practiced the ninety-day summer retreat should not be called bhikṣus who are the disciples of the Buddha. It is not only to practice in the causal state; it is practice-and-experience of the realized state. The all-enlightened World-Honored One, indeed, has practiced-and-experienced it through his whole life, without missing a single summer. Remember, it is the Buddha's experience in the realized state. A person who, nevertheless, does not practice-and-experience the ninety-day summer retreat and yet says, *"I may be a descendant of the Buddhist Patriarch,"* is laughable, and is a stupid person unworthy of laughter. Do not even listen to the words of people who speak like this. Do not talk with them. Do not sit with them. Do not walk with them on the same path. For in the Buddha-Dharma we treat evil people through the method of silence.[122] We must just understand, and maintain and rely upon, the ninety-day summer retreat as the Buddhist Patriarch himself. Its authentic transmission extends from the Seven Buddhas to Mahākāśyapa, and twenty-eight patriarchs in India have authentically transmitted it from rightful successor to rightful successor. The twenty-eighth patriarch personally manifested himself in China and caused Great Master Taiso Shoshu Fugaku, the second patriarch,[123] to receive its authentic transmission. Since the second patriarch it has been authentically transmitted from rightful successor to rightful successor, and it has been authentically transmitted to the present day. Having gone into China, in the order of a Buddhist patriarch [I] directly received its authentic transmission, and [I] am performing its authentic transmission in Japan. Now that we have actu-

---

120. India, China, Japan.

121. 一大事 (ICHIDAIJI) alludes to 一大事因縁 (ICHIDAIJI INNEN), "the one great purpose." The Lotus Sutra says that the buddhas appear in the world only by reason of one great purpose: to cause living beings to disclose the wisdom of Buddha, to show living beings the wisdom of Buddha, to cause living beings to realize the wisdom of Buddha, and to cause living beings to enter the state of truth, which is the wisdom of Buddha. See LS 1.88–90, and chap. 17, *Hokke-ten-hokke.*

122. "Silence" is 梵壇 (BONDAN), representing the Sanskrit *brahma-daṇḍa,* which lit. means "pure rod." This was a form of punishment in which the other members of a Buddhist order did not talk to a member of the order who had committed a sin.

123. Master Taiso Eka, the second patriarch in China.

ally practiced the ninety-day summer sitting in an order to which it has been authentically transmitted, we have received the authentic transmission of the Dharma of summer. To have practiced the retreat, living together with this person,[124] may be the true retreat. [The retreat] really has been transmitted in face-to-face transmission from rightful successor to rightful successor since the retreat of the Buddha's lifetime; therefore, we have directly received the authentic transmission of the face of the Buddha and the face of the patriarchs, and we have immediately experienced the body-and-mind of the Buddhist patriarchs. For this reason it is said that to meet the retreat is to meet Buddha, to experience the retreat is to experience Buddha, to practice the retreat is to practice Buddha, to hear the retreat is to hear Buddha, and to learn the retreat is to learn Buddha. In sum, that the buddhas and the patriarchs never go against or go beyond the ninety-day retreat is the Dharma. This being so, human kings, King Śakra, King Brahma, and so on, should become bhikṣus and, even if only for one summer, practice the retreat; this will be to meet Buddha. Human beings, celestial beings, and dragons, even if only for one period of ninety-days, should become bhikṣus or bhikṣuṇīs and practice the retreat; this will be to meet Buddha at once. To have joined the order of a Buddhist patriarch and practiced the ninety-day retreat is to have met Buddha already. That, fortunately, before our present dew-drop life has fallen, we have already practiced a summer retreat—whether in heaven above or in the human world—is to have had our own skin, flesh, bones, and marrow replaced by the skin, flesh, bones, and marrow of the Buddhist patriarchs. Because the Buddhist patriarchs come and practice the retreat through us, each person's practice of the retreat is the retreat's practice of each person. This being so, [we] who have experienced the retreat are simply called *"a thousand buddhas and myriad patriarchs."* The reason, if asked, is that the retreat is the very skin, flesh, bones, marrow, mind, and body of the Buddhist patriarchs; it is their brains and eyes; it is their fists and nostrils; it is their round form and Buddha-nature;[125] it is a fly whisk and a staff; it is a bamboo stick and a round cushion. The summer retreat is not the production of something new, and at the same time it is not the repeated use of something old.

[200] The World-Honored One addresses Bodhisattva Round Realization,[126] the great assemblies of monks, and all living beings: *"If you practice the retreat for three months from the beginning of summer, you will abide in the pure state of a bodhisattva, your mind will leave the state of a śrāvaka, and you will be beyond de-*

124. "This person" suggests Master Dogen himself, and at the same time, each individual person.

125. 円相 (ENSO), "round form," and 仏性 (BUSSHO), "Buddha-nature," allude to a story about Master Nāgārjuna quoted in chap. 22, *Bussho.*

126. A bodhisattva who appears in *Engaku-kyo (The Sutra of Round Realization).* The sutra is thought to have been written in China.

pendence on others. When the day of the retreat arrives, say before the Buddha the following words: 'In order that I, bhikṣu / bhikṣuṇī / upāsaka / upāsikā[127] *So-and-So, who ride upon the Bodhisattva-vehicle may perform tranquil practice; that I may harmoniously enter, dwell in, and maintain the pure real form; that I may make the great round realization into my temple; that body and mind may practice the retreat; and that the wisdom whose nature is balance, and the peaceful natural state of self, may be without hindrances; I now respectfully ask, without relying on the state of a śrāvaka, to practice the three-month retreat together with the tathāgatas of the ten directions and the great bodhisattvas. By virtue of enacting the great causes of the supreme and fine truth of the bodhisattva, I will not be involved with others.' Good sons! This is called a bodhisattva's manifestation of the retreat."*[128]

[201] Thus, bhikṣus, bhikṣuṇīs, upāsakas, and upāsikās, whenever they arrive at the three months of the retreat, inevitably enact the great causes of the supreme and fine truth together with the tathāgatas of the ten directions and the great bodhisattvas. Remember, upāsakas and upāsikās also should practice the retreat. This place of the retreat is the great round realization. That being so, Vulture Peak and Jetavana Park are both temples of the great round realization of the Tathāgata. We should listen to the World-Honored One's teaching that the tathāgatas of the ten directions and the great bodhisattvas all experience together three months of training in the retreat.

[202] *The World-Honored One practices a ninety-day retreat at one place. On the day of indulgence,*[129] *Mañjuśrī suddenly appears in the order. Mahākāśyapa asks Mañjuśrī, "This summer where have you practiced the retreat?" Mañjuśrī says, "This summer I have practiced the retreat at three places." At this, Mahākāśyapa assembles the monks. He is about to expel Mañjuśrī by striking the block,*[130] *but just as he lifts the clapper he sees countless Buddha-lands appear. At the place of every Buddha there is a Mañjuśrī, and there is a Mahākāśyapa lifting the clapper to expel Mañjuśrī. The World-Honored One thereupon addresses Mahākāśyapa, "Which Mañjuśrī are you now going to expel?" Then Mahākāśyapa is dumbfounded.*[131]

[203] Zen Master Engo,[132] in a discussion of the ancients, says, *"A bell not struck does not ring. A drum not hit does not sound. Mahākāśyapa is moored in the main harbor. Mañjuśrī instantly sits away the ten directions. At the present moment there is*

---

127. The four classes of Buddhists: monks, nuns, lay men, and lay women.

128. *Engaku-kyo (The Sutra of Round Realization).*

129. The day on which the restrictions of the summer retreat end. On this day, practitioners confess to each other the mistakes they have made during the retreat, and ask to be forgiven.

130. 白椎 (BYAKUTSUI), lit. "to strike the hammer," means to strike an octagonal wooden block, about three feet high, with a *tsui,* a small wooden clapper. The octagonal block and clapper are traditional instruments still seen in Buddhist temples in Japan today.

131. *Dai-ho-ko-hokyo-gyo (The Great Square and Wide Treasure Chest Sutra).* Also quoted in *Engo-ko-roku, (General Record of Engo [Kokugon]).*

132. Master Engo Kokugon (1063–1135), successor of Master Goso Ho-en, and editor of *Heki-gan-roku (Blue Cliff Record).*

a lovely scene of a Buddhist event. How regrettable to miss a move! As Old Master Śākyamuni said, "Which Mañjuśrī are you going to expel?" If [Mahākāśyapa] had immediately given the block a crack... imagine! What kind of total solution would the other[133] have performed?"[134]

[204] Zen Master Engo, in a eulogy to the ancients, says,

A big elephant does not play on a rabbit's path.
What do swallows and sparrows know of swans and storks?[135]
Obeying the rules is just like creating a style.
Breaking the standard is just like biting a [flying] arrow.[136]
The whole world is Mañjuśrī.
The whole world is Mahākāśyapa.
Facing one another, each is in the solemn state.
What is there to punish by lifting the clapper?
It is a nice instance of needlework.[137]
The golden dhūtas[138] have gotten rid of [all] obstacles.[139]

So the World-Honored One practices the retreat at one place and Mañjuśrī practices the retreat at three places, but neither ever fails to practice the retreat. One who does not practice the retreat is neither a buddha nor a bodhisattva. There is no example of a descendant of the Buddhist Patriarch failing to practice the retreat. We should recognize those who practice the retreat as the descendants of the Buddhist Patriarch. That which practices the retreat is the Buddhist Patriarch's body-and-mind, the Buddhist Patriarch's eyes, and the Buddhist Patriarch's very life. Those who do not practice the retreat are not the descendants of the Buddhist Patriarch, and are not Buddhist patriarchs. Buddhas and bodhisattvas of the present, [whether] of soil or wood, of white silk or gold, or of the seven treasures, should all practice a

---

133. The Buddha.

134. 合殺 (GASSATSU), lit. "total killing," suggests a complete solution, or the perfect restoring of tranquillity. *Engo-ko-roku (General Record of Engo)*, chap. 17.

135. In the first two lines Master Engo praises the exceptional personalities of Master Mahākāśyapa and Bodhisattva Mañjuśrī.

136. 破的 (TEKI *[o] yabu[ru koto]*), lit. "breaking the target" or "violating the mark," suggests Mañjuśrī's transcendence of idealistic rules. 噛鏃 (ZOKU *[o] ka[mu]*), lit. "biting an arrow," suggests behavior that is exactly right. The latter phrase alludes to a Chinese legend that when two excellent warriors, Toku Kunmo and O Reichi, had a competition to test each other's skill in archery, Toku Kunmo caught in his teeth an arrow shot by O Reichi. The story is recorded in *Taihei-ko-ki (Widely Extending Record of the Taihei Era)*, chap. 227.

137. Suggests sharp action in the moment of the present.

138. 頭陀 (ZUDA) represents the Sanskrit *dhūta*, which means a hard practice. In this case, "golden dhūtas" means the Indian practitioners themselves. See Book 1, Glossary.

139. "Gotten rid of [all] obstacles" is 落節 (RAKU-SETSU), lit. "dropped joints." The joint of a bamboo symbolizes something difficult to break, or a problem that is difficult to solve. *Engo-ko-roku (General Record of Engo)*, chap. 19.

summer sitting for three months in retreat. This is the ancient tradition of abiding in and maintaining the treasures of Buddha, Dharma, and Saṃgha, and it is the Buddha's instruction. In conclusion, people in the house of the Buddhist Patriarch decidedly must practice the summer sitting in retreat for three months.

Shobogenzo Ango

Preached to the assembly at Daibutsu-ji temple in Fukui prefecture on the 13th day of the 6th lunar month during the summer retreat in the 3rd year of Kangen.[140]

140. 1245.

[80]

佗心通

TASHINTSU

The Power to Know Others' Minds

Ta ***means "others,"*** ***shin*** *means "mind," and* ***tsu*** *(short for* ***jinzu****) means "mystical power." So* ***tashintsu*** *means "the mystical power to know others' minds." Some Buddhist groups believed it possible for Buddhist practitioners to attain a mystical power allowing them to see into others' minds. On this subject, there is a famous story concerning Master Nanyo Echu's questioning of an Indian monk called Daini Sanzo. The story was often discussed, and the interpretations of five famous Buddhist masters are given in this chapter. Master Dogen was not satisfied by their explanations and criticizes the views they expressed, in the process presenting us with his own views.*

[209] ***National Master Echu***[1] *of Kotaku-ji temple in the Western Capital,*[2] *is a man from Shoki in Esshu district.*[3] *His family name is Zen. After receiving the mind seal, he lives on Hakugai-zan mountain in Tosu-koku valley in Nan-yo district.*[4] *For more than forty years he never goes down from the Temple Gate, [but] rumor of his practice of the truth is heard even in the imperial capital. In the second year of Jogen,*[5] *during the reign of the Tang emperor Shukuso,*[6] *the Emperor sends his private messenger, Son Chosin, to convey the decree that [the Master] should come to the capital. [The Emperor] receives [Master Echu] with the courtesies shown to one's master, and installs him by imperial decree at Seizen-in monastery in the grounds of Senpuku-ji temple.*[7] *When the Emperor Daiso*[8] *takes the throne, he also sends for [the Master] and has him stay at Kotaku temple.*[9]

---

1. Master Nan-yo Echu (died 775), successor of Master Daikan Eno.

2. 西京 (SEIKEI). There were five capitals in ancient China with this name. In this case, the capital corresponds to the present-day city of Luoyang in north Honan, east China, in the Hwang basin.

3. A district in modern-day Chekiang province in east China.

4. In modern-day Honan province in east China.

5. 761.

6. 粛宗 (SHUKUSO), reigned 756 to 763. Also mentioned in chap. 12, *Kesa-kudoku,* notes to chap. 63, *Hensan* (from *Shinji-shobogenzo,* pt. 1, no. 26), and chap. 86, *Shukke-kudoku.*

7. The suffix 寺 (JI) is translated here as "temple," and the suffix 院 (IN) as "monastery."

8. 代宗 (DAISO), reigned 763 to 779. In chap. 86, *Shukke-kudoku,* para. [106], he is criticized alongside Shukuso for attaching to the throne. But he is praised in chap. 1, *Bendowa,* para. [52] for sitting in Zazen.

During sixteen years there, [the Master] preaches the Dharma according to [practitioners'] makings. At that time a certain Daini Sanzo[10] *from India arrives in the capital saying, "I have attained the eye that intuits the minds of others." The Emperor decrees that the National Master should examine him. As soon as Sanzo meets the Master he prostrates himself at once and stands to the [Master's] right.*

The Master says, "Have you got the power to know others' minds?"

[Sanzo] answers, "I would not be so bold [as to say so]."[11]

The Master says, "Tell me where [this] old monk is just now."

Sanzo says, "Master, you are the teacher of the whole country. Why have you gone to the West River to watch a boat race?"

The Master asks a second time, "Tell me where the old monk is just now."

Sanzo says, "Master, you are the teacher of the whole country. Why are you on Tientsin Bridge[12] *watching [someone] play with a monkey?"*

The Master asks a third time, "Tell me where the old monk is just now."

Sanzo takes a good while but he does not know where [the Master] has been. The Master scolds him, saying, "You ghost of a wild fox, where is your power to know others' minds?" Sanzo has no answer.[13]

[211] *A monk asks Joshu,*[14] *"Daini Sanzo does not see where the National Master is the third time. I wonder where the National Master is." Joshu says, "He is right on Sanzo's nostrils."*

[212] *A monk asks Gensa,*[15] *"If he is already on [Sanzo's] nostrils, why does [Sanzo] not see him?" Gensa says, "Simply because of being enormously close."*

---

9. In this case "temple" is 精藍 (SEIRAN). 精 (SEI) means "spiritual" or "pure." 藍 (RAN) is derived from the Sanskrit *saṃgha-arāma*, lit. "a resting place for a company [of monks]," a term equivalent to the Sanskrit *vihāra*.

10. 大耳三蔵 (DAINI-SANZO). 大耳 (DAINI) lit. means "Big Ears." 三蔵 (SANZO) represents the meaning of the Sanskrit *tripitaka*, the three baskets of *sūtra* (discourses), *vinaya* (discipline) and *abidharma* (commentaries). The title *Sanzo* was given to a person who was accomplished in studying the *tripitaka*.

11. 不敢 (FUKAN), lit. "I do not dare." In chap. 22, *Bussho*, para. [73], Master Dogen explains the characters as follows: *Obaku says, "I would not be so bold." In the land of Sung when you are asked about an ability that you possess, you say these words "I would not be so bold" to suggest that the ability is [your own] ability.* So Sanzo is suggesting that out of modesty he does not want to boast about his power.

12. Tientsin is a large city and port in northeast China, in Hopeh Province, southeast of Beijing.

13. Quoted directly from *Keitoku-dento-roku*, chap. 5. The story is also discussed in chap. 19, *Shin-fukatoku*, as are the following comments of the five venerable patriarchs.

14. Master Joshu Jushin (778–897), successor of Master Nansen Fugan. See also, for example, chap. 35, *Hakujushi*.

15. Master Gensa Shibi (835–907), successor of Master Seppo Gison. See also, for example, chap. 4, *Ikka-no-myoju*.

[212] *A monk asks Kyozan[16] "Why does Daini Sanzo not see the National Master the third time?" Kyozan says, "The first two times [the Master's] mind is concerned with external circumstances;[17] then he enters the samādhi of receiving and using the self,[18] and so [Sanzo] does not see him."*

[213] *Kai-e [Shu]tan[19] says, "If the National Master is right on Sanzo's nostrils, what difficulty could [Sanzo] have in seeing him? Above all, it has not been recognized that the National Master is inside Sanzo's eyeballs."*

[213] *Gensa chides Sanzo: "You! Say! Have you seen at all, even the first two times?" Zen Master Myokaku Juken[20] of Seccho says "I am defeated, I am defeated."[21]*

[214] The odorous fists are many who, since ancient times, have made comments on and assertions about the story of how National Master Daisho[22] tested Daini Sanzo, but there are five particularly venerable old fists among them. And although I do not deny that the insight and accuracy of each of these five venerable patriarchs are very insightful and accurate, there are many respects in which they have not glimpsed the conduct of the National Master. The reason, if asked, is that all concerned, past and present, have thought that the first two times Sanzo unerringly knew the National Master's situation. This is our ancestors' great error, and we students of later ages should not be ignorant of it. My present doubts about the five venerable patriarchs are twofold. First, [the venerable patriarchs] do not know the National Master's fundamental intention in examining Sanzo. Second, they do not know the National Master's body-and-mind.

[215] Now the reason I say that they do not know the National Master's fundamental intention in examining Sanzo is as follows: The first time the National Master says *"Tell me where [this] old monk is just now,"* his fundamental intention is to question whether Sanzo has eyes that see and hear the Buddha-Dharma. He is questioning whether Sanzo has within himself the power to know others' minds, which belongs to the Buddha-Dharma. At this time, if

---

16. Master Kyozan Ejaku (803–887), successor of Master Isan Reiyu.

17. 涉境心 (SHOKYOSHIN). 涉 (SHO, *wata[ru]*) lit. means cross over or float across, and 境 (KYO, *sakai*) means boundaries or external circumstances. In Master Kyozan's usage, the phrase 涉境心 (SHOKYOSHIN) suggests the mind that is attached to external things and events. But in his commentary, Master Dogen says that this mind and the balanced state (samādhi) are the same.

18. 自受用三昧 (JIJUYO ZANMAI), the state of natural balance.

19. Master Kai-e Shutan (1025–1072), successor of Master Yogi Ho-e.

20. Master Seccho Juken (980–1052), a successor of Master Chimon Koso. Zen Master Myokaku is his posthumous title.

21. In this chapter, the five comments are all quoted directly in Chinese characters, whereas in chap. 19, *Shin-fukatoku,* direct quotes from the Chinese are interspersed with words and phrases in Japanese *kana.* The order in which the comments are quoted also changes: Master Kyozan's comment comes first in *Keitoku-dento-roku,* third in this chapter, and last in *Shin-fukatoku.*

22. Posthumous title of Master Nan-yo Echu.

the Buddha-Dharma were present in Sanzo, when asked *"Where is the old monk just now?"* he would have a way of getting the body out; he would manifest a practical means that was familiar to him. The National Master's words *"Where is the old monk just now?"* are as if to ask "What is the old monk?" *"Where is the old monk just now?"* asks "Just now is what kind of moment?" *"Is where"* asserts that *"This place is where something ineffable exists."* [The Master's words] contain the truth of calling something ineffable *"the old monk."* The National Master is not necessarily an "old monk," but *the old monk* is always a fist.[23] Daini Sanzo does not know this idea because, although he has come from the faraway Western Heavens, he has not learned the Buddha's truth, and because he has only vainly learned the ways of non-Buddhists and the two vehicles. The National Master asks again *"Tell me where the old monk is just now."* And here again Sanzo offers futile words. The National Master asks once again, "Tell me where the old monk is just now." This time Sanzo takes a while but is dumbfounded and without a response. Then the National Master scolds Sanzo, saying, *"You ghost of a wild fox, where is your power to know others' minds?"* Even after being scolded like this, Sanzo still has nothing to say for himself. He does not respond. He has no through route. Nevertheless, the ancestors all think, in regard to the National Master's scolding of Sanzo, "The first two times [Sanzo] knew where the National Master was; he does not know and does not see only at the third time, and therefore he is scolded by the National Master." This is a great mistake. The National Master's scolding of Sanzo scolds Sanzo outright for never having seen the Buddha-Dharma from the beginning, even in a dream. He does not scold Sanzo for having known the first two times but not knowing the third time. He scolds [Sanzo] outright for boasting that he has attained the power to know others' minds when in fact he does not know others' minds. The National Master first tests [Sanzo] by asking whether the power to know others' minds exists in the Buddha-Dharma. By saying, *"I would not be so bold"* [Sanzo] seems to affirm that it exists. After that, the National Master thinks, "If we say that the power to know others' minds exists in the Buddha-Dharma, and if we cause the power to know others' minds to exist in the Buddha-Dharma, it should be in such-and-such a state. If expression of the state lacks the total manifestation of the state, it cannot be the Buddha-Dharma." Even if Sanzo narrowly managed to say something the third time, if it had anything in common with the first two attempts it would not include expression of the state, and [the Master] would have to scold him outright. In now venturing to ask three times, the National Master is asking again and again whether Sanzo is able to understand the National Master's question, and so he repeats the question three times.

---

23. The concept "old monk" is not always applicable to the National Master, but the self that he expressed as *the old monk* is always present.

[218] The second [doubt] is that none of the ancestors has known the body-and-mind of the National Master. What I have called "the body-and-mind of the National Master" cannot easily be seen or known by Dharma-teachers of the three baskets.[24] It is beyond even [bodhisattvas in] the ten sacred stages and the three clever stages,[25] and it is not clarified by [bodhisattvas] at the place of assignment[26] or in the state of balanced awareness.[27] How could a scholar of the three baskets, a common man, know the whole body of the National Master? We must affirm this principle with total certainty. To say that the body-mind of the National Master could be known or could be seen by a scholar of the three baskets is an insult to the Buddha-Dharma. To recognize that [the Master's body-and-mind] might be on the level of a teacher of sutras and commentaries is the utmost madness. Do not learn that a person who has attained the power to know others' mind might be able to know the place where the National Master is.

[219] From time to time there are people who acquire the power to know others' minds as an ethnic custom of the western country, India. [But] no example has ever been heard of a person who, without relying upon establishment of the bodhi-mind and without relying on the right viewpoint of the Great Vehicle, has attained the power to know others' minds and by virtue of the power to know others' minds has realized the Buddha-Dharma. Even after acquiring the power to know others' minds, if a person proceeds, as a common man, to establish the will and to undergo training, he will naturally be able to experience and to enter the Buddha's truth. If it were possible to know the Buddha's truth only by virtue of the power to know others' minds, all the past saints would have first learned the power to know others' minds and then used that ability to know the buddha-effect. During the appearance in the world of even a thousand buddhas and ten thousand patriarchs, such a thing will never be. Of what use are those who are unable to know the truth of the Buddhist patriarchs? We can say that they are of no use to Buddhism. One who has attained the power to know others' minds, and a common man who has not attained the power to know others' minds, may be exactly equal. In maintaining and relying upon the Buddha-nature a mind-

24. 三蔵法師 (SANZO-HOSHI), or "Dharma-teacher of the tripitaka." 法師 (HOSHI), "Dharma-teacher," like *Sanzo*, was a title sometimes used for scholar-priests and teachers of theory as opposed to monks who practiced Zazen. See also note 10.

25. 十聖三賢 (JUSHO-SANKEN), lit. "ten sacreds and three clevers." A bodhisattva is said to pass through fifty-two phases before becoming buddha: ten stages of belief (phases 1–10); then thirty phases classed as the three clever stages (11–40); then ten sacred stages (41–50); then the penultimate state of balanced awareness (51); and finally the ultimate state of subtle awareness (52).

26. 補処 (FUSHO), short for 一生補処の菩薩 (ISSHO-FUSHO *no* BOSATSU), lit. "a bodhisattva at the place of assignment in one life"—that is state no. 52, also called 妙覚 (MYOKAKU), subtle awareness.

27. 等覚 (TOKAKU), state no. 51.

reader and a common man may be the same. Students of the state of Buddha must never think that non-Buddhists and people of the two vehicles who have the five powers or the six powers[28] are superior to the common man. A person who has only the will to the truth yet hopes to learn the Buddha-Dharma may be superior to [a person who has] the five powers or six powers—as the song of the kalavinka,[29] even in the egg, is superior to [the songs of] ordinary birds. Furthermore, what is called in India *"the power to know others' minds,"* should be called "the power to know the images in others' minds."[30] [Mind readers] may dimly detect, on the outer edges of perception, images arising in the mind. In the absence of images in the mind, however, they are dumbfounded; that must be laughable. Moreover, the mind is not always mental images, and mental images are not always the mind. When the mind becomes the image,[31] the power to know others' minds cannot know it, and when the image becomes the mind, the power to know others' minds cannot know it. This being so, the five powers and the six powers of India are not equal to our mowing weeds and working the fields in this country. They are of no use at all. For this reason, all the past masters in and to the east of China have not liked to practice the five powers and the six powers, because there is no need to do so. Even a one-foot gem can be necessary, [but] the five powers and the six powers are not necessary. Even a one-foot gem is not a treasure, [but] every inch of time is vital. How could a person who attaches importance to time want to learn the five or six powers? In sum, we should decisively affirm the principle that the power to read others' minds cannot reach the boundary of the Buddha's wisdom.

[223] For each of the five venerable patriarchs to have thought, on the contrary, that at the first two times Sanzo knew the situation of the National Master, is greatly mistaken. The National Master is a Buddhist patriarch. Sanzo is a common man. How could we even discuss a meeting between the two of them? First the National Master says, *"Tell me where the old monk is just now."* There is nothing hidden in this question; it contains a clearly manifest

---

28. Explained in chap. 25, *Jinzu.*

29. The kalavinka is said to be a bird of the Himalayas whose voice is so beautiful that no-one ever tires of hearing it.

30. 佗念通 (TANENTSU), or "the power to know others' ideas." The first meaning of the noun 念 (NEN) is images in the mind—ideas, thoughts, illusions, wishes, dreams, Buddhist theories etc. The second meaning of 念 (NEN)—which is not always easy to distinguish from the first—is the state of awareness of reality, or the image of reality as reflected in the balanced state of action. See also the discussion of mindfulness in chap. 73, *Sanjushichi-bon-bodai-bunpo,* para. [14].

31. 心の念ならんとき (SHIN *no* NEN *nara n toki*) means "when the mind becomes the image," or "when the mind becomes awareness," or "when the mind becomes awareness of the image." The phrase suggests the state of undivided wholeness in the moment of the present—as for example, in the moment when an archer shoots an arrow at the target, or at the moment when a batter hits the ball.

expression of the state. That Sanzo does not know it is not his fault. That the five venerable patriarchs neither hear nor see it is a mistake. The National Master has said already, *"Where is the old monk just now?"* He never says, "Tell me where the old monk's mind is just now." He does not say "Where are the old monk's thoughts just now?" [What he says] is an expression of the state which is extremely necessary to observe and to inspect. Nevertheless, [the five venerable patriarchs] neither know nor see it. They neither hear nor see the National Master's expression of the state, and for that reason they do not know the body-and-mind of a National Master—because one in whom there is expression of the state is called "National Master," and because one who lacks expression of the state cannot be a National Master. Moreover, they cannot recognize that the National Master's body-mind is beyond big and small, and beyond self and others. They seem to have forgotten that he possesses the brains and possesses the nostrils. Though the National Master has no time free from practice, how could he intend to become Buddha! Therefore, we should not expect to meet him by referring to "Buddha." The National Master already possesses the body-mind of the Buddha-Dharma. We cannot fathom it through mystical powers and practice and experience, and we cannot suppose it by means of transcending thought and forgetting involvements. It is never hit by thinking or non-thinking. The National Master is beyond having the Buddha-nature, is beyond not having the Buddha-nature, and is beyond the body of space.[32] This state of the National Master's body-mind is utterly beyond recognition. In the present lineage from the order of Sokei, besides Seigen and Nangaku only the National Master Daisho is such a Buddhist patriarch.[33] Now I would like to test and to defeat each of the five venerable patriarchs.

[225] Joshu says that because the National Master is right on Sanzo's nostrils, [Sanzo] does not see him. This expression has no meaning. How could the National Master be right on Sanzo's nostrils? Sanzo has never had nostrils. If we affirm that nostrils are present in Sanzo, then the National Master, from his side, should meet with Sanzo. A meeting of the National Master and Sanzo, if we affirm that there is one, may simply be a pair of nostrils facing a pair of nostrils.[34] Sanzo cannot really meet with the National Master at all.

---

32. 虚空身 (KOKU-SHIN). The Garland Sutra lists 解境十仏 (GE-KYO-JUBUTSU), or "Ten States of Buddha Understood by Their Objective Circumstances," namely: the body of living beings, the body of a national land, the body of karmic reward, the śrāvaka-body, the pratyekabuddha-body, the bodhisattva-body, the body of the Tathāgata, the body of wisdom, the Dharma-body, and the body of space.

33. Master Daikan Eno transmitted the Dharma to these three masters on Mt. Sokei. Master Seigen Gyoshi became the ancestral master of Master Dogen's lineage. Master Nangaku Ejo's successors include the ancestral masters of the Rinzai Sect.

34. In this paragraph 鼻孔 (BIKU), "nostrils," firstly symbolizes the vigorous Buddhist state, which Sanzo lacks, and secondly means an ordinary pair of nostrils, which Sanzo has.

[226] Gensa says, *"Simply because of being enormously close."* Certainly, his *enormously close*[35] can be left as it is, but still he has missed the point. What is *enormous closeness?* I guess that Gensa has never known *enormous closeness* or experienced *enormous closeness*. The reason, if asked, is that he knows only that in being enormously close there is no seeing each other, but he does not know that mutual realization is *enormous closeness* itself.[36] We can say that in regard to the Buddha-Dharma he is the farthest of the far. To describe only the third time as enormously close would suggest that the state at the first two times was enormously distant. Now let us ask Gensa: What do you call *enormously close*? Are you describing a fist? Are you describing the Eye? From now on, do not say that nothing is seen in the state of *being enormously close*.

[227] Kyozan says, *"The first two times [the Master's] mind is concerned with external circumstances; then he enters the samādhi of receiving and using the self, and so [Sanzo] does not see him."* Kyozan! Though you live in an eastern land, you have extended your acclaim as a lesser Śākyamuni even to India in the west. Nevertheless, your words now contain a great error. The mind that is concerned with external circumstances, and the samādhi of receiving and using the self, are not different. Therefore you should not say that [Sanzo] does not see because of the difference between the mind that is concerned with external circumstances and the state of receiving and using the self. That being so, though you proffer a reason based upon the difference between the state of receiving and using the self and the mind that is concerned with external circumstances, your expression is not an expression at all. If you say, "When I enter the samādhi of receiving and using the self, other people cannot see me," then the state of receiving and using the self can never experience the state of receiving and using the self, and there can be no practice-and-experience. Kyozan! If you understand that Sanzo really believes that he sees where the National Master is the first two times, you are not yet a person who is learning Buddha. In short, Daini Sanzo neither knows nor sees where the National Master is, not only the third time, but also the first two times. And if you are as the above expression suggests, Sanzo is not the only one who does not know the situation of the National Master; we might say that Kyozan also has never known the situation of the National Master. Now I will ask Kyozan: *"Where is the National Master just now?"* And at that moment, if Kyozan makes to open his mouth, I will at once let out a yell.

Similarly, みる (*miru*), "to meet" or "to see," firstly suggests mutual realization between two buddhas, and secondly, two people meeting each other.

35. Master Dogen affirmed Master Gensa's comment as meaning that Sanzo could not see what was right there in front of him (right in front of his nose!).

36. Master Gensa only recognized the situation (for example, in a tightly-packed crowd) when two people do not notice each other because they are too close together. "Seeing each other" and "mutual realization" are originally the same characters, 相見 (SOKEN).

[229] Gensa chides Sanzo, saying, *"Have you seen [the National Master] at all, even the first two times?"* The present utterance *"Have you seen at all, even the first two times?"* sounds as if it says what needs to be said. [But] Gensa should study his own words. The excellence of this remark is as it is. At the same time, it is not right, because it seems only to suggest that [Sanzo's] seeing is like not seeing.[37] Hearing the above, Juken, Zen Master Myokaku of Seccho-zan mountain, says, *"I am defeated. I am defeated."* When we have seen Gensa's words as the truth we should say this, but when we do not see Gensa's words as the truth we should not say this.

[229] Kai-e [Shu]tan says, *"If the National Master is right on Sanzo's nostrils, what difficulty could [Sanzo] have in seeing him? Above all, it has not been recognized that the National Master is inside Sanzo's eyeballs."* This again discusses only the third time. It does not criticize [Sanzo] as he should be criticized, for never having seeing at all, even the first two times. How could [Kai-e] recognize that the National Master was on Sanzo's nostrils or inside his eyeballs? If he speaks like this, I must say that he has never heard the National Master's words. Sanzo has never had nostrils or eyes. Even supposing that Sanzo were to maintain and rely upon eyeballs and nostrils of his own, if the National Master came and entered those nostrils and eyeballs, Sanzo's nostrils and eyeballs would each instantly be split apart. Having been split apart, they would not be a haunt of the National Master.

[230] None of the five venerable patriarchs knows the National Master. The National Master is an eternal buddha through all the ages and a tathāgata for all the world. He has clarified and received the authentic transmission of the Buddha's right-Dharma-eye treasury, and has securely retained black bead eyes.[38] He passes the authentic transmission to the buddha of himself, and he passes the authentic transmission to the buddha of others. He has already experienced the same state as Śākyamuni Buddha, and yet he is investigating the state simultaneously with the Seven Buddhas. At the same time, he has experienced the same state as all the buddhas of the three times. He has realized the truth before Emptiness King,[39] he has realized the truth after Emptiness King, and he has realized the truth in the same state as, and just in the time of, the Buddha Emptiness King. The National Master has always seen the sahā-world as his national land; at the same time, "the sahā-[world]" is not necessarily present within his world of Dharma and not necessarily present

---

37. Master Dogen is interested in whether or not Sanzo could see where the National Master was—right there in front of him!

38. 木かん子眼 (MOKKANSU-GEN). 木かん子 (MOKKANSU) are the black spherical seeds of the fruit of the *aphananthe aspera*; each seed is about the size of a pupil. 眼 (GEN) means eyeball. Retaining black-bead eyes means remaining balanced and therefore detached. See also chap. 28, *Butsu-kojo-no-ji*, para. [65].

39. 空王 (KU-O), the name of a legendary eternal Buddha who ruled the world during the Kalpa of Emptiness (the eternal past).

within his whole Universe in ten directions. And Śākyamuni Buddha, as the ruler of sahā-nations, neither usurps nor restricts the national land of the National Master—just as, for example, former and latter Buddhist patriarchs each have countless realizations of the truth, but they neither detract from nor restrict each other. The situation is like this because former and latter Buddhist patriarchs' realizations of the truth are restricted, in each case, by realization of the truth itself.

[232] With Daini Sanzo's failure to know the National Master as evidence, we should decisively affirm the principle that śrāvakas and pratyekabuddhas, people of the small vehicle, do not know the periphery of a Buddhist patriarch. We should clarify and learn the National Master's intention in scolding Sanzo, as follows. Even if the National Master himself scolded [Sanzo] for knowing his situation the first two times and only failing to know the third time, that would be meaningless. To know two thirds of the whole is to know the whole itself. [Sanzo] would not deserve to be scolded for being like that. If he were scolded, it would not be for failing to know completely. Sanzo's attitude is an insult to the National Master. If [the National Master] scolded Sanzo on not being recognized only the third time, who could believe in the National Master? With ability that had been able to know the first two times, Sanzo might scold the National Master. The National Master's intention in scolding Sanzo is this: he scolds [Sanzo] for totally failing all three times, from the outset, to know the National Master's situation, his thoughts, and his body-mind. He scolds [Sanzo] for never having seen, heard, or learned the Buddha-Dharma at all. With this intention, from the first time to the third time, he questions [Sanzo] with the same words. At the first try Sanzo says, *"Master, you are the teacher of the whole country. Why have you gone to the West River to watch a boat race?"* Addressed thus, the National Master never agrees, "Yes Sanzo, you have truly recognized the situation of the old monk"; he only repeats the question again and again, three times. Failing to recognize and failing to clarify this fact, old veterans in all directions, for several centuries since the time of the National Master, have delivered comments and set forth theories at random. The comments of each past individual are wholly irrelevant to the original intention of the National Master, and they do not accord with the fundamental teaching of the Buddha-Dharma. It is pitiful that the old drills of the past have each blundered on in error. Now, if we say that there is the power to know others' minds in the Buddha-Dharma, there must be the power to know others' bodies, there must be the power to know others' fists, and there must be the power to know others' eyes. That being so, there must be the power to know our own mind, and there must be the power to know our own body. If the state is like this already, self-command of our own mind[40] may be nothing other than *the power to know our own mind.*[41]

40. 自心の自拈 (JISHIN *no* JINEN), or "taking hold by oneself of the mind of the self," sug-

When expressions like this are realized, the state may be the power to know others' minds [which naturally emerges] from the self itself and from the mind itself. Now let us ask: Is it right to command the power to know others' minds or is it right to command the power to know our own minds? Speak at once! Speak at once! Setting that aside, [we can conclude that] *"You have got my marrow"* is just the power to know others' minds.[42C]

Shobogenzo Tashintsu

Preached to the assembly at Daibutsu-ji temple in Etsu-u on the 4th day of the 7th lunar month in the 3rd year of Kangen.[43]

gests self-regulation of the whole self through the practice of Zazen. Various meanings of 拈 (NEN), including take hold, twirl, utilize, and comprehend are discussed in the notes to chap. 68, *Udonge.*

41. 自心通 (JISHINTSU).

42. The sentences from "Now let us ask" to the end of the paragraph are in Chinese characters only, but are almost certainly composed by Master Dogen himself.

43. 1245.

[81]

王索仙陀婆

O-SAKU-SENDABA

A King's Seeking of Saindhava

*O means "king," **saku** means "to seek," and **sendaba** is a phonetic rendering of the Sanskrit saindhava. Saindhava means "products of the Indus river basin." The Mahā-parinirvāṇa-sutra contains a story which uses the multiple meanings of words to express the ambiguity of reality. When a king needs to wash his hands and requests saindhava, his servant will bring water. When the king is eating a meal and requests saindhava, the servant will bring salt. When the king wants to drink water and requests saindhava, the servant will bring a cup. And when the king wants to go out and requests saindhava, the servant will bring a horse. Buddhist monks in China often used this story to discuss the multiple meanings of words and the ambiguous nature of reality. In this chapter Master Dogen explains the meaning of "A King's Seeking of Saindhava" from his own unique viewpoint.*

[237] *Words – no words;*
Real wisteria and real trees;
Feeding donkeys, feeding horses;
Clear water and transparent clouds.[1]

[238] Because this is the way it is already,

In the Sutra of the Great Parinirvāṇa[2] the World-honored One says, *"For example, it is like a great king telling his retainers, 'Bring saindhava!' Saindhava is one word for four products. The first is salt, the second is pots, the third is water, and the fourth*

---

1. This poem describes the world in which we live. The first line suggests that sometimes there are words to affirm things, and sometimes there are no words to affirm things. This is the first or intellectual phase. The second line suggests the concrete inter-relationship between real things—here wisteria, which relies on a tree for support. The line can also be seen as representing the negation of words, phrases, ideas (the first phase) and passage into the area of concrete things (second phase). In the third line people feed donkeys and people feed horses—suggesting action in daily life (third phase). The final line suggests that in reality, water is just water and clouds are just clouds—things as they are. The poem also alludes to the philosophical system, called 四句分別 (SHIKU-FUNBETSU), which was elucidated by Master Nāgārjuna, the fourteenth patriarch in India.

2. 大般涅槃経 (DAIHATSU-NEHAN-KYO), from the Sanskrit, *Mahāparinirvāṇa-sūtra.* Sometimes known as the *Sutra of the Great Demise.*

is horses. These four things each have the same name. [Yet] a wise retainer is able to know [the meaning of] this word. If the king requests saindhava when about to wash, [the retainer] at once serves water. If the king requests saindhava when eating, [the retainer] at once serves salt. If the king requests saindhava after eating, when he wants to drink water, [the retainer] at once serves a pot. If the king requests saindhava when he wants to go out, [the retainer] at once serves a horse. A wise retainer like this is able to understand in four ways a great king's secret talk."[3][4]

[240] This king's seeking of saindhava, along with the retainer's serving of saindhava, have come to us from long ago. They have been transmitted in common with the Dharma-robe. The World-honored One himself inevitably discussed them, and so his descendants have discussed them again and again. We can guess that those who have experienced the same state as the World-honored One have made saindhava into their own practice. To those who are not in the same state as the World-honored One: When you buy some straw sandals and tread one step forward on foot, you will have got it already![5C] Saindhava in the house of the Buddhist patriarchs has secretly leaked out already, and so saindhava is present in the residences of great kings.

[241] The eternal Buddha Wanshi[6] of Tendo-zan mountain in the Great Sung city of Keigen-fu,[7] in formal preaching in the Dharma Hall, preaches to the assembly, *"To quote: A monk asks Joshu[8] 'How is it when a king seeks saindhava?' Joshu bows with hands folded.[9] Seccho[10] comments, 'It was the seeking of salt and the serving of a horse.'"* The Master [Wanshi] says, *"Seccho is an excellent master of a hundred years ago; Joshu is an eternal buddha one hundred and twenty years of age. If Joshu is right, Seccho is wrong. If Seccho is right, Joshu is wrong. Now say: in the end, how is it? [I,] Tendo, cannot help adding a footnote. If we differ from it by a thousandth or a hundredth we miss it by a thousand miles.*

> *To understand is to beat about in the grass to scare snakes,*[11]
> *And not to understand is to burn money to attract demons.*[12]

---

3. 密語 (MITSUGO), "Secret Talk," is the title of chap. 51, *Mitsugo.*

4. *Daihatsu-nehan-kyo*, vol. 9, from the chapter entitled *Nyorai-sho (The Nature of the Tathāgata).* The sutra compares a king's request for saindhava with the situation that the Tathāgata's nirvāṇa is unchanging and eternal, but its manifestation is changing and momentary.

5. A Chinese expression for which no source has been traced, hence marked C.

6. Master Wanshi Shokaku (1091–1157), successor of Master Tanka Shijun. Master Wanshi is praised, for example, in chap. 27, *Zazenshin.*

7. Modern-day Ningpo, in northern Chekiang province in east China.

8. Master Joshu Jushin (778–897), successor of Master Nansen Fugan.

9. 叉手 (SHASHU). Left fist (with fingers of left hand curled around the thumb) placed palm down against the sternum. Right palm placed on back of the left hand. Forearms horizontal.

10. Master Seccho Juken (980–1052), successor of Master Chimon Koso.

11. A symbol of ineffective effort. Related words appear in the Chinese book *Inzui (Rhymes of Good Fortune).*

12. A symbol of unreasonable behavior. There was a custom at Chinese funerals of placing

Without preferences in regard to an uncultivated field is Old Gutei.[13]
Extending his hand, [he tackles] what he picks up just now.[14]

242] During formal preaching in the Dharma Hall my late Master, the eternal Buddha, would usually say, *"The eternal Buddha Wanshi."* But only my late Master, the eternal Buddha, has met the eternal Buddha Wanshi as an eternal buddha. In Wanshi's time there was a certain Soko, called "the Zen Master Dai-e of Kinzan mountain,"[15] who may have been a distant descendant of Nangaku.[16] The whole realm of the Great Sung thinks that Dai-e might be equal to Wanshi. Moreover, some have thought that he is more of a person of the fact than Wanshi. This mistake has arisen because both monks and lay people in the great kingdom of Sung, being negligent in learning, are not yet clear in their eyes for the truth, are without clarity in knowing people, and are without the ability to know themselves. In Wanshi's comment the real establishment of the will is present. We should learn in practice the principle of the eternal Buddha Joshu bowing with hands folded. Just at that moment, is it the king's seeking of saindhava, or not? And is it the retainer's service of saindhava, or not? We should learn in practice Seccho's teaching that *"It was the seeking of salt and the serving of a horse."* The *seeking of salt* and the *serving of a horse* is each the king's seeking of saindhava and the retainer's seeking of saindhava. The World-honored One seeks saindhava and Mahākāśyapa's face breaks into a smile. The first Patriarch seeks saindhava and the four disciples serve a horse, salt, water, and a pot.[17] We should learn the pivotal state which—at the moment when a horse, salt, water, or a pot and the seeking of saindhava become one—is the serving of a horse or the serving of water.[18]

45] *Nansen*[19] *one day on seeing To Inpo*[20] *coming towards him points to a water jar and says, "The jar is circumstances. Inside the jar there is water. Without disturbing the*

---

coins (called "money for the six realms") in the coffin. Later the authorities prohibited the burying of money, and the custom evolved of burning imitation paper money. Related words appear in the Chinese book *Mei-hoki (Chronicles of the Underworld).*

13. Master Gutei of Mt. Kinka, who was famous for his "one finger Zen." It is said that he answered questions by just raising one finger—see chap. 62, *Hensan*, para. [66].

14. Source untraced but possibly *Wanshi-koroku.*

15. Master Dai-e Soko (Ch. Ta-hui Tsung-kao) (1089–1163), a successor of Master Engo Kokugon. Dai-e Soko was a proponent of so-called "Koan Zen" who denigrated Master Wanshi's traditional practice of Zazen (see chap. 27, *Zazenshin*) as 黙照禅 (MOKUSHO ZEN), "silent-illumination Zen." Soko himself is denigrated in chap. 75, *Jisho-zanmai.*

16. Master Nangaku Ejo (677–744), successor of Master Daikan Eno. The Dharma was transmitted from Nangaku Ejo through Baso Do-itsu, Hyakujo Ekai, and Obaku Ki-un, to Rinzai Gigen, the founder of the Rinzai Sect. Dai-e Soko belonged to this lineage.

17. See chap. 46, *Katto.*

18. A horse, salt, water, and a pot are objective things. Seeking is the subjective function of the mind. At the place where object and subject are one, there is serving (action).

19. Master Nansen Fugan (748–834), successor of Master Baso Do-itsu.

20. Master Godai Inpo (dates unknown), also a successor of Master Baso Do-itsu. "To" was

circumstances, bring some water to this old monk." [In]po then brings the jar of water before Nansen and pours. Nansen leaves it at that.[21]

Thus,

Nansen seeks water,
The ocean having dried right to the bottom.
Inpo serves a pot,
Tipped over and emptied out completely.

And though they are like this, at the same time we should learn in practice that *in the reality*[22] *of circumstances there is water,*[23] and *in the reality of water there are circumstances.*[24] To disturb water is immature, and to disturb circumstances is immature.

[246] Great Master Kyogen Shuto,[25] the story goes, is asked by a monk, *"What is a king's seeking of saindhava?"*

[Kyo]gen says, "Pass there and come here."

The monk leaves.

[Kyo]gen says, "His stupid response [could] kill a person!"[26]

Now let us ask: Is the state Kyogen expressed as *"Pass there and come here"* the seeking of saindhava, or is it the serving of saindhava? Try, if you will, to say something![27] Is the monk's having left that place the state that Kyogen sought? Is it a state that Kyogen served? Is it what Kyogen originally expected? If it is not what [Kyogen] originally expected, he should not say *"His stupid response could kill a person!"* If it is what [Kyogen] originally expected, it could not be a stupid response that kills a person. What Kyogen has expressed is the total effort of his whole career; even so, he has not been

---

his family name before becoming a monk.

21. Suggests Master Nansen's affirmation of Master Inpo's behavior. *Keitoku-dento-roku,* chap. 8, and *Shinji-shobogenzo,* pt. 1, no. 64.

22. 中 (CHU) means "inside" (as in the story: "Inside the jar there is water."). At the same time, in Shobogenzo, 中 (CHU) sometimes means "in the state of," or "the reality of." See, for example, notes to chap. 22, *Bussho,* and chap. 38, *Muchu-setsumu.*

23. 境中有水 (KYO-CHU SUI *a[ri]*). This is Master Nansen's phrase with 境 (KYO) "circumstances" substituted for 缾 (HEI) "the jar." Master Dogen suggests that in concrete circumstances real things (like water) exist.

24. 水中有境 (SUI-CHU KYO *a[ri]*). The characteristic reversal of elements suggests the interdependence of subject and object.

25. Master Kyogen Chikan (died 898), successor of Master Isan Reiyu. Great Master Shuto is his posthumous title.

26. *Hekigan-roku (Blue Cliff Record),* no. 92.

27. 試請道看 *(kokoromi[ni] ko[u] i[e] mi[n])* is a more polite version of the phrase 試道看 *(kokoromi[ni] i[e] mi[n])* which is discussed in the notes at the end of chap. 68, *Soshi-sairai-no-i.* 請 *(ko[u]),* which literally means to request or to invite, is added to make the sentence more polite.

able to avoid losing his body and losing his life.[28] He is like the general of a defeated army still talking of his bravery. In sum, the brains and the eyes that preach the yellow[29] and describe the black[30] are, naturally, the painstaking and meticulous seeking and serving of saindhava. Who could claim not to understand the taking up of a staff or the holding up of a fly-whisk? At the same time, [the seeking and serving of saindhava] are not the state of people who play stringed instruments with bridges glued.[31] Because these people do not know that they are playing stringed instruments with bridges glued, they are not in the state.

[48] *The World-honored One, one day, ascends the seat [of preaching]. Mañjuśrī claps the sounding block[32] and says, "When we see into the Dharma of the Dharma-King, the Dharma of the Dharma-King is like this." The World-honored One descends from the seat. Juken, the Zen Master Myokaku[33] of Seccho-zan mountain, says:*

An excellent practitioner among the forest's sacred ranks,[34]
Knows that the Dharma-edict of the Dharma-King is not like that.
If any in the assembly is an exponent of saindhava,
Why does Mañjuśrī need to deliver a clap?

So what Seccho says is this: if *one clap* is flawlessness through the whole body,[35] to have delivered it and not to have delivered it both may be the liberated state of flawlessness. If in the state like this, one clap is saindhava itself. And [the person] may be a person of the ineffable already; that is, *an*

---

28. 喪身失命 (SOSHIN-SHITSUMEI), "losing body and losing life," suggests that Master Kyogen was defeated. At the same time, it suggests that, looking at the monk's behavior, Master Kyogen came back to reality.

29. 説黄 *(ou [o] to[ku])*, "preaching the yellow," means manifesting the Buddhist state. 黄 *(ou)*, "yellow," suggests the color of the earth in China, and thus alludes to something realistic or down to earth.

30. 道黒 *(koku [o] i[u])*, "describing the black," suggests the behaviour of Buddhist patriarchs. 黒 *(koku)*, "the black," means the misconceptions, wrong views, and bad habits that Buddhist patriarchs by skillful means bring to the attention of their students.

31. Alludes to the movable bridges positioned under the strings of a *koto*, or Japanese harp. Playing a *koto* with its bridges glued symbolizes blind adherence to fixed ideas or rules, inflexibility, and corresponding lack of sensitivity to actual conditions or real needs.

32. 白椎 (BYAKU-TSUI). 白 (BYAKU) lit. means "white," but here it is used as a verb meaning to make conspicuous, to sound. 椎 (TSUI) stands for 椎砧 (TSUI-CHIN) or "clapper and sounding block." The *tsui*, or "clapper," is a small wooden block used as a mallet to strike the *chin*, which is an octagonal wooden pillar usually three or four feet high. 白椎 (BYAKU-TSUI) means to attract everyone's attention by striking the sounding block.

33. Master Seccho Juken (see note 10). Zen Master Myokaku is his posthumous title.

34. 列聖叢中 (RESSHO-SO-CHU), lit. "inside a thicket of lines of the sacred," means in a monastery where many Buddhist practitioners are sitting in rows. 叢 (SO) stands for 叢林 (SORIN), lit. "thicket-forest," from the Sanskrit *piṇḍavana,* which means a place where many practitioners are gathered for Buddhist practice. See Glossary.

35. 渾身無孔 (KONSHIN-MUKU), lit. "the whole body without holes."

exponent of saindhava in sacred ranks united as one forest.[36] Thus, *The Dharma of the Dharma-King is like this.* To be able to use the twelve hours is to seek saindhava. To be used by the twelve hours is to seek saindhava. We should seek a fist and should serve a fist. We should seek a fly-whisk and should serve a fly-whisk. Nevertheless, people in the temples of great Sung China today who call themselves veterans have never realized the state of saindhava even in a dream. How painful it is, how painful it is, that the Patriarch's truth is going downhill.[37C] Do not shirk hard practice, and you will surely succeed to the life-blood of the Buddhist Patriarch. For example, when the question is put *"What is buddha?"* and the answer is given *"The mind here and now is buddha,"* what does that mean? Is this not saindhava? We should painstakingly investigate who is described by *"The mind here and now is buddha."* Does anyone know that it is saindhava jostling?

Shobogenzo O-saku-sendaba

Preached to the assembly at Daibutsu-ji temple in Esshu[38] on the 23rd day of the 10th lunar month in the 3rd year of Kangen.[39]

---

36. 列聖一叢 (RESSHO-ISSO). Master Dogen substituted 一叢 (ISSO), lit. "one thicket" or "the whole monastery" for Master Seccho's 叢中 (SO-CHU), lit. "inside a thicket" or "in a monastery." Master Dogen's intention may have been to eliminate any sense of disjuncture conveyed by the phrase 列聖 (RESSHO), "ranks of the sacred."

37. 苦哉苦哉、祖道陵夷 (*ku [naru] kana ku [naru] kana*, SODO-RYOI) looks like the words of Master Tendo Nyojo. 祖道陵夷 (SODO-RYOI), or "the decline of the Patriarch's truth," is a phrase used by Master Tendo in chap. 16, *Shisho*, para. [21].

38. 越州 (ESSHU) is another name for 越宇 (ETSU-U), the ancient district corresponding to present-day Fukui prefecture. 州 (SHU) means state or district and 宇 (U) means 1) sky or roof and 2) the boundary of a country. Master Dogen seems to use the two terms interchangeably.

39. 1245.

[82]

示庫院文

JI-KUIN-MON

Sentences to Be Shown in the Kitchen Hall

__Ji__ means "to show," __kuin__ means the Kitchen Hall of a temple, and __mon__ means "sentences." So __ji-kuin-mon__ means "sentences to be shown in the Kitchen Hall." This chapter was not originally included in Shobogenzo, but when Master Hangyo Kozen edited the 95-chapter edition in 1690, he included this chapter along with Bendowa and Ju-undo-shiki. Master Dogen placed great value on the activity of cooking in Buddhist temple life, and wrote his views down in a book called Tenzo-kyokun or "Instructions for the Chief Cook." The reason that he wrote the book, and the reason he revered the activity of cooking in the temple originates with his experiences in China. Just after arriving in China, he met an old monk who took pride in being the cook in his temple, and who explained to Master Dogen that cooking is Buddhist practice itself. Later, Master Dogen came across another old monk who was diligently drying seaweed for the monks' meals, and he realized how important is the activity of cooking meals for the practitioners in the temple.

3] **On the 6th day of the 8th lunar month** in the 4th year of Kangen[1] I preached to the assembly as follows:

> *In preparing meals for the Saṃgha,*
> *To do so with reverence is fundamental.*

During the authentic transmission of the Dharma from the distant land of India and the authentic transmission of the Dharma from the near nation of China, since the Tathāgata's passing, gods have served to the Buddha and the Saṃgha celestial offerings, and kings have served to the Buddha and the Saṃgha offerings of royal fare. In addition, [meals] were offered from the homes of rich people and householders, and offered from the homes of vaiśyas and śudras.[2] Acts of reverence, in each such instance of serving offerings, are polite and sincere. Beings in the heavens above and in the human world, by employing the most respectful courtesies and by showing their reverence with the most honorific words, are well able to make preparations for the service of meals and other offerings. This has profound meaning.

1. 1246.
2. Workers and servants, the third and fourth of the four classes in the Indian caste system.

Now, even though we are deep in remote mountains, we should directly receive the authentic transmission of the polite manners and words of a temple kitchen.[3] This, in the heavens above or in the human world, is to learn the Buddha-Dharma.

[5] For instance, call gruel[4] "honorable gruel" or call it "morning gruel"; do not call it [just] gruel. Call lunch "the honorable midday meal" or call it "lunch-time"; do not call it [just] lunch. Say "would you make the rice white"; do not say "pound the rice!" In regard to washing rice, say "would you cleanse the rice"; do not say "dunk the rice!" Say "please choose some ingredients for the honorable side-dish";[5] do not say "choose some vegetables!" Say "would you prepare some honorable soup"; do not say "boil the soup!" Say "would you prepare some honorable broth"; do not say "make the broth!" Say that "the honorable lunchtime rice" or "the honorable morning gruel" has been "cooked nicely." Treat with such respect all utensils containing rice and gruel. Disrespect invites misfortune and mistakes; it never has good effects. While the midday meal or the morning gruel is being prepared, people must not breathe on the rice, on the side-dish, or on any other item. Do not touch even dried items with a sleeve of your gown. If a hand has touched head or face do not, before washing, touch with the hand any mealware or the meals[6] themselves. If you scratch an itchy part of the body at any time during the preparation—from sorting the rice to cooking the rice and making the soup—be sure to wash the hand. At places where the meals are prepared, we may recite lines of Buddhist sutras and words of the ancestral masters, but do not speak worldly words or dirty talk. In general, use the polite form to describe the presence of rice, vegetables, salt, soy-sauce and the various other items. Do not say [in the plain form] "there is rice," or "there are vegetables." When monks and novices pass by a place where the midday meal or morning gruel are present, they should join hands and bow the head. Spilt vegetables, spilt rice, and so on, should be put to use[7] after the meal. As long as a meal is unfinished, do not violate [this rule]. Kindly protect and care for the utensils used in preparing the meals; and do not use them for other purposes. Do not let them be touched by the hand of anyone

---

3. 香積局 (KOSHAKU-KYOKU), lit. "Fragrance-Accumulation's office." The Vimalakīrti Sutra says that Buddhist layman Vimalakīrti obtained food from a Tathāgata called Fragrance-Accumulation with which to serve the Saṃgha.

4. Gruel and breakfast were synonymous.

5. "Side-dish" is 菜 (SAI), lit. "vegetables." In this case the character suggests 惣菜 (SOZAI) which means a side-dish. A standard meal in a Japanese temple consists of a large bowl of rice or gruel, a medium bowl of miso soup, a small bowl of pickles, and one or two side-dishes (usually vegetables, or an egg, tofu, et cetera).

6. "Meals" is 齋粥 (SAI-SHUKU) lit. "midday meal and [morning] gruel." These two were the only meals.

7. For example, to feed domestic animals.

who has come from lay society and who has not yet washed the hands. Vegetables, fruit, and so on that have come from lay people and that have yet to be purified should be rinsed, incensed, and exposed to fire, and then offered to the Three Treasures and to the monks of the Saṃgha. In the mountains and temples of great Sung China today, dumplings, dairy cakes, steamed cakes and so on that have come from lay people are re-steamed before being served to the monks. This purifies them. They are not served without being steamed.

These items are just a few among many. Understand their gist, venerable cooks of the Kitchen Hall,[8] and put them into practice. In all your myriad duties, never violate the standard.

Each of the aforementioned articles,
Is the lifeblood of the Buddhist patriarchs,
And the Eye of a patch-robed monk.
Non-Buddhists have never known them,
Celestial demons cannot abide them:
Only disciples of the Buddha
Are able to receive their transmission.
Main officers of the Kitchen Hall!
Understand them and do not forget them.[9]

Displayed[10] by the founding monk,
Dogen.

[The Master of] Eihei-ji temple,

Now addresses the main officers:
Henceforth,
If it is already past noon,
When a dānapati[11] *offers cooked rice,*
It will be kept for the next day.
[But] if [the offering] is cakes, fruit,
Or any kind of gruel or suchlike,
Even in the evening, let us eat it.[12]

---

8. 庫院香積 (KU-IN KOSHAKU), lit. "Koshakus of the Kitchen Hall." See note 3.

9. This paragraph is written (in the style of a gāthā) in Chinese characters only, but it was almost certainly written by Master Dogen himself.

10. 示 (JI, *shime[su]*), lit. "to show," appears in the concluding sentence of most chapters, and is translated as "preached [to the assembly...]." But this chapter was written in the form of a notice to be read by monks of the Kitchen Hall.

11. A donor.

12. In Buddhist monasteries in hot countries it is often forbidden to eat after the midday meal.

It is the "medicine"[13] *of the orders of Buddhist patriarchs.*
Moreover, it is an excellent trace of those in great Sung China
Who possessed the state of truth.

The Tathāgata permitted underclothes for monks in snowy mountains. On this mountain we too permit medicine during the season of snow.[14]

The founder of Eihei-ji temple,
Kigen (his seal)[15]

---

13. 薬石 (YAKU-SEKI), lit. "medicine-stone." One traditional interpretation is that, to keep warm, monks sometimes wrapped up a heated stone and kept it by their lower abdomen. The stone was called *yaku-seki,* and the same name was given to a supper that had the same warming effect. But this interpretation is open to doubt. A simpler explanation is that *seki* refers to the stone needle used in acupuncture treatment and thus *yaku-seki* is a single concept: "medicine." In relatively cold countries like China and Japan Buddhist monks ate meals in the evening, and they called the meals "medicine."

14. Master Dogen also wrote these sentences in Chinese characters, but they are separated from the preceding gāthā in the source text.

15. Kigen (希玄) is one of Master Dogen's names. Master Dogen signed the name "Kigen" and stamped his seal next to it.

[83]

出家

SHUKKE

Leaving Family Life

It was the custom in ancient India for people who wanted to pursue the truth to leave their family, and this custom was retained in Buddhist orders. It is said that Gautama Buddha first left his family life and began the life of a monk when he was 29 years old. For this reason, Buddhist orders revere the tradition of transcending family life in pursuit of the truth, and Master Dogen explains the custom in this chapter.

2] **Zen-en-shingi**[1] **says,** *"The buddhas of the three times all say that to leave family life*[2] *is to realize the truth. The twenty-eight patriarchs in India and six patriarchs in Tang China*[3] *who transmitted the Buddha-mind-seal, were all śramaṇas.*[4] *Perhaps it was by strictly observing the vinaya*[5] *that they were able to become universal models for the triple world. Therefore, in practicing [Za]zen and inquiring into the truth, the precepts are foremost. Without having departed from excess and guarded against wrong, how is it possible to realize the state of buddha and to become a patriarch? The method of receiving the precepts is [as follows]: The three robes*[6] *and pātra*[7] *must be provided, together with new and clean clothes. If you have no new clothes, wash [old clothes] clean. Never borrow robes and pātra to go onto the platform and receive the precepts. Concentrate*

---

1. *Zen-en-shingi (Pure Criteria for Zen Monasteries)* is a ten-fascicle text compiled by Master Choro Sosaku in 1103. This quotation from the first fascicle also appears in Shobogenzo, chap. 86, *Shukke-kudoku,* and chap. 94, *Jukai.*

2. 出家する (SHUKKE *suru*), lit. "to leave home," means 1) to transcend family life; that is, to transcend the values of secular society, and 2) concretely to leave family life, that is; to assume the forms of a Buddhist monk. In Shobogenzo, Master Dogen affirms lay people's pursuit of the Buddhist truth (which cannot begin without discarding the will to fame and gain—see chap. 5, *Ju-undo-shiki*); at the same time, he strongly affirms the forms of a Buddhist monk. As a noun, 出家 (SHUKKE) means "one who has left home"; that is, a monk.

3. The version in *Jukai* abbreviates the subject to "the ancestral masters of successive generations." The original text may have been abbreviated or expanded during copying in China. It is also possible that Master Dogen was quoting from memory.

4. Buddhist monks.

5. The rules of discipline, or precepts.

6. Kaṣāyas of five stripes, seven stripes, and nine or more stripes. See chap. 12, *Kesa-kudoku.*

7. The Buddhist food-bowl. See chap. 78, *Hatsu-u.*

wholeheartedly and be careful not to go against circumstances. To assume the form of the Buddha, to come into possession of the Buddha's precepts, to get what the Buddha received and used: these are not small matters. How could they be treated lightly? If we were to borrow robes and pātra, even if we mounted the platform and received the precepts, we would not get the precepts at all. Unless we received [the precepts] again, we would be people without precepts throughout our life, fraternizing without reason in the lineage of emptiness, and accepting devout offerings in vain. Beginners in the truth have not yet memorized the Dharma-precepts; it is masters, by not saying anything, who cause people to fall into this [wrongness]. Now I have spoken a stern exhortation. I dare to hope that you will engrave it on your hearts. If you have already received the śrāvaka precepts[8] *you should receive the bodhisattva precepts. This is the first sign of having entered the Dharma."*

[14] Clearly know, the buddhas' and the patriarchs' realization of the truth is nothing other than their leaving family life and receiving the precepts. The life-blood of the buddhas and the patriarchs is nothing other than their leaving family life and receiving the precepts. Someone who has not left family life is never a Buddhist patriarch. To see the buddhas and to see the patriarchs is to leave family life and to receive the precepts.

[15] *Mahākāśyapa,*[9] *following the World-honored One, seeks to leave family life and desires to deliver all things. The Buddha says, "Welcome, bhikṣu!" [Mahākāśyapa's] hair and beard fall off by themselves, and a kaṣāya covers his body.*[10]

When [a person] follows the Buddha and becomes free of all things, the excellent example of leaving family life and receiving the precepts is, in every case, like this one.

[15] The Great Prajña Sutra[11] fascicle 3 says, *The World-honored Buddha said, "If a bodhisattva-mahāsattva thinks, 'At some time, I will relinquish a throne and leave family life, on which day I will realize the supreme, right, and balanced state of bodhi; also on that day, I will turn the wonderful wheel of Dharma, causing countless, innumerable sentient beings to depart from dust and leave dirt, and causing them to have the pure Dharma-eye; at the same time, I will cause countless, innumerable sentient beings to end forever all excesses, and to liberate their mind and intuition; further, I will cause countless, innumerable sentient beings all to attain the state of not regressing or straying from the supreme, right, and balanced state of bodhi,' [then] this bodhisattva-mahāsattva who wants to realize those things should learn the prajña-pāramitā."*[12]

---

8. Suggests precepts taken by Hīnayāna Buddhists (of which there are 250 precepts for monks and 348 precepts for nuns), as opposed to the 16 bodhisattva precepts (explained in chap. 94, *Jukai*).

9. Master Mahākāśyapa, the Buddha's successor and the first patriarch in India.

10. *Keitoku-dento-roku,* chap. 1.

11. In Sanskrit, *Mahā-prajña-pāramitā-sūtra.*

12. This paragraph is also quoted in chap. 86, *Shukke-kudoku.*

16] In sum, the supreme state of bodhi is perfectly satisfied at the time of leaving family life and receiving the precepts. It never becomes perfect on a day other than the day of leaving family life. That being so, by bringing in the day of leaving family life, we actualize a day of realizing the supreme state of bodhi. And that which brings forth the day of realizing the supreme state of bodhi is a day of leaving family life. This leaving family life, which is to somersault, is the turning of the splendid Dharma-wheel. This leaving family life itself causes innumerable sentient beings not to regress or to stray from the supreme state of bodhi. Remember, the situation in which self-benefit and benefiting others become perfectly satisfied at this concrete place and there is neither regression nor straying from anuttara-samyak-saṃbodhi, is the leaving of family life and receiving of the precepts. Realizing the supreme state of bodhi, conversely, makes the day of leaving family life realize bodhi. Remember, in truth, that the day of leaving family life is beyond unity and difference. On the day we leave family life, we practice and experience three asaṃkhya kalpas. On the day we leave family life, we abide in the ocean of infinite kalpas and turn the splendid wheel of Dharma. The day of leaving family life is beyond the time of "meal-time,"[13] is beyond sixty minor kalpas, has transcended the three times, and has gotten free from the brain. The day of leaving family life has transcended already the day of leaving family life. And though this may be so, when nets and cages are broken open, the day of leaving family life is just the day of leaving family life, and the day of realizing the truth is just the day of realizing the truth.

18] The Great Commentary,[14] number 13, says: *The Buddha is at Jetavana Park. A drunken Brāhman comes to the Buddha's place, wanting to become a bhikṣu. The Buddha instructs the other bhikṣus to give [the Brāhman] a shaved head and to put a kaṣāya on him. When he sobers up, [the Brāhman] is astonished and bewildered to see that his form has suddenly changed into that of a bhikṣu, and he runs away at once. The other bhikṣus ask the Buddha, "Why did you permit the drunken Brāhman to become a bhikṣu, only now to go back [home]?" The Buddha says, "This Brāhman for countless eons was without the will to leave family life. Now, as a result of getting drunk, he has momentarily established a bit of the will. Because of this circumstance, he will leave family life in the future." There are many kinds of stories like this one. Breaking of the precepts having left family life is better than keeping the precepts as a lay person, because with the precepts of a lay person we do not realize liberation.*[15]

0] The point of the Buddha's instruction is clear. In the Buddha's teaching

---

13. Lit. "is beyond being called 'like meal-time.'"

14. 大論 (DAIRON) stands for 大智度論 (DAI-CHI-DO-RON), lit. "Discussion of the Accomplishment which is Great Wisdom," that is, the Chinese translation (by Kumārajīva) of the Mahā-prajña-pāramitopadeśa, a commentary on the Mahā-prajña-pāramitā-sūtra, attributed to Master Nāgārjuna.

15. A slightly different version of this paragraph is quoted in chap. 86, *Shukke-kudoku*.

just to leave family life is fundamental, and that which has not left family life is not the Buddha-Dharma. While the Tathāgata was in the world, when various non-Buddhists devoted themselves to the Buddha-Dharma, having discarded their own false ways, they always requested at the outset to leave family life. Either the World-honored One himself graciously offered the words *"Welcome bhikṣu!"* or he instructed the other bhikṣus to shave [the newcomer's] hair and beard and cause [the newcomer] to leave family life and receive the precepts. In each case, the means for leaving family life and receiving the precepts were provided at once. Remember, when the Buddha's teaching has already covered body-and-mind, hair naturally falls from the head and a kaṣāya clothes the body. Without the consent of the buddhas, hair and beard are not shaved off, the kaṣāya does not clothe the body, and the Buddhist precepts are impossible to receive. In sum, to leave family life and receive the precepts is [to experience] the personal affirmation of the buddha-tathāgatas.

[21] Śākyamuni Buddha says, *"Good sons! Seeing living beings who take pleasure in small things, whose virtue is scant and whose filthiness is accumulated, the Tathāgata to these people states, 'In my youth I left family life and attained anuttara-samyak-saṃbodhi.' And since I actually realized [the state of] buddha, [my] eternity has been such as it is. Only to teach and transform living beings, by expedient means, so that they will enter the Buddhist truth, do I make statements like this."*[16]

Thus, realization of the eternal is *"In my youth I left family life." Anuttara-samyak-saṃbodhi* is *"In my youth I left family life."* When [the Buddha] describes that *"In my youth I left family life,"* living beings who, with scant virtue and accumulated filthiness, take pleasure in small things, also realize *"In my youth I [will] leave family life."* At any place where we see, hear, and learn in practice the Dharma-preaching that *"In my youth I left family life,"* we meet the Buddha's state of anuttara-samyak-saṃbodhi. When [the Buddha] delivers living beings who are taking pleasure in small things, to these people he states, *"In my youth I left family life and attained anuttara-samyak-saṃbodhi."* Though I have described it like this, someone might ask, in conclusion, *"How important is the virtue of leaving family life?"* I would say to that person, *"As important as your head!"*

Shobogenzo Shukke

Preached to the assembly at Eihei-ji temple in Fukui prefecture on the 15th day of the 9th lunar month in the 4th year of Kangen.[17]

---

16. Lotus Sutra, *Nyorai-juryo (The Tathāgata's Lifetime).* See LS 3.16.
17. 1246.

[84]

三時業

SANJI-NO-GO

Karma in Three Times

San *means "three,"* ***ji*** *means "time" and* ***go*** *means "conduct." In this chapter,* ***sanji*** *means three kinds of time lag and* ***go*** *refers to both conduct and its effect.*[1] *Belief in cause and effect forms a central part of Buddhist philosophy. This is the reason why Master Dogen wrote the chapter of Shobogenzo titled* ***Shinjin-inga,*** *or "Deep Belief in Cause and Effect." He insisted that all things and phenomena in the Universe are governed by the law of cause and effect, perfectly and without any exception. In accord with this theory, we should deny the existence of indeterminate events. But in our daily life it often seems that such accidents happen. So if Buddhism insists that the law of cause and effect is all-encompassing, it is necessary to explain the apparent existence of accidents. Buddhism explains these apparent accidents with the theory that there are three kinds of time lag between our conduct and the effect of our conduct. The effect of an action sometimes manifests itself at once, sometimes after a short time, and sometimes after a very long time. In the second and third cases, it is often difficult to believe that the whole world is governed completely by the law of cause and effect. But if we affirm that there are three kinds of time lag between conduct and its effect, we can affirm the validity of the law of cause and effect in all cases without exception. Master Dogen explains the problem in this chapter.*

6] ***The nineteenth patriarch,*** *the Venerable Kumāralabdha, arrives at a country in central India, [where] a mahāsattva called Gayata*[2] *asks, "In my family, father and mother have always believed in the Three Treasures yet they have been beset by ill health and, in general, are disappointed in all their undertakings. My neighbor's family has long done the work of caṇḍālas,*[3] *yet their bodies are always in sound health and their doings harmoniously combine. What is their good fortune? And what is our guilt? The Venerable One says, "How could there be room for doubt? In short, retribution for good and bad has three times. Generally, people only see that to the good [comes] early death;*

---

1. 業 (GO), represents the Sanskrit *karman*, which means action or conduct. Like the word karma in current English usage, 業 (GO) suggests not only conduct itself, but also the effects generated by conduct. See Book 1, Glossary.

2. Became the twentieth patriarch in India. After receiving the Dharma from Master Kumāralabdha, he lived and taught in the city of Rājagṛha.

3. Outcasts, charged with such jobs as hunting, slaughter, and execution.

to the violent, long life; to the evil, fortune; and to the righteous, calamity; whereupon [people] say that there is no cause and effect and no wrongness or happiness. Particularly, they do not know that shadow and sound accord with [their sources], not differing by a thousandth or a hundredth and—even with the passing of a hundred thousand myriad kalpas—never wearing away."[4] *Then Gayata, having heard these words, at once relinquishes doubt.'*[5]

[28] The Venerable Kumāralabdha is, from the Tathāgata, the nineteenth recipient of the Dharma. The Tathāgata personally recorded his name. [Kumāralabdha] not only clarified and authentically received the Dharma of the one Buddha Śākyamuni; he also clearly realized the Dharma of all the buddhas of the three ages.[6] The Venerable Gayata, after asking the present question, practiced and learned the Tathāgata's right Dharma following the Venerable Kumāralabdha, and eventually became the twentieth ancestral master. In this case also, the World-honored One, from afar, had recorded that the twentieth patriarch would be Gayata. That being so, above all, we should learn the criteria of the Buddha-Dharma as thus decided by the ancestral masters. We should not mix with people of false views[7] in the world today who neither know cause and effect, nor understand karmic retribution, nor know the three ages, nor distinguish between good and bad.[8]

[29] These words *"Retribution for good and bad has three times"* mean 1) *retribution is received in the immediate present;* 2) *it is received in one's next life;* 3) *it is received latterly.*[9] These are called *"the three times."* In practicing and learning the truth of the Buddhist patriarchs, from the very beginning we study and clarify this principle of karmic retribution in three times. Because they are not like that, many make mistakes and fall into the false view. Not only do they fall into

---

4. These words are also quoted in chap. 89, *Shinjin-inga.*

5. *Keitoku-dento-roku,* chap. 2.

6. 三世 (SANZE), usually translated as "the three times" (past, present, and future), but translated here as "the three ages" in order to distinguish it from the 三時 (SANJI), "three times" of the chapter title.

7. 邪見 (JAKEN), "the false view," represents the Sanskrit *mithyā-dṛṣṭi,* which means false doctrine, heresy, or atheism—the view which negates cause and effect. It is the third of the five wrong views (in Sanskrit, *pañca-dṛṣṭayah*). See Book 1, Glossary.

8. The belief was widespread among people of Master Dogen's time, in the Kamakura period, that Mahāyāna Buddhism was not concerned with good and bad conduct.

9. In the Buddha's time the Brahmanistic belief was widely held that a person is reborn in a better or worse world according to his or her conduct in this life. The Buddha used the spiritualistic idea of Brahmanism to emphasize the existence of cause and effect in the real world. Buddhist masters through the ages have criticized the idea that the spirit is reborn (see, for example, chap. 1, *Bendowa,* and chap. 6, *Soku-shin-ze-butsu),* but expressions about past and future lives have remained in Buddhist explanations of cause and effect. At the same time, one human lifespan may be seen as consisting of a series of lives—as a schoolchild, trainee, worker, retiree, invalid, et cetera.

the false view; they [also] fall into bad states[10] and experience long periods of suffering. While they are failing to continue good roots, they lose much merit and the way to bodhi is long obstructed. Is it not regrettable? This karma in the three times covers [both] good and bad.

0] *1) Karma in which retribution is received in the immediate present: If, in this life, we produce and promote karma, and in this life we receive differently matured effects,*[11] *this is called "karma in which retribution is received in the immediate present."*

That is to say, a person doing in this life either good or bad and then receiving in this life the corresponding retribution is called *"karma in which retribution is received in the immediate present."*

1] An example of doing bad and receiving in this life bad retribution: *'Once there was a woodcutter who went into the mountains and lost his way in the snow. The time was approaching dusk; the snow was deep and the cold was freezing: [the woodcutter] would be dead before long. Then he advanced into a dense wood whereupon he saw, already there in the wood, a bear whose body color was deep blue and whose eyes were like two torches. The man was scared half to death. [But] this was really a bodhisattva who had for the present received a bear's body. Seeing the [woodcutter's] distress and fear, [the bear] soothed and admonished him, saying, "Now you must not be afraid. A father and mother sometimes are treacherous to a child, [but] I now am completely without ill will towards you." Then it stepped forward, lifted up [the woodcutter], and carried him into a cave to warm his body. After letting him recuperate, it picked various roots and fruits and encouraged him to eat what he liked, and, afraid lest [the woodcutter's] coldness would not thaw, it hugged and lay [with him]. It thus tenderly nursed him for six days, until, on the seventh day, the weather cleared and the path became visible. The man had the will to return. The bear, having recognized [this] already, again picked sweet fruits and served these [to the man] until he was satisfied. It escorted him out of the woods and politely bade him farewell. The man dropped to his knees and said in thanks: "How can I repay your kindness?" The bear said, "Now I want no other reward: I only hope that just as, in recent days, I have protected your body, you would act likewise towards my life." The man respectfully assented and, carrying his wood, he descended the mountain. He met two hunters, who asked him, "What kinds of creatures have you seen in the mountains?" The woodcutter replied, "I have not seen any other beast at all; I have only seen one bear." The hunters begged him, "Can you show us, or not?" The woodcutter answered, "If you can give me a share of two-thirds, I will show you." The hunters thereupon agreed and together they set off. At length they slew the bear and divided its flesh into three. As the woodcutter, with both hands, went to take the bear-meat, through the force of his bad karma both arms dropped off—like pearls on a string that is cut, or*

---

10. 悪道 (AKUDO). 三悪道 (SAN-AKUDO), or the three evil states, are: 1) the state of hell; 2) the state of hungry ghosts; 3) the state of animals.

11. 異熟果 (IJUKU-KA), from the Sanskrit *vipāka-phala* (maturation of effects). 異 (I), "different," emphasizes that different effects follow from different causes. See Book 1, Glossary.

like chopped lotus roots. The hunters were alarmed [by this] and in astonishment they asked the reason [for it]. The woodcutter, ashamed, related the plot in detail. These two hunters berated the woodcutter, saying, "The other already had for you this great benevolence! How could you have carried out now such evil treachery? It is a wonder that your body has not rotted!" At this, [the woodcutter] and the hunters together took the meat to donate to a saṃghārāma. Then an elder[12] *among the monks, who had got the fine wisdom [to know others'] wishes, immediately entered into the immovable state [of Zazen] and reflected what kind of meat this was. Thereupon he knew that this was the flesh of a great bodhisattva who had produced benefit and joy for all living beings. At length, he left non-movement and told the monks of this matter. The monks were shocked to hear it. Together, they gathered fragrant firewood to cremate the flesh, collected the remaining bones, erected a stūpa, performed prostrations, and served offerings.' Bad karma like this must—whether it waits for continuance or skips continuance—inevitably suffer its effect.*[13]

[34] Such is called *"karma in which retribution for bad conduct is received in the immediate present."* As a general rule, when we receive kindness, we should intend to repay it. In being kind to others, [however,] do not seek reward. One who would bring treachery and harm upon a kind person, as in the present [story], will inevitably suffer the corresponding bad karma. May living beings never have the mind of this woodcutter! Out of the woods, when bidding [the bear] farewell, he says *"How can I repay this kindness?"* Yet at the foot of the mountain, when he meets the hunters, he greedily seeks two thirds of the meat and, led by avarice, he slays that [which showed him] great kindness. May lay people and those who have left home never have this mind that does not know kindness! Cutting by the force of bad karma, when it severs both hands, is faster than the cutting of a sword.

[35] An example of doing good in this life and—with retribution being received in the immediate present—getting a good reward:

'Once upon a time, King Kaniṣka of the country of Gandhāra[14] *retained an androgyne who always supervised internal court affairs. On a temporary excursion beyond the city [walls],*[15] *he saw a herd of bulls, fully five hundred in number, being led into the city. He*

---

12. 上座 (JOZA), lit. "senior seat," represents the Sanskrit *sthavira,* "elder." See Book 1, Glossary.

13. *Daibibasha-ron* (*Abhidharma-mahāvibhāṣa-śāstra*) fascicle 114. This is a commentary said to have been compiled by Master Vasumitra, the seventh patriarch in India, in cooperation with five hundred arhats belonging to the Sarvāstivāda School.

14. A king called Kaniṣka is said to have established the country of Gandhāra in the first or second century A.D. JEBD states that King Kaniṣka became a great patron of Buddhism following conversion by Master Aśvaghoṣa, the 12th patriarch in India (though this raises a question as to the relative timing of the reign of King Kaniṣka and the compilation of the Abhidharma-mahāvibhāṣa-śāstra by the seventh patriarch Master Vasumitra).

15. 城 (JO) means "castle" or "city." Some ancient Indian cities were surrounded by fortified walls.

asked the herder, "What kind of bulls are these?" [The herder] replied, "These bulls are going to be castrated." At this, the androgyne immediately thought to himself, "I, through long-held karma, have received an emasculate body. Now I shall use my wealth to rescue these bulls from [that] hardship." Eventually he paid their price and had them all set free. Through the force of good karma, this androgyne was caused at once to recover a male body. He profoundly rejoiced. Then he went back into the city and, standing still at the palace gate, he sent a messenger to inform the King that he wished to enter for an audience. The King summoned him to enter and asked in wonder for an explanation. Thereupon the androgyne related the aforementioned episode in detail. The King, on hearing of it, was surprised and delighted. He generously bestowed precious treasures, promoted [the androgyne] to high office, and put him in charge of external affairs.' Good karma like this must—whether it waits for continuance or skips continuance—inevitably receive its effect.[16]

[37] Clearly, though the bodies of bulls and animals are not to be treasured, a person who saves them will receive good effects. How much more, by honoring the field of the kind and honoring the field of the virtuous,[17] will we enact many kinds of good! Such is called *"karma in which reward for good conduct is received in the immediate present."* There are many episodes like these, arising from good and from bad, but there is not time to quote them all.

[38] *2) Karma that receives [retribution] in the next life: If, in this life, we produce and promote karma, and in a second life we receive differently matured effects, this is called "karma that receives [retribution] in the next life."*

That is to say, if people have committed in this life the five actions [leading to] incessant [hell],[18] they will inevitably fall into hell in their next life. *"The next life"* means the life following this life. For lesser sins, there are those who fall into hell in their next life, and there are also those who, because they have deserved the influence of latterly received [karma], do not fall into hell in the next life; [their karma] becomes karma of latter [retribution]. [But] for these five actions [leading to] incessant [hell], we invariably fall into hell with karma that receives [retribution] in the next life. *The next life* is also called *"a second life."* The five actions [leading to] incessant [hell] are *1) to kill one's father, 2) to kill one's mother, 3) to kill an arhat, 4) to cause the*

---

16. *Daibibasha-ron*, fascicle 114.

17. Alludes 四福田 (SHI-FUKUDEN), "four fields of happiness": 1) 趣田 (SHUDEN), "field of the [animal] world," means happiness produced through kindness to animals; 2) 苦田 (KUDEN), "field of the suffering," means happiness produced through kindness to needy people; 3) 恩田 (ON DEN), "field of the kind," means happiness produced through repaying the kindness of one's parents; 4) 徳田 (TOKUDEN), "field of the virtuous," means happiness produced through repaying the kindness of the sacred practitioners of the three vehicles.

18. 五無間業 (GO-MUGEN-GO), from the Sanskrit *pañcāvīci-karmāṇi*. 無間 (MUGEN) stands for 無間地獄 (MUGEN-JIGOKU), "incessant hell," which represents the Sanskrit *Avīci*. See Glossary.

Buddha's body to bleed, and 5) to disrupt the Saṃgha of the Dharma-wheel.[19] These are called *"the five actions [leading to] incessant [hell],"* and also called *"the five deadly sins."* The first three are killing, and the fourth is conduct which applies to killing. There is no way for the Tathāgata to be killed by a person; only to cause his body to bleed is considered a deadly [sin]. Those who are not subject to early death are: *bodhisattvas in their last body, bodhisattvas obstructed by one life in Tuṣita Heaven,*[20] *[the angels of] the northern continent,*[21] *Jyotiṣka,*[22] *and the Buddha's doctor.*[23] Number five, the sin of disrupting the Saṃgha, is false and deceitful words. For these five deadly [sins] inevitably, with karma that receives [retribution] in the next life, we fall into hell. Devadatta[24] committed three of these five actions [leading to] incessant [hell]. That is to say, he killed the bhikṣuṇī Utpalavarṇā,[25] and this bhikṣuṇī was a great arhat. This is seen as his killing of an arhat. He attempted to kill the World-honored One by hurling a great boulder; the boulder then was blocked and shattered by a mountain god, [but] a splinter flew off and struck the Tathāgata's toes. The toes were broken and blood naturally bled. This was the sin of causing the Buddha's body to bleed. [Devadatta] exhorted five hundred novices and foolish bhikṣus to go [with him] to the peak of Mt. Gayā,[26] [where] he established separate practices. This was the sin of disrupting the Saṃgha. As a result of these three deadly sins, he fell into Avīci Hell. Today he is suffering incessant pain; even Devadatta, who was [formerly like] the four buddhas,[27] remains

---

19. 破法輪僧 (HA-HORIN-SO), "disrupting the Saṃgha of the Dharma-wheel," means establishing wrong theories. 破羯磨僧 (HA-KATSUMA-SO), "disrupting the Saṃgha of practice," means establishing wrong practices. The sin of disrupting the Saṃgha is divided into these two categories.

20. See, for example, Appendix 2, *Ippyaku-hachi-homyo-mon,* which is based on the preaching given by a bodhisattva in his last life in Tuṣita Heaven. He then descends to earth for one last life before becoming buddha.

21. In ancient Indian cosmology, human beings live on the continent south of Mt. Sumeru. The northern continent (in Sanskrit, *Uttara-kuruḥ),* is inhabited by angels.

22. A rich man and disciple of the Buddha who lived in Rājagṛha. It is said that he was born when his mother's body was cremated.

23. The Buddha's doctor was Jīvaka. He was the son of a courtesan and was abandoned by her shortly after birth, but was saved and brought up by a prince. As a young man he studied medicine for seven years at the famous university of Takkasīla (present-day Taxila in Pakistan). Thereafter he became the king's physician in Rājagṛha and a lay disciple of the Buddha.

24. Devadatta was a cousin of the Buddha. In the *Devadatta* chapter of the Lotus Sutra, the Buddha praised him as a good friend and predicted that he would become a buddha. Nevertheless, Devadatta turned against the Buddha, as explained in this paragraph.

25. See chap. 12, *Kesa-kudoku,* para. [87].

26. Short for Gayāśīrṣa. This mountain is the present-day Brahmayoni, one mile west of the city of Gayā, which is sixty miles southwest of Patna in Bengal. The Chinese name for the mountain is 象頭山 (ZOZU-SEN) "Elephant Head Mountain." The peak was said to have the shape of an elephant's head.

27. 四仏 (SHIBUTSU), "the four buddhas," are the four buddha images in the north, south, east, and west of a maṇḍala. These four buddhas attend Vairocana Buddha in the center. Used

in Avīci. The bhikṣu Kokālika,[28] in order to slander Śāriputra and Maudgalyāyana[29] in this life, groundlessly invoked the pārājika rule.[30] The World-honored One himself cautioned against it, and King Brahmā came down to prevent it, but [Kokālika] did not stop; he slandered the two venerable ones and fell into hell. When the bhikṣu [who mistook] the fourth dhyāna[31] confronted the end of his life, he fell into Avīci Hell as a result of slandering the Buddha. Such is called *"karma that receives [retribution] in the next life."*

[42] *3) Karma that receives [retribution] latterly: If, in this life, we produce and promote karma, and consequently in a third life, or even hundred thousands of kalpas beyond that, we receive differently matured effects, this is called "karma that receives [retribution] latterly."*

That is to say, if people, having committed in this life either good or bad, feel the effect of good or bad karma in a third life or in a fourth life or even after hundred thousands of lives, this is called *"karma that receives [retribution] latterly."* Most of a bodhisattva's three asaṃkhya kalpas[32] of virtue is *karma that receives [retribution] latterly.* Without knowing such truths as this, practitioners often harbor doubt—as the Venerable Gayata does when he is a layman, in the present [story]. If he had not met the Venerable Kumāralabdha, it might have been difficult for him to resolve that doubt. When a practitioner's consideration is good, bad immediately ceases. When consideration is bad, good instantly ceases.

44] *In the country of Śrāvastī[33] once upon a time there lived two people, one who always practiced good, and another who always committed bad. The one who practiced good deeds had always practiced good deeds throughout his life and had never committed bad. The one who committed bad deeds had constantly committed bad deeds throughout his life and had never practiced good. When the one who practiced good deeds came to the end of his life, through the influence of bad karma that receives [retribution] latterly, a middle existence[34] in hell suddenly appeared before him. Then he thought, "Throughout my life I have always practiced good deeds and have never committed bad. I should be born in a heaven realm. What reason is there for this middle existence to appear before*

---

here as an adjective, 四仏 (SHIBUTSU), suggests Devadatta's attitude, before he went astray, of service to the Buddha.

28. A disciple of Devadatta.

29. Two of the Buddha's ten great disciples.

30. A pārājika is a violation of the precepts warranting expulsion from the community. See Book 1, Glossary.

31. 四禅比丘 (SHIZEN-BIKU) is the title of chap. 90.

32. A bodhisattva is said to accumulate virtue for three asaṃkhya kalpas before becoming buddha.

33. Śrāvastī, the capital of Kośala, was sometimes treated as an independent country.

34. 中有 (CHU-U), represents the Sanskrit *antarā-bhava,* originally a Brahmanistic concept describing the soul in its middle existence between death and rebirth. See Book 1, Glossary.

me?" Eventually the following thought arose: "I surely must have bad karma which is receiving [retribution] latterly. Because [bad karma] is now maturing, this middle existence in hell has appeared before me." Then he remembered the good actions he had practiced through his life and he profoundly rejoiced. Because of his manifestation of [this] excellent consideration, the middle existence in hell disappeared at once and a middle existence in a heaven realm suddenly appeared before him. After this, when his life ended, he was born in the heavens above.[35]

[45] This person who has always practiced good deeds not only considers *"[Karma] which latterly receives [retribution] is present in my own body, which must inevitably suffer [retribution]"*; he also considers further *"For the good I have practiced throughout my life, also, I will surely receive [retribution] in future."* This is the reason that he profoundly rejoices. Because this notion is true, the middle existence in hell immediately disappears, a middle existence in a heaven realm suddenly appears before him, and, when his life is over, he is born in the heavens above. If this person were a bad person, when his life ended and a middle existence in hell appeared before him he would think, *"My practice of good throughout my life has been without merit. If good and bad exist, how could I be looking at a middle existence in hell?"* At this time he would negate cause and effect and slander the Three Treasures. If he were like that, his life would end at once and he would fall into hell. Because he is not like that, he is born in the heavens above. We should clarify and know this truth.

[46] *When the one who committed bad deeds came to the end of his life, through the influence of good karma that latterly receives [retribution], a middle existence in a heaven realm suddenly appeared before him. Then he thought, "Throughout my life I have constantly committed bad deeds and have never practiced good. I deserve to be born in hell. What reason is there for this middle existence to appear before me?" At length, the false view arose: he negated good and bad and different maturation of effects. Through the influence of the false view, the middle existence in a heaven realm disappeared at once and a middle existence in hell suddenly appeared before him. After this, when his life ended, he was born in hell.*[36]

[47] This person, as long as he has lived, has constantly committed bad and has never practiced a single act of good. Not only that: when his life ends and he sees a middle existence in a heaven realm appear before him, he does not recognize it as [karma] that latterly receives [retribution, and so he thinks] *"All my life I have committed bad but I am going to be born in a heaven realm. Clearly, there was no good and bad at all."* Through the influence of the false view which negates good and bad like this, the middle existence in a heaven realm suddenly vanishes, a middle existence in hell instantly appears before him, and when his life is over he falls into hell. Thus, it was because of the false

35. *Daibibasha-ron*, fascicle 69.
36. *Ibid.*

view that the middle existence in a heaven realm disappeared. Therefore, practitioners, you must never take the false view! Learn, until you use up your body, what is the false view and what is the right view. To begin with, negation of cause and effect, slandering of Buddha, Dharma, and Saṃgha, and negation of the three ages[37] and of liberation, are all the false view. Remember, our body in this life is not two and not three. If we idly fell into the false view and experienced, to no avail, the effects of bad karma, would that not be regrettable? When, while committing bad, we think that it is not bad, just because we wrongly consider that there will be no bad retribution, this does not mean that we will not experience the bad retribution.

[49] *Court Priest*[38] *Kogetsu asks Master Chosa [Kei]shin,*[39] *"A past master has said, 'After we have understood, karmic hindrances are originally void. Before we have understood, we must atone for long-held debts.' How is it possible that ones such as the Venerable Siṃha*[40] *and the Great Master the Second Patriarch*[41] *atoned for their debts [so] completely?"*

Chosa says, '"Virtuous One! You do not know the original void."

The other says, "What is the original void?"

Chosa says, "Karmic hindrances themselves."

[Kogetsu] asks again, "What are karmic hindrances?"

Chosa says, "The original void itself."

Kogetsu is wordless.

Chosa then teaches him with the following verse:

> *Supposed existence is fundamentally different from Existence.*
> *Termination of the supposed also is different from Nonexistence.*
> *The meaning of "Nirvana is atonement"*
> *Is that the one essential state is utterly without discrimination.*[42]

[50] Chosa's answer is no answer.[43] It does not possess the truth that

---

37. 三世 (SANZE), past, present, and future. See note 6.

38. 供奉 (GUBU), is the title of a priest who served the Buddha images in those rooms of a palace that were devoted to Buddhist practice.

39. Master Chosa Keishin (died 868), successor of Master Nansen Fugan.

40. Master Siṃha, the twenty-fourth patriarch in India, is said to have been executed by the king of Kaśmīra (present-day Kashmir).

41. Master Taiso Eka. He also is said to have been killed.

42. *Keitoku-dento-roku*, chap. 3.

43. The priest understood the original state of emptiness and the concrete restrictions of cause and effect as two separate things, so Master Chosa wanted to suggest undivided reality. His intention was that the priest need not consider past karma, because there is only real existence, here and now. But Master Dogen recognized in this a tendency to negate cause and effect.

Kumāralabdha teaches to Gayata. We should recognize that [Master Chosa] does not know the principle of karmic hindrances. When descendants of the Buddhist patriarchs pursue the truth through practice-and-experience, they must first unfailingly clarify and know, in the manner of the Venerable Kumāralabdha, this karma in three times. This [effort] is, already, the action of the ancestral patriarchs; we should not cease or neglect it. Besides this [karma in three times], there is indefinite karma,[44] and there are also eight kinds of karma;[45] we should broadly learn them in practice. People who have not clarified this truth of karmic retribution must not randomly call themselves the guiding teachers of human beings and gods. We will inevitably experience retribution in three times for bad karma, but if we confess and repent[46] that will transform a heavy [sin] and cause [retribution] to be received lightly; it will also end our wrongdoing and make us pure. Further, if we take delight in good karma, that will promote [good karma] more and more. Everything depends on whether the making of karma is black or white.[47]

[52] *The World-honored One said, "Even with the passing of hundreds of kalpas, the karma that we make does not perish. When causes and conditions come together, effects and results are naturally received."*

"You all should know! If your actions are purely black, you will experience the maturation[48] of purely black [effects]. If your actions are purely white, you will experience the maturation of purely white [effects]. If your actions are black and white, you will experience corresponding maturation of miscellaneous [effects]. For this reason, you should abandon actions that are purely black and that are a mixture of black and white. You should be diligent in practicing and learning actions which are purely white." Then all in the great assembly, having heard the Buddha's preaching, rejoiced and believed.[49]

44. 不定業 (FUJO-GO), short for 不定受業 (FUJO-JU-GO), "karma in which [retribution] is received indefinitely," or karma that operates in indefinite periods.

45. The eight kinds of karma are: good karma that operates in the three times and in indefinite times, and bad karma that operates in the three times and in indefinite times.

46. 懺悔 (SANGE) means, for example, reciting the following verse: 我昔所造諸悪業、皆由無始貪瞋痴、従身口意之所生、一切我今皆懺悔. (GA-SHAKU-SHOZO-SHOAKUGO, KAI-YU-MUSHI-DONJINCHI, JU-SHIN-KU-I-SHI-SHOSHO, ISSAI-GA-KON-KAI-SANGE), "The many bad actions that I have done in the past, / All have stemmed, since times without beginning, from greed, anger, and delusion. / They were produced from body, mouth, and mind. / I now totally confess and repent them all."

47. "Black or white" means wrong or right, bad or good.

48. 異熟 (IJUKU), short for 異熟果 (IJUKU-KA), lit. "different maturation of effects." See note 11.

49. *Dai-ho-shak-kyo* (*Mahāratnakūta-sūtra*), chap. 57.

Shobogenzo Sanji-no-go

Finished copying this, in the head monk's quarters at Eihei-ji temple, on the 9th day of the 3rd lunar month in the 5th year of Kencho.[50]

Ejo

50. 1253. This is one of the twelve chapters Master Dogen began in the last years of his life. The version translated here is the one included in the 95-chapter edition of Shobogenzo. The version contained in the 12-chapter edition is slightly longer.

[85]

四馬

SHIME

The Four Horses

Shi *means "four" and* ***me*** *means "horses," so* ***shime*** *means four horses. An ancient Buddhist scripture called Saṃyuktāgama contains a story about four kinds of horses: horses that know the rider's intention at the sight of the whip, horses that know the rider's intention when the whip touches their hair, horses that know the rider's intention when the whip touches their flesh, and horses that know the rider's intention when the whip reaches their bones. These differences between four kinds of horses are used as a simile for the differences between the levels of intuition that Buddhist students exhibit in studying Buddhism. Studying Buddhism is not based only on intellectual teachings; the ability to intuitively understand the Master's teachings is important, as Master Dogen explains in this chapter using the simile of the four kinds of horses.*

56] ***[A story of] the World-honored One:*** *one day a non-Buddhist visited the place where the Buddha was, and he asked the Buddha, "I do not ask for words. I do not ask for no words."*[1]

The World-honored One sat on his seat for a while.

The non-Buddhist did venerative prostrations and praised him, saying "How excellent, World-honored One! Your great benevolence and great compassion have opened my clouds of delusion, and made me able to enter [the truth]." Then he made a prostration and left.

After the non-Buddhist had left, Ānanda said to the Buddha, "Through what attainment did the non-Buddhist say that he had been able to enter [the truth] and [then] praise you and leave?"

The World-honored One said, "It was like a good horse in the world seeing the form of a whip and running."[2]

7] Since the ancestral Master's coming from the west until today, many good counselors have taken up this story and set it before people of learning in practice, at which times—either taking years or taking days and months—many have clarified it and believed and entered the Buddha-Dharma. It is

1. The intention of the non-Buddhist was to ask for teaching that transcends words.
2. *Keitoku-dento-roku*, chap. 27.

called *"the story of the non-Buddhist questioning the Buddha."* We should know that the World-honored One performed the two kinds of establishment of the teaching: sacred silence and sacred preaching. Those who are able to enter through this [story] are all *like good horses in the world seeing the form of a whip and running.* Those who are able to enter through that establishment of the teaching which is beyond sacred silence and sacred preaching, are also like this.[3]

[58] The ancestral Patriarch Nāgārjuna says, *"When I preach to people phrases [of Dharma], it is as if fast horses are seeing the form of a whip and at once entering the right path."* At any moment and in any circumstances, whether listening to the Dharma of appearance and non-appearance [or] listening to the Dharma of the three vehicles and the one vehicle,[4] we often tend towards wrong paths, but when we are frequently able to see the form of a whip, we then enter the right path. If, following a master, we have met a human being, there is no place which is not the preaching of phrases [of Dharma] and there is no time when we do not see the form of a whip. Those who see the form of a whip at once, those who see the form of a whip after three asaṃkhya kalpas, and those who see the form of a whip after countless kalpas, [all] are able to enter the right path.[5]

[59] The Saṃyuktāgama Sutra[6] says: *The Buddha told the bhikṣus, "There are four kinds of horses. The first sees the form of a whip, is startled at once, and follows the rider's will. The second is startled when [the whip] touches its hair, and then it follows the rider's will. The third is surprised after [the whip] touches its flesh. The fourth wakes up only after [the whip] has penetrated to the bone. The first horse is like one who hears of impermanence[7] in another community[8] and then is able to feel aversion.[9] The second horse is like one who hears of impermanence in his or her own community and then is able to feel aversion. The third horse is like one who hears of the impermanence of his or*

3. Those who are able to enter the truth through intuitional grasp of the state of just acting are like good horses.

4. The three vehicles are the ways of the śrāvaka (intellectual Buddhist), pratyekabuddha (sensual Buddhist), and bodhisattva (practical Buddhist). The one vehicle is the way of the buddha. The teaching of the three vehicles and the one vehicle is preached by Gautama Buddha in the third chapter of the Lotus Sutra; *Hiyu (A Parable).* See Shobogenzo, chap. 17, *Hokke-ten-hokke.*

5. 鞭影 (BEN-EI), "the form of a whip," or "the image of a whip," symbolizes the Buddha's instruction.

6. 雑阿含経 (ZO-AGON-GYO), lit. "Miscellaneous Āgama Sutra," the third of the four Āgamas in Chinese translation. It was translated in fifty fascicles by Guṇabhadra, during the Liu Sung Dynasty (420–479).

7. 無常 (MUJO), "impermanence" or "inconstancy," in this case means death or disaster.

8. 聚落 (SHURAKU), lit. colony or community, represents the Sanskrit *jana-kāya* or *grāma*. See Glossary.

9. 厭 (EN), "aversion," in this case means aversion to the impermanence, inconstancy, or unreliability of situations in secular society.

her own parent and then is able to feel aversion. The fourth horse is like one whose own body suffers sickness and only then is able to feel aversion."[10]

[60] This is *the four horses* of the Āgama [Sutra]. It is studied whenever the Buddha-Dharma is learned in practice. Those who, as true good counselors, manifest themselves in the human world and in the heavens above and, as emissaries of the Buddha, become ancestral masters, inevitably have learned this [teaching] in practice, and they transmit it for the benefit of their students. Those who do not know it are not good counselors to human beings and gods. Those students who are close with the Buddha's truth, as living beings who have thickly accumulated good roots,[11] are inevitably able to hear this [teaching]. Those who are far from the Buddha's truth neither hear it nor know it. So masters should plan to preach it without delay, and disciples should hope to hear it without delay. The meaning of this *"to feel aversion"* is as follows: *"When the Buddha expounds the Dharma with a single utterance, living beings each understand according to their type. Some have fear. Some rejoice. Some feel aversion and detachment. Some cut doubt."*[12]

[61] The Sutra of the Great [Demise] says: *The Buddha said, "Good sons! It is like training horses. Broadly there are four kinds [of horse]: Those which 1) are contacted through hair, 2) are contacted through skin, 3) are contacted through flesh, or 4) are contacted through bone, and which, according to those respective places of contact, obey the rider's will. The Tathāgata also is like that. With four kinds of Dharma, he controls and subdues living beings: 1) he preaches to them of life, and then they accept the Buddha's words, like [a horse], when its hair is touched, following the rider's will; 2) he preaches of life and aging, and then [living beings] accept the Buddha's words, like [a horse], when its hair and skin are touched, following the rider's will; 3) he preaches of life and also of aging and death, and then [living beings] accept the Buddha's words, like [a horse], when its hair, skin, and flesh are touched, following the rider's will; 4) he preaches of life and also of aging, sickness, and death, and then [living beings] accept the Buddha's words, like [a horse], when its hair, skin, flesh, and bone are touched, following the rider's will. Good sons! There is no certainty in a rider's training of a horse, [but] the World-honored Tathāgata's control and subjugation of living beings are assured and are never in vain. For this reason, the Buddha is titled 'Controller of Men.'"*[13]

[63] This is called the *"the four horses of the Nirvāṇa Sutra."* No students have failed to learn it, and no buddhas have failed to preach it. We hear it by following buddhas; whenever we meet and serve buddhas, we listen to it with-

---

10. *Maka-shikan-guketsu*, vol. 2, chap. 5.

11. 善根 (ZENKON) means good actions as the roots of happiness.

12. *Yuimakitsu-shosetsu-gyo* (*Vimalakīrti-nirdeśa*); *Bukkoku-bon (Buddha-land Chapter).*

13. *Daihatsu-nehan-gyo* (Sutra of the Great Demise—*Mahāparinirvāṇa-sūtra*); fascicle 18, *Bongyo-bon (Pure Conduct Chapter).* 調御丈夫 (CHOGO JOBU), lit. "controller-rider of stout men," represents the Sanskrit *puruṣa-damya-sārathi.* See Book 2, Glossary. This is one of ten epithets of the Buddha, which are listed in chap. 87, *Kuyo-shobutsu.*

out fail; and whenever we receive the transmission of the Buddha-Dharma our preaching to living beings of this [teaching] continues, without flagging, through successive kalpas. When we finally arrive at Buddhahood, we preach this [teaching] for bodhisattvas and śrāvakas, and for great orders of human beings and gods, as if it were the time of our first establishment of the will. For this reason, the seed of the treasures of Buddha, Dharma, and Saṃgha is uninterrupted. Because it is like this, the preaching of buddhas is far removed from the preaching of bodhisattvas. Remember, the methods of a horse trainer are broadly of four kinds: to touch hair, to touch skin, to touch flesh, and to touch bone. We cannot read what the object is that is caused to touch hair, but mahāsattvas of the Dharma transmission understand that it might be a whip. At the same time, among methods of training horses, there may be those that employ a whip and those that do not employ a whip; the training of horses may not always be limited to the whip. [Horses] with a standing height of eight feet are called *"dragon horses."* These horses are seldom trained in the human world. Further, there are horses called *"thousand-mile horses"* which run a thousand miles in a day. While running five hundred miles these horses sweat blood; after five hundred miles they are refreshed and swift. Few people can ride these horses, and few know how to train them. There are no such horses in China, [but] there are in other countries.[14] We do not read that every one of these horses [must] frequently be given the whip. Nevertheless, a past master has said, *"In training horses, we inevitably give them the whip. Without the whip, horses are not trained. Such is the method of training horses."* There are the present four methods: the touching of hair, skin, flesh, and bone. To touch skin and bone but not hair is impossible. To touch flesh and bone but not hair and skin is impossible. We have seen, therefore, that the whip is to be given. That this is not explained here in the present [quotation] is due to a lack in the sentences.[15] There are numerous places like this in all sutras. The Tathāgata, World-honored One, Controller of Men,[16] is also like that [horse trainer]: he uses four kinds of Dharma to control and subdue all living beings, *assuredly and never in vain.* That is to say, he preaches to them of life, whereupon some instantly accept the Buddha's words; he preaches to [living beings] of life and aging, whereupon some accept the Buddha's words; he preaches to [living beings] of life, aging, and sickness, whereupon some accept the Buddha's words; and he

---

14. It is said that in 138 B.C. a Chinese general called Chang Ch'ien traveled to Fergana (in present-day Uzbekistan) to buy some horses that, according to rumor, ran so fast that they sweated blood. The general found that in fact they bled because of a skin parasite. But he also learned that Fergana's merchants would pay a handsome price for silk. His emperor, Wu-ti, thereupon lifted an export ban that had been in force since the Chinese started weaving silk around 2000 B.C., and trading began along what was to become the Silk Route.

15. In the quotation from the *Daihatsu-nehan-gyo*, it is understood that what touches the horse's hair is a whip: the character 鞭 (BEN, *muchi*), "whip," does not appear in the quotation.

16. 如来世尊調御丈夫 (NYORAI-SESON-JOGOJOBU) are three of the ten epithets of the Buddha.

preaches to [living beings] of life, aging, sickness, and death, whereupon some accept the Buddha's words. Those who hear of the last three [can] never avoid the first one,[17] just as, in training horses in the world, aside from contact with hair there is no contact with skin, flesh, and bone. *"He preaches to them of life, aging, sickness, and death"* means that the Tathāgata, the World-honored One, preaches to others of life, aging, sickness, and death.[18] This is not in order to cause living beings to depart from life, aging, sickness, and death. He does not preach that life, aging, sickness, and death are just the truth, and he does not preach in order to make living beings understand that life, aging, sickness, and death are just the truth. His purpose is—by this preaching to others of life, aging, sickness, and death—to cause all living beings to grasp the reality of anuttara-samyak-saṃbodhi. Thus *the World-honored Tathāgata's control and subjugation of living beings are assured and are never in vain. For this reason, the Buddha is titled 'Controller of Men.'*

Shobogenzo Shime

On a day of the summer retreat in the 7th year of Kencho,[19] I finished copying this from the Master's draft.

Ejo

17. Buddhist preaching is sometimes about aging, sickness, and death, but it is always about life.

18. The Buddha, while venerated and honored as the most sacred of beings, preaches to others about concrete mundane matters.

19. 1255. This is one of the chapters of the 12-chapter edition of Shobogenzo that Master Dogen began in the last years of his life. Master Dogen died in 1253, two years before his successor Master Ko-un Ejo added the concluding note.

[86]

出家功徳

SHUKKE-KUDOKU

The Merit of Leaving Family Life

Shutsu *means "to get out of" or "to transcend."* ***Ke*** *means "house," "home," or "family life," and* ***kudoku*** *means "merit." So* ***shukke-kudoku*** *means the merit of leaving family life. In this chapter Master Dogen praised and emphasized the merit of leaving or transcending family life. Most people are brought up within a family, and the influence that our family has on us is often much stronger than we realize. The aim of studying Buddhism is to realize what the truth is. To achieve this, it is necessary for us to transcend our family life, because the habits we form and the influence that our family has on us tend to prevent us from seeing clearly what the truth is. This is why the merit of the tradition of leaving family life is revered in Buddhism, as Master Dogen explains here.*

[69] **Bodhisattva Nāgārjuna**[1] **said:** *Someone asks, "With the lay precepts,*[2] *we are able to be born in the heavens above, to attain the bodhisattva-way, and to attain nirvāṇa. Why then is it necessary to rely on the precepts of those who have left family life?"*[3]

I reply: Although both [lay people and monks] can attain salvation, still there is difficulty and ease. Lay people's livelihoods have all sorts of jobs and duties; if they want to concentrate their minds on the truth and the Dharma, their trade will deteriorate, and if they concentrate on practicing their trade, matters pertaining to the truth will deteriorate. They should be able to practice the Dharma without selecting and without abandoning [one or the other], which is called 'difficult.' If we leave family life and part from secular society, to eradicate miscellaneous irritations and disturbances, and to concentrate the mind solely on practice of the truth, is called 'easy.' Further, family life, being disorderly and noisy, with many jobs and many duties, is the root of hindrances and the seat of many sins. It is called 'very difficult.' If we leave family life, we are like, for example, a person going off to stay in a deserted place, among empty fields, and making the mind whole so that there is no mind and no concern: we are already rid of inner thoughts, and external matters also have departed. As a verse says,[4]

---

1. The fourteenth patriarch in India.

2. In Master Nāgārjuna's time, there were 250 precepts for monks and 348 for nuns. Lay Buddhists observed five precepts.

3. 出家 (SHUKKE), i.e. monks.

4. Master Nāgārjuna quoted the poem from an older Buddhist sutra or commentary.

We sit in quietness among the trees of the forest,
In the serene state, all evils evaporate.
We placidly get a whole mind.
This pleasure is beyond the pleasure of gods.

Others seek gain: wealth and status,
Fine clothes and comfortable bedding.
Such pleasures are not peaceful.
In seeking gain there is no satisfaction.

In patched robes we go begging for food,
In movement and in stillness, minds constantly whole.
With our own eyes of wisdom,
We reflect on the reality of all dharmas.

The many kinds of Dharma-gates,
All, through balance, are entered by reflection.
The mind of understanding and wisdom abides in serenity,
It is beyond the triple world.

Thus we see that when we leave family life, to observe the precepts and practice the truth is very easy. Further, leaving family life and observing the precepts gains countless criteria of virtue and regulation and puts us completely in possession of them all. For this reason, ones clothed in white[5] *should leave family life and receive ordination.*[6] *Further, in the Buddha-Dharma, the Dharma of leaving family life is the most difficult of all to practice, as [illustrated when] the Brāhman Jambukhādaka asked Śāriputra, "What is the most difficult thing in the Buddha-Dharma?"*

Śāriputra answered, "Leaving family life is [most] difficult."

[The Brāhman] asked further, "What difficulties are there in leaving family life?"

[Śāriputra] answered, "In leaving family life, to have inner comfort is difficult."

[The Brāhman asked] "When one has already attained inner comfort, what then is difficult?"

[Śāriputra answered,] "To practice good ways is difficult."

Thus, we should leave family life. Further, when a person leaves family life, the king of demons, in astonishment and sorrow, says, "This person has scarcely any hindrances or wants! [This person] will surely attain nirvāṇa and fall into the numbers of the Saṃgha-treasure!" Further, in the Buddha-Dharma, people who have left family life, even if they break the precepts and fall into sin, after they have expiated their sins, they can attain liberation, as the bhikṣuṇī Utpalavarṇā explains in the Jātaka sutra:[7] *When the Buddha is in the world, this bhikṣuṇī attains the six mystical powers and the state of an arhat. She*

5. Lay people.

6. 具足戒 (GUSOKUKAI), from the Sanskrit *upasaṃpadā,* means taking the 250 precepts for a monk or 348 precepts for a nun. See Book 1, Glossary.

7. 本性経 (HONSHO-KYO), legendary stories of the Buddha's past lives as a bodhisattva.

goes into the houses of nobles and constantly praises the Dharma of leaving family life, saying to all the aristocratic ladies, "Sisters! You should leave family life."

The noblewomen say, "We are young and in our prime and our figures are at the height of beauty. To keep the precepts would be difficult. Sometimes we might break the precepts."

The bhikṣuṇī says, "If you break the precepts, you break them. Just leave family life!"

They ask, "If we break the precepts we will fall into hell. Why should we risk breaking them?"

She answers, "If you fall into hell, you fall."

The noblewomen all laugh at this, saying, "In hell we would have to receive [retribution for our] sins. Why should we risk falling [into hell]?"

The bhikṣuṇī says, "I myself remember during a past life I became a prostitute, wore all sorts of clothes, and spoke archaic words. One day, as a joke, I put on a bhikṣuṇī's robe, and due to this as a direct and indirect cause, at the time of Kāśyapa Buddha[8] *I became a bhikṣuṇī. I was proud of my noble pedigree and fine features: vanity and arrogance arose in my mind, and I broke the precepts. Because of the wrongness of breaking the precepts I fell into hell and suffered for my various sins, but after suffering I finally met Śākyamuni Buddha, left family life, and attained the six mystical powers and the truth of an arhat. Thus, I know that when we leave family life and receive the precepts, even if we break the precepts, due to the precepts as direct and indirect causes we can attain the truth of an arhat. If I had only done bad, without the precepts as direct and indirect causes, I could not have attained the truth. In the past I fell into hell in age after age. When I got out of hell I became a bad person, and when the bad person died, I went back into hell, and there was no gain at all. Now therefore I know from experience that when we leave family life and receive the precepts, with this as a direct and indirect cause—even if we break the precepts—we can attain the bodhi-effect."*[9]

] *Further, when the Buddha was at Jetavana Park, a drunken Brāhman came to the Buddha's place and sought to become a bhikṣu. The Buddha instructed Ānanda to give him a shaved head and to clothe him in the Dharma-robe. Having woken from his drunkenness, [the Brāhman] was dismayed that his body had suddenly become that of a bhikṣu, and he ran away at once. All the bhikṣus asked the Buddha, "Why did you permit this Brāhman to become a bhikṣu?"*

The Buddha said, "This Brāhman for countless kalpas had never had any will at all to leave family life. Now, because of being drunk, he has temporarily established a bit of the will. With this as a direct and indirect cause, in the future he will leave family life and attain the truth."

---

8. Kāśyapa Buddha is the sixth of the seven ancient buddhas, the seventh being Śākyamuni Buddha.

9. *Daichido-ron* (from the Sanskrit Maha-prajña-pāramitopadeśa), chap. 30. The Maha-prajña-pāramitopadeśa is considered to be Master Nāgārjuna's commentary on the Pañcaviṃśati-sāhasrikā Prajña-pāramitā-sūtra (see notes 60 and 61). This section of *Daichido-ron* is also quoted in chap. 12, *Kesa-kudoku,* para. [87].

In various stories like this, the merit of leaving family life is immeasurable. Thus, those clothed in white, even if they possess the five precepts,[10] are not equal to those who have left family life.[11]

[76] The World-honored One thus permitted the drunken Brāhman to leave family life and receive the precepts, seeing it as the first planting of the seed of attainment of the truth. Clearly, from ancient times until today, living beings who lack the merit of leaving family life have been forever unable to attain the buddha-state of bodhi. This Brāhman, because he was slightly[12] drunk, momentarily established a bit of the will and, having his head shaved and receiving the precepts, he became a bhikṣu. The period before he sobered up was not so long, but the principle that this merit[13] should be preserved, and should be promoted as a good root of attainment of the truth, is present in the World-honored One's golden words of true philosophy, and is the Tathāgata's original wish in manifesting himself in the world. All living beings, in the past, present, and future, definitely should believe and devoutly practice [this principle of leaving family life]. Truly, the establishment of the will and the attainment of the truth inevitably occur relying upon kṣāṇas.[14] This Brāhman's momentary merit of leaving family life is also like that. Still more, how could the merit of leaving family life and receiving the precepts for the whole of our present human lifetime and life be inferior to [the merit of] the drunken Brāhman? Sacred wheel-rolling kings[15] appeared more than eighty thousand years ago and ruled the four continents, being abundantly furnished with the seven treasures. At that time these four continents were all like the Pure Land.[16] The pleasure enjoyed by the wheel kings is beyond expression in words. There are some [wheel-kings], it is said, who rule a three-thousandfold world. There are distinctions between [kings of] gold, silver, copper, and iron wheels, who rule one, two, three, or four continents,[17] [but] the bodies of them all are invariably free of the ten evils.[18]

---

10. 五戒 (GOKAI), "five precepts," from the Sanskrit *pañca-śīlāni*: 1) not to kill, 2) not to steal, 3) not to commit adultery, 4) not to lie, 5) not to drink alcohol. These five precepts are still a standard observed by lay people in Hīnayāna Buddhist countries such as Thailand.

11. *Daichido-ron*, chap. 30. See also chap. 83, *Shukke*, para. [18].

12. The diminutive わずかに... *(wazukani)*, "slightly," suggests that, relative to the importance of leaving family life, the fact that the Brāhman was drunk was not so important.

13. The merit of wanting to leave family life.

14. Moments. It is said that one click of the fingers takes 65 kṣāṇas.

15. 転輪聖王 (TENRINJO-O), "sacred wheel-rolling kings," from the Sanskrit *cakravarti-rāja*, feature in sutras such as the Lotus Sutra. See, for example, LS 2.60. See Book 1, Glossary.

16. 浄土 (JODO), from the Sanskrit *Sukhāvatī*, suggests an ideal realm.

17. For example, it was said that a king with a gold wheel rules all four continents; a king with a silver wheel rules the east, west, and south continents; a king with a copper wheel rules the east and south continents; and a king with an iron wheel rules only the southern continent.

18. Killing, stealing, adultery, lying, flattery, abusive words, two-faced speech, greed, anger, wrong views.

Even though such a sacred wheel-rolling king is thus abundantly provided with pleasures, when a single white hair grows on his head, he abdicates the throne to the crown prince and with his own body he at once leaves family life, puts on the kaṣāya, and enters the mountains or forest to train, so that when his life ends, he is inevitably born in a brahma-heaven. He puts this white hair from his own head into a silver casket, to be kept in the royal palace and transmitted to the next wheel-king. The next wheel-king, when he too grows a white hair, does exactly the same as the previous king. The length of the life remaining to a sacred wheel-rolling king after leaving home is beyond comparison with that of people today. A wheel-king is said to be already over eighty thousand [years old], and his body is endowed with the thirty-two signs;[19] people today cannot equal him. Nevertheless, when he sees a white hair and realizes impermanence, he inevitably leaves home and practices the truth, in order to accomplish merit by performing spotless conduct. The kings of today cannot match the sacred wheel-rolling kings. If they waste precious time amid greed, and fail to leave family life, they may regret it in future ages. Still more, in a minor nation in a remote land, although there are kings in name they do not have the virtue of kings; they are unable to confine their greed. [But] if they leave family life and practice the truth many gods will gladly protect them, dragon deities will respectfully guard them, and the Buddha-eyes of the buddhas might definitely authenticate them and rejoice. In her past as a prostitute, [the Nun Utpalavarṇā] put on the bhikṣuṇī-robe not out of belief, but as a joke. Although this likely carried the sin of making light of the Dharma, by virtue of clothing her body in this robe, she met the Buddha-Dharma in a second age. *"The bhikṣuṇī robe"* means the kaṣāya. By virtue of jokingly wearing the kaṣāya she met Kāśyapa Buddha in a second life, she left family life and received the precepts, and she became a bhikṣuṇī. Even though, as a result of breaking the precepts, she fell into hell and received [retribution for] her sins, because the merit [of wearing the kaṣāya] had not decayed, she finally met Śākyamuni Buddha. Meeting buddha, hearing the Dharma, establishing the will, and doing training, she parted from the triple world forever and became a great arhat, equipped with the six powers and the three kinds of knowledge. Undoubtedly [her state] must have been the supreme truth. Therefore when, from the beginning, solely for the sake of the supreme state of bodhi, we distill pure belief and we believe in and receive the kaṣāya, the maturation of that merit will be swifter than [the maturation of] the merit of the prostitute. Still more, when for the sake of the supreme state of bodhi we establish the bodhi-mind, leave family life, and receive the precepts, that merit might be immeasurable. Without a human body, this merit is rarely accomplished. In the Western Heavens and the Eastern Lands[20], as monks or as laymen, bodhi-

19. Refers to the thirty-two distinguishing marks on the body of a buddha.

20. India and China.

sattvas and ancestral masters have been many, but none has equaled the ancestral Master Nāgārjuna. Only the ancestral Master Nāgārjuna quoted stories such as those of the drunken Brāhman and the prostitute, in order to encourage living beings to leave family life and receive the precepts. This is the ancestral Master Nāgārjuna's exact record of the golden speech of the World-honored One.

[81] The World-honored One said, *"On the southern continent*[21] *there are four kinds of supreme excellence: 1) meeting Buddha, 2) hearing the Dharma, 3) leaving family life, and 4) attaining the truth."*

Clearly remember, these four kinds of supreme excellence are beyond the northern continent[22] and beyond the various heavens. Now that, led by the power of long-accumulated good roots, we have received a supremely excellent body,[23] we should rejoicingly leave family life and receive the precepts. Do not waste the supremely excellent body of goodness, leaving its dew-drop life at the mercy of the wind of inconstancy. If we accumulate life after life of leaving family life, that will be *the piling up of merit and heaping up of virtue.*[24]

[82] The World-honored One said, *"In the Buddha-Dharma the effects and results of leaving family life are unthinkable. Even if a person erected a stūpa of the seven treasures as high as the thirty-three gods,*[25] *the merit gained would be inferior to that of leaving family life. Why? Because a stūpa of the seven treasures can be demolished by greedy and malicious stupid people, [but] the merit of leaving family life is indestructible. Therefore if [someone] teaches men and women [of this merit], or sets free male and female servants, or permits citizens, or with his or her own body leaves family life and enters the truth, the merit is immeasurable."*[26]

[83] The World-honored One, clearly knowing the amount of the merit, made a comparison like this. Śrīvaddhi,[27] on hearing it, though he was an old

---

21. 南洲 (NANSHU), suggests Jambudvīpa, the continent south of Mt. Sumeru on which human beings are living; that is, the human world.

22. 北洲 (HOKUSHU), from the Sanskrit *Uttara-kura,* the northern continent; an ideal realm of everlasting bliss.

23. A human body.

24. 積功累徳 (SHAKKU-RUITOKU). The expression originates in the Lotus Sutra. See, for example, LS 2.218–220.

25. 三十三天 (SANJUSAN-TEN), "thirty-three gods," representing the Sanskrit *Trāyastriṃśa,* are said to live on the top of Mt. Sumeru in the second of the six heavenly realms of the world of desire. Śakra-devānām-indra is in the center surrounded by eight gods in each of the four quarters. See Book 3, Glossary.

26. *Kengu-kyo,* fascicle 4.

27. 福増 (FUKUZO), lit. "Wealth-Increaser," represents the Sanskrit *Śrīvaddhi,* the name of a wealthy man from Rājagṛha who appears in fascicle 4 of *Kengu-kyo.* Already a centenarian, he asked Śāriputra if he could become a monk, but Śāriputra refused, saying that Śrīvaddhi was too old. The Buddha, however, thereafter allowed him to become a monk.

man of 120 years, was compelled to leave family life and receive the precepts; he sat alongside children in the end-seats, underwent training, and became a great arhat. Remember, the human body of our present life is temporarily formed through direct and indirect combinations of the four elements and the five aggregates, and it always has the eight kinds of pain.[28] Furthermore, kṣāṇa by kṣāṇa, it appears and disappears, utterly without cease. Still more, during a click of the fingers sixty-five kṣāṇas appear and disappear, but because we are dull we never know it. Altogether, in the passing of one day and night there are 6,400,099,980 kṣāṇas,[29] [in each of which] the five aggregates appear and disappear, but we do not know it. It is pitiful that, even as we appear and disappear, we ourselves do not know it. This duration of the appearance and disappearance of a kṣāṇa was known only by the World-honored Buddha and by Śāriputra; though other saints have been many, not one of them has known it. Again, by virtue of just this fact of instantaneous appearance and disappearance, living beings produce good or bad karma. By virtue of this fact of instantaneous appearance and disappearance, living beings establish the will and attain the truth. [Our human body] is a human body which appears and disappears like this; even if we treasure it, it cannot stand still. Since time immemorial, there has never been a single person who, by begrudging [the human body], stood still. The human body is thus not our own, but if we utilize it to leave family life and receive the precepts, we will experience the buddha-state that is as imperishable as a diamond, the anuttara-samyak-saṃbodhi experienced by the buddhas of the three times. What wise person would not gladly pursue [this state]? Hence, the eight sons of the past Buddha Sun-Moon-Light all renounced a royal position of dominion over four continents, and left family life.[30] The sixteen sons of the Buddha Universal-Surpassing-Wisdom each left family life.[31] While Universal-Wisdom had entered the immovable state, they preached to the assembly the Flower of Dharma,[32] and they have now become tathāgatas of the ten directions. *Eight myriad koṭis of people among the masses led by the sacred wheel-rolling king,*[33] their royal father, on seeing the sixteen princes leave family life, also sought to leave family life, whereupon the king at once permitted them. The two sons of the King Resplendent, together with their royal father and his queen, all left family life.[34] Remember, it is evident that whenever great saints have appeared, they have inevitably considered leaving family life to

---

28. The eight kinds of pain are the pain of 1) birth; 2) aging; 3) sickness; 4) death; 5) separation from loved ones; 6) association with hated ones; 7) seeking what cannot be attained; 8) building up of the five aggregates (strong desire).

29. Sixty-four hundred million, ninety-nine thousand, nine hundred and eighty.

30. Alludes to Lotus Sutra, *Jo (Introductory).* See LS 1.42–44.

31. Lotus Sutra, *Kejo-yu (Parable of the Magic City).* See LS 2.58.

32. Ibid. See LS 2.62.

33. Ibid. See LS 2.60.

34. Lotus Sutra, *Myoshogon-o-honji (Story of the King Resplendent).* See LS 3.302.

be the right Dharma. We should not say that these people left family life out of stupidity; knowing that they left family life out of wisdom, we should hope to do the same. In the time of the present Buddha Śākyamuni, Rāhula,[35] Ānanda,[36] and so on, all left family life. Further, there is [the example of] the thousand Śākyas leaving family life and the twenty thousand Śākyas leaving family life;[37] we should call these excellent examples. From the five bhikṣus who left family life at the beginning[38] to Subhadra who left family life at the end,[39] [all] people who devoted themselves to the Buddha immediately left family life. Remember, its merit is immeasurable. Therefore, if people of the world have compassion for their children and grandchildren, they should let them leave family life without delay. If they have compassion for their fathers and mothers, they should recommend them to leave family life. For this reason, a verse says:

If there were no past ages,
There could be no past buddhas.
If there were no past buddhas,
There would be no leaving family life and receiving ordination.[40]

This verse is a verse of the buddha-tathāgatas. It destroys the non-Buddhist assertion that past ages do not exist. So remember, leaving family life and receiving ordination are the Dharma of the past buddhas. While fortunately meeting a time to leave family life and to receive ordination—which actions are the wonderful Dharma of the Buddhas—if we idly fail to leave family life and receive the precepts it would be hard to know what obstacle was the cause. With the subsisting body,[41] the lowest kind of thing, we can accomplish the highest kind of merit. It may be the highest kind of merit in Jambudvīpa and in the triple world. While this human body in Jambudvīpa has still not disappeared, we should, without fail, leave family life and receive the precepts.

---

35. The Buddha's son.

36. The Buddha's cousin and the second patriarch in India.

37. Śākya was the name of the clan into which the Buddha was born, hence the name Śākyamuni, which means "Sage of the Śākyas."

38. Ājñāta-kauṇḍinya, Aśvajit, Bhadrika, Mahānāman, and Daśabala-kāśyapa. These five were ordered by the Buddha's father, the king of the Śākyas, to accompany the Buddha in his ascetic practice. They left the Buddha when he discarded asceticism, but when they heard his first turning of the Dharma wheel, they became the first monks of the Buddha's order.

39. Subhadra was a Brāhman who, shortly before the Buddha's death, became the last of the Buddha's disciples to become a monk.

40. *Daibibasha-ron*, chap. 76. Also quoted in chap. 87, *Kuyo-shobutsu*.

41. 依身 (ESHIN). 依 (E) means "to rely upon," and 身 (SHIN) means "body." 依身 (ESHIN) means the body as the basis of consciousness; that is, the physical body.

3] An ancient saint[42] said, *"People who have left family life, even if they break the precepts, still surpass lay people who receive and keep the precepts. Therefore the sutras solely encourage people to leave family life, and that benevolence is hard to repay. Further, to encourage [people] to leave family life is just to encourage people to practice venerable conduct; the effects and results gained [by this encouragement] surpass King Yama,*[43] *the wheel-kings, and the God Śakra. Therefore the sutras solely encourage people to leave family life, and that benevolence is hard to repay. Such facts do not exist in encouraging people to receive and keep the precepts of a lay follower, and so the sutras do not verify it."*[44]

] Remember, if we have left family life, even if we break the precepts, that is better than not breaking the precepts as a lay person. As [acts of] devotion to the Buddha, leaving family life and receiving the precepts are, in every case, most excellent. The effects and results of encouraging others to leave family life are beyond the excellence of King Yama, beyond the excellence of a wheel-king, and beyond the excellence of the God Śakra. Even a vaiśya[45] or a śudra,[46] by leaving family life, will surpass a kṣatriya,[47] and indeed surpass King Yama, surpass the wheel-kings, and surpass the God Śakra. The lay precepts are not like this; therefore we should leave family life. Remember, what the World-honored One taught, though unfathomable, was widely collected by a World-honored One and five hundred great arhats.[48] Truly, [therefore,] we have been able to know that truths in the Buddha-Dharma should be evident. Ordinary teachers of recent ages cannot fathom even the wisdom of the three kinds of knowledge and the six powers of one saint, much less [the wisdom of] the five hundred saints. [The five hundred] have known what ordinary teachers of recent ages do not know, have seen what [ordinary teachers] do not see, and have realized what [ordinary teachers] do not realize, but nothing known by ordinary teachers is unknown to [the five hundred saints]. So do not compare the dismal and foolish explanations of ordinary teachers with the words of saints of the three kinds of knowledge.

---

42. Refers to the seventh Indian patriarch, Master Vasumitra who, together with a large number of collaborators known as the five hundred arhats, compiled the Abhidharma-mahāvibhāṣa-śāstra (the Chinese translation is called *Daibibasha-ron* in Japan) about four hundred years after the Buddha's death.

43. In Sanskrit Yama-rāja, the king of the underworld who decides the fate of the dead according to their virtue.

44. *Daibibasha-ron*, fascicle 66. 故経不証 *(yue [ni] kyo [ni] sho[se]zu)*. *Daibibasha-ron* has 故経不説 *(yue [ni] kyo [ni] to[ka]zu)*; "therefore the sutras do not mention it."

45. A peasant or worker belonging to the third of the four castes in the ancient Indian social system. See Book 1, Glossary.

46. A servant belonging to the lowest of the four castes, whose only business was to serve the three higher classes: brāhmana, kṣatriya, and vaiśya. See Book 1, Glossary.

47. A member of the military or ruling class, the second of the four castes. See Book 1, Glossary.

48. Again, this refers to Master Vasumitra and the five hundred arhats who compiled the Abhidharma-mahāvibhāṣa-śāstra at the Fourth Council, held in the Kingdom of Kaniṣka.

[91] The Abhidharma-mahāvibhāṣa-śāstra, [fascicle] 120, says, *"Even one who establishes the will and leaves family life is already called a sacred being; how much more one who has attained the state of indulgence towards the Dharma."*[49]

Remember, to establish the will and leave family life is to be called a sacred being.

[91] In Śākyamuni Buddha's five hundred great vows,[50] vow no. 137 is: *"In future, after I have realized the right state of truth, if there are any men who, in my Dharma, want to leave family life, I vow that they will be free of hindrances—namely, infirmity; loss of mindfulness; confusion; pride; lack of awe; being stupid and without wisdom; abundant preoccupations; and distraction of the mind. Otherwise, I shall not realize the right state of truth." Vow no. 138 is: "In future, after I have realized the right state of truth, if there are any women who want, in my Dharma, to leave family life, to learn the truth, and to receive the great precepts, I vow that I will cause them to accomplish [this]. Otherwise, I shall not realize the right state of truth." Vow no. 314 is: "In future, after I have realized the right state of truth, if there are any living beings who lack good roots*[51] *but while experiencing a good root feel love and delight in their mind, I shall cause them, in the Buddha-Dharma in a future age, to leave family life and learn the truth, and shall cause them peacefully and steadfastly to abide by the sacred and pure ten precepts.*[52] *Otherwise, I shall not realize the right state of truth."*

[93] Remember, the good sons and good daughters who have left family life today all have been assisted by the power of the great vows made in the ancient past by the World-honored One, and [thus] they have been able, without hindrances, to leave family life and receive the precepts. The Tathāgata already, through his vowing, is causing us to leave family life. Clearly we have seen that it is the most valuable and the highest great merit.

[94] The Buddha said, *"Moreover, if there is anyone who, following me, shaves beard and hair and wears a kaṣāya without receiving the precepts, even those who serve offerings to this person will be able at last to enter the castle of fearlessness. For such reasons do I preach like this."*[53]

---

49. 忍法 (NIN PO), or "indulgence towards the Dharma," is traditionally interpreted as an expression of the state in which a person recognizes the Four Noble Truths. 忍 (NIN) represents the Sanskrit *ksānti*, which MW defines as "patience, indulgence; the state of saintly abstraction." At the same time, 忍 (NIN) can be interpreted as representing the character 認 (NIN), "recognition." See Book 1, Glossary.

50. *Hige-kyo* (the Chinese translation of the Karuṇā-puṇḍarīka-sūtra) actually lists only 335 vows. In chap. 12, *Kesa-kudoku,* Master Dogen also quotes vows from *Hige-kyo* and refers to the five hundred great vows.

51. 善根 (ZENKON), "good roots," means good actions as the roots of happiness.

52. The ten serious prohibitions are included in the sixteen bodhisattva precepts which, by Master Dogen's time, were taken by both monks and laymen in China and Japan. These sixteen precepts are a condensed version of the 250 precepts observed by monks and the 348 precepts observed by nuns in Hīnayāna Buddhism. (See chap. 94, *Jukai*).

53. *Daishu-kyo* (in Sanskrit, Mahā-saṃnipāta-sūtra), fascicle 53.

Clearly we see that if [a person] shaves beard and hair and wears the kaṣāya, even without receiving the precepts, people who serve offerings to this [person] will enter the castle of fearlessness.

95] Further he said, *"If, again, there is a person who, for my sake, has left family life and who, even without taking the precepts, shaves beard and hair and wears a kaṣāya, those who, through non-Dharma, trouble or harm this [person], will even injure the Dharma-bodies and reward-bodies*[54] *of the buddhas of the three times, because they will eventually be filled with the three evil states."*[55]

95] The Buddha said, *"If there are any living beings who, for my sake, have left family life and who shave beard and hair and wear the kaṣāya, even if they do not retain the precepts, they all have been stamped already by the seal of nirvāṇa.*[56] *Further, if anyone, through non-Dharma, disturbs those who have left family life without retaining the precepts, or reviles and humiliates them, or insults them, or strikes, binds, or cuts them using hand, sword, or stick; or steals their robes and pātra; or steals miscellaneous necessities of life, then such a person injures the real reward-bodies of the buddhas of the three times and offends the eyes of all human beings and gods—because this person wants to conceal the seeds that the buddhas possess of the right Dharma and of the Three Treasures; because [this person] prevents gods and human beings from getting benefit and causes them to fall into hell; and because [this person] promotes and replenishes the three evil states."*[57]

Remember, if [people] shave their hair and [wear] the dyed robe, even if they do not retain the precepts, they are stamped by the seal of supreme and great nirvāṇa. If a person troubles them, [this person] injures the reward-bodies of the buddhas of the three times. That may be equal to a deadly sin. Clearly, we have seen that the merit of leaving family life is directly proximate to the buddhas of the three times.

7] The Buddha said, *"In general, those who have left family life should not commit wrong. If they commit wrong, that is not to have left family life. The body and mouth of a person who has left family life should be in mutual accord. If they are not in mutual accord, that is not to have left family life. Forsaking father, mother, brothers, wife and child, relatives, and acquaintances, I left family life to practice the truth. That was just*

---

54. 法身 (HOSSHIN), "Dharma-body," from the Sanskrit *dharma-kāya,* means a buddha's body seen as an inclusive entity with real value or meaning. See Book 1, Glossary. 報身 (HOJIN), "reward-body," from the Sanskrit *saṃbhoga-kāya* (lit. enjoyment body), means the concrete physical body seen as the result of actions and circumstances in the past. See Book 2, Glossary.

55. The three evil states are the states of beings in hell, hungry ghosts, and animals.

56. 涅槃印 (NEHAN-IN), "the seal of nirvāṇa," is the fourth of four 法印 (HO-IN), "Dharma-seals," (in Sanskrit *Dharmoddāna*): 1) All is suffering; 2) All dharmas are without self; 3) All actions are inconstant; 4) The quiet and still state of nirvāṇa. These four Dharma-seals, or concrete characteristics of the Buddha-Dharma, are said to distinguish the teaching of Buddhism from non-Buddhism.

57. *Daishu-kyo,* fascicle 53.

the time [when I was able to] accumulate virtuous realizations; it was never a time to accumulate non-virtuous realizations. 'Virtuous realization' means having compassion for all living beings, as if they were babies. Non-virtuous realization is different from this."[58]

In general, the inherent nature of leaving family life is *to have compassion for all living beings as if they were babies.* This state is just *not committing wrong* and is *body and mouth in mutual accord.* When such behavior is present already in leaving family life, its merit is as described now.

[98] The Buddha said, *"Furthermore, Śāriputra,*[59] *if bodhisattva-mahāsattvas want, on the very day of leaving family life, to realize anuttara-samyak-saṃbodhi; and [want], on that very day, to turn the Dharma wheel, so that when they turn the Dharma wheel countless asaṃkhyas of living beings depart from dust and leave dirt and amidst all dharmas attain purity of the Dharma-eye, and [so that] countless asaṃkhyas of living beings attain the state beyond perception of all dharmas; and [if bodhisattva-mahāsattvas want] to attain liberation from the mind of excesses, and [want] to enable countless asaṃkhyas of living beings to attain the state of not regressing or straying from anuttara-samyak-saṃbodhi, [then bodhisattva-mahāsattvas] should learn the prajñā-pāramitā."*[60]

This *"bodhisattvas who learn the prajñā-pāramitā"* means the patriarchs. At the same time, [the truth of] anuttara-samyak-saṃbodhi, in every case, is accomplished *on the very day of leaving family life.* However, when [bodhisattvas] practice and experience [the truth] for three asaṃkhya kalpas or practice and experience it for countless asaṃkhya kalpas, they do not taint it with "limited" and "limitless." Students should remember this.

[100] The Buddha said, *"If a bodhisattva-mahāsattva thinks, 'At some time, I will relinquish a throne and leave family life, on which day I will realize the supreme, right, and balanced state of bodhi; also on that day, I will turn the wonderful wheel of Dharma, causing countless, innumerable sentient beings to depart from dust and leave dirt, and causing them to have the pure Dharma-eye; at the same time, I will cause countless, innumerable sentient beings to end forever all excesses, and to liberate their minds and intuition; further, I will cause countless, innumerable sentient beings all to attain the state of not regressing or straying from the supreme, right, and balanced state of bodhi,' [then]*

---

58. *Daihatsu-nehan-gyo* (Sutra of the Great Demise—in Sanskrit, *Mahāparinirvāṇa-sūtra*), fascicle 23.

59. Śāriputra, who died while the Buddha was still alive, was one of the Buddha's ten great disciples. The Prajña-pāramitā-hṛdya-sūtra (or Heart Sutra) is addressed to Śāriputra, and represents the heart of all Sanskrit prajña-pāramitā literature. See Shobogenzo, chap. 2, *Maka-hannya-haramitsu.*

60. *Maka-hannya-haramitsu-kyo,* fascicle 1. *Maka-hannya-haramitsu-kyo* is Kumārajīva's translation of the Pañcaviṃśati-sāhasrikā Prajña-pāramitā-sūtra.

this bodhisattva-mahāsattva who wants to realize those things should learn the prajña-pāramitā."[61]

This is [the Buddha's] gracious expounding of the merit of his descending to be born in a royal palace, as a bodhisattva in the last body, and his *relinquishing the throne, realizing the right truth, and turning the Dharma wheel to save living beings.*

[101] *"The Prince Siddhārtha*[62] *took from Chandaka's*[63] *side a sword whose hilt of the seven treasures was adorned with maṇi*[64] *and miscellaneous embellishments. He grasped that sword in his right hand and drew it from its scabbard. With the left hand he at once took hold of the conch-like topknot of his hair, which was deep blue, the color of an utpala.*[65] *Wielding the sharp sword himself in his right hand, he cut off [the topknot]; with his left hand he held it aloft and threw it into the air. At this Śakra-devānām-indra greatly rejoiced, with a mind he had rarely experienced, and held aloft the Prince's topknot, not letting it fall to the ground. With a fine celestial robe, [Śakra] received [the topknot] and kept it. Then the gods served to it their most excellent celestial offerings."*[66]

[102] This is how Śākyamuni Tathāgata, when formerly a prince, scaled the ramparts in the middle of the night, went in the daytime to the mountains, and cut the hair from his own head. At that time, gods of the Heavens of Pure Abiding[67] came [down] to shave his head and to offer him the kaṣāya. Such [actions] are always the auspicious omens of a tathāgata's manifestation in the world, and [such] are the usual methods of the world-honored buddhas. There are no buddhas who realized buddha while remaining in family life, [not] even one buddha among all the buddhas of the three times and the ten directions. Because in the past there were buddhas, the merit of leaving family life and receiving the precepts exists. Living beings' attainment of the truth inevitably depends upon their leaving family life and receiving the precepts. In sum, the merit of leaving family life and receiving the precepts is that they are just the usual method of the buddhas, and therefore their merit is immeasurable. Within the sacred teaching there is expla-

---

61. *Dai-hannya-haramitsu-kyo*, fascicle 3. *Dai-hannya-haramitsu-kyo*, translated from Sanskrit into Chinese by Genjo in 659, is a 600-fascicle collection of the 16 prajña-pāramitā sutras which make up the great bulk of prajña-pāramitā literature. The second of these 16 sutras is the Pañcaviṃśati-sāhasrikā Prajña-pāramitā-sūtra.

62. Siddhārtha; lit. "he who has fulfilled the aim (of his coming)," was the Buddha's given name as a prince.

63. A servant employed by King Śūddhodana as Prince Siddhārtha's charioteer.

64. Pearls or jewels.

65. A blue lotus.

66. *Butsu-hongo-jikkyo*, fascicle 18. *Butsu-hongo-jikkyo* is a 60-fascicle biography of the Buddha translated into Chinese by Jñānagupta.

67. 浄居天 (JOGOTEN) or "Heavens of Pure Abiding," are described as the realm where an anāgāmin (one not subject to returning) is reborn. There are said to be five of these heavens, located in the fourth dhyāna heaven in the world of matter.

nation of lay realization of buddha, but it is not the authentic tradition. There is explanation of the female body realizing buddha, but this also is not the authentic tradition.[68] [The tradition] that the Buddhist patriarchs authentically transmit is to leave family life and realize buddha.

[103] *[At the time of] the fourth patriarch, the Venerable Upagupta, there is a rich man's son called Dhītika.*[69] *He comes to bow before the Venerable One, and seeks to leave family life. The Venerable One says, "Will you leave family life with body or leave family life with mind?"*

[Dhītika] replies, "My seeking to leave family life is not for the sake of body and mind."

The Venerable One says, "If not for the sake of the body-and-mind, who leaves family life at all?"

[Dhītika] replies, "In general, those who leave family life are without me and mine. Because they are without me and mine, the mind does not arise and pass.[70] *Because the mind does not arise and pass, the state is just the normal state of truth.*[71] *Buddhas, similarly, are normal. Their mind is without shape or form. And their body also is like that."*

The Venerable One says, "You will realize great realization and your mind will naturally penetrate to the ultimate. It is good that, through devotion to Buddha, Dharma, and Saṃgha, you will inherit the sacred seeds and cause them to flourish."[72] *Then he lets [Dhītika] leave family life and receive ordination.*[73]

[105] Now to meet the Dharma of the buddhas and to leave family life is the most excellent effect and result. Its method is neither for the sake of *me*, nor for the sake of *mine*, nor for the sake of *body and mind:* it is not that *body and mind* leave family life. The truth that leaving family life is beyond *me and mine* is like this. Because it is beyond *me and mine,* it may be the method of the buddhas. It is simply the usual method[74] of the buddhas. Because it is the usual method of the buddhas, it is beyond *me and mine* and beyond *body and mind.* It is beyond comparison with the triple world. Because it is like this, leaving family life is the supreme method. It is neither sudden nor gradual; it is neither constancy[75] nor a state without constancy; it is neither an arrival nor a departure; it is neither to abide nor to become; it is neither wide nor

---

68. When a person leaves family life and realizes the state of buddha, that person's social standing and gender are irrelevant.

69. A native of Magadha. He eventually succeeded Master Upagupta, becoming the fifth patriarch.

70. In other words, the mind is realized in each moment of the present.

71. 常道 (JODO). 常 (JO) means constant, usual, or normal. 道 (DO), "way," frequently represents the Sanskrit *bodhi* which means the Buddhist state of truth. See Book 1, Glossary.

72. The causes of the state of buddha.

73. *Keitoku-dento-roku,* chap. 1.

74. 常法 (JOHO). 常 (JO), "usual," appears in Master Dhītika's phrase 常道 (JODO), "the normal state of truth"—see note 71. 法 (HO) means method or Dharma.

75. 常 (JO), as in notes 71 and 74.

restricted; it is neither great nor small. It is beyond becoming and beyond non-becoming. Ancestral masters of the one-to-one transmission of the Buddha-Dharma, without exception, leave family life and receive the precepts. The truth of Dhītika meeting now, for the first time, with the Venerable Upagupta and seeking to leave family life, is like this. He left family life and received ordination, learned in practice under Upagupta, and eventually became the fifth ancestral master.

07] *The seventeenth patriarch, the Venerable Saṃghanandi, is the son of the King Treasure-Adornment*[76] *of the city of Śrāvastī.*[77] *Able to speak from birth, he always praises Buddhist matters. At the age of seven he grows averse to worldly pleasures and, in verse, he addresses his parents as follows:*

> *Bowing to the ground before my great benevolent father,*
> *With vandana*[78] *to the mother of my bones and blood,*
> *I now desire to leave family life.*
> *Hopefully, I beseech you, because you are compassionate.*

His father and mother firmly put a stop to this. At last, when he goes all day without eating, they permit him to leave home at home.[79] *They name him Saṃghanandi,*[80] *and order the śramaṇa Zenrita*[81] *to be his teacher. [Thus] he accumulates nineteen years without ever regressing or growing weary. [But] the Venerable One is always thinking to himself, "My body resides in the royal palace. How can this be called leaving family life?" One evening a celestial brightness falls upon [the earth], and [Saṃghanandi] sees a path, flat and level. Unconsciously he walks slowly forward. About ten miles on he arrives before a great rock containing a stone cavern, inside which he at once settles into quietness.*[82] *The father, having missed his son, banishes Zenrita out of the country in search of his son, [but] they do not know where he is. In the following ten years the Venerable One attains the Dharma and receives affirmation, after which he goes, teaching as he travels, to the kingdom of Madai.*[83]

08] The term *"leaving home at home"* was first heard at this time. But, aided by long-accumulated good, [Saṃghanandi] found the level road in the celestial brightness and he finally left the royal palace and went to the stone cavern—

---

76. 宝荘厳王 (HO-SHOGON-O). Sanskrit equivalent not traced.

77. Capital of the ancient Indian kingdom of Kośala.

78. The Sanskrit *vandana* means to venerate or to perform an act of veneration.

79. 在家出家 (ZAIKE-SHUKKE). He remained at home in the royal palace but formally became a monk.

80. "Saṃgha-Joy."

81. His life history is not known. Zenrita represents the sound of the Sanskrit, but the Sanskrit itself has not been traced.

82. 燕寂 (ENJAKU) stands for 燕坐寂静 (ENZA-JAKUJO), or "settled sitting in quietness," an expression for Zazen. 燕 (EN) is used interchangeably with 安 (AN), which means peaceful, stable, or settled.

83. Sanskrit equivalent not known. This story is quoted from *Keitoku-dento-roku*, chap. 2.

truly an excellent example. Those who dislike worldly pleasures and abhor secular dust are the sacred ones. Those who love the five desires[84] and forget about getting free are the common and the stupid. Though the emperors Daiso and Shukuso[85] frequently associated with monks, they still were greedy for the royal position, which they never abdicated. Layman Ro,[86] having left his parent, became a patriarch; [that] is the merit of leaving family life. Layman Ho[87] threw away treasure but failed to throw away dust; [that] might be called extremely stupid. Mister Ro's bodhi-power and Mister Ho's emulation of the ancients do not deserve to be compared. Those who are clear inevitably leave family life. Those who are dull end [their lives] at home, which is the cause and conditions of black karma.

[110] *Zen Master Nangaku Ejo one day spontaneously speaks the following praise: "In general, leaving family life is Dharma without appearance.*[88] *In the heavens above and in the human world, there is nothing to surpass it."*[89]

"Dharma without appearance" means the right Dharma of the Tathāgata; therefore, in the heavens above and in the human world, it is supreme. As to the meaning of *"the heavens above,"* there are the six heavens in the world of desire, there are eighteen heavens in the world of matter, and four kinds [of state] in the world of non-matter, [but] none is on a par with the truth of leaving family life.

[111] Zen Master Banzan Hoshaku says, *"Zen friends! Appropriate learning of the truth is like the earth holding aloft a mountain without recognizing the mountain's solitary steepness, or like a stone containing a jewel without recognizing the jewel's flawlessness. If [learning the truth] is like this, we call it leaving family life."*[90]

The Buddhist Patriarch's right Dharma is not necessarily connected with

---

84. Five desires corresponding to the five senses: desires for sights, sounds, smells, tastes, and sensations.

85. Tang dynasty emperors who lived at the time of Master Nan-yo Echu. See chap. 80, *Tashintsu.*

86. 盧居士 (RO KOJI). 盧 (RO) was the family name of Master Daikan Eno, the sixth patriarch in China. The story of him leaving his mother is recorded in chap. 30, *Gyoji.* The concept 居士 (KOJI), which represents the Sanskrit *gṛhaparti,* or "householder," is explained in chap. 8, *Raihai-tokuzui.* See Book 1, Glossary.

87. Layman Ho-on (?–808). Originally a disciple of Master Sekito Kisen, he later received the Dharma from Master Baso Do-itsu, although he never became a monk. See also chap. 73, *Sanjushichi-bon-bodai-bunbo* and *Shinji-shobogenzo,* pt. 1, nos. 5, 88, 99.

88. 無生 (MUSHO) means "without appearance" or "non-birth." In the latter meaning, it is sometimes used as a synonym for nirvāṇa. In the former meaning, "without appearance," describes 1) the eternity of time, which is without a beginning; and 2) the reality of the present moment, which is cut off from the past and future and therefore without appearance or disappearance. See also discussion in chap. 23, *Gyobutsu-yuigi.*

89. *Tensho-koto-roku,* chap. 8.

90. *Keitoku-dento-roku,* chap. 7.

recognition and non-recognition. Leaving family life is the Buddhist Patriarch's right Dharma, and so its merit is evident.

12] Zen Master Gigen[91] of Rinzai-in temple in Chinshu[92] says, *"In general, those who have left family life should be able to intuit the normal and true view: to intuit [the state of] buddha, to intuit [the state of] demons, to intuit the true, to intuit the false, to intuit the common, and to intuit the sacred. If they are able to intuit like this, they are called true leavers of family life. If they do not distinguish between demons and buddhas, they have just left one nest and entered another nest, and they are called ordinary beings who are producing karma; they still cannot be called true leavers of family life."*[93]

This *"normal and true view"* means deep belief in cause and effect, deep belief in the Three Treasures, and so on. *"To intuit buddha"* means to be clear in mindfulness of the virtues of buddha [both] in the causal process and in the resultant state. We definitely distinguish between the true and the false, and the common and the sacred. If we are unclear with regard to demons and buddhas, we sacrifice learning of the truth and regress and deviate in learning the truth. When we sense the doings of demons, if we do not follow those doings, pursuit of the truth does not regress. This is called the method of a true leaver of family life. Those who randomly consider demon-doings to be the Buddha-Dharma are many; it is a wrongness of recent ages. Students, without delay, should know [the state of] demons and should clarify and practice-and-experience [the state of] buddha.

14] *At the time of the Tathāgata's parinirvāṇa,*[94] *Bodhisattva Mahākāśyapa said to the Buddha, "World-honored One! A tathāgata is perfectly equipped with the power to know the nature of others.*[95] *You surely knew that Sunakṣatra*[96] *would cut off his good roots. Through what causes and circumstances did you permit him to leave family life?"*

The Buddha said, "Good son! In the past, when I first left family life, my younger brother Nanda,[97] *my cousins Ānanda and Devadatta, my son Rāhula, and suchlike,*[98] *all*

---

91. Master Rinzai Gigen (c. 815–867), successor of Master Obaku Ki-un.

92. In modern-day Hopeh province in northeast China.

93. *Rinzai-esho-zenji-goroku.*

94. The term *pari-nirvāṇa,* "complete extinction," represents the Buddha's death, as distinct from *nirvāṇa,* "extinction," which represents the state of non-attachment that the Buddha realized during his lifetime. See Book 1, Glossary.

95. One of the ten powers of a tathāgata. See note 100.

96. 善星 (ZENSHO), lit. "Good Star," represents the Sanskrit *Sunakṣatra.* It is said that Sunakṣatra served the Buddha as an attendant monk, but later returned to the secular world and slandered the Buddha and his teaching. The *Dai-hatsu-nehan-kyo* cites him as an example of an *icchantika* (one who pursues personal desires in the extreme), in whom arose the wrong view that there is no Buddha, Dharma, or nirvāṇa. As a result, he fell into Avīci hell even during his lifetime.

97. Nanda was the son of the Buddha's father, King Śuddhodana, by Śuddhodana's second wife, Mahāprajāpatī. The Buddha's mother, Mahāmāyā, died soon after the Buddha's birth.

98. Suggests other members of the Śākya clan who were in line to become king.

followed me in leaving family life and practicing the truth. If I had not allowed Sunakṣatra to leave family life, that man in due course would have been able to inherit the position of king; free to exercise that power, he would have destroyed the Buddha-Dharma. In view of these causes and circumstances, I immediately permitted him to leave family life and practice the truth. Good son! If the bhikṣu Sunakṣatra had not left family life but still cut off his good roots, in countless ages there would have been no benefit at all. Now, after leaving family life, although he has cut off good roots, he has been able to receive and to retain the precepts; to serve and to venerate aged veterans, eminent patriarchs, and people of virtue; and to practice and to learn from the first dhyāna to the fourth dhyāna.[99] *These are called good causes. Good causes like these can give rise to good ways. Once good ways have arisen, we can practice and learn the truth. Once we have practiced and learned the truth, we will be able to attain the state of anuttara-samyak-saṃbodhi. For this reason, I allowed Sunakṣatra to leave family life. Good son! If I had not allowed the bhikṣu Sunakṣatra to leave family life and receive the precepts I could not be called a tathāgata equipped with the ten powers.*[100] *Good son! A buddha reflects whether living beings possess good ways or non-virtuous ways. This man [Sunakṣatra], although he possesses both such ways, before long may cut off all good roots and possess [only] non-virtuous roots. For what reasons? [Because] ordinary beings like him do not associate with good friends, do not listen to the right Dharma, do not think of good, and do not act in accord with the Dharma. Due to such causes and circumstances, he may cut off good roots and possess [only] non-virtuous roots."*[101]

[117] Remember, although the Tathāgata, the World-honored One, is clearly aware that ordinary beings might become cutters of good roots,[102] in order to bestow upon them the causes of good, he permits them to leave family life: it is great benevolence and great compassion. Becoming a cutter of good roots is the result of not associating with good friends, not listening to the right Dharma, not thinking of good, and not acting in accord with the Dharma. Students today, without fail, should associate closely with good friends. *"A good friend"* means one who maintains that buddhas exist and who teaches that there is wrongness and happiness. One who does not negate

---

99. The four dhyānas are a categorization of the state in Zazen into four stages. See chap. 90, *Shizen-biku.*

100. 如来具足十力 (NYORAI-GUSOKU-JURIKI), or "the ten powers with which a tathāgata is equipped," represents the Sanskrit *daśa-tathāgata-balāni.* See Glossary. A traditional interpretation of the ten powers is as follows: 1) knowing right and wrong; 2) knowing which karmic effects follow from which causes; 3) knowing the various balanced states (four dhyānas, eight states of liberation, three samādhis, et cetera); 4) knowing the superior or inferior makings of others; 5) knowing the desires of others; 6) knowing the states of others; 7) knowing the destinations of others (nirvāṇa, hell, et cetera); 8) knowing the past; 9) knowing life and death; 10) knowing how to end excesses.

101. *Dai-hatsu-nehan-kyo,* fascicle 33.

102. 断善根 (DAN-ZENKON), "cutter of good roots," represents the Sanskrit *icchantika,* which means one who pursues to the end wishes, desires, or inclinations, and who therefore has no belief in the Buddha and no interest in doing good and not doing wrong. See Book 2, Glossary.

cause and effect is called *"a good friend"* and called *"a good counselor."* The preaching of such a person is the right Dharma itself. To think about this truth is *to think good*. To act in this manner may be *to act in accord with the Dharma*. Therefore, irrespective of whether ordinary beings are familiar to us or unfamiliar, we should just encourage them to leave family life and receive the precepts. Do not heed whether or not they will regress in future and do not worry whether or not they will practice. This may truly be Śākyamuni's right Dharma.

[118] *The Buddha addressed the bhikṣus: "Remember, King Yama once opined, 'I will some day get free from this suffering. I will be born in the human world. By obtaining a human body, I will then be able to leave family life, shave beard and hair, wear the three Dharma-robes, and learn the truth as one who has left family life.' Even King Yama had this idea. Much more, you all now have obtained a human body and have been able to become śramaṇas. Therefore, bhikṣus, you should mindfully practice the actions of body, mouth, and mind and should not cause imperfections to occur. You should eliminate the five fetters*[103] *and cultivate the five roots.*[104] *Bhikṣus such as you are should do such training." Then the bhikṣus, hearing the Buddha's preaching, rejoiced and devoutly practiced.*[105]

[119] Clearly we have seen, the longing for a life in the human world, even of King Yama, is like this. A human being who has already been born should, without delay, shave beard and hair, wear the three Dharma-robes, and learn the Buddha's truth. These are the merits of the human world which are beyond other worlds. To have been born in the human world yet nonetheless wantonly to pursue a political path or a worldly career, idly spending one's life as the servant of kings and ministers, encircled by dreams and illusions, and in later ages to proceed towards pitch darkness still without anything upon which to rely, is extremely stupid. Not only have we received the rarely-received human body; we have [also] encountered the rarely-encountered Buddha-Dharma. We should immediately cast aside all in-

---

103. 五結 (GOKETSU). The five fetters, according to one interpretation, are: 1) greed, 2) anger, 3) conceit, 4) envy, 5) meanness. At the same time, 結 (KETSU), "that which ties or hinders," represents the Sanskrit *kleśa*, "affliction." The *Vijñavāda* enumerates six *mūla-kleśa* or fundamental afflictions: 1) *rāga* (vehement desire), 2) *pratigha* (anger), 3) *mūḍha* (confusion), 4) *māna* (self-conceit), 5) *vicikitsā* (doubt), and 6) *dṛṣṭi* (wrong views). Sometimes the former five are regarded as one group, and the five wrong views, *pañca dṛṣṭayah*, are regarded as a second group. See Book 1, Glossary.

104. 五根 (GOKON), from the Sanskrit *pañcendriyāṇi*. In Sanskrit they are: 1) *śraddhā* (belief), 2) *vīrya* (diligence), 3) *smṛti* (mindfulness), 4) *samādhi* (the balanced state), and 5) *prajñā* (wisdom). See Glossary. These roots of good conduct are listed in chap. 73, *Sanjushichi-bon-bodai-bunbo* and in the penultimate chapter of the 12-chapter edition of Shobogenzo, *Ippyaku-hachi-homyo-mon*. See Appendices.

105. *Ki-se-in-hongyo*, fascicle 4. The lit. meaning of 起世因本経 (KI-SE-IN-HONGYO) is "Sutra of Past Occurrences of Causes in the World."

volvements and should swiftly leave family life and learn the truth. Kings, ministers, wives, children, and relatives, inevitably, are encountered everywhere, [but] the Buddha-Dharma, like the uḍumbara flower,[106] is hardly ever encountered. In conclusion, when impermanence suddenly arrives, kings, ministers, friends and relatives, servants, wives and children, and precious treasures, are of no help; each person simply proceeds to the underworld[107] alone. What accompanies us is only our good or bad karma. When we are about to lose the human body, our regret at the loss of the human body might be deep. While we retain a human body we should quickly leave family life. Just this may be the right Dharma of the buddhas of the three times.

[121] For those who have thus left family life there are four kinds of practice of the Dharma, namely, *"the four reliances:"*[108] *1) throughout one's life to sit beneath trees, 2) throughout one's life to wear robes of rags, 3) throughout one's life to beg for food, 4) throughout one's life, in case of illness, to take old medicine.*[109] *One who practices each of these methods truly is called one who has left family life, and truly is called a monk. If we do not practice them we are not called monks. For this reason, they are called practices of the Dharma by those who have left family life.*

Now, in the Western Heavens and the Eastern Lands, what is authentically transmitted by the Buddhist patriarchs is just *practices of the Dharma by those who have left family life.* The state of *a whole life without leaving the temple-forest*[110] is directly furnished with these practices of the Dharma, the four reliances. This is called *"practicing the four reliances."* If [someone] goes against this and establishes five reliances, remember, it is false Dharma: who could believe in it, and who could affirm it? What is authentically transmitted by the Buddhist patriarchs is the right Dharma. To leave family life in accordance with this [right Dharma] is the highest and most valuable human happiness. Therefore, in the Western Heavens of India, Nanda, Ānanda, Devadatta, Aniruddha,[111] Mahānāma[112] and Bhadrika,[113] who were all grand-

---

106. The uḍumbara is a kind of mulberry tree that grows in India. Its flowers form a peel, so it appears to have no flowers. Ancient Indians used the uḍumbara flower as a symbol of something very rare, saying that the flower bloomed only once every three thousand years. See chap. 68, *Udonge.*

107. 黄泉 (OSEN), lit. "yellow spring." In the Taoist tradition in China, yellow represents the earth.

108. 四依 (SHI-E), "the four reliances," are listed in *Daijogi-sho,* fascicle 2.

109. 陳棄薬 (CHINKIYAKU). *Zengaku-daijiten* says that this referred to medicines that had fallen out of use in secular society, such as compounds made from the feces and urine of cattle.

110. 一生不離叢林 (ISSHO-FURI-SORIN). Words of Master Joshu Jushin. See chap. 39, *Dotoku.*

111. Aniruddha was a cousin of the Buddha and one of the Buddha's ten great disciples, said to be foremost in supernatural vision. He lost his eyesight but was excellent at seeing intuitively.

112. This may refer to Mahānāma, who, like Ānanda and Aniruddha, was a son of Śuddhodana's brother Droṇodana (but is said not to have become a monk). Or it may refer to

sons of King Siṃhahanu,[114] and who were of the most noble kṣatriya caste, quickly left family life. It may be an excellent example for later generations. Those today who are not kṣatriyas should not begrudge their bodies. For those who are not even princes, what could there be to begrudge? [The royal Śākyas], coming from the noblest [position] in Jambudvīpa, arrived at the noblest [position] in the Triple World:[115] this was just leaving family life. Kings of lesser nations, and the Licchavi[116] multitudes, vainly treasuring what did not deserve to be treasured, taking pride in what did not warrant pride, and staying where they should not have stayed, failed to leave family life: who could not see them as inept, and who could not see them as extremely stupid? The Venerable Rāhula was the son of the Bodhisattva, and the grandson of King Śuddhodana, who would have bequeathed the throne to him. Nevertheless, the World-honored One pointedly caused him to leave family life. Know that the Dharma of leaving family life is supremely valuable. As the disciple foremost in exact observance,[117] [Rāhula] even today has not yet entered nirvāṇa, but actually abides in the world as a field of happiness for living beings. Among the ancestral masters of the Western Heavens who transmitted the Buddha's right-Dharma-eye treasury, the princes who left family life have been many. Now the first patriarch in China was the third royal son of the king of Koshi.[118] Not attaching importance to his royal status, he received and retained the right Dharma: we have been able clearly to see that leaving family life is supremely valuable. Having a body that cannot rank alongside those [princes], yet being in a position to leave family life, how could we not hasten [to do so]? For what kind of tomorrow should we wait? If we leave family life in haste, without waiting for [the next] exhalation or inhalation, that might be wise. We should remember also that the benevolence of the master under whom we leave family life and receive the precepts may be exactly equal to that of a father and mother.

125] *Zen-en-shingi, fascicle 1, says "The buddhas of the three times all say that to leave family life is to realize the truth. The twenty-eight patriarchs of the Western Heavens and six patriarchs of the Land of Tang who transmitted the Buddha-mind-seal were all*

Mahānāma-koliya, who was one of the five bhikṣus to whom the Buddha delivered his first preaching (but was of the Koliya clan, not the Śākya clan).

113. Bhadrika was one of the five bhikṣus. He belonged to the Śākya clan.

114. King Siṃhahanu, lit. "Having the Jaws of a Lion," was the name of the father of King Śuddhodana and the grandfather of Gautama Buddha.

115. 三界 (SANGAI), "the triple world," in this case means the whole world or the whole Universe.

116. The republic of the Licchavi tribe, with its capital at Vaiśalī, was one of the main republics of the central Gangetic plain in the Buddha's time.

117. 密行第一 (MITSUGYO-DAIICHI), lit. "number one in exact conduct." Each of the Buddha's ten great disciples was known as the foremost in some virtue. Rāhula was said to be foremost in exact observance of śīla.

118. An ancient state of southern India. Sanskrit not traced.

śramaṇas. Perhaps it was by strictly observing the vinaya that they were able to become universal models for the triple world. Therefore, in practicing [Za]zen and inquiring into the truth, the precepts are foremost. Unless we have already departed from excess and guarded against wrong, how can we realize the state of buddha and become patriarchs?"[119]

Even if a temple-forest[120] is in decay, still it may be a gardenia-grove,[121] a place beyond common trees and common grass.[122] Or it is like milk diluted with water. When we want to use milk, we should use this milk diluted with water [but] should not use any other substance. Therefore, the authentic tradition, which is that *the buddhas of the three times all say that to leave family life is to realize the truth,* is supremely valuable. There are no buddhas of the three times who fail to leave family life. Such is the right-Dharma-eye treasury, the fine mind of nirvāṇa, and the supreme [truth of] bodhi, which the buddhas and the patriarchs authentically transmit.

Shobogenzo Shukke-kudoku

A day of the summer retreat in the 7th year of Kencho.[123]

---

119. *Zen-en-shingi,* fascicle 1. This quotation also appears in Shobogenzo, chap. 83, *Shukke,* and chap. 94, *Jukai.*

120. 叢林 (SORIN), lit. "clump of forest," from the Sanskrit *piṇda-vana,* suggests a Buddhist monastery as a place where monks are clustered together. See also note 110. See Glossary.

121. Trees and shrubs of the genus *Gardenia* have fragrant, showy white or yellow flowers.

122. Even in those Buddhist monasteries where the precepts were not obeyed strictly, Master Dogen still felt something in the life of Buddhist monks that was valuable, and beyond the profane situations of the secular world.

123. 1255. This is one of the chapters of the twelve-chapter edition of Shobogenzo written by Master Dogen in the last years of his life. Master Dogen died in 1253. He had given a short lecture on leaving family life (chap. 83, *Shukke*) in 1246. It seems likely that, with a view to giving a longer lecture on the merit of leaving family life, Master Dogen selected many relevant excerpts from sutras and prepared comments on them, and that after Master Dogen's death his successor Master Ko-un Ejo edited Master Dogen's draft and added this concluding note.

[87]

供養諸仏

KUYO-SHOBUTSU

Serving Offerings to Buddhas

Kuyo *means "to serve offerings,"* ***shobutsu*** *means "buddhas," and so* ***kuyo-shobutsu*** *means "to serve offerings to buddhas." There is a tradition in Buddhism of believers serving offerings to buddhas, that is, people who have attained the truth. It is a very natural action, therefore, to serve offerings to buddhas. People who have a purely spiritual viewpoint may feel it unnecessary to serve material offerings, believing that religious reverence is sufficient. Buddhism, however, is not a spiritual religion but a religion of reality, and so it reveres conduct. Thus Buddhism values the action of making real offerings, and affirms the serving of offerings as a demonstration of sincere belief, whether or not the offerings are materially valuable or not. The value is in the serving of the offering itself, which is just Buddhist conduct.*

127] **The Buddha said:**

> *If there were no past ages,*
> *There could be no past buddhas.*
> *If there were no past buddhas,*
> *There would be no leaving family life and receiving ordination.*[1]

Clearly remember, in the three ages,[2] without fail, buddhas exist. Now, with regard to past buddhas, do not say that they have a beginning, and do not say that they have no beginning. If we falsely suppose the existence or nonexistence of a beginning and an end, we are not learning the Buddha-Dharma at all. Those who serve offerings[3] to past buddhas and, leaving family life, follow and obey them, inevitably become buddhas. They become buddhas by virtue of serving buddhas. How could living beings who have never served offerings to even a single buddha themselves become buddha? There can be no becoming buddha without cause.

---

1. *Daibibasha-ron,* chap. 76. Also quoted in the preceding chapter, *Shukke-kudoku.*

2. 三世 (SANZE), or "the three times"; past, present and future; eternity.

3. 供養 (KUYO), "serving offerings," in Buddhist sutras represents the Sanskrit *pūjana,* See Glossary.

[129] *Butsu-hongyo-jikkyo* (*chapter 1, Serving Offerings*)[4] says: *The Buddha told Maudgalyāyana,*[5] *"I remember in the past, in the orders of countless infinite world-honored ones, I planted many good roots and sought after anuttara-samyak-saṃbodhi.*

"Maudgalyāyana! I remember in the past, I assumed the body of a sacred wheel-rolling king and met thirty koṭis of buddhas, all who shared one name and were named Śākya. The Tathāgata[6] *and a host of śrāvakas worshipped them, waited upon them, venerated them, and served offerings to them, furnishing them with the four things: namely, clothes, food and drink, bedding, and medicine. At that time those buddhas did not give me the affirmation that 'You will attain anuttara-samyak-saṃbodhi, and [become] Understander of the World, Teacher of Gods and Human Beings, and World-honored Buddha. In a future age you will be able to realize the right state of truth.'*

"Maudgalyāyana! I remember in the past, I assumed the body of a sacred wheel-rolling king and met eight koṭis of buddhas, all who shared one name and were named Burning Torch.[7] *The Tathāgata and a host of śrāvakas worshipped and venerated them and served them offerings of the four things: namely, clothes, food and drink, bedding, and medicine; and banners, canopies, flowers, and incense. At that time those buddhas did not give me the affirmation that 'You will attain anuttara-samyak-saṃbodhi, and [become] Understander of the World, Teacher of Gods and Human Beings, and World-honored Buddha.'*

"Maudgalyāyana! I remember in the past, I assumed the body of a sacred wheel-rolling king, and met three koṭis of buddhas, all who shared one name and were named Puṣya. The Tathāgata and a host of śrāvakas furnished them completely with offerings of the four things. At that time those buddhas did not give me the affirmation that 'You will become buddha.'"

[131] Besides these, he served offerings to innumerable other buddhas. In the body of a sacred wheel-rolling king he would invariably have ruled four continents; materials for serving offerings to buddhas, truly, must have been plentiful. If he was a great wheel-rolling king he would have been the king of a three-thousandfold world; the service of offerings at that time would be beyond the imagination of common [people] today. Even if the Buddha explained it, it might be hard to comprehend.

[131] *Butsuzo-kyo*[8] (*Chapter 8, The Pure View*) *says: The Buddha told Śāriputra,*[9] *"I remember in the past, seeking after anuttara-samyak-saṃbodhi, I met thirty koṭis of buddhas, all named Śākyamuni. I then, for every one of them, became a sacred wheel-*

---

4. The words in parenthesis are in small characters in the source text—they may have been added by a later editor.

5. One of the Buddha's ten great disciples, foremost in mystical power.

6. The Buddha is referring to himself.

7. 然燈 (NENTO), "Burning Torch," represents the meaning of the Sanskrit *Dīpaṃkara*, the name of a mythical buddha.

8. 仏蔵経 (BUTSUZO-KYO), "The Buddha's Treasury Sutra," from the Sanskrit *Buddhagarba-sūtra*. This was translated from Sanskrit into Chinese by Kumārajīva.

9. One of the Buddha's ten great disciples.

rolling king and throughout a lifetime, for the purpose of seeking after anuttara-samyak-saṃbodhi, I served to buddha and disciples offerings of clothes, food and drink, bedding, and medicine. Yet those buddhas did not affirm me [by saying,] 'In a coming age you will be able to become buddha.' Wherefore? Because I had expectation of gain.[10]

"Śāriputra! I remember in the past, I was able to meet eight thousand buddhas, all named Constant Light.[11] *I then, for every one of them, became a sacred wheel-rolling king and throughout a lifetime, for the purpose of seeking after anuttara-samyak-saṃbodhi, I served to buddha and disciples offerings of clothes, food and drink, bedding, and medicine. Yet those buddhas did not affirm me [by saying,] 'In a coming age you will be able to become buddha.' Wherefore? Because I had expectation of gain.*

"Śāriputra! I remember in the past I met sixty thousand koṭis of buddhas, all named Brightness.[12] *I then, for every one of them, became a sacred wheel-rolling king and throughout a lifetime, for the purpose of seeking after anuttara-samyak-saṃbodhi, I served to buddha and disciples offerings of clothes, food and drink, bedding, and medicine. Yet those buddhas also did not affirm me [by saying,] 'In a coming age you will be able to become buddha.' Wherefore? Because I had expectation of gain.*

"Śāriputra! I remember in a past age I met three koṭis of buddhas, all named Puṣya. I then, for every one of them, became a sacred wheel-rolling king and served offerings of the four things. All did not affirm me—because I was expecting gain.

"Śāriputra! I remember in a past age I was able to meet eighteen thousand buddhas, all named Mountain-King.[13] *The kalpa was called "the Upper Eight." In the orders of all these eighteen thousand buddhas, I shaved my hair and dyed a robe, and I trained in anuttara-samyak-saṃbodhi. All did not affirm me—because I was expecting gain.*

"Śāriputra! I remember in a past age I was able to meet five hundred buddhas, all named Flowers-Above.[14] *I then, for every one of them, became a sacred wheel-rolling king and served offerings of every kind to the buddhas and their disciples. All did not affirm me—because I was expecting gain.*

"Śāriputra! I remember in the past I was able to meet five hundred buddhas, all named Majestic Virtue.[15] *I served offerings to them all. All did not affirm me—because I was expecting gain.*

"Śāriputra! I remember in a past age, I was able to meet two thousand buddhas, all named Kauṇḍinya.[16] *I then, for every one of them, became a sacred wheel-rolling king and served*

---

10. 有所得 (USHOTOKU) means "gain" or "to be after gain" (out to get something) or "expectation" or "grasping" (though it is not necessarily confined to grasping for material possessions). In this case, it means having an ulterior motive other than just serving offerings. The antonym 無所得 (MUSHOTOKU), "non-gaining" or "non-attainment" or "non-expectation," appears in the Heart Sūtra. See chap. 2, *Maka-hannya-haramitsu.*

11. 定光 (JOKO), is another rendering of the Sanskrit name *Dīpaṃkara.* See note 7.

12. 光明 (KOMYO), representing the Sanskrit *Prabhā.*

13. 山王 (SAN-O). The Sanskrit name has not been traced.

14. 華上 (KAJO). The Sanskrit name has not been traced.

15. 威徳 (ITOKU). The Sanskrit name has not been traced.

to the buddhas offerings of every kind. All did not affirm me—because I was expecting gain.

"Śāriputra! I remember in a past age, I met nine thousand buddhas, all named Kāśyapa. I served offerings of the four things to the buddhas and their hosts of disciples. All did not affirm me—because I was expecting gain.

"Śāriputra! I remember in the past, for ten thousand kalpas no buddha appeared. In the first five hundred kalpas of that period, there were ninety thousand pratyekabuddhas. Throughout lifetimes I served them all offerings of clothes, food and drink, bedding, and medicine; and I worshipped and praised them. In the next five hundred kalpas, I served offerings of the four things to a further eighty-four thousand koṭis of pratyekabuddhas, and I worshipped and praised them.

"Śāriputra! After these thousand kalpas there were no more pratyekabuddhas. I then died in Jambudvīpa and was born in a brāhma world, becoming Great King Brahmā. Thus I proceeded for five hundred kalpas, always being born in a brāhma world and becoming Great King Brahmā, never being born in Jambudvīpa. After these five hundred kalpas, I was born down in Jambudvīpa, and I governed Jambudvīpa. [But] when my life ended I was born in the Heaven of the Four Quarter Kings.[17] *When my life there ended, I was born in Trāyastriṃśa Heaven,*[18] *becoming Śakra-devānām-indra. Thus I proceeded, completing five hundred kalpas [before] being born in Jambudvīpa, [then] completing five hundred kalpas being born in a brāhma world and becoming Great King Brahmā.*

"Śāriputra! In nine thousand kalpas, only once was I born in Jambudvīpa. For nine thousand kalpas I was born only in the heavens above. At the time of the holocaust which ends a kalpa, I was born in the Heaven of Luminous Sound,[19] *[but] once the world was created I was again born in a brāhma world. For nine thousand kalpas, I was never [again] born among human beings.*

"Śāriputra! In these nine thousand kalpas, there were no buddhas or pratyekabuddhas, and many living beings fell into evil ways.

"Śāriputra! After the passing of these ten thousand kalpas, there appeared in the world a buddha named Universal Protector Tathāgata,[20] *One who Deserves Offerings,*[21]

---

16. The Sanskrit *Kauṇḍinya* means "coming from Kuṇḍina." Kuṇḍina is the name of a *ṛṣi* (a legendary patriarchal Indian sage), and of a place.

17. 四天王天 (SHI-TEN-O-DEN), from the Sanskrit *Cātur-mahārāja-kāyikā,* the first and lowest of the six heavens in the world of desire. It is said to be located half way down the side of Mt. Sumeru.

18. Trāyastriṃśa Heaven is the second of the six heavens in the world of desire. The Sanskrit *Trāyastriṃśa* means "thirty-three," referring to Śakra-devānām-indra who lives in the center of the heaven and the thirty-two gods who surround him.

19. 光音天 (KO-ON-TEN), from the Sanskrit *Ābhāsvara,* is one of the second group of heavens in the world of matter. Legend says that when gods in this heaven speak, pure light shines from their mouths and turns into words. However, because *Ābhāsvara* belongs in the world of matter, it may be interpreted as a less idealistic place than a brāhma heaven.

20. 普守如来 (FUSHU-NYORAI). 普守 (FUSHU) represents the meaning of an untraced Sanskrit name. 如来 (NYORAI), "Thus-Come," or "One Who Has Arrived at the State of Reality," repre-

Rightly All-Enlightened One,[22] *One who is Perfect in Knowledge and Action,*[23] *One who has Fared Well,*[24] *Understander of the World,*[25] *Supreme One,*[26] *Controller of Men,*[27] *Teacher of Gods and Human Beings,*[28] *World-honored Buddha.*[29] *At that time, when my life finished in a brāhma world and I was born in Jambudvīpa, I became a sacred wheel-rolling king named Communal Heaven,*[30] *whose human life span was ninety thousand years. I spent [this] lifetime serving offerings of all kinds of comforts to that buddha and to ninety koṭis of bhikṣus for ninety thousand years, for the purpose of seeking after anuttara-samyak-saṃbodhi. This Buddha, Universal Protector, also did not affirm me [by saying,] 'In a coming age you will be able to become buddha.' Wherefore? [Because] at that time, I could not fully understand that all dharmas are real form, and I was greedily attached to the gaining view of the calculating self.*

"Śāriputra! During that kalpa there appeared a hundred buddhas, each named differently. I then, for every one of them, became a sacred wheel-rolling king and spent a lifetime serving offerings to buddha and disciples, for the purpose of seeking after anuttara-samyak-saṃbodhi. Yet these buddhas also did not affirm me [by saying,] 'In a coming age you will be able to become buddha.' This was because I was expecting gain.

"Śāriputra! I remember in the past, during the seven hundredth asaṃkhya of kalpas, I was able to meet a thousand buddhas, all named Jambūnada.[31] *I spent lifetimes serving them offerings of the four things. They also did not affirm me—because I was expecting gain.*

"Śāriputra! I remember in the past, again during the seven hundredth asaṃkhya of kalpas, I was able to meet six hundred and twenty myriad buddhas, each named Seeing All Forms.[32] *I then, for every one of them, became a sacred wheel-rolling king, and throughout a lifetime I served offerings of all comforts to buddha and disciples. They also did not affirm me—because I was expecting gain.*

"Śāriputra! I remember in the past, again during the seven hundredth asaṃkhya of kalpas, I was able to meet eighty-four buddhas, all named Imperial Form.[33] *I then, for every one of them, became a sacred wheel-rolling king, and throughout a lifetime I served offerings*

---

sents the Sanskrit *Tathāgata,* which is the first of the ten epithets of a buddha. The other nine epithets follow.

21. 応供 (OGU), from the Sanskrit *arhat.*
22. 正遍知 (SHOHENCHI), from the Sanskrit *samyak-saṃbuddha.*
23. 明行足 (MYOGYOSOKU), from the Sanskrit *vidyā-caraṇa-saṃpanna.*
24. 善逝 (ZENZEI), from the Sanskrit *sugata.*
25. 世間解 (SEKENGE), from the Sanskrit *lokavit.*
26. 無上士 (MUJOJI), from the Sanskrit *anuttara.*
27. 調御丈夫 (CHOGO-JOBU), from the Sanskrit *puruṣa-damya-sārathi.*
28. 天人師 (TENNINSHI), from the Sanskrit *śāstā-deva-manuṣyānām.*
29. 仏世尊 (BUTSU-SESON), or "One in the State of Truth Who Is Honored by the World," from the Sanskrit *buddha-bhagavat.*
30. 共天 (GUTEN). The Sanskrit name has not been traced.
31. In China and Japan this Buddha is usually called 閻浮檀金 (ENBUDAN-GON), "Jambūnada-Gold," representing the Sanskrit *Jambūnada-suvarṇa.*
32. 見一切儀 (KEN-ISSAI-GI). The Sanskrit name has not been traced.
33. 帝相 (TEISO). The Sanskrit name has not been traced.

of all comforts to buddha and disciples. They also did not affirm me—because I was expecting gain.

"Śāriputra! I remember in the past, again during the seven hundredth asaṃkhya of kalpas, I was able to meet fifteen buddhas, all named Sun Bright.[34] *I then, for every one of them, became a sacred wheel-rolling king, and throughout a lifetime I served offerings of all comforts to buddha and disciples. They also did not affirm me—because I was expecting gain.*

"Śāriputra! I remember in a past age, again during the seven hundredth asaṃkhya of kalpas, I was able to meet sixty-two buddhas, all named Good Serenity.[35] *I then, for every one of them, became a sacred wheel-rolling king, and throughout a lifetime I served them offerings of all comforts. They also did not affirm me—because I was expecting gain.*

"Thus I proceeded until I met the Buddha Constant Light,[36] *and instantly attained realization of non-appearance.*[37] *Immediately [the Buddha Constant Light] affirmed me, saying, 'In an age to come, after the passing of asaṃkhya kalpas, you will be able to become a buddha named Śākyamuni Tathāgata, One Who Deserves Offerings, Rightly All-Enlightened One, One Who Is Perfect in Knowledge and Action, One Who Has Fared Well, Understander of the World, Supreme One, Controller of Men, Teacher of Gods and Human Beings, World-honored Buddha.'"*

[141] From meeting in the beginning with thirty koṭis of Śākyamuni Buddhas and serving offerings to them throughout lifetimes until meeting with Constant Light Tathāgata, in all cases he constantly spends lifetimes serving offerings in the body of a sacred wheel-rolling king. Sacred wheel-rolling kings may often be more than eighty-thousand years of age. [His service of offerings] is the service of offerings of all kinds of comforts throughout a lifetime of sometimes ninety thousand years and [sometimes] eighty thousand years. *"Constant Light Buddha"* means Burning Torch Tathāgata.[38] [In both sutras] he meets thirty koṭis of Śākyamuni Buddhas: the preaching of the *Butsu-hongyo-jikkyo* and of the *Butsuzo-kyo* are the same.

[141] *Śākya Bodhisattva in the first asaṃkhya met, attended, and served offerings to*

---

34. 日明 (NICHIMYO). The Sanskrit name has not been traced.

35. 善寂 (ZENJAKU). The Sanskrit name has not been traced.

36. Dīpaṃkara Buddha.

37. 無生忍 (MUSHONIN) stands for 無生法忍 (MUSHO-HO-NIN), which means indulgence towards, or realization of, the Dharma which is without appearance. 忍 (NIN) represents the Sanskrit *kṣānti*, or "indulgence"; at the same time, 忍 (NIN) can be interpreted as representing the character 認 (NIN), "recognition," or "realization." 忍法 (NINPO), or "indulgence towards the Dharma," is a traditional expression of the state in which a person realizes the Four Noble Truths. See chap. 86, *Shukke-kudoku*, para. [91]. 無生 (MUSHO), "non-appearance" or "non-birth," expresses the state, or teaching, or fact, of both instantaneousness and eternity.

38. Master Dogen identified the names Constant Light (the rendering of Dīpaṃkara used in the *Butsuzo-kyo*) and Burning Torch (the rendering of Dīpaṃkara used in the *Butsu-hongyo-jikkyo*). See notes 7 and 11.

seventy-five thousand buddhas, the first named Śākyamuni and the last named Jewel-Topknot.[39] *In the second asaṃkhya he met, attended, and served offerings to seventy-six thousand buddhas, the first that same Jewel-Topknot and the last named Burning Torch.*[40] *In the third asaṃkhya he met, attended, and served offerings to seventy-seven thousand buddhas, the first that same Burning Torch and the last named Excellent Reflection.*[41] *While cultivating the signs*[42] *and karma of different maturation*[43] *for ninety one kalpas, he met, attended, and served offerings to six buddhas, the first that same Excellent Reflection and the last named Kāśyapa.*[44]

142] In general, in his service of offerings to buddhas for three great asaṃkhyas of kalpas, there was nothing spared at all, beginning with [his own] body and life, through kingdoms and cities, wives and children, the seven treasures, male and female [servants], and so on. It is beyond the common intellect. He served offerings of silver bowls filled to the brim with golden millet, or of gold and silver bowls filled to the brim with seven-treasure millet. Or he served offerings of azuki beans, or flowers of water and land, or sandalwood, aloes, and other incense. Or he served to the Buddha Burning Torch offerings of five-stalked blue lotus flowers bought for five hundred pieces of gold and silver.[45] Or he served this [Buddha] with the offering of a deer-skin robe.[46] As a general rule in making offerings to buddhas, it is not that we serve offerings of what might be essential to buddhas: without delay, while life remains to us, without passing any time in vain, we serve offerings. Of what benefit to buddhas are even gold and silver? Of what benefit to buddhas are even incense and flowers? Rather, that [buddhas] accept is due to great kindness and great compassion in allowing living beings to increase merit.

144] The Mahāparinirvāṇa-sūtra[47] (fascicle 22) says: *The Buddha preached, "Good sons! I remember countless infinite nayutas of kalpas ago, when the world was called Sahā, there was a World-honored Buddha named Śākyamuni Tathāgata, One Who Deserves Offerings, Rightly All-Enlightened One, One Who Is Perfect in Knowledge and*

---

39. 宝髻 (HOKEI), represents the meaning of the Sanskrit *Ratnaśikhin.*

40. Dīpaṃkara.

41. 勝観 (SHOKAN), represents the meaning of the Sanskrit *Vipaśyin.* Vipaśyin is the first of the seven ancient Buddhas. In chap. 15, *Busso,* Vipaśyin Buddha is called 広説 (KOSETSU), "Universal Preaching."

42. 相 (SO) refers to 三十二相 (SANJUNISO), the thirty-two signs which distinguish the body of a buddha.

43. 異熟業 (IJUKU-GO), i.e., performing various good deeds. See chap. 84, *Sanji-no-go.*

44. The sixth of the seven ancient buddhas, the last being Śākyamuni Buddha himself. *Kusha-ron* (*Abhidharma-kośa-śāstra*), fascicle 18.

45. *Butsu-hongyo-jikkyo* says *"For two asaṃkhya kalpas he served offerings of seven blue lotus flowers to the Buddha Burning Torch."*

46. Ibid. *"He served offerings to the Buddha Burning Torch by spreading a deer-skin robe, and his own hair, over the mud."*

47. *Dai-hatsu-nehan-kyo (Sutra of the Great Demise).*

Action, One Who Has Fared Well, Understander of the World, Supreme One, Controller of Men, Teacher of Gods and Human Beings, World-honored Buddha. For many great assemblies he expounded the Great Nirvāṇa Sutra like this. I at that time, turning from a place of good friends, heard that that Buddha was going to preach the Great Nirvāṇa Sutra to a great assembly. After I had heard this, my heart rejoiced, and I wanted to prepare a service of offerings. Being of humble abode and without possessions, I intended to barter my own body. Unfortunately it did not sell. Then, intending to return home, I met a man on the road and told him, "I want to sell my body. Could you not buy me, sir?"

The man replied, "The work I have at my home is beyond human endurance. If you could do it, I would buy you."

I then asked him, "What work is there that is beyond human endurance?"

Veritably, that man replied, "I have a terrible illness, for which a good doctor has prescribed [the following] medicine: I am to take, daily, three pounds of human flesh. If you can really supply me with three pounds of your body's flesh every day, I will give you five gold coins."

Then, having heard this, I rejoiced in my heart. I told him further, "If you give me the coins and allow me seven days, when I have finished my own business, I will be obliged to return at once and work for you."

Veritably, that man replied, "Seven days is impossible. If you are able to do exactly as [I have] described, I will permit you one day."

Good sons! I then took those coins and returned to the place of the Buddha. I bowed my head and face to his feet and offered to him all that I possessed. After that, with a sincere mind, I listened to this Sutra. At this time, being dull and stupid, although I was able to hear the Sutra, I was only able to receive and retain the words of one verse:

> *The Tathāgata experienced nirvāṇa,*
> *And forever eradicated life and death.*
> *If, with sincerity, you listen,*
> *Constantly you will attain boundless joy.*

After receiving this verse, I went straight back to the home of that sick man. Good sons! Although then I indeed gave him three pounds of flesh every day, with remembrance of the verse as a direct and cooperating cause, I completed a month without feeling pain and without missing a day. Good sons! Due to this direct and cooperating cause, the illness was cured and my own body healed without even a scar. At that time, seeing that my body was perfectly sound, I instantly established the will to anuttara-samyak-saṃbodhi. The power of even a single verse can be like this; how much more might be [the power] of completely receiving, retaining, reading, and reciting [the Sutra]! Seeing that this Sutra has such efficacy, I established the will over and over, and vowed that in future, if I were able to realize the Buddhist truth, I would be named Śākyamuni Buddha. Good sons! It is by virtue of the direct and cooperating influence of this single verse that I am today caused to expound [the Sutra] completely to the gods and human beings in the great assembly. Good sons! Therefore this heavenly state of nirvāṇa is unthinkable. It ac-

complishes countless and infinite merits. Just this is the profound secret treasury of the buddha-Tathāgatas."

148] The bodhisattva of that age who sold his body is the antecedent of the Śākyamuni Buddha of the present age. By referring to other sutras [we can know that] the beginning of the first asaṃkhya of kalpas was the time when he served offerings to the old Śākyamuni Buddha. In that age he was a tiler, and his name was Great Brightness. When he served offerings to the old Śākyamuni Buddha and disciples, he made offerings of three kinds: straw cushions,[48] sugared drinks, and torches.[49] At that time he made the following vow: *"[My] national land, name, life span, and disciples shall be exactly the same as those of this Śākyamuni Buddha."* The vow he made then has already been realized today. Therefore, when thinking of serving offerings to buddhas, never say that your body is destitute, and never say that your household is destitute. [This story of] selling one's own body in order to serve offerings to buddhas is the right Dharma of the present Great Master Śākyamuni. Who could not be overjoyed by it? In it [the bodhisattva] meets a taskmaster who every day slices off three pounds of body flesh: [this] would be beyond the endurance of any other person, even a friend in virtue. Yet aided by a profound will to serve offerings, [the bodhisattva] possesses the virtue [described] now. Our listening now to the Tathāgata's right Dharma may be body flesh from that distant age being distributed. The present four-line verse is beyond being traded for five gold coins. During three asaṃkhyas [of kalpas] or one hundred great kalpas, in the reception of lives and the relinquishment of lives, it has not been forgotten; and in the orders of that buddha and this buddha it has continued to be substantiated: truly, it may possess unthinkable virtue. Disciples to whom the Dharma has been bequeathed should receive and retain it with profound humility. The Tathāgata himself has already proclaimed that *"The power of even a single verse can be like this."* [The virtue of the verse] may be immensely profound.

50] The Lotus Sutra says:

> *If people, to stūpas and shrines,*
> *To jewel images and painted images,*
> *With flowers, incense, banners, and canopies*
> *Reverently serve offerings;*
> *[Or] if they cause others to make music,*
> *To beat drums, to blow horns and conchs,*
> *[To play] panpipes, flutes, lutes, lyres,*
> *Harps, gongs, and cymbals,*
> *And many fine sounds such as these*

---

48. 艸座 (SOZA), lit. "seats of grass," from the Sanskrit *tṛṇa-śayyā*, lit. "bed of grass."

49. 然燈 (NENTO), lit. "Burning Torch" (as in the Chinese rendering of the name of Dīpaṃkara Buddha), in this case suggests small paper torches, tapers, or candles.

They bring forth entirely as offerings;
Or [if] with joyful hearts,
They sing the praises of the Buddha's virtue,
Even in one small sound,
They all have realized the Buddha's truth.
If people whose mind is distracted
With even a single flower
Serve offerings to a painted [Buddha] image,
They will gradually see numberless buddhas.
Again, people who do prostrations
Or who simply join palms,
Even those who raise a hand
Or slightly lower the head,
And thus serve an offering to an image
Will gradually see countless buddhas,
Will naturally realize the supreme truth,
And will widely save numberless multitudes.[50]

[151] This is the very brains and eyes of the buddhas of the three times, and we should strive headlong to meet the sages and emulate them. Do not pass time in vain! Great Master Sekito Musai says, *"Do not pass time in vain!"*[51] Virtue like this, in every case, realizes buddha. Past, present, or future, it must be the same: there can never be two or be three.[52] People who, due to the cause of serving offerings to buddhas, realize the effect of becoming buddha, are like this.

[152] The ancestral Master Nāgārjuna[53] said:

When we are pursuing the buddha-effect,
To praise a single verse,
To chant a single 'namas,'[54]
To burn a single pinch of incense,
To offer a single flower:
Small actions like these,
Without fail, enable us to become buddha.[55]

---

50. Lotus Sutra, *Hoben (Expedient Means).* See LS 1.116.

51. 光陰莫虚度 (KOIN MUNA*[shiku]* WATA*[ru koto]* NAKA*[re]*), appears at the end of the verse *Sandokai* by Master Sekito Kisen (700–790), successor of Master Seigen Gyoshi.

52. In other words, one law applies in the past, present, and future. The expression mirrors an expression in another part of Lotus Sutra, *Hoben.* See LS 1.106.

53. The fourteenth patriarch in India, to whom *Daichidoron* is attributed.

54. The Sanskrit *namas* means "bowing," "obeisance," or "reverential salutation." In this case it suggests the reciting of devotions to Buddha, Dharma, and Saṃgha. See chapter 88, *Kie-sanbo.*

55. *Daichidoron,* fascicle 7.

Although this is the preaching of the ancestral Master and Bodhisattva Nāgārjuna alone, we should devote our life to it. Still more, it is the preaching of the Great Master Śākyamuni Buddha, as authentically transmitted and upheld by the ancestral Master Nāgārjuna. That we now, climbing the treasure-mountain of the Buddha's truth and entering the treasure-ocean of the Buddha's truth, fortunately have obtained treasure, is most joyful. It may be the influence of vast kalpas of offerings to buddhas. We must not doubt that *without fail, we are able to become buddha*: it is assured. The preaching of Śākyamuni Buddha is like this.

[153] *Furthermore, there are cases of a small [direct] cause having a great effect, and of small circumstantial causes having great results. When we are pursuing the Buddha's truth, to praise one verse, to chant 'namas buddha' once, or to burn one pinch of incense, inevitably enables us to become buddha. Still more, if we hear and know that all dharmas are real form,*[56] *beyond appearance and disappearance and beyond non-appearance and non-disappearance, then whatever causal and circumstantial karma we enact, we will never fail at all.*[57]

The ancestral Master Nāgārjuna has intimately received the authentic transmission of the World-honored One's preaching, which is as conspicuous as this. [This preaching] possesses the right and traditional transmission of the golden words of genuine truth. Even if it is the preaching of ancestral Master Nāgārjuna himself, it should not be compared with the preaching of other masters. That we have been able to meet his authentic transmission, and propagation, of that which the World-honored One displayed, is most joyful. Do not randomly compare these sacred teachings with the empty elaborations of common teachers of the eastern land.

[154] The ancestral Master Nāgārjuna said: *Furthermore, because buddhas revere Dharma, they serve offerings to Dharma and make the Dharma their teacher. Why? [Because] the buddhas of the three times all make 'all dharmas are real form' into their teacher.*

[Someone] asks, "Why do they not serve offerings to the Dharma within their own bodies, but [only] serve offerings to the Dharma in others?" [I] answer: They follow the way of the world. When a bhikṣu wants to serve offerings to the treasure of Dharma, he does not serve offerings to the Dharma within his own body, but serves offerings to others who are retaining Dharma, who know Dharma, and who understand Dharma. Buddhas also are like this. Even though the Dharma is present in their own bodies, they serve offerings to the Dharma in other buddhas.

[Someone] asks, "Given that buddhas do not seek to gain merit, for what reason do they serve offerings?" [I] answer: Buddhas, for countless asaṃkhyas of kalpas, cultivate all virtues and constantly practice all forms of good, but not in pursuit of reward. Because

---

56. 諸法実相 (SHOHOJISSO), from LS 1.68, is the title of chap. 49, *Shoho-jisso.*

57. *Daichidoron*, fascicle 7.

they revere virtue [itself], therefore they perform the service of offerings. For instance when the Buddha was living there was a blind bhikṣu who, though his eyes saw nothing, sewed robes by his own hand. Once his needle came unthreaded and he said, "Is there any lover of merit who will thread the needle for me?" Then the Buddha came there and told the bhikṣu, "I am a person who loves merit, so I have come to thread your needle for you." This bhikṣu recognized the Buddha's voice. He promptly stood up, put on a robe, and bowed at the Buddha's feet. He said to the Buddha, "The Buddha has already fully accomplished virtue. Why did you say that you love merit?" The Buddha replied, "Although I have accomplished virtue already, I profoundly know the causes of virtue, the effects and results of virtue, and the power of virtue. That I now have attained pre-eminence among all living beings stems from this virtue. For this reason, I love it." The Buddha, having praised virtue for this bhikṣu, then spontaneously preached to him the Dharma. This bhikṣu attained purity of the Dharma-eye whose clarity was beyond eyes of flesh.[58]

[157] I heard this story long ago during a night-time talk in the room of my late Master. Thereafter I was able to check it against the sentences of *[Dai]chidoron*. The instruction of the ancestral Master of the Dharma-transmission had been clear and he had left nothing out. These sentences are in *[Dai]chidoron* [fascicle] number 10. That the buddhas invariably treat *all dharmas are real form* as their great teacher is evident. Śākyamuni also approved the usual method of all the buddhas. Their treating *all dharmas are real form* as their great teacher means their service of offerings to and veneration of the three treasures of Buddha, Dharma, and Saṃgha. Buddhas, for countless asaṃkhyas of kalpas, accumulate innumerable virtues and good roots without seeking any reward at all; they simply serve offerings in veneration of virtue itself. Having arrived at the state that is the buddha-effect of bodhi, they still love small [acts of] virtue, and so [the Buddha] threads the needle for the blind bhikṣu. If we hope to clarify the virtue that is the buddha-effect, the present story is an exact account of it. Therefore, the virtue which is the buddha-effect of bodhi, and the truth which is *all dharmas are real form*, are not as in the thoughts of common men in the world today. Common men today think that *all dharmas are real form* might apply to the commitment of wrongs, and they think that the buddha-effect of bodhi might only relate to gain.[59] False views like these, even if they see eighty thousand kalpas, never escape the essentialist view of past kalpas[60] and the trivialist view of future kalpas.[61]

---

58. *Daichidoron*, fascicle 10.

59. 有所得 (USHOTOKU). See note 10.

60. 本劫本見 (HONGO-HONKEN), the view that essences are eternal (e.g. the Platonic view), is a traditional expression of idealism. This view is more commonly represented as 常見外道 (JOKEN-GEDO), lit. "eternity-view non-Buddhism" (see, for example, chap. 89, *Shinjin-inga*).

61. 末劫末見 (MATSUKO-MAKKEN) represents the materialist view, which is trivial because it does not recognize that good actions in the present will produce good effects in the future. This view is more commonly represented as 断見外道 (DANKEN-GEDO), lit. "cutting view non-

How can they perfectly realize the *all dharmas are real form* that *buddhas alone, together with buddhas,*[62] perfectly realize? The reason [they cannot] is that what *buddhas alone, together with buddhas,* perfectly realize is just *all dharmas are real form.*

59] *Broadly there are ten kinds of service of offerings, namely: 1) serving offerings to a person; 2) serving offerings to a caitya; 3) serving offerings to what is actually present; 4) serving offerings to what is not actually present; 5) service of offerings performed by oneself; 6) service of offerings performed by others; 7) serving offerings of property; 8) serving offerings of excellence; 9) untainted service of offerings; 10) serving offerings of attainment of the state of truth.*[63]

60] Among these, "*Number One, serving offerings to a person,*" is [explained] as follows: *Performing the service of offerings to a buddha's physical body is called serving offerings to a person.*

60] *Number two: making offerings to a Buddha's shrine is called serving offerings to a caitya.*[64] *Sogi-ritsu*[65] *says, "One containing bones*[66] *is called a stūpa.*[67] *One without bones is referred to as a caitya." Some say that both are called caityas. Further, the Sanskrit word stūpa,*[68] *pronounced "chuba,"*[69] *is here*[70] *translated as "square tomb" or "shrine." The Āgamas say "shicha."*[71]

Buddhism," that is the nihilistic, or materialistic view, which denies continuation into the future of the moral cause and effect relation. In the compound 本末 (HONMATSU), 本 (HON) and 末 (MATSU) form a pair of opposites: beginning and end, substance and detail, origin and future, essence and trivialities, et cetera. Therefore the parallel expressions 本劫本見 (HONGO-HONKEN) and 末劫末見 (MATSUKO-MAKKEN) include a double play on words: 本 (HON) means 1) essence, and 2) past; and 末 (MATSU) means 1) trivialities, and 2) future.

62. 唯仏与仏 (YUIBUTSU-YOBUTSU), again from LS 1.68, is the title of Shobogenzo, chap. 91.

63. *Daijogi-sho,* fascicle 14.

64. 支提 (SHIDAI) is a purely phonetic transliteration of the Sanskrit *caitya.* MW defines a caitya as "a funeral monument or stūpa or pyramidal column containing the ashes of deceased persons." In LSW, on the other hand, a distinction is drawn between a caitya as a pagoda in which sutras are deposited, and a stūpa as a pagoda in which sacred relics are deposited.

65. 僧祇律 (SOGI-RITSU), short for 摩訶僧祇律 (MAKASOGI-RITSU), a 40-fascicle translation of the vinaya of the Mahāsaṃghika School, or School of the Great Saṃgha, one of the two principal Hīnayāna schools, the other being the Sthavira School (School of the Elders; in Pali *Theravāda*). The Chinese translation of *Maka-sogi-ritsu* was accomplished by Buddhabhadra and Hokken during the Eastern Ch'in dynasty (317 to 419).

66. 舎利 (SHARI) represents the sound of the Sanskrit *śarīra,* which means bones or relics. See Book 1, Glossary.

67. 塔婆 (TOBA), represents the sound of the Sanskrit *stūpa.* At the same time, 塔 (TO) means tower, pagoda, or stūpa. See Book 1, Glossary.

68. 塔婆 (TOBA), as in the preceding note.

69. 偸婆 (CHUBA), a closer transliteration of the Sanskrit *stūpa,* using Chinese characters whose meaning is not relevant.

70. China.

71. 支徴 (SHICHO) is a purely phonetic transliteration of the Sanskrit *caitya.* A note in small characters in the source text indicates that, in this case, 徴 (CHO) should be pronounced not as *cho* but as *cha.*

Whether we call it a stūpa or whether we call it a caitya, it appears to be the same. On the other hand, Great Zen Master Nangaku [E]shi's[72] *Hokke-senbo*[73] says: *"Whole-heartedly we bow in veneration to the śarīras, to the images of honored ones, to the caityas, to the wonderful stūpas, and to the Tathāgata Abundant Treasures and the treasure-stūpa that is his whole body,*[74] *of worlds in the ten directions."* Clearly, [in these words] caityas and stūpas, śarīras and images of honored ones, seem to be separate.

[162] *Sogi-ritsu* (fascicle 33) says: *Dharma regarding stūpas: The Buddha was staying in the kingdom of Kośala and wandering. On one occasion a Brāhman who was plowing the earth saw the World-honored One going by. Holding his ox-stick on the ground for support, he bowed to the Buddha. The World-honored One, having seen this, smiled. The [accompanying] bhikṣus said to the Buddha, "For what reason did you smile? We solely desire to hear."*

The Buddha then told the bhikṣus, "This Brāhman now has bowed to two world-honored ones."

The bhikṣus said to the Buddha, "Which two buddhas?"

The Buddha told the bhikṣus, "In his bowing to me, right under his stick there was a stūpa of Kāśyapa Buddha."

The bhikṣus said to the Buddha, "We beg to see the stūpa of Kāśyapa Buddha."

The Buddha told the bhikṣus, "You must request from this Brāhman this plot together with its mass of earth."

The bhikṣus at once requested it, whereupon the Brāhman at once donated it. Having obtained [the land], the World-honored One then manifested a seven-treasure stūpa of Kāśyapa Buddha. Its height was one yojana, and the width of its front was a half yojana. The Brāhman, upon seeing it, immediately said to the Buddha, "World-honored One! My family name is Kāśyapa. This will be my Kāśyapa's stūpa."

Then the World-honored One, at that same abode, fashioned a stūpa for Kāśyapa Buddha. The bhikṣus said to the Buddha, "World-honored One! May we contribute mud and earth, or not?"

The Buddha said, "You may contribute them." Then he preached the following verse:

> *Hundreds of thousands of pounds of pure gold,*[75]
> *Brought for alms-giving,*
> *Do not equal a single ball of mud*
> *Used, with devout mind, to build a Buddha's stūpa.*

---

72. Master Nangaku Eshi (515–577), the second patriarch of the Tendai Sect in China. "Great Zen Master" is his title in the Tendai Sect.

73. 法華懺法 (HOKKE-SENBO), short for 法華三昧懺儀 (HOKKE-ZANMAI-SENGI), which is said to have been written by Master Tendai Chigi, the third patriarch of the Tendai Sect.

74. Alludes to Lotus Sutra, *Ken-hoto (Seeing the Treasure-Stūpa)*. See LS 2.172.

75. 擔 (TAN) is a unit of weight approximately equal to 132 pounds, or 60 kilos.

64] *At that time the World-honored One himself constructed the stūpa for Kāśyapa Buddha. Its base was four-sided and was surrounded by a handrail. [The mound] was of circular construction, in two layers, with square tusks protruding in the four [directions]. The top, which was decked with banners and canopies, showed a long spire of rings.*[76] *The Buddha said, "The method of building a stūpa should be like this." The stūpa had been completed. The World-honored One, because he venerated the buddhas of the past, then personally performed prostrations. The bhikṣus said to the Buddha, "World-honored One! May we perform prostrations, or not?" The Buddha said, "You may." Then he preached the following verse:*

> *People's hundreds of thousands of [gifts of] gold,*
> *Brought for alms-giving,*
> *Do not equal one good mind*
> *Bowing in veneration to a Buddha's stūpa.*

65] *At that time people of the world, hearing that the World-honored One had built the stūpa, came bearing incense and flowers to offer to the World-honored One. The World-honored One, because he served offerings to the buddhas of the past, then received the incense and flowers and took them to serve as offerings to the stūpa. The bhikṣus said to the Buddha, "May we serve offerings, or not?" The Buddha said, "You may." Then he preached the following verse:*

> *Hundreds of thousands of carts of pure gold,*
> *Brought for alms-giving,*
> *Do not equal one good mind*
> *With flowers and incense serving offerings to a stūpa.*

65] *At that time a great gathering came together like a cloud. The Buddha told Śāriputra, "You will preach the Dharma for [these] people." The Buddha then preached the following verse:*

> *Hundreds of thousands of Jambudvīpas,*
> *Filled with alms of pure gold,*
> *Do not equal one gift of Dharma*[77]
> *That causes others accordingly to train.*

At that time, among those seated in the assembly, there were some who attained the truth. The Buddha then preached the following verse:

> *Hundreds of thousands of worlds,*
> *Filled with alms of pure gold,*

---

76. 輪相 (RINSO). This refers to an ornament still often seen on top of stūpas in Tibet and Nepal, and pagodas in China and Japan; a vertical pole spears a row of rings (usually nine rings) that get smaller as they go higher.

77. 法施 (HOSE), "giving of Dharma," from the Sanskrit *dharma-dāna,* is one of the three kinds of giving. The other two are 財施 (ZAISE), "giving of goods," from the Sanskrit *āmiṣa-dāna,* and 無畏施 (MUISE), "giving of fearlessness," from the Sanskrit *abhaya-dāna.*

Do not equal one gift of Dharma
According to which we see the genuine truth.

[166] *At that time the Brāhman attained indestructible belief. At once he set before the stūpa a meal for the Buddha and the Saṃgha. Then King Prasenajit,*[78] *upon hearing about the World-honored One building Kāśyapa Buddha's stūpa, ordered seven hundred carts to be loaded with tiles and he visited the Buddha's place. He bowed his head and face to the [Buddha's] feet and said to the Buddha, "World-honored One! I desire to extend this stūpa. May I do so, or not?" The Buddha said, "You may." The Buddha told the great King, "During a past age, at the time of Kāśyapa Buddha's parinirvāṇa, there was a king named Good Fortune*[79] *who intended to build a stūpa of the seven treasures. Then a retainer said to the King, 'In a future age people who are against the Dharma will appear and will destroy this stūpa, acquiring heavy sin. Solely I beseech you, Great King, make [the stūpa] out of tiles, and cover the surface with gold and silver. If someone takes the gold and silver, the stūpa will still be able to remain intact.' The King, as the retainer advised, built [the stūpa] out of tiles and covered it with gold leaf. Its height was one yojana, and the width of its front was a half yojana. The handrail was made of copper. After seven years, seven months, and seven days [the stūpa] was built. After its completion, [the King] served offerings of incense and flowers to [Kāśyapa] Buddha and to the Saṃgha of bhikṣus." King Prasenajit said to the Buddha, "That king was abundant with merit and he possessed rare treasures. Now I shall build, but I will not be able to equal that king." Immediately he started building and after seven months and seven days [the stūpa] was complete. After completing [the stūpa], [King Prasenajit] served offerings to the Buddha and to the Saṃgha of bhikṣus.*

[168] *The method of building a stūpa: The base is four-sided and surrounded by a handrail. [The mound] is of circular construction, in two layers, with square tusks protruding in the four [directions]. The top is decked with banners and canopies, and shows a long spire of rings. If [people] say that the World-honored One, having dispelled greed, anger, and delusion, [still] has recourse to such a stūpa, for that they will acquire a sin [equal to] transgressing the vinaya, because the karmic retribution will be heavy. This is called "the method of building a stūpa."*

[168] *Stūpa construction: When building a saṃghārāma,*[80] *first survey in advance good land to make into the site for a stūpa. Stūpas must not be located in the south and must not be located in the west. They should be located in the east or should be located in the north. The monks' land must not encroach on the Buddha's land, and the Buddha's land must not encroach on the monks' land. If a stūpa is close to a forest [containing] corpses, and if dogs might carry in leftovers and desecrate the site, a perimeter fence should be built. Monks' quarters should be built in the west or in the south. Water from the monks' land must not be allowed to run onto the Buddha's land, [but] water from the Buddha's land*

---

78. The king of Kośala, and a lay disciple of the Buddha.

79. 吉利 (KITSURI) may represent the meaning of a Sanskrit name or it may be a transliteration from Sanskrit. The original Sanskrit name has not been traced.

80. A monastery or temple.

may run onto the monks' land. A stūpa should be built on a high and prominent site. It is not permissible, within the stūpa perimeter, to wash or to dye robes or to dry them in the sun, or to wear leather shoes, or to cover the head, or to cover the shoulder,[81] *or to hack and spit on the ground. If [people] speak as follows: "Does the World-honored One, already having dispelled greed, anger, and delusion, [still] need such a stūpa?" then they will acquire a sin [equal to] transgressing the vinaya, because the karmic retribution will be heavy. This is called "stūpa construction."*

70] *Stūpa niches: At that time King Prasenajit visited the Buddha, bowed head and face at his feet, and said to the Buddha, "World-honored One! In building the stūpa for Kāśyapa Buddha, may we make niches, or not?" The Buddha said, "You may. During a past age, after Kāśyapa Buddha's parinirvāṇa, the King Good Fortune erected a stūpa for [Kāśyapa] Buddha, and in its four aspects he built niches. For their upper parts he fashioned images of lions and all sorts of colorful paintings; for their fronts he made railings. [The niches] were a place to put flowers. Inside the niches he hung banners and canopies." If people say that the World-honored One, having dispelled greed, anger, and delusion, still takes pleasure in his own glorification, they will acquire a sin [equal to] transgressing the vinaya and the karmic retribution will be heavy. This is called "stūpa niches."*

71] Clearly we have seen that, in the state beyond the buddha-effect of bodhi, to erect a *stūpa* to eternal buddhas and to perform prostrations and offerings to it, is the usual method of the buddhas. Episodes like this are numerous, but for the present I shall just quote this one. With respect to the Buddha-Dharma, the Existence School[82] is supreme, and within that [School] the vinaya[83] is most fundamental. The vinaya was first brought [to China] by Hokken,[84] after he had cleared a way through brambles and thorns to India

---

81. The kaṣāya is usually worn over the left shoulder, with the right shoulder bared.

82. 有部 (UBU) stands for 説一切有部 (SETSU-ISSAI-U-BU), lit. "School that Preaches that All Things Exist." In a narrow sense, this represents the Sarvāstivāda School. In a broader sense, it may be interpreted as the lineage which, through Zazen, affirms real existence.

83. 僧祇律 (SOGI-RITSU), lit. "Saṃgha-Discipline," in a narrow sense, stands for 磨訶僧祇律 (MAKASOGI-RITSU) which was the name of the vinaya of the Mahāsaṃghika School (see note 65). In a broader sense, 僧祇律 (SOGI-RITSU) may simply be interpreted as the authentically-transmitted vinaya of the Buddha. From a scholarly point of view, the Mahāsaṃghika School and the Sarvāstivāda School are opposed. JEBD notes: *"According to the Sarvāstivādin tradition, the Buddhist order split into two schools as a result of Mahādeva's heresy: his followers formed the Mahāsaṃghika School, while the more conservative monks who rejected his new theories formed the Sthavira. In the third century after the demise of the Buddha, the Sarvāstivāda School emerged from the Sthavira."* On the one hand, this historical opposition of the two schools may not have been recognized in Master Dogen's time. On the other hand, it may be argued that Master Dogen strongly revered the true Buddhist lineage which affirms the existence of this world and at the same time he strongly revered the traditional vinaya which belongs to that lineage, without discriminating between one sect and another.

84. Became a monk in his childhood and departed for India in 399. After a six-year journey filled with hardships (brambles and thorns), he traced the history of the Buddha, learnt Sanskrit, and obtained Sanskrit texts of the tripiṭaka (sūtra, vinaya, and abhidharma), before returning to

and climbed Vulture Peak. The Dharma that has been authentically transmitted from patriarch to patriarch is exactly in conformity with the Doctrine of Existence.

[172] *Number 3, to serve offerings to what is actually present, means directly to face the bodies of buddhas, and caityas, and to perform the service of offerings.*

[172] *Number 4, to serve offerings to what is not actually present, means widely to perform the service of offerings to buddhas and caityas that are not actually present. That is to say, both in their presence and not in their presence, we serve offerings to buddhas and to caityas and stūpas: we also make offerings to buddhas and to caityas and stūpas that are not actually present. Serving offerings to what is actually present acquires great merits. Serving offerings to what is not actually present acquires great great merits, because the state is magnanimous and wide. Serving offerings to the present and the non-present [alike] acquires the greatest of great merits.*

[173] *Number 5, service of offerings performed by oneself, means serving offerings with one's own body to buddhas and to caityas.*

[173] *Number 6, service of offerings performed by others to buddhas and to caityas, means causing others, if they have some small possession, not to be lazy in offering it. That is to say, regarding service of offerings by self and by others, we do either one, equally. Service of offerings performed by oneself acquires great merits. Causing others to serve offerings acquires great great merits. Serving offerings [in the state of unity] of self-and-others acquires the greatest of great merits.*

[174] *In number 7, serving offerings of property to buddhas and to caityas, stūpas, and śarīras, there are said to be three kinds of property: 1) offerings of necessity-goods,*[85] *namely clothing, food, and so on; 2) offerings of venerative goods, namely incense, flowers, and so on; and 3) offerings of decorative goods, namely all other treasures, adornments, and so on.*

[174] *In number 8, serving offerings of excellence, there are three kinds of excellence: 1) just devotedly to perform the service of miscellaneous offerings; 2) with pure believing mind, to believe in the weight of the Buddha's virtue and to serve offerings accordingly; and 3) while experiencing the will to transfer merit and the will to pursue the state of buddha, to perform the service of offerings.*

[175] *In number 9, untainted service of offerings, there are two kinds of untaintedness: 1) the mind being untainted, being free from all transgressions; and 2) property being untainted, being free from violations of the Dharma.*

[175] *Number 10 is serving offerings of attainment of the state of truth. That is to say, service of offerings following [realization of] the effect is called "serving offerings of*

China via Sri Lanka in 414. Back in China, he translated *Maka-sogi-ritsu,* together with Buddhabhadra, and other works. He died aged 82 (one account says 86).

85. 資具 (SHIGU) stands for 資生具 (SHISHOGU), lit. "contributing-to-life goods," i.e. necessities of life. The latter expression appears in chapter 86, *Shukke-kudoku,* para. [95].

attainment of the state of truth." The buddha-effect is the state to be attained, and the practice of serving offerings, which can attain that state, is [itself] called "attainment of the state of truth." Serving offerings of attainment of the state of truth is either called serving offerings of Dharma or called serving offerings of deeds. Within it there are three [categories]: 1) serving offerings of property may be serving offerings of attainment of the state of truth; 2) serving offerings of joy may be serving offerings of attainment of the state of truth; and 3) serving offerings of practice may be serving offerings of attainment of the state of truth.

The service of offerings to Buddha includes these ten services of offerings [listed] already. For Dharma and for Saṃgha similar categories also apply. Namely, to serve offerings to Dharma means to serve offerings to the teaching of principles and the methods of practice that the Buddha expounded, and also to serve offerings to volumes of the sutras. To serve offerings to Saṃgha means to serve offerings to all sacred beings of the three vehicles, and to their caityas, statues, and stūpas, and to monks who are common men.

7] *Next, the mind in serving offerings is of six kinds: 1) the supreme mind of the field of happiness;*[86] *within the field of happiness, it produces the greatest excellence; 2) the supreme mind [which recognizes] benevolence; all virtuous joys have appeared by virtue of the three treasures; 3) the appearance of the mind that is supremely excellent among all living beings; 4) the mind that is as hard to meet as the uḍumbara flower;*[87] *5) the singular and independent undivided mind [which is one with] the three-thousand-great-thousandfold world; 6) the mind which, in all worldly areas and areas beyond the world, is completely equipped with reliable criteria—for example, the Tathāgata, being in complete possession of worldly and world-transcendent methods, is able to provide for living beings a basis upon which to rely: this is called being completely equipped with reliable criteria. If with these six minds we serve offerings to the three treasures, even if it is only something small, we will be able to secure countless and infinite merits, how much more if that [offering] is plentiful?*

8] Such service of offerings we should perform unfailingly with sincere mind. It has been performed without fail by the buddhas. Stories about it are evident throughout the sutras and vinaya. At the same time, the Buddhist patriarchs themselves have personally handed down its authentic transmission. Days and months of waiting in attendance and doing work are just times of serving offerings. The standards for placement of statues and śarīras, for serving offerings and doing prostrations, and for building stūpas and building caityas, have been authentically transmitted only in the house of the Buddhist patriarchs. They are not authentically transmitted to anyone other than the descendants of the Buddhist patriarchs. Further, if [standards] are not authentically transmitted in accordance with the Dharma, they will

86. 福田 (FUKUDEN) suggests the state in Zazen. The kaṣāya is called 福田衣 (FUKUDEN-E), "the field of happiness robe."

87. The uḍumbara flower is a symbol of the Buddha's state of mind, which, like the uḍumbara flower, is rarely encountered. See chap. 68, *Udonge.*

contravene the Dharma-standards. When the service of offerings contravenes the Dharma-standards, it is not genuine. If the service of offerings is not genuine, its merit is spare. Without fail we should learn, and receive the authentic transmission of, the method of serving offerings which accords with the Dharma. Zen Master Reito[88] spent years and months tending to the site of Sokei's stūpa; and the temple servant Ro,[89] not resting day or night, pounded rice to serve to the assembly: [these instances] were entirely the service of offerings in accordance with the Dharma. They are a small sample of such [instances], which I do not have time to quote extensively. We should serve offerings like this.

Shobogenzo Kuyo-shobutsu

A day during the summer retreat in
the 7th year of Kencho.[90]

---

88. Master Sokei Reito (666–760). He became a monk under Master Daikan Eno, whom he served until Master Daikan Eno's death. Then he took care of a pagoda in which Master Daikan Eno's kaṣāya was preserved. He declined the Emperor's invitation several times, staying on Sokei mountain until his own death, aged 95. His posthumous title was Master Daigyo.

89. Master Daikan Eno (638–713). Sokei is the name of the mountain on which he and Master Reito lived. Master Daikan's family name was Ro. Before formally becoming a monk he worked on the temple grounds as a servant, pounding rice for the monks. See chap. 30, *Gyoji*.

90. 1255. This is one of the chapters of the twelve-chapter edition of Shobogenzo. The structure of this chapter is similar to that of chap. 86, *Shukke-kudoku*, with Master Dogen adding brief comments to excerpts from sutras. Master Dogen died in 1253, two years before this concluding note was added, presumably by Master Ko-un Ejo.

[88]

帰依三宝

KIE-SANBO

Taking Refuge in the Three Treasures

***Kie** means "devotion to," or "taking refuge in," and **sanbo** means "the Three Treasures": Buddha, Dharma, and Saṃgha. Buddha means Gautama Buddha and other people who have attained the same state as Gautama Buddha. Dharma means reality. Saṃgha means the Buddhist community of monks, nuns, laymen, and laywomen. The Three Treasures are of supreme value in Buddhism and Master Dogen emphasized the importance of devoting ourselves to them. He says that devotion to the Three Treasures is the beginning and the end of Buddhism.*

[81] ***Zen-en-shingi* says,** "Do you revere Buddha, Dharma, and Saṃgha, or not?" (One hundred and twenty, question one).

Clearly, in the Western Heavens and the Eastern Lands, what the Buddhist patriarchs have authentically transmitted is reverence for Buddha, Dharma, and Saṃgha. If we do not take refuge in them,[1] we do not revere them; and if we do not revere them, we cannot take refuge in them. We accomplish the merit of this taking refuge in Buddha, Dharma, and Saṃgha whenever sympathetic communication of the truth[2] takes place. Whether we are in the heavens above, the human world, hell, or states of demons and animals, if sympathetic communication of the truth occurs, we take refuge without fail. Once we have taken refuge, we develop [merit] in every life, in every age, in every location, and at every place; we pile up merit and heap up virtue, and we accomplish [the truth of] anuttara-samyak-saṃbodhi. Even if we happen to be led by bad friends and encounter hindrances of demons, so that we temporarily become one who cuts off good roots, or become an icchantika,[3] eventually we will continue with good roots, whose merit will develop. The

---

1. 帰依 (KIE), lit. "returning to and depending upon," represents the Sanskrit *śaraṇa,* which means "refuge" or "taking refuge." See Glossary.

2. 感応道交 (KANNO-DOKO) means mystical communication between buddhas and living beings, or between the Universe and living beings.

3. The Sanskrit *icchantika,* here represented phonetically, means one who pursues desires to the end. See Book 2, Glossary. The meaning of the Sanskrit *icchantika* was represented in Chinese either by 断善根 (DAN-ZENKON), "one who cuts off good roots," or by 信不具足 (SHIN-FUGUSOKU), "one who does not possess belief." See also chap. 86, *Shukke-kudoku.*

merit of taking refuge in the Three Treasures is, in the end, not subject to decay. This *"taking refuge in the Three Treasures"* means, with concentrated pure belief—whether the age is one in which the Tathāgata is alive or whether it is after the Tathāgata's extinction—holding the palms together, lowering the head, and orally reciting the following:

> *I, so and so,*
> *From my present body until attainment of the Buddha's body,*
> *Take refuge in Buddha,*
> *I take refuge in Dharma,*
> *I take refuge in Saṃgha.*
> *I take refuge in Buddha, most honored of bipeds.*
> *I take refuge in Dharma, honored as beyond desire.*
> *I take refuge in Saṃgha, honored among communities.*
> *I have taken refuge in Buddha,*
> *I have taken refuge in Dharma,*
> *I have taken refuge in Saṃgha.*[4]

[184] Resolving upon the distant buddha-effect of bodhi, we should thus bring into being a saṃnāha.[5] Then, although [this] body-and-mind, kṣāṇa by kṣāṇa, even now is appearing and disappearing, the Dharma-body will long continue to thrive and will accomplish the state of bodhi, without fail. As for the meaning of *"to take refuge,"* [lit. "to return to and to depend upon"] *to return* is *to devote oneself to*, and *to depend upon* is *to submit to;* for this reason, we call it *"taking refuge."* The form of *devotion* is, for example, like a child belonging to its father. *Submission* is, for example, like a people depending upon their king. These are words for, in another word, *salvation*. Because Buddha is our great teacher, we take refuge in him. Because Dharma is good medicine, we take refuge in it. Because Saṃgha are excellent friends, we take refuge in them. *[Someone] asks: "For what reason do we take refuge solely in these three?" The answer is; "Because these three kinds [of treasure] are ultimate places of refuge and they can cause living beings to get free from life and death and to experience the great state of bodhi. Therefore we take refuge in them. These three kinds [of treasure], in conclusion, are of unthinkable merit."*[6] *Buddha*[7] in India is pronounced *buddaya*[8] and in China is translated as "the state of truth"[9]—the supreme, right and balanced state of

---

4. Quoted from *Zen-en-shingi*, pt. 9. See also chap. 94, *Jukai*.
5. The Sanskrit *saṃnāha* means a suit of armor. See Glossary.
6. From *Daijo-gi-sho*, a 20-fascicle commentary on Mahāyāna Buddhism written in China during the Sui Dynasty (589–618).
7. 仏 (*hotoke*) is the Chinese character meaning "Buddha."
8. 仏陀耶 (BUDDAYA) is a transliteration of the Sanskrit *Buddha*.
9. 覚 (KAKU), concludes the phrase 無上正等覚 (MUJO-SHOTO-KAKU), "the supreme, right and balanced state of truth," which represents the meaning of the Sanskrit *anuttara-samyak-saṃbodhi*. See Book 1, Glossary.

truth. *Dharma* in India is pronounced *daruma*[10]—or pronounced *donmu*,[11] which is a variant of the Sanskrit sound—and in China is translated as "the Law." All dharmas, good, bad, and indifferent, are called "dharmas," but the present *Dharma* as an object of devotion within the Three Treasures is Dharma as the Law. *Saṃgha* in India is pronounced *sogya*[12] and in China is translated as "harmonious community." [The Three Treasures] have been praised like this.

86] *"The Three Treasures as what abides and is maintained": statues and stūpas are the Buddha-Treasure; yellow paper on a red rod is the transmitted Dharma-Treasure; shaving of the head, dyeing of robes, and the conventional form of the rules of discipline are the Saṃgha-Treasure.*

"The Three Treasures as [related to the Buddha's] teaching forms": Śākyamuni, the World-honored One, is the Buddha-Treasure; the Dharma-wheel he turned, and the sacred teachings that he propagated, are the Dharma-Treasure; the five men, Ājñāta-kauṇḍinya and the others,[13] *are the Saṃgha-Treasure.*

"The Three Treasures as the body of theory": the Dharma-body of five divisions[14] *is called the Buddha-Treasure; the truth of cessation,*[15] *the state without intention, is called the Dharma-Treasure; and the merits of students and those beyond study*[16] *are the Saṃgha-Treasure.*

"The Three Treasures [each] as a totality": experience and understanding of the great state of truth is called the Buddha-Treasure; purity, being beyond taintedness, is called the Dharma-Treasure; and ultimate principles making harmony, being without hesitation and without stagnancy, is called the Saṃgha-Treasure.[17]

[Past Buddhists] took refuge in the Three Treasures [as described] like this. Living beings of scant good fortune and small virtue do not hear even the names of the Three Treasures; how much less are they able to take refuge?

---

10. 達磨 (DARUMA) is a transliteration of the Sanskrit *Dharma*.

11. 曇無 (DONMU) is a transliteration of the Pali *Dhamma*.

12. 僧伽 (SOGYA) is a transliteration of the Sanskrit *Saṃgha*.

13. The five bhikṣus: Ājñāta-kauṇḍinya, Aśvajit, Bhadrika, Mahānāman, and Daśabala-kāśyapa, who accompanied the Buddha in his ascetic practice and became the first monks of the Buddha's order.

14. 五分法身 (GOBUN-HOSSHIN), from the Sanskrit *asamasama-pañca-skandha*. The five divisions are represented in Chinese as 戒身 (KAISHIN), the precepts-body; 定身 (JOSHIN), the body of the balanced state; 慧身 (ESHIN), the body of wisdom; 解脱身 (GEDATSU-SHIN), the body of liberation; and 解脱知見身 (GEDATSU-CHIKEN-SHIN), the body of knowledge of liberation.

15. 滅諦 (METTAI), the third of the Four Noble Truths.

16. 無学 (MUGAKU), lit. "no study," means one who has nothing more to study; that is, an arhat. Later in this chapter, the Sanskrit word *arhat* is represented phonetically and also by the term 四果 (SHIKA), "the fourth effect." Arhathood is the fourth and final stage of a śrāvaka of the small vehicle (one who studies Buddhism intellectually).

17. Quoted from an untraced sutra.

[188] The Sutra of the Flower of Dharma says:

> *These living beings of many sins,*
> *With their bad conduct as direct and indirect causes,*
> *Even if they pass asaṃkhyas of kalpas*
> *Do not hear the name of the Three Treasures.*[18]

The Sutra of the Flower of Dharma is *the one great purpose*[19] of the buddha-tathāgatas. Of all the sutras preached by the Great Teacher Śākyamuni, the Sutra of the Flower of Dharma is the great king and is the great teacher. Other sutras and other Dharmas are all the subjects and the retinue of the Sutra of the Flower of Dharma. What is preached in the Sutra of the Flower of Dharma is just the truth; what is preached in other sutras always includes an expedient means, which is not the Buddha's fundamental intention. If we evoked preaching contained in other sutras in order to compare and appraise the Sutra of the Flower of Dharma, that would be backwards. Without being covered by the influence of the merit of the Flower of Dharma, other sutras could not exist. Other sutras are all waiting to devote themselves to the Flower of Dharma. In this Sutra of the Flower of Dharma there is the present preaching. Remember, the merits of the Three Treasures are supremely valuable and are supreme.

[189] The World-honored One said, *"Ordinary people, fearing oppression, often seek refuge in mountains and parks and in forests, solitary trees, caityas,*[20] *and so on. Such seeking for refuge is not excellent and such seeking for refuge is not valuable. It is not possible, through such seeking for refuge, to be liberated from the many kinds of suffering. If beings take refuge in Buddha and take refuge in Dharma and Saṃgha, they will, in the reality of the Four Noble Truths, constantly observe with wisdom, knowing suffering, knowing the accumulation of suffering, knowing eternal transcendence of the many kinds of suffering, and knowing the eightfold noble path*[21] *that leads to the balanced and peaceful state of nirvāṇa. This taking refuge is most excellent and this taking refuge is supremely valuable. It is always possible, by thus taking refuge, to be liberated from the many kinds of suffering."*[22]

[190] The World-honored One clearly set it out for all living beings: living beings should not, fearing oppression, vainly seek refuge in mountain-deities, demon-deities, and the like, or seek refuge in non-Buddhist caityas. [Living beings] are never liberated through such seeking for refuge. Typically, following the wrong teachings of non-Buddhism, [people adhere to]

---

18. Lotus Sutra, *Nyorai-juryo (The Tathāgata's Lifetime).* See LS 3.32.

19. 一大事因縁 (ICHIDAIJI-INNEN). Lotus Sutra, *Hoben (Expedient Means).* See LS 1.88–90.

20. In this case (as is clarified in Master Dogen's commentary) caityas means non-Buddhist shrines.

21. 八支聖道 (HASSHI *[no]* SHODO). See chap. 73, *Sanjushichi-bon-bodai-bunbo.*

22. *Kusha-ron* (Sanskrit: *Abhidharma-kośa*), fascicle 14.

the ox precepts,[23] *the deer precepts, the rākṣasa*[24] *precepts, the demon precepts, the mute's precepts, the deaf person's precepts, the dog precepts, the chicken precepts, or the pheasant precepts; or they coat the body with ash; or they make their long hair into forms;*[25] *or they sacrifice a sheep*[26]*—at which time they first recite dhāraṇīs and then kill it—or they perform fire rituals for four months;*[27] *or they take air for seven days;*[28] *or they serve to various gods offerings of hundred thousand koṭis of flowers; and all their desires by this means they [strive to] accomplish. There is no affirmation that such methods can become the cause of liberation. [Such methods] are not praised by the wise; they are to suffer in vain without good results.*[29] Because it is so, we must definitely be clear that we are not idly devoted to wrong ways. Even if a method is different from these precepts, if its principle corresponds to the principle of [seeking refuge in] *solitary trees, caityas, and so on,* do not seek refuge through it. The human body is hard to receive, and the Buddha-Dharma is rarely met. If we idly spent a lifetime as the follower of a demon-deity, or if we passed many lives as beings descended from the false view, that would be lamentable. By swiftly taking refuge in the Three Treasures of Buddha, Dharma, and Saṃgha, we should not only be liberated from the many kinds of suffering: we should accomplish the state of bodhi.

[93] The Sutra of Rare Occurrences[30] says: *Teaching the four continents and the six heavens of [the world of] desire, so that all attain the fourth effect, does not equal the merit of one human being's reception of the Three Devotions.*[31]

---

23. Adherence to the ox precepts means imitating the life of an ox in one's daily life—a kind of ascetic practice.

24. A demon that feeds on human flesh.

25. Refers to the matted-hair ascetics (in Sanskrit *jaṭila*) of the Buddha's time.

26. Blood-sacrifices were common in ancient India. It is credited to the historical influence of Buddhism that the ritual sacrifice of animals is no longer widely practiced in India.

27. Various forms of fire cult existed in ancient India. For example, a Vedic-Brahmin fire-sacrifice was carried out by professional Brahmins, who observed elaborate cultic prescriptions in order that the fire-god Agni would carry the sacrifice up to the gods. Other fire-ritualists tried to purify their own souls by burning their impurities in sacred flames.

28. 服風 (FU *[o] fuku[su]*), "take air [as medicine]" probably suggests fasting. At the same time, an air cult is included in a list of twenty kinds of non-Buddhism.

29. Quotation from an untraced Chinese text.

30. 希有経 (KE-U-KYO), short for *Bussetsu-ke-u-koryo-kudoku-kyo,* lit. "Sutra of the Buddha's Preaching on Comparison of the Merits of Rare Occurrences." The sutra was translated from Sanskrit by Jñānagupta (522–600) during the Sui dynasty (589–618). The sutra does not contain the exact words quoted here; it is likely that this quotation was taken from a summary of the sutra.

31. 受三帰 (SANKI *[o] ukuru*), "to receive the Three Devotions," means to take refuge in Buddha, Dharma, and Saṃgha at the beginning of the precepts ceremony. Receiving the precepts means receiving these Three Devotions, followed by the Three Summarized Precepts, followed by the Ten Bodhisattva Precepts. See chap. 94, *Jukai.*

"The four continents" are the eastern, western, southern, and northern continents. Of these, the northern continent cannot be reached by the teaching of the three vehicles:[32] to teach all living beings in that place, and to make them into arhats, would be seen as a very rare occurrence indeed. Even if such benefit existed, it could never equal the merit of guiding one human being to receive the Three Devotions. The six heavens, also, are imagined to be a place where living beings who can attain the truth are rare. Even if we caused those [living beings] to attain the fourth effect, that could never equal the greatness and the profundity of the merit of one human being's reception of the Three Devotions.

[194] The Ekottarāgama Sutra[33] says: *There was a god of Trāyastriṃśa*[34] *whose laments—when the five signs of decay*[35] *appeared—that it would be born as a wild boar, were heard by Śakra-devānām-indra. Śakra, upon hearing this [god], summoned it and told it; "You should take refuge in the Three Treasures." It immediately did as it had been instructed and thereby escaped birth as a wild boar. The Buddha preached the following verse:*

> *Beings that take refuge in Buddha,*
> *Do not fall into the three evil states.*[36]
> *They end excesses and live [in the world] of humans and gods.*
> *They will arrive at nirvāṇa.*

After [the god] had received the Three Devotions it was born into a rich man's family. Further, it was able to leave family life and to realize the state of one beyond study.

In sum, the merit of taking refuge in the Three Treasures is beyond consideration: it is inestimable and infinite.

[195] When the World-honored One was in the world, twenty-six koṭis of hungry dragons came together to the Buddha's place and, all of them shedding tears like rain, they addressed him: *"Solely we beseech you! Have pity and save us, All-compassionate World-honored One! We remember during a past age, although we were able to leave family life in the Buddha-Dharma, we perpetrated to the*

---

32. The continent north of Mt. Sumeru is inhabited only by angels, and is thus out of bounds to Buddhists of the three vehicles; namely, śrāvakas, pratyekabuddhas, and bodhisattvas.

33. One of the four Āgamas in the Chinese version, said to have been first translated into Chinese by Dharmanandi in 384. The Dharmanandi translation, however, is lost. A later translation, which survives, was made by Gautama Saṃghadeva in 397.

34. Trāyastriṃśa means the heaven of thirty-three gods, which is the second highest of the six heavens in the world of desire, situated on top of Mt. Sumeru. Śakra-devānām-indra presides, surrounded by eight gods in each of the four directions. See Book 3, Glossary.

35. The five signs that a celestial being is about to die are; 1) its crown of flowers fades, 2) sweat flows from under its arms, 3) its clothes become soiled, 4) its body loses its glow, and 5) it becomes reluctant to sit in its original place.

36. 三悪道 (SAN-AKUDO): hell, the state of hungry ghosts, and the state of animals.

full various bad actions like these,[37] *and because of the bad actions we expended countless bodies in the three evil states. Further, because of residual retribution, we have been born in the world of dragons, and have suffered extremely-great agonies." The Buddha told the dragons, "Now you must all receive the Three Devotions and single-mindedly perform good. By virtue of this cause you will meet, during the Kalpa of the Wise,*[38] *the last Buddha therein, whose name will be Tower-Arrival.*[39] *In the age of that Buddha you will be able to expiate your sins." Then, when the dragons had heard these words, they all exhausted their lives with utmost sincerity, and each received the Three Devotions.*[40]

[96] The Buddha himself, in saving the dragons, possessed no other method and no other technique: he simply imparted to them the Three Devotions. [The dragons] had received the Three Devotions in a past age when they left family life but, as a result of karmic retribution, they had become hungry dragons, at which time no other method could save them. Therefore [the Buddha] imparted to them the Three Devotions. Remember, the World-honored One already has certified, and living beings should duly believe, that the merit of the Three Devotions is supremely valuable and is supreme, profound, and unthinkable. [The Buddha] did not cause them to recite the names of the buddhas of the ten directions: he simply imparted to them the Three Devotions. The Buddha's intention is profound: who can fathom it? Living beings today, rather than vainly reciting the name of every single buddha, should swiftly receive the Three Devotions. Do not be so dull as to squander great merit.

[97] *At that time in the gathering there was a blind dragon-woman. The inside of her mouth was swollen and inflamed and filled with all kinds of grubs, as if it were excrement; it was as foul as the uncleanness within a female organ—the stink of fish being hard to bear—and all kinds of things were feeding off it so that pus and blood oozed out. All parts of her body were constantly being bitten by mosquitoes, wasps, and various poisonous flies. The stinking organs of her body hardly bore perceiving. At that time, the World-honored One, with great compassion, seeing that dragon-woman's blindness and her suffering of such distress, asked her, "Little sister! What circumstances caused you to acquire this wretched body? In past ages what actions have you done?" The dragon-woman answered, "World-honored One! This body of mine is now beset with all kinds of suffering, and I do not have a moment of respite. Even if I wanted to describe [the suffering], it would be impossible to explain. I remember the past thirty-six koṭis [of years]. For hundreds of thousands of years I have been suffering like this in the state of a wretched dragon, without so much as a kṣāṇa of respite, day or night. The reason is that*

---

37. Refers to an account earlier in the sutra.

38. 賢劫 (KENGO) represents the Sanskrit *bhadra-kalpa*, which is the present kalpa, so called because many buddhas will manifest themselves within its duration. See Book 1, Glossary.

39. 楼至 (ROSHI), lit. "Tower Arrival," may represent the meaning of a Sanskrit name or it may be a transliteration of the Sanskrit sound. The original Sanskrit has not been traced.

40. *Daishu-kyo* (Sanskrit: *Mahā-saṃnipāta-sūtra*), fascicle 44.

in the distant past, during the ninety-first kalpa, I became a bhikṣuṇī in the Dharma of Vipaśyin Buddha[41] *but I thought about matters of desire more than would a drunken man; even though I had left family life, I was unable to accord with the Dharma: I spread bedding in a saṃghārāma*[42] *and committed any number of impure acts in order to indulge in passion and to feel great pleasure; or sometimes, greedily seeking the property of others, I appropriated an abundance of the offerings of the faithful. For such reasons as these, during the ninety-first kalpa I was always unable to receive the body of a god or a human being. I constantly stewed in the fires of the three evil states." The Buddha asked further, "If it is so, at the end of these middle kalpas, little sister, where will you be born?" The dragon-woman answered, "With the force of my past karma as causes and conditions, even if I am born in another world, when that kalpa finishes I will be blown back by the winds of bad karma and reborn in this state." Then that dragon-woman, having spoken these words, made the following plea: "All-compassionate World-honored One! Please save me! Please save me!" At that time the World-honored One scooped some water in his hand and told the dragon-woman, "This water is called the medicine of wish-fulfilling joy.*[43] *Now, honestly speaking, I say to you: In the distant past I cast aside body and life in order to save a dove, and to the end I did not waver in resolve or feel stinginess arise in my mind. If these words [of yours] are true, you will be completely cured of your terrible affliction." Then the World-honored Buddha took the water in his mouth and showered the body of that blind dragon-woman. All her terrible afflictions and stinking organs were totally cured. Already cured, she pleaded as follows: "I now beg the Buddha that I may receive the Three Devotions." At this the World-honored One at once imparted to the dragon-woman the Three Devotions.*

[200] This dragon-woman, in the distant past in the Dharma of Vipaśyin Buddha, became a bhikṣuṇī: although she broke the precepts, she may have seen and heard what is penetrable and what is impenetrable in the Buddha-Dharma. Now she personally meets with Śākyamuni Buddha and begs that she might [again] receive the Three Devotions. Receiving the Three Devotions from the Buddha must be said to be [due to] densely-accumulated good roots. The merit of [her] meeting the Buddha must inevitably have derived from the Three Devotions.[44] We are not blind dragons and are not in the bodies of animals, but we neither see the Tathāgata nor receive the Three Devotions under the Buddha. [Our] meeting Buddha is distant, and we should be ashamed. The World-honored One himself imparted [to the

41. The first of the seven ancient buddhas. See chap. 15, *Busso*.

42. Lit. "a resting place for the Saṃgha"; that is, a temple.

43. 瞋陀留脂薬和 (SHINDARUSHI-YAKUWA). 瞋陀 (SHINDA) represents the Sanskrit *cintā*, which means thought or wish (as in *cintāmaṇi*, the wish-fulfilling gem). 留脂 (RUSHI) represents Sanskrit that has not been traced. 薬和 (YAKUWA) means medicine or medicinal compound. The phrase is often rendered in Chinese characters as 如意楽水 (NYO-I-RAKU-SUI), "water of wish-fulfilling joy."

44. That is, her devotions to Buddha, Dharma, and Saṃgha when becoming a bhikṣuṇī in the Dharma of Vipaśyin Buddha.

dragon-woman] the Three Devotions: remember the merit of the Three Devotions is profound and immeasurable. When God-king Śakra did prostrations to a wild fox and received the Three Devotions, everything rested upon the profundity of the merit of the Three Devotions.[45]

[201] *When the Buddha was staying in a banyan[46] grove by the city of Kapilavastu,[47] Śākya-mahānāma[48] came to the Buddha's place and spoke thus: "What is an upāsaka?"[49] The Buddha then explained to him, "If any good son or good daughter is in sound possession of their faculties and receives the Three Devotions, this person is then called an upāsaka." Śākya-mahānāma said, "World-honored One! What is a one-part upāsaka?" The Buddha said, "Mahānāma! If [a person] receives the Three Devotions and also receives one precept,[50] this person is called a one-part upāsaka."[51]*

Becoming a disciple of the Buddha invariably rests upon the Three Devotions. Whichever precepts we receive, we invariably receive the Three Devotions [first] and after that receive the precepts. Therefore, [only] through the Three Devotions is it possible to obtain the precepts.

[203] *The Dhammapada[52] says: Once upon a time the God-king [Śakra], inwardly knowing that when his life ended he would be reborn as a donkey, lamented interminably and said, "The only one who can save me from this agony and misfortune is the Buddha, the World-honored One." Then he went to the Buddha's place, bowed his head to and prostrated himself upon the ground, and took refuge in the Buddha. His life ended there and then, before he had risen, and he was reborn in the womb of a donkey. The mother donkey broke her bit and smashed some clay pots at a china shop. The potter struck her. In due course this caused injury to her womb and [Śakra] reentered the body of a god-king. The Buddha said, "As you let go of life, you were taking refuge in the Three Treasures; returns from your sins have already ceased." God-king [Śakra], on hearing this, attained the first effect.[53]*

---

45. The story of Śakra and the wild fox is recorded later in this chapter (see para. [206]).

46. 尼拘陀 (NIKUDA) is a transliteration of the Sanskrit *nyagrodha,* which lit. means "growing downwards" and thus represents the banyan, or Indian fig-tree, whose fibers descend from its branches to the earth, where they take root and form new stems.

47. Kapilavastu was the name of the kingdom, and the capital thereof, inhabited by the Śākya clan, into which Gautama Buddha was born.

48. Mahānāma was a member of the Buddha's family (the Śākyas) who devoted himself to the Buddha's order as a layman.

49. Upāsaka means a (male) lay Buddhist.

50. The five precepts taken by lay people in the Buddha's time were sometimes taken one at a time.

51. *Daihatsu-nehan-gyo,* fascicle 34.

52. 法句経 (HOKKUKYO), lit. Sutra of Dharma-phrases. This is the first of fifteen books in the Khuddaka-nikāya, and the fifth of the five Nikāyas in the Pali canon. The Dhammapada comprises 423 verses.

53. 初果 (SHOKA), "the first effect," means the stage of the *srotāpanna* (stream-enterer), the first stage of a śrāvaka on the way to the fourth effect of arhathood. See Book 1, Glossary.

[204] In general, in saving us from the agonies and misfortunes of the world, the Buddha, the World-honored One, is unsurpassed. For this reason God-king [Śakra] hastens to the place of the World-honored One. While he is still prostrate on the ground his life ends and he is reborn in the womb of a donkey. Due to the merit of [Śakra's] devotion to the Buddha, the mother donkey breaks her bit and tramples on some pots at a china shop. The potter strikes her. This injures the body of the mother donkey, and the donkey in the womb is destroyed, whereupon [Śakra] reenters the body of a god-king. That upon hearing the Buddha's preaching [Śakra] attains the first effect is the influence of the merit of taking refuge in the Three Treasures. Therefore, the [power] which swiftly frees us from the agonies and misfortunes of the world, and which causes us to grasp in experience the supreme [truth of] bodhi, may be, in every case, the power of taking refuge in the Three Treasures. In general, the power of the Three Devotions not only frees us from the three evil states: it [also] re-enters the body of God-king Śakra. It not only attains effects and rewards in the heavens above: it [also] becomes sacred beings who are srotāpannas. Truly, the ocean of the merit of the Three Treasures is immeasurable and infinite. When the World-honored One was in the world human beings and gods experienced such happiness. Now, in a latter five-hundred-year period following the extinction of the Tathāgata, how can human beings and gods do anything? At the same time, the Tathāgata's statues, śarīras, and so on, are still abiding in the present in the world. By taking refuge in these, we also will gain the kind of merit described above.

[206] *Mizo-u-kyo*[54] *says: The Buddha said, "I remember numberless kalpas ago, on Mt. Śita in the great kingdom of Vima,*[55] *there was a wild fox being chased by a lion, about to become prey. While running away, [the fox] fell into a well. It could not get out and spent three days there until, resigning itself to death, it spoke the following verse:*

What a miserable fate!
Beset today by hardships,
I will lose my life in a hillside well.
All myriad things are inconstant.
I regret that my body was not eaten by the lion.
Namas! I take refuge in the buddhas of the ten directions.
May they be notified that my mind is pure and unselfish.

Then God-king Śakra heard the naming of the buddhas. Awed, his hair standing on end, he became mindful of eternal buddhas. He thought to himself, 'I am alone and unprotected and without a guiding teacher; and addiction to the five desires is drowning me.' At once, accompanied by a host of eighty thousand gods, he flew down to the well intending to

---

54. 未曾有経 (MIZO-U-KYO), stands for 未曾有因縁経 (MIZO-U-INNEN-KYO), lit. "The Sutra of Unprecedented Episodes."

55. Mt. Śita and the kingdom of Vima are legendary places in Jambudvīpa, the continent south of Mt. Sumeru where human beings live.

investigate in full. Then he saw the wild fox at the bottom of the well, paws clawing the earth, unable to get out. God-king [Śakra] again thought to himself, and said, 'Saintly person, perhaps you consider that you are without ways or means. Although I now see the figure of a wild fox, you are assuredly a bodhisattva, not a common instrument; for, kind gentle person, [the verse] you spoke previously was not common words. I beg you to preach for the gods the pivot of the Dharma.' At this the wild fox called up in reply, 'Though you are a god-king, you are uneducated. While a teacher of Dharma is down below, you yourself remain up above: entirely failing to practice courtesy, you ask [to hear] the pivot of the Dharma! The water of Dharma is pure and is able to save people. How can you intend to obtain for yourself [such a] tribute?' God-king [Śakra] on hearing this was greatly ashamed. [But] the gods in attendance laughed in surprise, [saying,] 'If the celestial king alighted there would be no benefit at all.' God-king [Śakra] thereupon addressed the many gods: 'Pray, do not harbor surprise or fear at this. It is [due to] my being stubborn and closed and lacking in virtue. Without fail we must hear from this [fox] the pivot of the Dharma.' Then [Śakra] hung down a celestial precious robe, taking hold of which the wild fox emerged above. The gods served to it a meal of nectar. The wild fox, taking sustenance, gained the will to live. Unexpectedly, in the midst of calamity, it had come upon such good fortune that its mind was set dancing and its joy was boundless. The wild fox widely preached, for God-king [Śakra] and all the gods, the pivot of the Dharma."

[208] This is called the story of God-king [Śakra's] doing prostrations to an animal and making it his teacher. Clearly we have seen, God-king [Śakra's] making a wild fox into his teacher may be proof of how hard it is to hear the name of Buddha, the name of Dharma, and the name of Saṃgha. The present fact that, aided by long-accumulated good, we are meeting the Dharma bequeathed by the Tathāgata, and that, night and day, we are hearing the precious appellations of the Three Treasures, will not regress with [the passing of] time. Just this may be the pivot of the Dharma. Even celestial marāpāpīyas[56] may escape affliction by taking refuge in the Three Treasures. How much more may other beings be able, in respect of the merit of the Three Treasures, to *pile up merit and heap up virtue*? How could we fail to ponder it? In sum, in practicing the truth as disciples of the Buddha, we first, without fail, make venerative prostrations to the Three Treasures of the ten directions, request the presence of the Three Treasures of the ten directions,[57] burn incense and scatter flowers before them, and we then, in due course, perform all practices. This is just an excellent vestige of the ancestors and an eternal convention of the Buddhist patriarchs. If any have never practiced the con-

56. Idealistic devils who inhabit the world of desire and deprive Buddhist practitioners of life.

57. For example, by walking around in a circle three times at the place of a ceremony, while reciting 南無仏陀耶、南無達磨耶、南無僧伽耶、南無祖師菩薩。In Japan, traditionally pronounced, "NAMU-FUDOYA, NAMU-TABOYA, NAMU-SUGYAYA, NAMU-SUSUBUSA"; "Namas Buddha! Namas Dharma! Namas Saṃgha! Namas the ancestral masters and bodhisattvas!"

vention of taking refuge in the Three Treasures, know that theirs is the Dharma of non-Buddhists, and know that it may be the Dharma of celestial demons. The Dharma of the buddhas and the patriarchs inevitably has, at its beginning, a ceremony of taking refuge in the Three Treasures.

Shobogenzo Kie-sanbo

On a day of the summer retreat in the 7th year of Kencho,[58] I finished copying from the late Master's initial draft. He had yet to reach the stage of an intermediate draft, a fair copy, and so on. Doubtless during the Master's revision there would have been additions and deletions. Now such procedures are impermissible and so the Master's draft reads as it is.[59]

58. 1255; two years after Master Dogen's death.

59. The final comment was almost certainly added by Master Dogen's successor, Master Ko-un Ejo. This chapter is included in the twelve-chapter edition of Shobogenzo compiled by Master Dogen in his last years.

[89]

深信因果

SHINJIN-INGA

Deep Belief in Cause and Effect

__Shin__ means "deep" and __shin__ (in this case pronounced __jin__) means "belief." __In__ means "cause," and __ka__ (in this case pronounced __ga__) means "effect." So __shinjin-inga__ means "deep belief in cause and effect." It is clear that Buddhism believes in cause and effect. But many so-called Mahayana Buddhists say that the Buddhist theory of belief in cause and effect belongs to Hinayana Buddhism, and that Mahayana Buddhists are able to transcend the rule of cause and effect. This belief, however, is wrong. Master Dogen emphasizes in this chapter that to understand Buddhism it is very important to believe in the law of cause and effect. Chinese Buddhism contains a widely-known story about a Buddhist priest who fell into the body of a wild fox because he denied the law of cause and effect, but who was saved by the words of Master Hyakujo Ekai. Many Buddhist students thought mistakenly that this story illustrates transcendence of cause and effect. But Master Dogen points out their mistakes in this chapter. He explains clearly the true meaning of the story, and he affirms Buddhism's profound belief in the rule of cause and effect.

[3] **When Master Ekai, the Zen Master Daichi of Hyakujo,**[1] gives his informal preaching, generally present there is an old man. He always listens to the Dharma along with the assembly, and when the people in the assembly retire, the old man also retires. Then suddenly one day he does not retire. The Master eventually asks him, *"What person is this, standing before me?"*

The old man answers, *"I am not a person. In the past age of Kāśyapa Buddha,*[2] *I used to preside on this mountain. Once a student asked me, 'Do even people in the state of great practice fall into cause and effect, or not?' I answered, 'They do not fall into cause and effect.' Since then I have fallen into the body of a wild fox for five hundred lives. Now I beg you, Master, to say for me words of transformation.*[3] *I long to be rid of the body of*

---

1. Master Hyakujo Ekai (749–814), successor of Master Baso Do-itsu. Ekai was his monk's name used during his lifetime. Zen Master Daichi is his posthumous title. He lived on Mt. Hyakujo in Kiangsi province in southeast China.

2. Kāśyapa Buddha is the sixth of the seven ancient buddhas, and so the time of Kāśyapa Buddha suggests the eternal past.

3. 一転語 (ICHITENGO), lit. "one-turn words," or "turning words," means words that have the power to transform another. See chap. 61, *Kenbutsu*, note 9.

a wild fox." Then he asks, *"Do even people in the state of great practice fall into cause and effect, or not?"*

The Master says, "Do not be unclear about cause and effect."

The old man, under these words, realizes the great realization. He does prostrations and says, *"I am already rid of the body of a wild fox, and would like to remain on the mountain behind this temple. Dare I ask the Master to perform for me the rites for a deceased monk?"*

The Master orders the supervising monk[4] to strike the block[5] and to tell the assembly, *"After the meal, we will see off a deceased monk."*

All the monks discuss this, [saying,] *"The whole Saṃgha is well and there is no sick person in the Nirvāṇa Hall.[6] What is the reason for this?"*

After the meal, the Master is simply seen leading the monks to the foot of a rock on the mountain behind the temple, and picking out a dead fox with a staff. They then cremate it according to the formal method. In the evening the Master preaches in the Hall and discusses the preceding episode.

Obaku[7] then asks, *"The man in the past answered mistakenly with words of transformation, and fell into the body of a wild fox for five hundred lives. If he had gone on without making a mistake, what would have become of him?"*

The Master says, *"Step up here. I will tell you."*

Obaku finally steps up and gives the Master a slap. The Master claps his hands and laughs, and says, *"You have just expressed that a foreigner's[8] beard is red, but it is also a fact that a red-beard is a foreigner."*[9]

[6] This story is in *Tensho-koto-roku.*[10] Still, people of learning in practice are not clear about the truth of cause and effect, and they make the mistake of idly negating cause and effect. It is pitiful that, with a wind of decay blowing all around, the Patriarch's truth[11] has slipped into decline. *"They do not fall into cause and effect"* is just the negation of cause and effect, as a result of which [the negator] falls into bad states. *"Do not be unclear about cause and effect"*

---

4. 維那 (INO), supervisor of monks in the Zazen Hall, or rector; one of the six main officers.

5. 白椎 (BYAKU-TSUI), means to beat the top of an octagonal wooden pillar with a small wooden block *(tsui)* in order to call the monks together.

6. Name of the temple infirmary.

7. Master Obaku Ki-un (died between 855 and 859), successor of Master Hyakujo.

8. 胡 (KO) originally indicated a person from the area to the northwest of China; that is, Russia.

9. *Tensho-koto-roku,* chap. 8, and *Shinji-shobogenzo,* pt. 2, no. 2. Also quoted in Shobogenzo, chap. 76, *Dai-shugyo.*

10. *Tensho-koto-roku,* the second of the Five Records of the Torch, was completed in the Tensho Era of the Sung Dynasty, about thirty years after *Keitoku-dento-roku.* Its 30 chapters were compiled by Ri Junkyoku.

11. In this case the Patriarch's truth means Master Bodhidharma's Buddhism, centered in Zazen.

evidently is deep belief in cause and effect, as a result of which the listener gets rid of bad states. We should not wonder [at this], and should not doubt it. Among people of recent generations who profess to be "students of the way of Zen practice," most have negated cause and effect. How do we know that they have negated cause and effect? Namely [because] they have considered that *"do not fall"* and *"do not be unclear"* amount to the same and are not different. Hence, we know that they have negated cause and effect.

[7] The nineteenth patriarch, the Venerable Kumāralabdha, says, *"In brief, retribution for good and bad has three times. Common people only see that to the good [comes] early death; to the violent, long life; to the evil, fortune; and to the righteous, calamity; whereupon [common people] say that cause and effect is nonexistent and that 'wrongness' and 'happiness' are meaningless. Particularly, they do not know that shadow and sound accord with [their sources], without a discrepancy of a thousandth or a hundredth and—even with the passing of a hundred thousand myriad kalpas—never wearing away."*[12]

Clearly we have seen that the ancestral Patriarch never negates cause and effect. That present students of later ages do not clarify the ancestral Founder's benevolent instruction is [due to] negligence in emulating the ancients. Those who are negligent in emulating the ancients and yet randomly call themselves good counselors to human beings and gods, are great nuisances to human beings and gods and are the enemies of practitioners. You people before and behind me! Never preach, with the purport of negating cause and effect, to junior students and late learners. That is false doctrine. It is not the Dharma of the Buddhist patriarchs at all. It is due to sparse study that you have fallen into this false view.

[9] Patch-robed monks and the like of present-day China often say; *Though we have received the human body and have met the Buddha-Dharma, we do not know even the facts of one life or two lives. The former Hyakujo who became a wild fox has been able to know five hundred lives. Clearly, he might be beyond falling down as the result of karma. It may be that "Even if held by golden chains and black barriers, he does not abide. He goes forward among alien beings and, for the present, lets the wheel turn."*[13] The views and opinions of those who are called great good counselors are like this. But it is difficult to place such views and opinions inside the house of the Buddhist patriarchs. There are those among human beings, or among foxes, or among other beings, who innately possess the power to see a while back into former states,[14] but it is not the seed of clear understanding: it is an

12. *Keitoku-dento-roku*, chap. 2. Also quoted in Shobogenzo, chap. 84, *Sanji-no-go*.

13. These are the concluding two lines of a poem by Master Do-an Josatsu—one of ten of his poems quoted in *Keitoku-dento-roku*, chap. 29. Master Do-an Josatsu belongs to a side lineage of Master Seigen Gyoshi. These lines suggest that our efforts to order our lives are always in vain, so we should live freely and independently without worrying about cause and effect.

14. 宿通 (SHUKUTSU) stands for 宿住通 (SHUKU-JU-TSU), the power to know former states of

effect felt from bad conduct. The World-honored One has broadly expounded this principle for human beings and gods; not to know it is the utmost negligence in study. It is pitiful. Even knowing a thousand lives or ten thousand lives does not always produce the Buddha's teaching. There are non-Buddhists who already know eighty thousand kalpas [but their teaching] is never esteemed as the Buddha's teaching. To know barely five hundred lives is no great ability. The greatest ignorance of recent Zen practitioners of the Sung Dynasty lies just in their failure to recognize that *not falling into cause and effect* is a doctrine of the false view. It is pitiful that, in a place where the Tathāgata's right Dharma has spread, and while meeting the authentic transmission from patriarch to patriarch, they form wrong groups who negate cause and effect. Zen practitioners should urgently clarify the truth of cause and effect. The truth of the present Hyakujo's *not being unclear about cause and effect* is "not to be ignorant of cause and effect."[15] So the principle is evident that if we initiate a cause we will feel the effect. [This] may be the assertion of the buddhas and the patriarchs. As a general rule, before clarifying the Buddha-Dharma, do not randomly preach the Dharma to human beings and gods.

[11] The ancestral Master Nāgārjuna[16] says, *"If we deny the existence of cause and effect in the world, as do people of non-Buddhism, then there is no present or future; and if we deny the existence of cause and effect beyond the world,[17] then there are no Three Treasures, Four Truths, or four effects of a śramaṇa."*[18]

Clearly we should know that to deny the existence of cause and effect, whether in the world or beyond the world, must be non-Buddhism. "Denial of the present" means: *The physical form exists at this place, but the spiritual essence since time immemorial has belonged to the state of enlightenment. The spiritual essence is just the mind, for the mind is not the same as the body.* Such understanding is just non-Buddhism. Some say: *When human beings die, they unfailingly return to the ocean of spiritual essence;*[19] *even if they do not practice and learn the Buddha-Dharma, they will naturally return to the ocean of enlightenment, whereupon the wheel of life and death will turn no more. For this reason, there will be no future.* This is the nihilist view of non-Buddhism.[20] Even if in form they resemble bhikṣus, those who

---

existence. See chap. 25, *Jinzu.*

15. Master Dogen explained the Chinese character 昧 (MAI), "unclear," with the Japanese word 暗し *(kurashi),* which means unclear, dark, or ignorant.

16. The fourteenth patriarch in India.

17. 出世 (SHUSSE), "out of the world," means the Buddhist area as opposed to the secular world.

18. The four effects are 1) *srotāpanna,* 2) *sakṛdāgāmin,* 3) *anāgāmin,* and 4) *arhat.* See Book 1, Glossary. *Maka-shikan,* chap. 33.

19. 性海 (SHOKAI), or "the spirit world." The same term appears in chap. 1, *Bendowa.*

20. 断見外道 (DANKEN-GEDO), lit. "cutting-off view non-Buddhism," represents the Sanskrit *uccheda-dṛṣṭi.* This view denies continuation into the future of the moral cause and effect

hold such wrong opinions are not the Buddha's disciples at all. They are just non-Buddhists. In sum, because they negate cause and effect, they wrongly opine that the present and the future do not exist. Their negation of cause and effect is the result of failing to learn in practice under a true good counselor. One who has long studied under a true good counselor can never hold wrong opinions such as the negation of cause and effect. We should profoundly believe in and admire, and should humbly receive upon the head[21] the benevolent instruction of the ancestral Master Nāgārjuna.

3] Master Genkaku, the Great Master Shinkaku of Yoka,[22] is an eminent disciple of Sokei.[23] Previously he has studied the Flower of Dharma of the Tendai [Sect],[24] sharing a room with Great Master Sakei Genro.[25] While he is reading the Nirvāṇa Sutra,[26] golden light floods the room and he attains forever the realization in which there is no birth. He proceeds to visit Sokei [mountain] and reports his experience to the sixth Patriarch. The sixth Patriarch in time gives his seal of approval. Later [Master Genkaku] produces *"The Song of Experiencing the Truth,"*[27] in which he says; *"'Emptiness'*[28] *run wild negates cause and effect; and, in a morass of looseness, invites misfortune and mistakes."*[29] Clearly we should know, *the negation of cause and effect* is *the invitation of misfortune and mistakes*. Past masters in former ages all were clear about cause and effect. Late learners in recent ages all are deluded about cause and effect. [But] even in the present age, those who, with a dauntless bodhi-mind, learn the Buddha-Dharma for the sake of the Buddha-Dharma, will be able to clarify cause and effect as did the masters of the past. To say that there are no causes and no effects is just non-Buddhism.

---

relation. It is opposed to 常見外道 (JOKEN-GEDO), "eternity view non-Buddhism," from the Sanskrit *śāśvata-dṛṣṭi*. These two opposing views are known as 辺見 (HENKEN), "the extreme views," from the Sanskrit *antagrāha-dṛṣṭi*. See Glossary and note 38.

21. 頂戴 (CHODAI) literally means humbly to receive some revered object (such as the kaṣāya) upon the head, as a sign of reverence. See chap. 12, *Kesa-kudoku*.

22. Master Yoka Genkaku. Great Master Shinkaku is his posthumous title. Yoka is the name of the city where he was born. The information about him recorded here is contained in *Keitoku-dento-roku*, chap. 5.

23. Master Daikan Eno (638–713), the sixth patriarch in China.

24. Tendai is the name of a mountain, of Master Tendai Chigi who lived there, and of the Tendai Sect which he founded. The Tendai Sect is based on the study of the Lotus Sutra (the Sutra of the Flower of Dharma).

25. The eighth patriarch of the Tendai Sect. Died 754, aged 82.

26. That is, the *Mahāparinirvāṇa-sūtra (Sutra of the Great Demise)*.

27. 証道歌 (SHODOKA). This work is still commonly recited in Soto Sect temples in Japan today.

28. 空 (KU), "emptiness," in this case suggests the concept of *śūnyatā* as understood in idealistic interpretations: the view that all is nothing; indifference, vacuity. See Book 1, Glossary.

29. 過 (KA), "mistakes" in the orginal *Shodoka* is 禍 (KA, *wazawai*), "calamity."

[15] The eternal Buddha Wanshi[30] comments on the aforementioned instance of cause and effect, in a eulogy to the ancients, as follows:

One foot of water and a one-fathom wave.[31]
[What happened] five hundred lives ago is of no consequence.
Even as [people] discuss 'not falling' and 'not being unclear,'
Still they are forcing themselves into nests of entanglement.[32]
Ha! Ha! Ha!
Do you understand, or not?
If you are free and easy,
There is nothing to prevent me going "Ta! Ta! Wa! Wa!"[33]
Gods sing, spirits dance, and music naturally plays.
In between hand claps, a chorus of hoorays.

The present words *"Even as [people] discuss 'not falling' and 'not being unclear,' still they are forcing themselves into nests of entanglement"* just mean that *not falling* and *not being unclear* may amount to the same. In short, this instance of cause and effect has not completely expressed the theory thereof. The reason, if asked, is that although [Wanshi] has manifested before us the shedding of the body of a wild fox, he does not say that [the former Hyakujo], after escaping the body of a wild fox, will then be born in the human world, he does not say that [the former Hyakujo] will be born in the heavens above, and he does not say that [the former Hyakujo] will be born in any other state. [But these] are the areas of people's doubt. If he deserves, once rid of the body of a wild fox, to be born in a good state, he will be born in the heavens above or the human world; if he deserves to be born in an evil state he will be born in a state such as the four evil states.[34] After getting rid of the body of a wild fox, he cannot emptily exist without a place of appearance. The assertions that when living beings die they return to the ocean of spiritual essence, or that they return to the universal self, are both the views of non-Buddhists.

[17] Master Kokugon,[35] the Zen Master Engo of Kassan mountain, in a eulogy to the ancients, says:

Fishes swim and water gets muddy,
Birds fly and feathers fall.

---

30. Master Wanshi Shokaku (1091–1157), a successor of Master Tanka Shijun. See also, for example, chap. 27, *Zazenshin.*

31. Concrete things here and now.

32. 葛藤 (KATTO), see chap. 46, *Katto.*

33. The sounds of a baby, suggesting Master Wanshi's unworried state.

34. Hell, the world of *pretas* (hungry ghosts), the world of animals, and the world of *asuras* (angry demons).

35. Master Engo Kokugon (1063–1135), successor of Master Goso Ho-en, and editor of *Heki-gan-roku (Blue Cliff Record).* See also chap. 66, *Shunju,* and chap. 74, *Tenborin.*

The supreme mirror [36] *is inescapable,*
Great space is desolate and wide open.
Once a thing has passed, it is utterly distant.
Five hundred lives originate solely from the great practice that is
cause and effect.
A thunderbolt breaks the mountain and wind shakes the ocean,
[But] pure gold forged a hundred times does not change its color. [37]

Even this poem of praise has a tendency towards negation of cause and effect. At the same time, it has a tendency towards the eternity view.[38]

[8] Master Soko,[39] the Zen Master Dai-e of Kinzan mountain in Koshu,[40] in a poem of praise, says:

'Not falling' and 'not being unclear':
Are stones and clods,
Met along the path by any rice paddy.
Having crushed the silver mountain,
I clap my hands and laugh, ha! ha!, in every situation.
In Minshu[41] *there lived that foolish Happy Buddha.*[42]

People of the Sung Dynasty today consider someone like this to be an instructing patriarch. But the view and understanding of Soko has never arrived [even] at the idea of bestowing the Buddha-Dharma through expedients. If anything, he has a tendency towards the view and understanding of naturalism. In all, for this [one] story, there are eulogies to the ancients and

---

36. A mirror symbolizes a standard, a criteria, or a law—in this case, used as a concrete simile for the law of cause and effect.

37. This world is very changeable, but at the same time, it has an immutable essence. *Engo-zenji-goroku*, chap. 19.

38. 常見 (JOKEN), "the eternity view." In general, 常見 (JOKEN), "the eternity view," and 断見 (DANKEN), "the cutting-off view," may be interpreted as traditional expressions of the two extreme views that modern philosophy calls idealism (championed by Hegel) and materialism (championed by Marx). See also note 20.

39. Master Dai-e Soko (1089–1163), successor of Master Engo Kokugon. Master Soko was a leading proponent of so-called *koan zen*, as opposed to the *mokusho zen* (silent reflection) of Soko's contemporary, Master Wanshi Shokaku. Master Dogen often praised Master Wanshi as an eternal buddha (see, for example, chap. 27, *Zazenshin*), but strongly criticized Master Dai-e Soko (see, for example, chap. 48, *Sesshin-sessho*, and chap. 75, *Jisho-zanmai*).

40. Present-day Hangchou, capital city of Chekiang province at the head of Hangchou Bay.

41. A district in the east of present-day Chekiang province.

42. 布袋 (HOTEI), or "Canvas Bag," so called because he wandered through China from temple to temple carrying a big bag containing all his belongings. He is the original "Happy Buddha" portrayed in statues with a fat belly and a happy smile. According to one account, he died in 916. Another account dates his death as in the Tenpuku era of the Tang dynasty (901 to 903). Quoted from *Dai-e-zenji-goroku*, chap. 10.

discussions of the ancients by more than thirty people. Not even one of them has suspected that *"they do not fall into cause and effect"* is the negation of cause and effect. It is pitiful that these fellows, without clarifying cause and effect, have uselessly idled away a lifetime in a state of confusion. In learning in practice the Buddha-Dharma, the first priority is to clarify cause and effect. Those who negate cause and effect are likely to beget the false view that craves profit, and to become a cutter of good roots.[43] In general, the truth of cause and effect is vividly apparent and is not a personal matter: those who commit evil fall down, and those who practice good rise up, without a thousandth or a hundredth of a discrepancy. If cause and effect perished and became void, buddhas could not appear in the world, and the ancestral Master could not come from the west. In sum, it would be impossible for living beings to meet Buddha and to hear the Dharma. The truth of cause and effect is not understood by the likes of Confucius and Lao-tzu.[44] It is clarified and transmitted only by the buddhas and the patriarchs. Students in [this] degenerate age, being of sparse good fortune, do not meet a true teacher and do not hear the right Dharma, and for this reason they do not clarify cause and effect. If we negate cause and effect, as a result of this error, in a *morass of looseness,* we will suffer *misfortune and mistakes.* Even before we have committed any evil other than negating cause and effect, the poison of this view, to begin with, will be terrible. Therefore, if people of learning in practice, seeing the bodhi-mind as foremost, wish to repay the vast benevolence of the Buddhist patriarchs, they should swiftly clarify causes and effects.

Shobogenzo Shinjin-inga

On a day of the summer retreat in the 7th year of Kencho,[45] I copied this from the Master's rough draft. He had yet to reach the stage of an intermediate draft or a fair copy. Doubtless there would have been revisions.

Ejo[46]

---

43. 断善根 (DAN-ZENKON), "cutter of good roots," represents the Sanskrit *icchantika,* which suggests one who is interested only in selfish ends. See Book 2, Glossary.

44. The founders of Confucianism and Taoism.

45. 1255.

46. Master Dogen's successor, Master Ko-un Ejo. Master Dogen died in 1253, two years before Master Ejo wrote this. This chapter is one of the chapters of the 12-chapter edition of Shobogenzo, which Master Dogen compiled in the final years of his life.

[90]

四禅比丘

SHIZEN-BIKU

The Bhikṣu in the Fourth Dhyāna

__Shi__ means four. __Zen__ represents the Sanskrit word dhyāna, which means Zazen or "the state in Zazen." __Biku__ represents the Sanskrit word bhikṣu, which means a Buddhist monk. __Shizen-biku__, or the bhikṣu who had attained the fourth state in Zazen, refers to a monk who mistakenly thought that his own state was the state of the arhat, a Buddhist practitioner who has reached the fourth and ultimate stage of practice. When he was dying, an apparition appeared before this monk; something not usually seen by someone who has attained the fourth state in Zazen, so he felt that Gautama Buddha had deceived him. And because of his mistaken idea, he fell into hell. Master Dogen quotes this story as an example of the wrong approach to Buddhism. In addition, in this chapter he warns strongly against the serious mistake of believing that Buddhism, Confucianism, and Taoism all teach the same thing.

23] **The fourteenth Patriarch,** the ancestral Master Nāgārjuna, said: *Among the Buddha's disciples there was one bhikṣu who, on attaining the fourth dhyāna, became highly self-conceited*[1] *and thought he had attained the fourth effect.*[2] *When he first attained the first dhyāna he thought he had attained the state of a srotāpanna;*[3] *when he attained the second dhyāna he thought it was the state of a sakṛdāgāmin;*[4] *when he attained the third dhyāna he thought it was the state of an anāgāmin;*[5] *and when he attained the fourth dhyāna, he thought it was arhathood. He thus became proud of himself and did not seek to progress further. When his life was about to end, he saw coming to him the form of a middle netherworld*[6] *for [one who has] the fourth dhyāna, and there arose in him the false view. He thought, "There is no nirvāṇa. The Buddha has deceived me." Because of [this] evil false view, he lost the middle netherworld for the fourth dhyāna and saw the form of*

---

1. 増上慢 (ZOJOMAN) represents the Sanskrit *abhimāna*, one of the seven categories of *māna* (arrogance). See Glossary.

2. 四果 (SHIKA), the state of an arhat.

3. A stream-enterer. See Book 1, Glossary.

4. One who will return only once more. (ibid.)

5. One who is not subject to returning. (ibid.)

6. 中陰 (CHU-IN), represents the Sanskrit *antarā-bhava*, the middle existence between death and regeneration, usually rendered into Chinese characters as 中有 (CHU-U), "middle existence." See Book 1, Glossary.

a middle netherworld in Avīci-niraya.[7] *When his life ended, he was at once born in Avīci-niraya. The bhikṣus asked the Buddha, "When the life of [this] araṇya-bhikṣu*[8] *ended, where was he born?" The Buddha said, "This person was born in Avīci-niraya." The bhikṣus were greatly surprised: Could sitting in Zazen and keeping the precepts lead to that? The Buddha answered as before, and said, "Everything stemmed from his conceit. When he attained the fourth dhyāna he thought he had attained the fourth effect. [Then] when he came to the end of his life and saw the form of a middle netherworld for the fourth dhyāna, there arose in him the false view. He thought, 'There is no nirvāṇa. I am an arhat; now, nonetheless, I am to be reborn. The Buddha has committed a deceit.' He thereupon saw the form of a middle netherworld to Avīci-niraya and as soon as his life ended he was born in Avīci-niraya." Then the Buddha preached in verse, saying:*

> *Even with abundant knowledge, observance of precepts, and dhyāna,*
> *He had yet to attain the Dharma by which excesses are ended.*
> *Although he possessed this virtue,*
> *This fact was hard for him to believe.*
> *That he fell into hell was because he slandered the Buddha.*
> *It was not connected with the fourth dhyāna.*[9]

[26] This bhikṣu is called *"the bhikṣu in the fourth dhyāna,"* and is also called *"the bhikṣu of no knowledge."* [The story] warns against mistaking attainment of the fourth dhyāna for the fourth effect, and it also warns against the false view which slanders the Buddha. All in the great order of human beings and gods have known [this story]: from the time when the Tathāgata was in the world until today, both in the Western Heavens and the Eastern Lands, in order to warn against attaching to what is wrong as if it were right, [human beings and gods] say in derision, "That is like attaining the fourth dhyāna and thinking it is the fourth effect!" The wrongs of this bhikṣu, if I now briefly summarize them, are threefold.[10] Firstly, although he is somebody of no knowledge who cannot distinguish between the fourth dhyāna and the fourth effect, he vainly departs from teachers and idly lives alone in the araṇya. Happily, this is the time when the Tathāgata is in the world. If [this bhikṣu] regularly visited the place of the Buddha, so that he were constantly meeting Buddha and hearing the Dharma, the mistakes described here could never be. Instead, living alone in the araṇya, he does not visit the place of the Buddha and does not meet Buddha and hear the Dharma at last, which is why he is like this. Even if he fails to visit the place of the Buddha, he should go to the orders of the great arhats and receive their instruction. Vainly to live in

---

7. *Avīci*, lit. "waveless," is the name of a particular hell. *Niraya* means hell.

8. *Araṇya* means forest, wilderness, or deserted place. The bhikṣu lived alone in the wilderness without visiting reliable teachers.

9. *Daichido-ron*, fascicle 17.

10. The first two mistakes are listed in this paragraph. The third mistake is described in para. [34].

solitude is a mistake born of self-conceit. Secondly, when he attains the first dhyāna he thinks it is the first effect, when he attains the second dhyāna he thinks it is the second effect, when he attains the third dhyāna he thinks it is the third effect, and when he attains the fourth dhyāna he thinks it is the fourth effect. This is his second mistake. The forms of the first, second, and third dhyānas, and the forms of the first, second, and third effects, are beyond comparison: how could we draw [a comparison]? This [mistake] derives from the fault of being without knowledge, a fault which [itself] derives from not serving a teacher and from ignorance.

[28] *Among the disciples of Upagupta*[11] *there is a bhikṣu who, with devout mind, has left his family life and got the fourth dhyāna, but he thinks it is the fourth effect. Upagupta, using expedient means, causes him to go to a distant place and makes a band of robbers materialize on the road thereto. He also materializes five hundred merchants. The robbers attack the merchants and there is a massacre. Seeing it, the bhikṣu becomes afraid. At once he thinks to himself, "I am not an arhat. This must be the third effect." After the merchants are dead, there [only] remains the daughter of a wealthy [merchant]. She says to the bhikṣu, "Solely I beg you, virtuous monk, take me with you!" The bhikṣu replies, "The Buddha does not permit me to walk with a woman." The girl says, "I will follow you from a distance, virtuous monk." The bhikṣu takes pity on her; in sight of each other they walk on. The Venerable One then materializes a big river. The woman says, "Virtuous monk, will you cross with me?" The bhikṣu is downstream, the woman upstream. The girl suddenly falls into the water and calls, "Virtuous monk, save me!" Then the hands of the bhikṣu reach to her and rescue her. He thinks about her smoothness and lust arises in his mind—at once he recognizes that he is not an anāgāmin. But feeling intense love for this woman, he leads her to a secluded place, wanting to have intercourse with her. On seeing that this is the Master, he is greatly ashamed and stands with head bowed. The Venerable One says, "You considered yourself to be an arhat. How could you want to do such a bad deed?" He led [the bhikṣu] into the Saṃgha, made him confess, explained to him the pivot of the Dharma, and caused him to attain the state of arhat.*[12]

[31] This bhikṣu initially makes the mistake of having views, but on witnessing the massacre he becomes afraid. At that time he thinks, "I am not an arhat." Still, he is mistaken in thinking that he might be in the third effect. After that, because of thinking about the [woman's] smoothness, he causes lust to arise in his mind and knows that he is not an anāgāmin. He has no thought of slandering the Buddha, no thought of slandering the Dharma, and no thought of turning against the sacred teachings; he is not the same as the bhikṣu in the fourth dhyāna. This bhikṣu possesses the ability of one who has learned the sacred teachings, and so he knows himself that he is not an arhat and not an anāgāmin. People without knowledge today neither know what

---

11. The fourth patriarch in India. See chap. 15, *Busso.*

12. Fascicle 5, pt. 4 of *Maka-shikan-hogyo-den-guketsu,* a commentary on Master Tendai Chigi's *Maka-shikan.* Master Tendai Chigi was founder of the Tendai Sect.

arhat is nor know what buddha is; therefore they do not know themselves that they are not arhats and not buddhas. That they just randomly think and say, "I am buddha," may be a great mistake and a profound fault. Students first should learn what buddha is.

[32] *A master of the past said, "Therefore we know that those who learn the sacred teachings know the proper order from the beginning; and transgressions, even if they occur, are easily resolved."*[13]

How true are the words of the master of the past! Even if they make the mistake of having views, people who have learned even a bit of the Buddha-Dharma will never be deceived by themselves and will never be deceived by others.

[33] *I have heard; there was a person who thought that he had become a buddha, and when the sky did not clear as he expected, he thought it must be due to the hindrances of demons. [The sky] did clear, but after that he did not see King Brahmā requesting him to preach the Dharma. He knew that he was not a buddha; he thought that he must be an arhat. But then when others spoke ill of him his mind became temperamental, and he knew that he was not an arhat; so he thought he must be in the third effect. But then when he saw a woman and thought lewd thoughts he knew that he was not a sacred person. Here also, because [a person] honestly recognized the form of the teachings, he was [able to be] like this.*[14]

[34] Now, those who know the Buddha-Dharma sense their own wrongness like this and swiftly get rid of mistakes. Those who do not know idly remain for their whole lives in stupidity; and even if they receive life after life, still it will be so. This disciple of Upagupta, having attained the fourth dhyāna, thinks he is in the fourth effect, but thereafter he has the wisdom that *"I am not an arhat."* If the bhikṣu of no knowledge, on coming to the end of his life and being able to see the middle netherworld for the fourth dhyāna, had the recognition *"I am not an arhat,"* then he could not be guilty of slandering the Buddha. Still more, it has been a long time since he attained the fourth dhyāna; why has he failed to recognize, by reflecting upon himself, that he is not in the fourth effect? If he were aware already of not being in the fourth effect, how could he fail to correct himself? [Instead,] he vainly sticks to his wrong consideration, hopelessly sunk in a false view. Thirdly, when his life ends, he makes an enormous mistake, the wrongness of which is so grave that he has duly fallen into Avīci Hell. [Monk of no knowledge,] even if you have spent your whole life thinking that the fourth dhyāna is the fourth effect, if you are able, when your life is ending, to see the middle netherworld for the fourth dhyāna, you should confess your lifelong mistake and consider that you were never in the fourth effect. How could you think, "The Buddha has

---

13. *Maka-shikan-hogyo-den-guketsu,* fascicle 5, pt. 4.
14. Ibid.

deceived me; though nirvāṇa does not exist, he has fabricated that nirvāṇa exists"? This is a wrongness [born of] no knowledge. This sin, already, is to have slandered the Buddha. Because of this, the middle netherworld to Avīci appears to him and, when his life ends, he falls down into Avīci Hell. How could anyone, even a saint of the fourth effect, equal the Tathāgata? Śāriputra has long been a saint of the fourth effect. Collect [all] the wisdom that exists in a three-thousand-great-thousandfold world, see [the wisdom] of others—excluding the Tathāgata—as one division, and compare a sixteenth of Śāriputra's wisdom with the wisdom that remains in the three-thousand-great-thousandfold world: [that remaining wisdom] will not equal the one-sixteenth of Śāriputra's wisdom. Nevertheless, on hearing the Tathāgata preach Dharma that he has never preached before, Śāriputra does not think, "This is different from the Buddha's preaching at former and latter times; [the Buddha] is deceiving me." He says in praise, *"Pāpīyas has nothing like this."*[15] The Tathāgata delivers Wealth-Increaser,[16] Śāriputra does not deliver Wealth-Increaser: the great difference between the fourth effect and the Buddha-effect is like this. If the world in the ten directions were full of the likes of Śāriputra and the other disciples, and together they tried to fathom the Buddha's wisdom, it would be impossible.[17] K'ung-tzu and Lao-tzu[18] have never had such virtue. Who among students of the Buddha-Dharma could fail to fathom Confucius and Lao-tzu? [But] no student of K'ung-tzu and Lao-tzu has ever fathomed the Buddha-Dharma. People today of the great kingdom of Sung mostly uphold the principle of agreement between K'ung-tzu and Lao-tzu and the Buddha's truth. It is the gravest of wrong views, as later I shall expand. When the bhikṣu in the fourth dhyāna, seeing his own wrong view as true, considers that the Buddha has deceived him, he turns his back on the Buddha's truth forever. The enormity of his stupidness may be equal to that of the six teachers.[19]

---

15. Lotus Sutra, *Hiyu (A Parable): "The World-honored One preaches the real truth./Pāpīyas has no such thing."* See LS 1.142. See Book 3, Glossary *(pāpīyas).*

16. 福増 (FUKUZO) represents the meaning of the Sanskrit *Śrīvaddhi,* the name of a rich man said to be already one hundred when he resolved to become a monk. Śāriputra refused to let him, saying he was too old. Later, Śrīvaddhi asked the Buddha, and the Buddha allowed it. Śrīvaddhi is described in fascicle 4 of *Kengu-kyo,* and also mentioned in Shobogenzo, chap. 86, *Shukke-kudoku.*

17. Alludes to Lotus Sutra, *Hoben.* See LS 1.72.

18. 孔老 (KORO) stands for 孔子 (KOSHI), K'ung-tzu, and 老子 (ROSHI), Lao-tzu. K'ung-tzu (555–479 B.C.), that is, Confucius, is the founder of Confucianism. Lao-tzu (also c. 6th century B.C.) is regarded as the founder of Taoism.

19. 六師 (ROKUSHI) stands for 六師外道 (ROKUSHI-GEDO), the six non-Buddhist teachers: Pūraṇa-kassapa (who denied the existence of good and evil), Makkali-gosāla (a fatalist), Sañjaya-velaṭ-ṭhiputta (a skeptic), Ajita-kesakambarin (a materialist), Pakuda-kaccāyana (who explained the universe by seven elemental factors), and Nigaṇṭha-nātaputta (the founder of Jainism).

[38] *A master of the past said, "Even when the Great Master was in the world, there were people of wrong consideration and views. How much worse, after [the Tathāgata's] extinction, are those without a teacher who are unable to attain any dhyāna."*[20]

The present *"Great Master"* means the World-honored Buddha. Truly, even those who left family life and received ordination when the World-honored One was in the world had difficulty, due to lack of knowledge, in avoiding the mistake of wrong consideration and the holding of views. How much less could we, in a remote and inferior time and place, in the fifth five-hundred-years after the Tathāgata's extinction, be without mistakes? Even one who established the fourth dhyāna was like this. How much less deserving of discussion are those who are not up to establishing the fourth dhyāna and who idly sink into greed for fame and love of gain, or those who crave official promotion or secular careers. In the great kingdom of Sung today there are many ill-informed and foolish people. They say that the Buddha-Dharma and the methods of K'ung-tzu and Lao-tzu are in accord and not divergent.

[39] *In the great Sung era of Katai,*[21] *there was a monk Shoju*[22] *who edited and presented*[23] *the record Futo-roku*[24] *in thirty volumes. He said, "Your subject has heard the words of Kozan Chi-en*[25] *that, 'My truth is like a three-legged cauldron, and the three teachings are like its legs. If one leg were missing, the cauldron would tip up.' Your subject has long since admired this person and contemplated his preaching, whereupon I have recognized that the essence of what Confucianism teaches is integrity, the essence of what the Tao teaches is detachment, and the essence of what Śākyamuni teaches is seeing the nature.*[26] *Integrity, detachment, seeing the nature: different in name, same in substance. When we master the point at which they converge, there is nothing that does not concur exactly with this truth..."*[27]

[40] People like this of wrong consideration and views are very many; they are not only Chi-en and Shoju. The mistake of these people is more grave than that of one who has attained the fourth dhyāna and thinks it is the fourth effect. They are slandering the Buddha, slandering the Dharma, and slandering the Saṃgha. Already, they are negating salvation, negating the three times, and negating cause and effect. That *in a morass of looseness, they invite*

---

20. *Maka-shikan-hogyo-den-guketsu,* fascicle 4, pt. 1.

21. 1201 to 1205.

22. Master Rai-an Shoju. A successor of Master Getsudo Dosho. Died 1208, aged 67.

23. That is, presented to the emperor.

24. *Katai-futo-roku (Katai Era Record of the Universal Torch),* completed 1201. Contains stories of both monks and lay people.

25. A monk of the Tendai Sect. Died 1022, aged 47.

26. 見性 (KENSHO), "seeing the nature" or "enlightenment": the concept 見性 (KENSHO) is generally used by people who regard the experience of "enlightenment" as an aim outside of practice.

27. Quoted from the preface to *Katai-futo-roku.*

misfortune and calamity,[28] is beyond doubt. They are equal to those who have thought that there are no *Three Treasures, Four Truths, or four effects of a śramaṇa.*[29] The essence of the Buddha-Dharma is never *seeing the nature*. Where has any of the Seven Buddhas or the twenty-eight patriarchs of India said that the Buddha-Dharma is only *seeing the nature*? The Sixth Patriarch's *Platform Sutra*[30] contains the words *seeing the nature*, but that text is a fake text; it is not the writing of one to whom the Dharma-treasury was transmitted, and it is not the words of Sokei. It is a text upon which descendants of the Buddhist Patriarch absolutely never rely. Because Shoju and Chi-en never knew one corner of the Buddha-Dharma, they produced this wrong consideration about one cauldron with three legs.

] *A master of the past said, "Even Lao-tzu and Chuang-tzu*[31] *themselves never recognized the subject of attachment and the object of attachment or the subject of detachment and the object of detachment of the small vehicle;*[32] *much less actual attachment and actual detachment*[33] *within the Great Vehicle. For this reason, they are not even slightly similar to the Buddha-Dharma. Yet the stupid people of the secular world are deluded by concepts and forms, and people of indiscriminate Zen stray from the true theory. They would like to equate the concepts of 'the merit of the Tao'*[34] *and 'the amble,'*[35] *with the preaching of salvation through the Buddha-Dharma; but how could that be possible?"*[36]

---

28. Alludes to a line in Master Yoka Genkaku's *Shodoka*: *"Emptiness run wild negates cause and effect; and in a morass of looseness, invites misfortune and calamity."* See also chap. 89, *Shinjin-inga*.

29. Alludes to Master Nāgārjuna's words, quoted in chap. 89, *Shinjin-inga*: *"When they deny the existence of cause and effect beyond the world, then there are no Three Treasures, Four Truths, or four effects of a śramaṇa."*

30. 六祖壇経 (ROKUSO-DANKYO) was said to have been compiled by Hokai and other disciples of Master Daikan Eno, the Sixth Patriarch. There are several editions, including the Tonko edition (Tonko was a station on the Silk Road), the Kosho-ji edition (Kosho-ji is a temple in Kyoto), and the Korean edition.

31. Lao-tzu is said to be the founder of Taoism, and Chuang-tzu is said to be his student. The Chinese texts of Taoism are named after the authors to whom those texts are ascribed. So the name "Chuang-tzu" represents both Taoist teaching and the name of the supposed teacher.

32. The small vehicle means intellectual Buddhism in which subject and object are separated.

33. 若著若破 (NYAKU-JAKU NYAKU-HA), lit. "possibility of attachment, possibility of breaking [attachment]." 若 (NYAKU) expresses possibility, but Master Dogen used the character to represent actuality, or the fact of already having happened. In chap. 22, *Bussho*, para. [14], Master Dogen identifies 若至 (NYAKU-SHI), "if it has arrived," and 既至 (KI-SHI), "it has already arrived."

34. 道徳 (DOTOKU). There is a text ascribed to Lao-tzu called 老子道徳経 (ROSHI-DOTOKU-KYO), *The Scripture of the Merit of the Tao of Lao-tzu.*

35. 逍遥 (SHOYO), lit. walk, amble, or stroll, expresses the fundamental ideal in the teaching of Chuang-tzu: to walk amid nature in a state of perfect ease.

36. *Maka-shikan-hogyo-den-guketsu*, fascicle 3, pt. 4.

Since olden times those deluded by concepts and forms and those who do not know the true theory have equated the Buddha-Dharma with Chuang-tzu and Lao-tzu. Of those who possess, with respect to the Buddha-Dharma, even slight esteem for the ancients, not one person since olden times has attached importance to Chuang-tzu or Lao-tzu.

[43] *Shojo-hogyo-kyo*[37] *says, "The Bodhisattva Moon Light*[38] *there they call Gankai;*[39] *the Bodhisattva Light and Purity*[40] *there they call Chuji;*[41] *the Bodhisattva Kāśyapa there they call Lao-tzu..."*[42]

Since olden times, quoting the preaching of this sutra, [people] have said that K'ung-tzu, Lao-tzu, and so on are bodhisattvas and so their preaching may be, at heart, equal to the Buddha's preaching, and they may be, moreover, the Buddha's emissaries, whose preaching might naturally be the Buddha's preaching. These opinions are all wrong. *A master of the past said, "Those who have referred to the catalogues [of the sutras], all consider this sutra to be a fake..."*[43] Relying now upon this preaching, [we can say that] the Buddha-Dharma and K'ung-tzu and Lao-tzu may be ever more widely divergent. [K'ung-tzu and Lao-tzu] are bodhisattvas already; they cannot compare with the Buddha-effect. Furthermore, the virtue of *softening one's light and harmonizing one's traces*[44] is the Dharma only of the buddhas and bodhisattvas of the three times. It is not an ability of common men in [the world of] secular dust. How can a common man occupied in his business be free to harmonize traces? K'ung-tzu has never had any saying about harmonizing traces. Still less do K'ung-tzu and Lao-tzu know causes in the past or explain effects in

---

37. 清浄法行経 (SHOJO-HOGYO-KYO), lit. "Sutra of Pure Dharma-Conduct," is not contained in the *Daizo-kyo* or complete collection of Buddhist sutras. The sutra was likely a fake, written in China as if it were written in India.

38. 月光 (GEKKO) represents the meaning of the Sanskrit *Candraprabha*. The image of this bodhisattva, along with that of 日光菩薩 (NIKKO-BOSATSU), the Bodhisattva Sun Light, (from the Sanskrit *Sūryaprabha*) are usually arranged on either side of the image of 薬師如来 (YAKUSHI-NYORAI), lit. "Medicine-Master Tathāgata," the Buddha of Healing (in Sanskrit *Bhaiṣajya-guru*, or *Bhaiṣajya-guru-vaiḍūryaprabha-tathāgata*). Statues of these three have been very popular in China and Japan from ancient times.

39. 顔回 (GANKAI), said to be the most excellent of the ten great disciples of K'ung-tzu.

40. 光浄 (KOJO); Sanskrit name not traced.

41. 仲尼 (CHUJI), another name of Confucius.

42. *Maka-shikan-hogyo-den-guketsu*, fascicle 6, pt. 3.

43. Ibid.

44. 和光応迹 (WAKO-OJAKU). 和光 (WAKO), "softening light," describes the practice of buddhas and bodhisattvas of concealing the brightness of their own state, so as not to bedazzle the living beings whom they wish to save. 応迹 (OJAKU), "harmonizing traces," describes the practice of buddhas and bodhisattvas of flexibly showing different forms as befits living beings who must be saved (see, for example, LS 3.252). Applying the theory of 和光応迹 (WAKO-OJAKU), people in China and Japan have argued that Confucianist and Taoist teachers, and Shinto gods, are manifestations of buddhas and bodhisattvas.

the present. They see as the aim the art of serving a lord and managing a household through the loyalty and filial piety of merely one age; they have no preaching at all about future ages. They may be, already, the descendants of nihilists. Those who, despising Chuang-tzu and Lao-tzu, have said, *"They know not even the small vehicle, much less the Great Vehicle,"* are the clear teachers of antiquity. Those who say that the three teachings are at one are [as] Chi-en and Shoju; they are the dim-witted common men of a later degenerate age. You [Chi-en and Shoju], what excellence do you have to disregard the preaching of the ancestral masters of antiquity and to claim at random that the Buddha-Dharma might be equal to K'ung-tzu and Lao-tzu? Your views are never fit for discussing the penetrable and the impenetrable in the Buddha-Dharma. Carrying your backpacks, you should go to learn under a clear teacher. Chi-en and Shoju! You have never known either the great or the small vehicle. You are more ignorant than [the monk] who, having attained the fourth dhyāna, thought it was the fourth effect. It is sad that, where winds of decay are blowing, there are many demons like this.

6] *A master of the past said, "According to the words of K'ung-tzu*[45] *and Kitan*[46] *and the writings of the three emperors and the five rulers,*[47] *a household is regulated through filial piety, a nation is regulated through loyalty, and the people benefit through assistance. But this is limited within one age; it does not extend into the past or the future. It never compares with the Buddha-Dharma's benefiting of the three times. How could [such a comparison] not be mistaken?"*[48]

How true they are, the words of the past master. They have nicely arrived at the ultimate principle of the Buddha-Dharma, and they are clear with regard to the principles of secular society. The words of the three emperors and the five rulers can never equal the teachings of the sacred wheel-rolling kings and should never be discussed alongside the preachings of King Brahmā or the god Śakra. The areas [Chinese emperors] govern, and the effects and results they attain may be far inferior. [But] not even the wheel kings, King Brahmā, and the god Śakra equal a bhikṣu who has left family life and received ordination. How much less could they equal the Tathāgata? The writings of K'ung-tzu and Kitan, moreover, cannot equal the eighteen great scriptures of India,[49] and they do not bear comparison with the four books of the Vedas.[50] The Brahamanist teaching of the Western Heavens is

---

45. 孔丘 (KOKYU), another name of Confucius. 丘 (KYU) was his first name.

46. 姫旦 (KITAN) means the ancient Chinese emperor 周公 (SHUKO), who laid down guidelines for an effective political system.

47. 五帝 (GOTEI). The legendary period of Chinese history (2852 B.C. to 2205 B.C.) is known as 五帝紀 (GOTEI-KI), "the age of the five rulers."

48. There is a similar passage in *Maka-shikan-hogyo-den-guketsu,* fascicle 10, pt. 2.

49. The scriptures of Brahmanism: four Vedas, six commentaries, and a further eight commentaries.

50. The Sanskrit *veda* lit. means divine knowledge (see Glossary). The Vedas, which are

never equal to the Buddha's teaching, nor even equal to the teachings of śrāvakas of the small vehicle. It is pitiful that, in the minor and remote nation of China, there is the false doctrine that the three teachings are at one.

[48] The fourteenth patriarch, Bodhisattva Nāgārjuna, said, *"The great arhats and pratyekabuddhas know eighty thousand great kalpas. The great bodhisattvas and [buddhas] know countless kalpas."*[51]

The likes of K'ung-tzu and Lao-tzu never know past and future within one generation. How could they have the power to know one past life or two past lives? How much less could they know one kalpa? How much less could they know a hundred kalpas or a thousand kalpas? How much less could they know eighty thousand great kalpas? And how much less could they know countless kalpas? Compared with the buddhas and bodhisattvas who illuminate and know these countless kalpas more clearly than one looking at the palm of a hand, the likes of K'ung-tzu and Lao-tzu do not even deserve to be called dim. Covering the ears, do not listen to the words that the three teachings are at one. It is the wrongest doctrine among wrong doctrines.

[49] Chuang-tzu said, *"Nobility and lowliness, suffering and joy, right and wrong, gain and loss: all these are just the natural state."*[52]

This view, already, is the descendant of non-Buddhists of the naturalistic view in the Western Kingdom.[53] Nobility and lowliness, suffering and joy, right and wrong, gain and loss, are all the effect of good or bad conduct. Because [Chuang-tzu] neither knows *fulfilling karma*[54] and *pulling karma*[55] nor understands the past and the future, he is ignorant of the present; how could he be equal to the Buddha-Dharma? Some say: *The buddha-tathāgatas widely substantiate the worlds of Dharma. Therefore Dharma-worlds of atoms*[56] *are all substantiated by the buddhas. That being so, both forms of [karmic] result, circumstances and the subject,*[57] *amount to the preaching of the Tathāgata, and therefore mountains,*

---

thought to have been compiled between c. 2000 and c. 500 B.C., consist of 1) *ṛg-veda*, the oldest collection of hymns; 2) *sāma-veda*, hymns (mainly from the *ṛg-veda*) set to music for use in rituals; 3) *yajur-veda*, spells used in rituals; and 4) *atharva-veda*, spells used in daily rites.

51. *Daichido-ron*, chap. 5.

52. *Maka-shikan*, fascicle 10, pt. 1.

53. 西国 (SAIKOKU), a variation of 西天 (SAITEN), "Western Heavens": India.

54. 満業 (MAN GO), sometimes called 別報業 (BEPPO-GO), "karma of distinct results," is a technical term in Chinese Buddhism to describe karma that produces the individual differences between a man or a woman, the wise and the unwise, the rich and the poor, et cetera.

55. 引業 (INGO) means karma that produces general results, such as birth as a human being.

56. Suggests the material realms of the Taoists. This section in italics represents an attempt to identify the materialist or naturalistic view with the Buddha-Dharma.

57. 依正二報 (E-SHO-NIHO) means 正報 (SHOHO) and 依報 (EHO). 正報 (SHOHO), lit. "the true result," means the human subject as the result of past karma. 依報 (EHO), lit. "dependence-results," means the circumstances upon which the subject's existence depends. 依正 (ESHO) is

rivers, and the Earth, the sun, the moon, and the stars, the four illusions[58] *and the three poisons,*[59] *all are what the Tathāgata preached. To see the mountains and rivers is to see the Tathāgata. The three poisons and the four illusions are nothing other than the Buddha-Dharma. To see atoms is the same as seeing the world of Dharma, and every instant is the state of saṃbodhi.*[60] *This is called "the great liberation." This is called "the directly transmitted and immediately accessible truth of the patriarchs."* Fellows who speak like this are as [common as] rice, flax, bamboo, and reeds; the government and the people are full of them. It is not clear, however, whose descendants these fellows are, and they do not know the truth of the Buddhist patriarchs at all. While [mountains, rivers, and the Earth] may be what the buddhas preach, it is not impossible for mountains, rivers, and the Earth momentarily to be what the common man sees. [Those fellows] do not learn and do not hear the principle of what constitutes the preaching of buddhas. For them to say that seeing atoms is the same as seeing the world of Dharma is like subjects saying they are the same as a king. Moreover, why do they not say that seeing the world of Dharma is the same as seeing atoms? If the view of these fellows could be esteemed as the great truth of the Buddhist patriarchs, the buddhas need not have appeared in the world, the ancestral Master need not have manifested himself, and living beings would not be able to attain the truth. Even if [those fellows] physically realize that *appearance is just non-appearance,*[61] [the truth] is beyond this principle.

Paramārtha Sanzo[62] *said, "In China there are two blessings. The first is that there are no rākṣasas.*[63] *The second is that there are no non-Buddhists."*[64]

These words were in fact imported by a non-Buddhist Brahmin from the Western Kingdom. Even if there is no-one able to penetrate non-Buddhism, that does not mean there cannot be people who beget non-Buddhist views.

---

commonly used as an expression of object and subject.

58. 四倒 (SHI-TO) is short for 四顛倒 (SHI-TENDO), lit. "the four inversions." 顛倒 (TENDO) represents the Sanskrit *viparyāsa*, which means overturning, inversion, perverseness, or delusion (see Glossary). The four illusions are 1) the illusion of permanence (*nitya-viparyāsa*); 2) the illusion of pleasure (*sukha-viparyāsa*); 3) the illusion of purity (*śuci-viparyāsa*); and 4) the illusion of self (*ātma-viparyāsa*).

59. 三毒 (SANDOKU); anger, greed, and ignorance.

60. The inclusive state of truth.

61. 生即無生 (SHO-SOKU-MUSHO), or "birth is non-birth," is a principle in the Sanron Sect which suggests going beyond conventional thinking: what is conventionally called "birth" or "appearance" is, in reality, a momentary state in which there is no change.

62. 真諦三蔵 (SHINTAI-SANZO). 真諦 (SHINTAI), lit. "True Philosophy," represents the meaning of the Sanskrit *Paramārtha*, the monk's name. 三蔵 (SANZO) was a title for a scholar of the tripiṭaka. Paramārtha (449–569), a native of western India, was invited to China by Emperor Wu of the Liang Dynasty in 546. He translated 64 sutras and other Buddhist books into Chinese, including the *Konkomyo-kyo (Golden Light Sutra)*.

63. Evil or malignant demons.

64. *Maka-shikan*, fascicle 10, pt. 1, and *Maka-shikan-hogyo-den-guketsu*, fascicle 10, pt. 2.

Rākṣasas have never been seen, but that does not mean there are no descendants of non-Buddhists. The reason [China] is a minor nation in a remote land, and therefore not the same as India, the center,[65] is that although [the Chinese] have learned the Buddha-Dharma a little, there is no-one who has grasped the state of experience as [it was grasped] in India.

[53] *A master of the past said, "Today there are many who have returned to secular society.*[66] *Afraid of having to perform king's service,*[67] *they enter into non-Buddhism but steal the principles of the Buddha-Dharma in order secretly to understand Lao-tzu and Chuang-tzu. They duly create confusion, deluding beginners about which is true and which is false, calling this the view that is able to unfold the Dharma of the Vedas."*[68]

Remember, those who cause confusion, not knowing which is true and which is false between the Buddha-Dharma and Lao-tzu and Chuang-tzu, and those who delude beginners, are just the present Chi-en and Shojo and their like. Not only is it the grossest stupidity: it is the utmost lack of esteem for the ancients. [This] is obvious and is evident. Among the monks of the Sung dynasty in recent days, there had not been even one who knew that K'ung-tzu and Lao-tzu are inferior to the Buddha-Dharma. Although people who had become descendants of the Buddhist Patriarch,[69] like rice, flax, bamboo, and reeds, filled the mountains and fields of the nine states, there was not one person or half a person upon whom it had dawned that, beyond K'ung-tzu and Lao-tzu, the Buddha-Dharma is outstanding in its excellence. Only my late Master Tendo, the eternal Buddha, clearly understood that the Buddha-Dharma and K'ung-tzu and Lao-tzu are not one. He instituted this teaching day and night. Though [others] were famous as teachers of sutras and commentaries or as lecturers, it had not dawned on any of them that the Buddha-Dharma far surpasses the areas of K'ung-tzu and Lao-tzu. For the last hundred years or so many lecturers have studied the conventions of people who practice [Za]zen and learn the state of truth, hoping to steal their understanding. We can say that they are utterly mistaken. In the writings of K'ung-tzu there is the *person of innate intelligence.*[70] In the Buddha's teaching there are no people of innate intelligence.[71] In the Buddha-Dharma there is

---

65. 中印度 (CHU-INDO), lit. "middle-India," suggests India as the center of civilization.

66. 還俗 (GENZOKU) describes a person giving up the life of a Buddhist monk and going back to secular life.

67. 王役 (O-EKI), was a kind of labor in lieu of tax. In this age, the Chinese government supported Taoism, and burdened Buddhist monks by forcing them to perform such service.

68. *Maka-shikan*, fascicle 10, pt. 1.

69. Suggests people who have become descendants of Master Bodhidharma, by practicing Zazen.

70. 生知者 (SHOCHISHA), or "those who know from birth." This term is also discussed in chap. 26, *Daigo*.

71. Because knowing derives from effort.

explanation of the śarīra.[72] K'ung-tzu and Lao-tzu do not know of the existence or nonexistence of the śarīra. Even if they intend to make [the three teachings] into one and mix them up, penetration or non-penetration of a detailed explanation will be beyond them at last.

[56] *Rongo*[73] *says, "[Those] who know it from birth are the best. Those who know through study are next. Those who learn it with difficulty are after that. Those who fail to learn even with difficulty, the people will see as the lowest."*[74]

If [this says] there is inborn intelligence, it is guilty of negating causality. In the Buddha-Dharma there is no doctrine that negates causality. When the bhikṣu in the fourth dhyāna comes to the end of his life, he falls into the sin of slandering the Buddha momentarily. If [students] think that the Buddha-Dharma is equal to the teachings of K'ung-tzu and Lao-tzu, their sin, to slander the Buddha through a lifetime, must be grave indeed. Students should swiftly throw away the opinion that falsely considers the Buddha-Dharma and K'ung-tzu and Lao-tzu to be at one. Those who harbor this view and fail to discard it will eventually fall into an evil state. Students, you must clearly remember: K'ung-tzu and Lao-tzu neither know the Dharma in the three times nor know the truth of cause and effect. They do not know the peaceful establishment of one continent;[75] how much less could they know the peaceful establishment of the four continents.[76] They do not even know about the six heavens; how much less could they know the Dharma of the triple world of nine realms?[77] They do not know a small thousandfold world and they are not able to know a middle thousandfold world; how could they see and how could they know the three-thousand-great-thousandfold world? Even in the solitary realm of China [K'ung-tzu and Lao-tzu] are only minor retainers who have not ascended to the rank of emperor; they cannot be compared with the Tathāgata, who is the king of the three-thousand-great-thousandfold world. In the Tathāgata's case, Brahmadeva, the god Śakra, and sacred wheel-rolling kings, day and night are venerating him and standing guard over him and perpetually requesting him to preach the Dharma. K'ung-tzu and Lao-tzu are without such merit; they are only common men wandering in

---

72. Sacred bones, especially of the Buddha. See, for example, Lotus Sutra (LS 2.154) and Shobogenzo, chap. 71, *Nyorai-zenshin*.

73. 論語 (RONGO), *The Discourses of Confucius*, the fundamental text of Confucianism.

74. *Rongo*, fascicle 8.

75. 一洲 (ISSHU), "one continent," means the southern continent of Jambudvīpa upon which human beings are living.

76. 四洲 (SHISHU), "the four continents," from the Sanskrit *catvāro-dvīpāh*, are Jambudvīpa (south), Pūrva-videha (east), Apara-godāna (west), and Uttara-kuru (north). See Glossary.

77. 三界九地 (SANGAI-KUJI), here represents the whole real world. The triple world comprises the worlds of desire, matter, and non-matter. It is said that the world of desire is one realm with hell at the bottom and the six heavens at the top. The worlds of matter and non-matter have four realms each.

the mundane circuit. They have never known the truth of transcendence and salvation; how could they perfectly realize, in the manner of the Tathāgata, that *all dharmas are real form*. If they have never perfectly realized [this] how could they be seen as equal to the World-honored One? K'ung-tzu and Lao-tzu are without inner virtue and without outer usefulness; they can never arrive at the level of the World-honored One. How could we disgorge the false doctrine that the three teachings are at one? K'ung-tzu and Lao-tzu cannot penetrate the existence of boundaries and the nonexistence of boundaries of the world. Not only do they fail to see and fail to know the wide and fail to see and fail to know the great; they [also] fail to see the smallest material forms and fail to know the length of a kṣāṇa.[78] The World-honored One clearly sees the smallest material forms and knows the length of a kṣāṇa; how could we liken him to K'ung-tzu and Lao-tzu? K'ung-, Lao-, and Chuang-tzu, and Hui-tzu[79] and suchlike, are just common men. They could not reach the level of even a srotāpanna[80] of the small vehicle; how much less could they reach the level of the second [effect] or the third [effect] or an arhat of the fourth [effect]? That students, however, out of ignorance, put them on a par with the buddhas, is *in the midst of delusion, deepening delusion*. K'ung-tzu and Lao-tzu are not only ignorant of the three times and ignorant of the many kalpas; they are not able to know one instant of mindfulness and not able to know one moment of the mind. They do not bear comparison even with the gods of the sun and the moon and they cannot equal the four great kings[81] and the hosts of gods. Whether in the secular sphere or beyond the secular sphere, [seen] in comparison with the World-honored One, they are straying in delusion.

[59] *The Biographies*[82] *say: "Ki was a great man of the Chou [dynasty].*[83] *He was skilled in astrology and once saw a celestial anomaly. Following it eastward, he met, as he had expected, Lao-tzu, whom he asked to write a book of five thousand words. Ki wished to go forth*[84] *so that he could follow Lao-tzu.*[85] *Lao-tzu said, 'If you are determined to go forth, bring the heads of seven people including your father and mother, and then you will be able to go forth.' Ki immediately did as he had been told, whereupon the seven heads all turned into the heads of pigs." A master of the past said, "In contrast, Confucianists*

---

78. An instant. See chap. 70, *Hotsu-bodaishin*, para. [201]: "Only the Tathāgata clearly knows the length of this kṣāṇa..."

79. 恵子 (KEISHI) was a scholar and orator who became a prime-minister during the Wei dynasty (220–265).

80. One who has entered the stream, the first of the four effects leading to arhathood.

81. The Four Quarter Kings who guard the four continents. In Sanskrit *catvāro mahā-rājikāḥ*.

82. 列伝 (RETSUDEN) refers to the biographical section of the Chinese book called 史記 (SHIKI), *(History)*.

83. The Chou dynasty prevailed in China from c. 1122 B.C. to c. 222 B.C.

84. He wished to quit his position in Chou society.

85. Lao-tzu is here called by the name 耼 (TAN).

who are [versed in] secular scriptures and dutiful to their parents honor even [their parent's] wooden images. [But] when Lao-tzu established his instruction, he made Ki kill his parents. In the lineage of the Tathāgata's teaching, great benevolence is the foundation. How could Lao-tzu make a deadly sin the starting point of his instruction?"[86]

61] In the past there were wrong groups who compared Lao-tzu with the World-honored One, and today there are stupid fellows who say that both K'ung-tzu and Lao-tzu compare with the World-honored One. How could we not pity them? K'ung-tzu and Lao-tzu cannot equal even the sacred wheel-rolling kings who, through the ten kinds of good,[87] govern the secular world. How could the three emperors and the five rulers be equal to the wheel-rolling kings of the gold, silver, copper, and iron [wheels], who are furnished with the seven treasures and a thousand things and who either govern four continents or rule a three-thousandfold world? K'ung-tzu and Lao-tzu can never be compared with even these [three emperors and five rulers]. The buddhas and the patriarchs of the past, present, and future have each considered the starting point of instruction to be dutiful obedience to parents, teacher-monks, and the Three Treasures; and service of offerings to sick people and so on. They have never, since time immemorial, considered harming one's parents to be the starting point of instruction. So Lao-tzu and the Buddha-Dharma are not one. To kill one's father and mother, in every case, is karma [felt] in the next life, in which falling into niraya is assured. For all Lao-tzu's random discussion of "the void," those who harm their father and mother will not escape the arising of retribution.

2] *Dento-roku says: The Second Patriarch*[88] *constantly lamented, saying, "The teachings of K'ung-tzu and Lao-tzu are [only] the art of decorum and criteria for behavior, and the writings of Chuang-tzu and the I-ching*[89] *are imperfect in regard to exquisite truths. Recently I have heard that the great man Bodhidharma is residing at Shaolin. A consummate human being may not be far away. [Under him] I shall mold the profound state."*[90]

People today should definitely believe that the authentic transmission into China of the Buddha-Dharma was solely due to the Second Patriarch's power of learning in practice. Though the First Patriarch had come from the west, without the Second Patriarch, the Buddha-Dharma would not have

---

86. *Maka-shikan-hogyo-den-guketsu,* fascicle 5, pt. 6.

87. 十善 (JUZEN) are abstention from the ten wrongs: 1) killing, 2) stealing, 3) adultery, 4) lying, 5) two-faced speech, 6) abusive speech, 7) useless chatter, 8) greed, 9) anger, 10) wrong views.

88. Master Taiso Eka, successor of Master Bodhidharma. See, for example, chap. 30, *Gyoji.*

89. 易 (EKI), "divination," stands for 易経 (EKI-KYO), lit. "The Divination Scripture," that is the I-ching. This work was written during the Chou dynasty, based on the study of yin and yang.

90. *Keitoku-dento-roku,* chap. 3.

been transmitted. If the Second Patriarch had not transmitted the Buddha-Dharma, in the eastern lands today there would be no Buddha-Dharma. In general the Second Patriarch must not be grouped among others.

[63] *Dento-roku says: The monk Shinko[91] was a man of broad accomplishments. For a long time he lived in I-raku.[92] He was widely read in many texts, and was well able to discuss profound truths.[93]*

The Second Patriarch's wide reading of many texts in former days may be far beyond the reading of [a few] volumes by people today. After he attained the Dharma and received the transmission of the robe, he had no words to the effect that, "In former days when I thought the teachings of K'ung-tzu and Lao-tzu were [only] the art of decorum and criteria for behavior, that was a mistake." Remember, the Second Patriarch had clearly realized that K'ung-tzu and Lao-tzu are unable to equal the Buddha-Dharma. Why do his distant descendants today turn their backs on their ancestral father and say that [K'ung-tzu and Lao-tzu] and the Buddha-Dharma are at one? Just know that it is a false doctrine. Among distant descendants of the Second Patriarch, who could rely upon the explanations of Shoju and the like? If you want to be a descendant of the Second Patriarch, never say that the three teachings are at one.

[65] *When the Buddha was in the world, there was a non-Buddhist called "Debating-Power"[94] who thought that in debate there was no-one who could equal his learning, his power being the greatest; for this reason, he was called "Debating-Power." At the request of five hundred Licchavīs,[95] he compiled five hundred salient enigmas and came to pester the World-honored One. Coming to the Buddha's place, he asked the Buddha, "Is there one ultimate truth, or are there many ultimate truths?"*

The Buddha said, "There is only one ultimate truth."

Debating-Power said, "We teachers each assert that we have the ultimate truth. Among non-Buddhists, we each consider ourself to be right and disparage the ways of others; we find in each other rightness and wrongness: therefore there are many truths."

The World-honored One at that time had already converted Deer-Head,[96] who had realized the effect of one beyond study.[97] He was standing by the Buddha. The Buddha asked Debating-Power, "Among the many truths, whose is foremost?"

---

91. Master Taiso Eka. Shinko was his monk's name in his youth.

92. The district bordered by two rivers pronounced in Japanese as *I* and *Raku*.

93. *Keitoku-dento-roku*, chap. 3.

94. 論力 (RONRIKI). Sanskrit name not traced.

95. An ethnic group inhabiting the republic of Vaiśālī. Its capital, also called Vaiśālī, was located at the present Besarb, twenty-seven miles north of Patna.

96. 鹿頭 (ROKUTO), from the Sanskrit *Migasīsa*. He was a brahmin from Kośala, who formerly practiced magic techniques, but later took refuge in the Buddha and became an arhat.

97. 無学果 (MUGAKUKA), "the effect of one beyond study," is a synonym for the state of arhat.

Debating-Power said, "Deer-Head is foremost."

The Buddha said, "If he is foremost, why has he discarded his own truth,[98] *become my disciple, and entered my state of truth?"*

Seeing this, Debating-Power hung his head in shame. He took refuge and entered the truth. Then the Buddha preached a philosophic verse, saying:

> *Everyone claims the ultimate,*
> *Each attaching to themselves,*
> *Each seeing themselves as right and others as wrong:*
> *This is never the ultimate.*
> *Such people enter controversies,*
> *And strive to elucidate intellectual nirvāṇa.*
> *Disputing with each other right and wrong,*
> *Winners and losers feel sadness or joy.*
> *The winners fall into the pit of conceit;*
> *The losers fall into a hell of gloom.*
> *Therefore, those who have wisdom*
> *Do not fall into these two ways.*
> *Debating-Power, you should know:*
> *In the Dharma of my disciples*
> *There is neither nothingness nor substance.*
> *What are you after?*
> *If you want to destroy my arguments,*
> *There is, at last, no basis for this.*
> *It is impossible to clarify total knowledge;*
> *By this [effort] you will only ruin yourself.*[99]

7] Now the golden words of the World-honored One are like this. The stupid and dull living beings of the eastern lands must not indiscriminately turn their backs on the Buddha's teaching and say that there are truths equal to the Buddha's truth. That would just be slandering the Buddha and slandering the Dharma. [People] of the Western Heavens, from Deer-Head and Debating-Power to the brahmin Long-Nails,[100] the brahmin Senika,[101] and so on: these were people of wide learning, [such as] have never existed since ancient times in the eastern lands. K'ung-tzu and Lao-tzu could never equal them at all. All of them discarded their own truths and took refuge in the Buddha's truth. If we were now to compare the secular people K'ung-tzu

98. 道 (DO), lit. "way" or "truth," represents the Sanskrit *bodhi*. In this context it suggests Dear-Head's former way, outlook, or philosophy of life.

99. *Maka-shikan-hogyo-den-guketsu*, fascicle 10, pt. 2, and *Daichido-ron*, fascicle 18.

100. 長爪 (CHOSO), represents the Sanskrit *Dīrghanakha*, the name of a brahmin who did not cut his nails, described in *Zo-agon-kyo*.

101. A brahmin described in the Garland Sutra. See, for example, chap. 1, *Bendowa*, and chap. 6, *Soku-shin-ze-butsu*.

and Lao-tzu with the Buddha-Dharma, even those who listened would be guilty of a sin. Furthermore, even arhats and pratyekabuddhas will all eventually become bodhisattvas: not one of them will finish in the small vehicle. [But] as for K'ung-tzu and Lao-tzu, who never entered the Buddha's truth, how could we say that they are equal to the buddhas? That would be an enormously wrong view. In conclusion, the fact that the World-honored Tathāgata far surpasses all is praised and known unanimously by the buddha-tathāgatas, the great bodhisattvas, Brahmadeva, and the god Śakra. The twenty-eight patriarchs of India all know it. In sum, all those who have the power of learning in practice know it. Living beings of the present degenerative age must not heed the mad utterance of the dimwits of the Sung Dynasty, that the three teachings are at one. It is the utmost ignorance.

Shobogenzo Shizen-biku

On a day during the summer retreat in the 7th year of Kencho,[102] I finished the copying from the Master's first draft.

Ejo

102. 1255. Master Dogen had died two years previously. This is one of the twelve chapters Master Dogen began or rewrote after deciding to make a 100-chapter edition of Shobogenzo. The twelve chapters are: chap. 12, *Kesa-kudoku;* chap. 70, *Hotsu-bodaishin;* chap. 84, *Sanji-no-go;* chap. 85, *Shime;* chap. 86, *Shukke-kudoku;* chap. 87, *Kuyo-shobutsu;* chap. 88, *Kie-sanbo;* chap. 89, *Shinjin-inga;* chap. 90, *Shizen-biku;* chap. 94, *Jukai;* chap. 95, *Hachi-dainingaku;* and *Ippyaku-hachi-homyo-mon.*

[91]

唯仏与仏

YUI-BUTSU-YO-BUTSU

Buddhas Alone, Together With Buddhas

Yui *means "only" or "solely,"* ***butsu*** *means "buddha" or "buddhas" and* ***yo*** *means "and" or "together with." So* ***yui-butsu-yo-butsu*** *means "buddhas alone, together with buddhas."* ***Yui-butsu-yo-butsu*** *is a phrase from a well-known quotation from the Lotus Sutra. The full quotation is: "buddhas alone, together with buddhas are directly able to perfectly realize that all dharmas are real form." In this chapter, Master Dogen explains what buddhas are.*

[1] **The Buddha-Dharma** cannot be known by people. For this reason, since ancient times, no common man has realized the Buddha-Dharma and no-one in the two vehicles[1] has mastered the Buddha-Dharma. Because it is realized only by buddhas, we say that *"buddhas alone, together with buddhas, are directly able perfectly to realize it."*[2] When we perfectly realize it, while still as we are, we would never have thought previously that realization would be like this. Even though we had imagined it, it is not a realization that is compatible with that imagining. Realization itself is nothing like we imagined. That being so, to imagine it beforehand is not useful. When we have attained realization,[3] we do not know what the reasons were for our being [now] in the state of realization.[4] Let us reflect on this. To have thought, prior to realization, that it will be like this or like that, was not useful for realization. That it was different from how we had supposed it to be, in all our miscellaneous prior thoughts, does not mean that our thinking, being very bad, had no power in it. Even the thinking of that time was realization itself, but because we were then directing it the wrong way round, we thought and said that it was powerless. Whenever we feel that [we are] useless, there is something

1. The vehicles of the śrāvaka and pratyekabuddha.

2. Lotus Sutra, *Hoben*. See LS 1.68.

3. さとりぬる *(satori nuru)* is here used, in the present perfect, as an intransitive verb, lit. "to have been enlightened, to have understood." Used as a transitive verb, it means "to realize." In general, the term "enlightenment" has been avoided because of its idealistic connotations. The noun さとり *(satori)*, similarly, has been translated as "realization" in preference to "enlightenment." See chap. 26, *Daigo*.

4. Or "When we have been enlightened, we do not know what the reasons were for our being enlightened."

that we should know; namely, that we have been afraid of becoming small.[5] If realization appears through the force of thoughts prior to realization, it might be an unreliable realization. Because it does not rely upon, and it has come far transcending the time prior to realization, realization is assisted solely by the force of realization itself. Delusion, remember, is something that does not exist. Realization, remember, is something that does not exist.

[74] When the supreme state of bodhi is a person, we call it "buddha." When buddha is in the supreme state of bodhi, we call it *"the supreme state of bodhi."* If we failed to recognize the features of the moment of being in this truth, that might be stupid. Those features, namely, are untaintedness. Untaintedness does not mean forcibly endeavoring to be aimless and free of attachment and detachment; nor does it mean maintaining something other than one's aim. Actually, without being aimed at or attached to or detached from, untaintedness exists. [But,] for example, when we meet people, we fix in mind what their features are like, and [when we see] a flower or the moon, we think upon them an extra layer of light and color. Again, we should recognize that, just as it is inescapable for spring to be simply the spirit of spring itself, and for autumn likewise to be the beauty and ugliness of autumn itself, even if we try to be other than ourselves, we are ourselves. We should reflect also that even if we want to make these sounds of spring and autumn into ourself, they are beyond us. Neither have they piled up upon us, nor are they thoughts just now existing in us. This means that we cannot see the four elements and five aggregates of the present as ourself and we cannot trace them as someone else. Thus, the colors of the mind excited by a flower or the moon should not be seen as self at all, but we think of them as ourself. If we consider what is not ourself to be ourself, even that can be left as it is, but when we illuminate [the state in which] there is no possibility of either repellent colors or attractive ones being tainted, then action that naturally exists in the truth is the unconcealed original features.

[76] A man of old[6] said that the whole earth is our own Dharma-body—but it must not be hindered by a "Dharma-body." If it were hindered by a "Dharma-body," to move the body even slightly would be impossible. There should be a way of getting the body out. What is this way by which people get the body out? For those who fail to express this way of getting the body out, the life of the Dharma-body ceases at once, and they are long sunk in the sea of suffering. If asked a question like this, what should we express, to let the Dharma-body live and so as not to sink into the sea of suffering? At such a time we should express, *"The whole earth is our own Dharma-body."* If this truth is present, the moment expressed as *"The whole earth is our own Dharma-body"* is

---

5. Because we are worried about becoming small, we try to become better, instead of realizing ourselves in the present.

6. Master Chosa Keishin; see following paragraph.

beyond expression. Moreover, when it is beyond expression we should promptly notice the possibility of not expressing it. There is an expression of an eternal buddha who did not express it: [namely,] in death there are instances of living;[7] in living there are instances of being dead;[8] there are the dead who will always be dead;[9] and there are the living who are constantly alive. People do not forcibly cause it to be so: the Dharma is like this. Therefore, when [buddhas] turn the wheel of Dharma they have light and they have sound like this, and we should recognize that in their *manifesting the body to save the living*[10] also, they are like this. This state is called *"the wisdom of non-birth."*[11] Their *manifesting the body to save the living* is their *saving the living to manifest the body.* When we behold their *saving,* we do not see a trace of *manifestation,* and when we watch them *manifesting,* they may be free of concern about *salvation.* We should understand, should preach, and should experience that in this *saving,* the Buddha-Dharma is perfectly realized. We hear and we preach that both *manifesting* and *the body* are as one with *saving.* Here also, [the unity of] *manifesting the body to save the living* makes it so. When [buddhas] have substantiated this principle, from the morning of their attaining the truth to the evening of their nirvāṇa, even if they have never preached a word, words of preaching have been let loose all around.

[79] An eternal buddha said:[12]

The whole earth is the real human body,
The whole earth is the gate of liberation,
The whole earth is the one Eye of Vairocana,[13]
The whole earth is our own Dharma-body.[14]

The point here is that *the real* is the real body. We should recognize that *the whole earth* is not our imagination; it is the body which is real. If someone asks, "Why have I not noticed this so far?" we should say, "Give me back my words that *the whole earth is the real human body."*[15] Or we might say, "That *the*

---

7. For example, a person on a battlefield establishes the will to the truth.

8. For example, a person wastes time regretting something that has already happened.

9. People laid to rest in cemeteries, et cetera.

10. 現身度生 (GENSHIN-DOSHO). See LS 3.252.

11. 無生の知見 (MUSHO *no* CHIKEN). 無生 (MUSHO), "non-appearance" or "non-birth," expresses reality, which is both instantaneousness (in the moment there is no appearance) and eternal (reality has no birth or beginning). 無生 (MUSHO) is also used as a synonym for nirvāṇa. 知見 (CHIKEN), " knowledge" or "knowing," is used many times in the Lotus Sutra to represent prajñā or the Buddha's wisdom. See, for example, LS 1.68; LS 1.88–90.

12. Master Chosa Keishin (d. 868), a successor of Master Nansen Fugan.

13. The Sun Buddha, a symbol of universal light.

14. A slightly different version of Master Chosa's words is quoted in *Engo-zenji-goroku,* chap. 6.

15. A person who can only understand the words intellectually does not deserve to have the words.

whole earth is the real human body, we know like this!" Next, *the whole earth is the gate of liberation* describes there being nothing at all to tangle with or to embrace. The words *the whole earth* are familiar to Time, to the years, to the mind, and to words: they are immediate, without any separation. We should call that which is limitless and boundless *the whole earth.* If we seek to enter this *gate of liberation,* or seek to pass through it, that will be utterly impossible. Why is it so? We should reflect on the asking of the question. Even if we hope to visit a place that does not exist, that is not feasible. Next, *the whole earth is the one Eye of Vairocana:* though buddha is one Eye, do not think that it must necessarily be like a person's eye. In people there are two eyes,[16] but when speaking of [our] Eye,[17] we just say "the human eye"; [18] we do not speak of two or three. When those who learn the teaching, also speak of the Buddha's Eye, the Dharma-Eye, the Supernatural Eye,[19] and so on, we are not studying eyes. To have understood them as if they were eyes is called unreliable. Now we should just be informed that the Buddha's Eye is one, and in it the whole earth exists. There may be a thousand Eyes[20] or ten thousand Eyes, but to begin with *the whole earth* is one among them. There is no error in saying that it is one among so many; at the same time, it is not mistaken to recognize that in the state of Buddha there is only one Eye. Eyes may be of many kinds. There are instances of three being present, there are instances of a thousand Eyes being present, and there are instances of eighty-four thousand being present; so the ears should not be surprised to hear that the Eye is like this. Next, we must hear that *the whole earth is our own Dharma-body.* To seek to know ourself is the inevitable will of the living. But those with Eyes that see themselves are few: buddhas alone know this state. Others, non-Buddhists and the like, vainly consider only what does not exist to be their self. What buddhas call themselves is just the whole earth. In sum, in all instances, whether we know or do not know ourselves, there is no whole earth that is other than ourself. The matters of such times we should defer to people of yonder times.[21]

[82] In ancient times a monk asked a venerable patriarch,[22] "*When a hundred*

16. 目 (ME) means ordinary eyes.

17. まなこ *(manako)* is the Japanese pronunciation of 眼 (GEN), which means not only eyes but also Eye, view, experience, et cetera—as in 正法眼蔵 (SHOBOGENZO), the right-Dharma-Eye treasury.

18. 人眼 (NINGEN). Here 眼 (GEN) means not only the concrete eye, but also the function of seeing.

19. 天眼 (TENGEN) refers to 天眼通 (TENGENZU), the power of supernatural vision, one of the six mystical powers. See chap. 25, *Jinzu.*

20. 千眼 (SENGEN) alludes to the thousand eyes of Bodhisattva Avalokiteśvara. See chap. 33, *Kannon.*

21. We should rely on traditional expressions of the truth.

22. Master Chinshu Hoju (dates unknown), a successor of Master Hoju Ensho, who was the successor of Master Rinzai Gigen. Another of Master Chinshu's conversations is quoted in

thousand myriad circumstances converge all at once, what should I do?" The venerable patriarch said, *"Do not try to manage them."*[23] The meaning is, "Let what is coming come! In any event, do not stir!" This is immediate Buddha-Dharma: it is not about circumstances. These words should not be understood as an admonition; they should be understood as enlightenment in regard to reality. [Even] if we consider how to manage [circumstances], they are beyond being managed.

[83] An ancient buddha said, *"Mountains, rivers, and the Earth, and human beings, are born together. The buddhas of the three times and human beings have always practiced together."* Thus, if we look at the mountains, rivers, and Earth while one human being is being born, we do not see this human being now appearing through isolated superimposition upon mountains, rivers, and Earth that existed before [this human being] was born. Having said this, still the ancient words may not be devoid of further meaning. How should we understand them? Just because we have not understood them, we should not disregard them; we should resolve to understand them without fail. They are words that were actually preached, and so we should listen to them. Having listened to them, then we may be able to understand them. A way in which to understand them [is as follows]: Who is the person that has clarified, by investigating this birth[24] from the side of this human being being born, just what is, from beginning to end, this thing called "birth"? We do not know the end or the beginning, but we have been born. Neither indeed, do we know the limits of mountains, rivers, and the Earth, but we see them here; and at this place, it is as if they are walking.[25] Do not complain that mountains, rivers, and the Earth are not comparable with birth. Illuminate mountains, rivers, and the Earth as they have been described, as utterly the same as our being born.

[85] Again, *the buddhas of the three times* have already through their practice accomplished the truth and perfected realization. How, then, are we to understand that this state of buddha is the same as us? To begin with, we should understand the action of buddha. The action of buddha takes place in unison with the whole Earth and takes place together with all living beings. If it does not include all, it is never the action of buddha. Therefore, from the establishment of the mind until the attainment of realization, both realization and practice are inevitably done together with the whole Earth and together with all living beings. Some doubts may arise in regard to this:

Shinji-shobogenzo, pt. 1, no. 40.

23. 莫管佗 (*ta [o] kan[suru koto] naka[re]*), or "Do not care about them." *Keitoku-dento-roku,* chap. 12.

24. 生 (SHO) means both "birth" and "life."

25. Master Fuyo Dokai said, *"The blue mountains are constantly walking."* See chap. 14, *Sansuigyo.*

when we seek to clarify that which seems to be mixed into ideas that are unknowable, such [doubting] voices are heard; but we should not wonder whether [the state of oneness] is the situation of [other] people. This is a teaching to be understood, and so we should recognize that when we establish, and practice, the mind of the buddhas of the three times, the principle is inevitably present that we do not let our own body-and-mind leak away. To have doubts about this is actually to disparage the buddhas of the three times. If we quietly reflect on ourselves, the truth exists in the fact that our own body-and-mind has been practicing in the same manner as the buddhas of the three times, and the truth is evident also that we have established the mind. If we reflect upon and illuminate the moment before and the moment behind this body-and-mind, the human being under investigation is not I and is not [another] person; in which case, as what stagnant object can we see it, and thereby consider it to be separated from the three times? All such thoughts do not belong to us. When the truth is being practiced by the original mind of the buddhas of the three times, how is it possible for anything at all to hinder that moment? The truth, in short, should be called "beyond knowing and not knowing."

[87] An ancient person said:[26]

Even the crashing down [of illusions] is nothing different;
Fluency[27] *is beyond discussion.*
Mountains, rivers, and the Earth,
Are just the total revelation of the Dharma-King's body.

People today also should learn in accordance with the saying of [this] person of ancient times. [Mountains, rivers, and the Earth] already are the body of a King of Dharma. Therefore there existed a King of Dharma who understood that even the crashing down was nothing different. This idea is like the mountains being on the earth, and like the earth bearing the mountains. When we understand, the time when we did not understand does not return to impede understanding. At the same time, there is no case of understanding being able to destroy past non-understanding. Still, both in understanding and in non-understanding, there is the mind of spring and the voice of autumn. The reason we have not understood even them is that, although [spring and autumn] have been preaching at the top of their voices, those voices have not entered our ears—our ears have been idly wandering inside the voices. Understanding will take place when, with the voice already having entered the ears, samādhi becomes evident. We should not think, though, that this understanding is small whereas the non-understanding was great.

---

26. Master Kokyo Shoju, quoted in *Sekimon-rinkan-roku (Sekimon's Forest Record)*, vol. 1.

27. 縦横 (JU-O), lit. "vertical and horizontal," describes the fluency of a buddha's preaching of Dharma. The same words appear in the opening paragraph of chap. 1, *Bendowa: "When we speak [of Dharma], it fills the mouth: it has no restriction vertically or horizontally."*

We should remember that, because we are beyond matters that we have conceived privately, *the Dharma-King* is like this. As to the meaning of *"the body of the Dharma-King,"* the Eye is like the body and the mind may be equal to the body. It may be that both the mind and the body, without the slightest separation, are *totally revealed.* We understand that in the brightness of light and in the preaching of Dharma, there exists, as described above, the body of the Dharma-King.

89] There is a saying from ancient times that none other than fish knows the mind of fish, and none other than birds can follow the traces of birds. Few people have been able to know this principle. Those who have interpreted only that human beings do not know the mind of fish and that human beings do not know the mind of birds, have misconstrued [the saying]. The way to understand it is [as follows]: Fish together with fish always know each other's mind. They are never ignorant [of each other] as human beings are. When they are going to swim upstream through the Dragon's Gate,[28] this is known to all, and together they make their mind one. The mind to get through the nine [rapids] of Chekiang,[29] also, is communicated in common. [But] none other than fish know this [mind]. Again, when birds are flying through the sky, walking creatures never imagine even in a dream the knowing of these tracks or the seeing and the following of these traces; [walking creatures] do not know that such [traces] exist, and so there is no example of [walking creatures] imagining [such traces]. Birds, however, can see in many ways that hundreds or thousands of small birds have flocked together and flown away, or that these are the traces of big birds that have gone south, or flown north, in so many lines. [To birds, those traces] are more evident than wheel-tracks in a lane, or a horse's hoofprints visible in the grass. Birds see the traces of birds. This principle also applies to buddhas. They suppose how many ages buddhas have spent in practice, and they know small buddhas and great buddhas, even among those who have gone uncounted. These are things that, when we are not buddha, we never know at all. There might be someone who asks, "Why can I not know it?" Because it is with the Eye of buddha that those traces can be seen; and those who are not buddha are not equipped with the Eye of buddha. Buddhas are counted among those that count things; without knowing, [however,] they are totally able to trace the tracks of the paths of buddhas. If, with [our own] eyes we can see these traces, we may be in the presence of buddhas and we may be able to compare their footprints. In the comparing, buddhas' traces are known, the length and depth of buddhas' traces are known, and, through consideration

---

28. The Dragon's Gate is the name of a set of rapids on the Yellow River. It is said that a carp that gets through the Dragon's Gate becomes a dragon.

29. 九浙 (KYU-SETSU). 九 (KYU), "nine," means many. 浙 (SETSU) means 浙江 (SEKKO), which is the name of a province (Chekiang) and a fast-flowing river in which there are many rapids.

of buddhas' traces, the illumination of our own traces is realized. To realize these traces may be called the Buddha-Dharma.

Shobogenzo Yui-butsu-yo-butsu

This was copied under the southern eaves of the guest quarters of Eihei-ji temple on Kichijo-zan mountain, in Shibi manor in the Yoshida district of Esshu,[30] at the end of the last month in spring in the 11th year of Ko-an.[31]

30. Corresponds to modern-day Fukui prefecture.

31. 1288, 35 years after Master Dogen's death. The date on which Master Dogen completed the chapter is not recorded.

[92]

生死

SHOJI

Life-and-Death

*Sho means "life" and ji means "death," so **shoji** means "life and death." Although the words "life" and "death" exist in all languages, Master Dogen says that we are not able to understand intellectually what our life and death are. He says that their meaning is embedded in our real day-to-day life itself. In this chapter he explains life-and-death as the real momentary state at the present moment. In our daily life, life and death both exist in undivided wholeness.*

[93] **Because in life-and-death** there is buddha, there is no life and death. Again, we can say: Because in life-and-death there is no "buddha," we are not deluded in life-and-death.[1] [This] meaning was expressed by Kassan[2] and Jozan.[3] [These] are the words of the two Zen Masters; they are the words of people who had got the truth, and so they were decidedly not laid down in vain. A person who wishes to get free from life and death should just illuminate this truth. If a person looks for buddha outside of life-and-death, that is like pointing a cart north and making for [the south country of] Etsu, or like facing south and hoping to see the North Star. It is to be amassing more and more causes of life and death, and to have utterly lost the way of liberation. When we understand that only life-and-death itself is nirvāṇa, there is nothing to hate as life and death and nothing to aspire to as nirvāṇa. Then, for the first time, the means exist to get free from life and death. To understand that we move from birth[4] to death is a mistake. Birth is a state at one moment; it already has a past and will have a future. For this reason, it is

1. These are Master Dogen's variations of expressions that appear in *Keitoku-dento-roku*, chap. 7: Jozan says to Kassan, *"Because in life-and-death there is no buddha, then it is not life-and-death."* Kassan says, *"Because in life-and-death there is buddha, then we are not deluded by life-and-death."*

2. Master Kassan Zen-e (805–881), a successor of Master Sensu Tokujo. At the suggestion of Master Dogo Enchi, he visited Master Sensu and attained the truth under him (see chap. 14, *Sansui-gyo*, and *Shinji-shobogenzo*, pt. 1, no. 90). Later he lived and taught on Mt. Kassan. His posthumous title was Great Master Denmyo.

3. Master Jozan Shin-ei (dates unknown), a successor of Master Isan Reiyu.

4. 生 (SHO) means "birth," "life," "arising," or "appearance."

said in the Buddha-Dharma that appearance is just non-appearance.[5] Extinction[6] also is a state at one moment; it too has a past and a future. This is why it is said that disappearance is just non-disappearance.[7] In the time called *life*, there is nothing besides life. In the time called *death*, there is nothing besides death. Thus, when life comes it is just life, and when death comes it is just death; do not say, confronting them, that you will serve them,[8] and do not wish for them.

[95] This life-and-death is just the sacred life of buddha. If we hate it and want to get rid of it, that is just wanting to lose the sacred life of buddha. If we stick in it, if we attach to life-and-death, this also is to lose the sacred life of buddha. We confine ourselves to the condition of buddha. When we are without dislike and without longing, then for the first time we enter the mind of buddha. But do not consider it with mind and do not say it with words! When we just let go of our own body and our own mind and throw them into the house of buddha, they are set into action from the side of buddha; then when we continue to obey this, without exerting any force and without expending any mind, we get free from life and death and become buddha. Who would wish to linger in mind?

[97] There is a very easy way to become buddha. Not committing wrongs; being without attachment to life-and-death; showing deep compassion for all living beings, venerating those above and pitying those below; being free of the mind that dislikes the ten thousand things and free of the mind that desires them; the mind being without thought and without grief: this is called buddha. Look for nothing else.

Shobogenzo Shoji

Year not recorded.

---

5. 生すなはち不生 (SHO *sunawachi* FUSHO). 不生 (FUSHO), "non-appearance," expresses instantaneousness. See, for example, chap. 3, *Genjo-koan*.

6. 滅 (METSU) means "extinction," "death," "cessation," or "disappearance." In general 生死 (SHOJI) suggests "life and death," whereas 生滅 (SHOMETSU) suggests "appearance and disappearance"; but 滅 (METSU) also means "death."

7. 滅すなはち不滅 (METSU *sunawachi* FUMETSU). 不滅 (FUMETSU), "non-disappearance," also expresses instantaneousness—the moment of the present is independent, so it does not appear from the past and it does not disappear into the future.

8. "Serving life," or "being a slave to life," means, for example, the attitude of a hypochondriac, or the excessively health-conscious. "Serving death" describes the attitude of a drug addict, or of someone who drives unreasonably fast. "Confronting" suggests separation.

[93]

道心

DOSHIN

The Will to the Truth

Doshin *represents the Sanskrit bodhicitta.* ***Do****, which means "way" or "truth," is a translation of the Sanskrit word bodhi, and* ***shin*** *means "mind/consciousness" or "will." In this chapter, Master Dogen preaches the will to the truth, devotion to the Three Treasures, the making of buddha-images, and practicing Zazen. The teachings in this chapter are rather concrete and direct, and some Buddhist scholars suppose that this chapter may have been written and preached for laypeople.*

9] **In pursuing the Buddha's truth,** we should see the will to the truth as foremost. People who know what the will to the truth is like are rare. We should inquire into it under people who know it clearly. Among people of the world there are people who are said to have the will to the truth but who really do not have the will to the truth. There are people who really have the will to the truth but are not known by [other] people. Thus, it is hard to know of its existence and nonexistence. For the most part, we do not believe and do not listen to the words of people who are stupid and bad. At the same time, we must not see our own mind as foremost. We should see as foremost the Law that the Buddha has preached. Constantly, night and day, we should obsess our minds with how the will to the truth should be; and we should hope and pray that somehow true bodhi might exist in this world. In a degenerate age there is almost no-one with a genuine will to the truth. Nevertheless, applying the mind for a while to inconstancy, we should not forget the unreliability of the world and the precariousness of human life. We need not be conscious that "I am thinking about the unreliability of the world." Deliberately attaching weight to the Dharma, we should think light of "my body" and "my life." For the sake of the Dharma we should begrudge neither body nor life.

01] Next, we should profoundly venerate the Three Treasures of Buddha, Dharma, and Saṃgha. We should desire to serve offerings to and venerate the Three Treasures, even through exchanging a life or exchanging the body.[1] Asleep and awake, we should consider the merit of the Three Treasures.

---

1. In the Mahāparinirvāṇa-sūtra, for example, a bodhisattva barters his body in order to be able to serve offerings to buddhas. See chap. 87, *Kuyo-shobutsu.*

Asleep and awake, we should chant the Three Treasures. Even between abandoning this life and being born in a next life—in which period there is said to be a "middle existence" whose life is seven days—even during that period, we should intend to chant the Three Treasures without ever lulling the voice. After seven days we [are said to] die in the middle existence, and then to receive another body in the middle existence, for seven days. At the longest [this body] lasts seven days. At this time we can see and hear anything without restriction, as if with the supernatural Eye.[2] At such a time, spurring the mind, we should chant the Three Treasures; we should chant without pause, not forgetting to recite *"namu-kie-Butsu, namu-kie-Ho, namu-kie-So."*[3] When, having passed out of the middle existence, we are drawing close to a father and mother, we should steel ourselves and—even when, due to the presence of right wisdom, we are in the womb-store [world][4] that will commit us to the womb—we should chant the Three Treasures. We might not neglect to chant even while being born. We should profoundly desire that, through the six sense organs, we might serve offerings to, chant, and take refuge in the Three Treasures. Again, it may be that when this life ends [a person's] two eyes become dark at once. At that time, knowing already that it is the end of our life, we should strive to chant *"namu-kie-Butsu."* Then the buddhas of the ten directions will bestow their compassion. Even sins for which—due to the presence of contributing causes—we might go to an evil world, will be transformed, and we will be born in the heavens above; being born before the Buddha, we will worship the Buddha and hear the Dharma which the Buddha preaches. After darkness comes before our eyes, we should strive unflaggingly to recite the three devotions, not letting up even until the middle existence, and even until the next birth. In this manner, exhausting life after life in age after age, we should recite [the Three Devotions]. Even until we arrive at the buddha-effect of bodhi, we should not let up. This is the truth practiced by the buddhas and bodhisattvas. It is called "profoundly to realize the Dharma," and is called "the Buddha's truth being present in the body." We should desire never to mix it with different ideas.

[104] Again, within our lifetime we should endeavor to make a buddha. Having made it, we should serve to it the three kinds of offerings. The three kinds are seats of straw, sugared drinks, and lights. We should serve these as offerings.

---

2. 天眼 (TENGEN), one of the six mystical powers. See chap. 25, *Jinzu*.

3. 南無帰依仏 (NAMU-KIE-BUTSU), "Namas! I take refuge in Buddha"; 南無帰依法 (NAMU-KIE-HO), "Namas! I take refuge in Dharma"; 南無帰依僧 (NAMU-KIE-SO), "Namas! I take refuge in Saṃgha." These are the three devotions or refuges. The Sanskrit *namas* is a reverential salutation.

4. 胎蔵 (TAIZO) stands for 胎蔵界 (TAIZOKAI), lit. "womb-store world" (from the Sanskrit *garbha-dhātu*), a term used in esoteric Buddhism to describe a world produced by the Buddha's benevolence. It is the subject of one of the two major maṇḍalas of esoteric Buddhism.

[104] Again, during this life we should produce [copies of] the Sutra of the Flower of Dharma. We should write them, should print them, and should retain them. Constantly we should receive them upon the head in reverence, make prostrations to them, and offer them flowers, incense, lights, food and drink, and clothing. Constantly keeping the head clean, we should humbly receive them upon the head.

[105] Again, constantly we should wear the kaṣāya and sit in Zazen. There are past examples of the kaṣāya [leading to] attaining the truth in a third life.[5] Already it is the attire of the buddhas of the three times: its merit is unfathomable. Zazen is not a method of the triple world:[6] it is the method of the Buddhist patriarchs.

Shobogenzo Doshin

Date not recorded.

5. See, for example, the story of the prostitute who wore the kaṣāya as a joke, in chap. 12, *Kesa-kudoku*.

6. 三界 (SANGAI), the world of desire, matter, and non-matter; the world of ordinary people.

[94]

受戒

JUKAI

Receiving the Precepts

***Ju** means "to receive," and **kai** means the Buddhist precepts. So **jukai** means "receiving the precepts." The traditional way of entering the Buddhist order is by receiving the Buddhist precepts. It is a ceremony marking entry into Buddhist life; becoming a Buddhist. Master Dogen put great value on receiving the precepts; in this chapter he explains what that value is, and gives an outline of the precept-receiving ceremony.*

107] **Zen-en-shingi[1] says,** *"The buddhas of the three times all say that to leave family life is to realize the truth. The ancestral masters of successive generations who transmitted the Buddha-mind-seal, were all śramaṇas.[2] Perhaps it was by strictly observing the vinaya that they were able to become universal models for the triple world. Therefore, in practicing [Za]zen and inquiring into the truth, the precepts are foremost. If we do not depart from excess and guard against wrong, how is it possible to realize the state of buddha and to become a patriarch? The method of receiving the precepts: The three robes, and pātra, must be provided, together with new and clean clothes. If you have no new clothes, wash [old clothes] clean. Do not borrow the robes and pātra of another to go onto the platform and receive the precepts. Concentrate whole-heartedly and be careful not to go against circumstances. To assume the form of the Buddha, to come into possession of the Buddha's precepts, to get what the Buddha received and used: these are not small matters. How could they be treated lightly? If we were to borrow the robes and pātra of another, even if we mounted the platform and received the precepts, we would not get the precepts at all. Having failed to receive them, we would become people without precepts throughout a lifetime, fraternizing without reason in the lineage of emptiness, and consuming devout offerings in vain. Beginners in the truth have not yet memorized the Dharma-precepts; it is masters, by not saying anything, who cause people to fall into this [wrongness]. Now herewith a stern exhortation has been spoken. It is keenly hoped that you will engrave it on your hearts. If you have already received the śrāvaka*

---

1. *Zen-en-shingi (Pure Criteria for Zen Monasteries)* is a ten-fascicle text compiled by Master Choro Sosaku in 1103. This quotation from the first fascicle also appears in Shobogenzo, chap. 83, *Shukke*, and chap. 86, *Shukke-kudoku*.

2. The Sanskrit *śramaṇa* means one who makes effort, a striver, a Buddhist monk.

precepts[3] *you should receive the bodhisattva-precepts. This is the beginning of entering the Dharma."*

[109] In the Western Heavens and the Eastern Lands, wherever the transmission has passed between Buddhist patriarchs, at the beginning of entering the Dharma there is inevitably the receiving of the precepts. Without receiving the precepts we are never the disciples of the buddhas and never the descendants of the ancestral masters—because they have seen *"departing from excess and guarding against wrong"* as *"practicing [Za]zen and inquiring into the truth."* The words *"the precepts are foremost"* already are the right-Dharma-eye treasury itself. To *realize buddha and become a patriarch* inevitably is to receive and maintain the right-Dharma-eye treasury; therefore, ancestral masters who receive the authentic transmission of the right-Dharma-eye treasury inevitably receive and maintain the Buddhist precepts. There cannot be a Buddhist patriarch who does not receive and maintain the Buddhist precepts. Some receive and maintain them under the Tathāgata, which in every instance is to have received the life-blood. The Buddhist precepts now authentically transmitted from buddha to buddha and from patriarch to patriarch were exactly transmitted only by the ancestral Patriarch of Sugaku[4] and, transmitted five times in China, they reached the founding Patriarch of Sokei.[5] The authentic transmissions from Seigen, Nangaku, and so on,[6] have been conveyed to the present day, but there are unreliable old veterans and the like who do not know it at all. They are most pitiful. That *"we should receive the bodhisattva-precepts; this is the beginning of entering the Dharma"* is just what practitioners should know. The observance in which *"we should receive the bodhisattva-precepts"* is authentically transmitted, in every case, by those who have long learned in practice in the inner sanctum of the Buddhist patriarchs; it is not accomplished by negligent and lazy people. In that observance, in every case, we burn incense and perform prostrations before the patriarch-master,[7] and ask *to receive the bodhisattva precepts*. Once granted permission, we bathe and purify ourselves, and put on new and clean clothes. Or we may wash [existing] clothes, then scatter flowers, burn incense, perform prostrations and show reverence, and then put them on.

---

3. Suggests precepts taken by Hīnayāna Buddhists (of which there are 250 precepts for monks and 348 precepts for nuns), as opposed to the 16 bodhisattva-precepts enumerated in this chapter.

4. Master Bodhidharma, the first patriarch in China.

5. Master Daikan Eno, the sixth patriarch in China.

6. Master Seigen Gyoshi and Master Nangaku Ejo were two of Master Daikan Eno's several successors. The lineages of masters of the Soto, Unmon, and Hogen sects trace back to Master Seigen Gyoshi. The lineages of masters of the Igyo and Rinzai sects trace back to Master Nangaku Ejo.

7. 祖師 (SOSHI) is usually translated as "ancestral master," and is often used to refer to Master Bodhidharma. In this case it means a living master who is a patriarch.

Widely we perform prostrations to the statues and images, perform prostrations to the Three Treasures, and perform prostrations to venerable patriarchs; we get rid of miscellaneous hindrances; and [thus] we are able to make body-and-mind pure. Those observances have long been authentically transmitted in the inner sanctum of the Buddhist patriarchs. After that, at the practice-place, the presiding ācārya duly instructs the receiver to do prostrations, to kneel up,[8] and, with palms together,[9] to speak these words:

[112] *"I take refuge in Buddha, take refuge in Dharma, take refuge in Saṃgha.*

I take refuge in Buddha, honored among bipeds.[10]

I take refuge in Dharma, honored as beyond desire. I take refuge in Saṃgha, honored among communities.

I have taken refuge in Buddha, have taken refuge in Dharma, have taken refuge in Saṃgha." (Said three times.)

"The Tathāgata, the ultimate, supreme, right and balanced state of truth, is my great teacher, in whom I now take refuge. From this time forward, I shall not be devoted to wicked demons and non-Buddhists. It is due to [the Tathāgata's] compassion. It is due to his compassion." (Repeated three times.)

[113] *"Good sons!*[11] *Now that you have discarded the false and devoted yourself to the true, the precepts already are surrounding you. You shall receive the Three Summarized Pure Precepts."*

"One: The precept of observance of rules. From your present body until attainment of the Buddha's body, can you keep this precept, or not?" Answer: *"I can keep it."* Asked three times, answered three times.

"Two: The precept of observance of the moral Law. From your present body until attainment of the Buddha's body, can you keep this precept, or not?" Answer: *"I can keep it."* Asked three times, answered three times.

"Three: The precept of abundantly benefiting living beings. From your present body until attainment of the Buddha's body, can you keep this precept, or not?" Answer: *"I can keep it."* Asked three times, answered three times.

"The preceding Three Summarized Pure Precepts each must not be violated. From your present body until attainment of the Buddha's body, can you keep these precepts, or not?" Answer: *"I can keep them."* Asked three times, answered three times.

---

8. 長跪 (CHOKI), lit. "extended kneeling": knees on the floor, thighs and torso extending in a straight line.

9. 合掌 (GASSHO). Palms held together, fingertips pointing upwards at the level of the nostrils.

10. In the source text, taking refuge in the Buddha is recorded on a separate line, as a mark of reverence.

11. 善男子 (ZENNANSHI), short for 善男子善女人 (ZENNANSHI-ZENNYONIN), "good sons and good daughters." These words are commonly spoken by the Buddha in Buddhist sutras. See, for example, LS 3.56.

"These things thus you should keep." The receiver performs three prostrations, and kneels up with palms together.

[115] *"Good sons! You already have received the Three Summarized Pure Precepts. You shall receive the Ten Precepts. They are just the pure and great precepts of the buddhas and bodhisattvas."*

"One: Not to kill. From your present body until attainment of the Buddha's body, can you keep this precept, or not?" Answer: *"I can keep it."* Asked three times, answered three times.

"Two: Not to steal. From your present body until attainment of the Buddha's body, can you keep this precept, or not?" Answer: *"I can keep it."* Asked three times, answered three times.

"Three: Not to lust. From your present body until attainment of the Buddha's body, can you keep this precept, or not?" Answer: *"I can keep it."* Asked three times, answered three times.

"Four: Not to lie. From your present body until attainment of the Buddha's body, can you keep this precept, or not?" Answer: *"I can keep it."* Asked three times, answered three times.

"Five: Not to sell liquor. From your present body until attainment of the Buddha's body, can you keep this precept, or not?" Answer: *"I can keep it."* Asked three times, answered three times.

"Six: Not to discuss the transgressions of other bodhisattvas, be they lay people or those who have left family life. From your present body until attainment of the Buddha's body, can you keep this precept, or not?" Answer: *"I can keep it."* Asked three times, answered three times.

"Seven: Not to praise yourself or to criticize others. From your present body until attainment of the Buddha's body, can you keep this precept, or not?" Answer: *"I can keep it."* Asked three times, answered three times.

"Eight: Not to begrudge Dharma or material possessions. From your present body until attainment of the Buddha's body, can you keep this precept, or not?" Answer: *"I can keep it."* Asked three times, answered three times.

"Nine: Not to become angry. From your present body until attainment of the Buddha's body, can you keep this precept, or not?" Answer: *"I can keep it."* Asked three times, answered three times.

"Ten: Not to insult the Three Treasures. From your present body until attainment of the Buddha's body, can you keep this precept, or not?" Answer: *"I can keep it."* Asked three times, answered three times.

"The preceding Ten Precepts each must not be violated. From your present body until attainment of the Buddha's body, can you keep these precepts, or not?" Answer: *"I can keep them."* Asked three times and answered three times. *"These things thus you should keep."* The receiver performs three prostrations.

8] *"The preceding Three Devotions, Three Summarized Pure Precepts, and Ten Serious Prohibitions are what the buddhas have received and kept. From your present body until attainment of the Buddha's body, these sixteen precepts thus you should keep."* The receiver performs three prostrations. Then we do the Sanskrit [chant, which begins] *"Shi-shi-kai...,"*[12] after which we say:

"I take refuge in Buddha, take refuge in Dharma, take refuge in Saṃgha." Then the receiver leaves the practice-place.

8] This observance of receiving the precepts has been authentically transmitted by Buddhist patriarchs without fail. The likes of Tanka Ten-nen[13] and Śramaṇera Ko of Yakusan[14] have similarly received and kept [these precepts]. There have been ancestral masters who did not receive the bhikṣu-precepts[15] but there has never been an ancestral master who failed to receive *these bodhisattva-precepts authentically transmitted by the Buddhist patriarchs.* We receive and keep them without fail.

Shobogenzo Jukai

Year not recorded.

---

12. The Chinese verse, originally a Sanskrit chant, can be found in the first volume of the sutra *Bussetsu-chojitsumyo-zanmai-kyo*. The four lines of the poem are as follows: 処世界如虚空、如蓮華不著水、心清浄超於彼、稽首礼無上尊。(SHI-SHI-KAI-JI-KI-KUN / JI-REN-KA-FU-JA-SHI / SHIN-SHINJIN-CHO-I-HI / KI-SHU-RIN-BU-JO-SON), *"To be in the world is [to be] as space; / As a lotus flower not touching water. / The mind is pure and beyond the objective world. / I strike my head in prostration to the one who is supremely venerable."*

13. Master Tanka Ten-nen (739–824). A disciple of Master Sekito Kisen, he was famous for having burned a wooden buddha to keep warm, and other unorthodox behavior. He also studied under Master Baso Do-itsu. *Keitoku-dento-roku*, chap. 14, records that he received the bodhisattva precepts but not the 250 bhikṣu-precepts.

14. A disciple of Master Yakusan Igen. See chap. 21, *Kankin*. After leaving Master Yakusan's order, he lived in a hut by a road, and taught the travelers who passed by. He is also mentioned in *Keitoku-dento-roku*, chap. 14 as someone who took the bodhisattva precepts, but not the 250 bhikṣu-precepts.

15. 比丘戒 (BIKU-KAI) means the 250 precepts that evolved in India during the age of Hīnayāna Buddhism.

[95]

八大人覚

HACHI-DAININGAKU

The Eight Truths of a Great Human Being

__Hachi__ means "eight." __Dainin__ means "a great human being," that is, a buddha. And __kaku__, pronounced here as __gaku__, means "an intuitive reflection or truth." Gautama Buddha preached the eight truths of a great human just before he died, and they are recorded in the Yuikyo-gyo (The Sutra of Bequeathed Teachings); they were his last teachings. Master Dogen preached this chapter when he felt his death was not far away, and in his case, too, it was his last teaching. This chapter thus forms the last chapter in the 95-chapter edition of Shobogenzo.

[21] ***Buddhas are great human beings.*** *[The Dharma] that great human beings realize*[1] *is therefore called "the eight truths of a great human being." To realize this Dharma is the cause of nirvāṇa.*[2]

It was the last preaching of our Original Master, Śākyamuni Buddha, on the night that he entered nirvāṇa.[3]

[22] *1) Small desire.*[4] *(Not widely to chase after those among objects of the five desires*[5] *that are as yet ungained, is called "small desire.")*[6]

The Buddha said, *"You bhikṣus should know that people of abundant desire abundantly seek gain, and so their suffering also is abundant. People of small desire, being free of seeking and free of desire, are free of this affliction. You should practice and learn small desire just for itself. Still more, small desire can give rise to all virtues: people of small desire never curry favor and bend in order to gain the minds of others. Further, they are*

---

1. 覚知 (KAKUCHI). The first half of the compound, 覚 (KAKU), here means to feel, to be aware, to reflect, to realize, et cetera. In the chapter title, the same character, 覚 (KAKU), "truth," means the object of buddhas' feeling, awareness, reflection, or realization.

2. The serene and peaceful state.

3. Nirvāṇa here means pari-nirvāṇa, that is, complete extinction, death.

4. 少欲 (SHOYOKU), from the Sanskrit *alpecchuḥ*. See Glossary.

5. The desires of the eyes, ears, nose, tongue, and skin. Also explained as desires for wealth, sensual contact, food, fame, comfort.

6. The words in parentheses are in small Chinese characters in the source text, as if added to the original sutra by way of commentary.

not led by the sense organs. Those who practice small desire are level in mind; they are without worries and fears; when they come into contact with things they have latitude; and they are constantly free from dissatisfaction. Those who have small desire just have nirvāṇa. This is called 'small desire.'"[7]

[123] *2) To know satisfaction.*[8] *(To take within limits from among things already gained, is called "to know satisfaction.")*

The Buddha said, *"If you bhikṣus desire to get rid of all kinds of suffering, you should reflect on knowing satisfaction. The practice of knowing satisfaction is the very place of abundance, joy, and peace. People who know satisfaction, even when lying on the ground, are still comfortable and joyful. Those who do not know satisfaction, even when living in a heavenly palace, are still not suited. Those who do not know satisfaction, even if rich, are poor. People who know satisfaction, even if poor, are rich. Those who do not know satisfaction are constantly led by the five desires; they are pitied by those who know satisfaction. This is called 'to know satisfaction.'"*

[124] *3) To enjoy tranquillity.*[9] *(Departing from all kinds of noise and living alone in an empty space is called "to enjoy tranquillity.")*

The Buddha said, *"If you bhikṣus wish to pursue tranquil and unintentional peace and joy, you should depart from noise and live alone in seclusion. People of quiet places are revered alike by the god Śakra and all the gods. For this reason you should abandon your own groups and other groups, live alone in an empty space, and think of dissolving the root of suffering. Those who take pleasure in groups suffer many troubles—like a flock of birds gathering on a great tree and then worrying that it will wither or break. [Those] fettered by and attached to the world are immersed in many kinds of suffering—like an old elephant drowning in mud, unable to get out by itself. This is called 'distancing.'"*

[126] *4) To practice diligence.*[10] *(It is ceaselessly to endeavor to perform good works, and so it is called "devoted effort"—'devotion' without adulteration, and 'effort' without regression.*[11]*)*

The Buddha said, *"If you bhikṣus practice diligence, nothing will be difficult. For this reason you should practice diligence—as a trickle of water that constantly flows is able to drill through rock. If the mind of a practitioner often tires and quits, that is like [a person] twirling a stick to start a fire and resting before it gets hot: although [the person] wishes to obtain fire, fire is unobtainable. This is called 'diligence.'"*

---

7. 遺教経 (YUIKYO-GYO), lit. "The Sutra of Bequeathed Teaching," short for *Bussui-hatsunehan-ryakusetsu-kyokai-gyo*. The original Sanskrit version of this sutra has been lost.

8. 知足 (CHISOKU), from the Sanskrit *saṃtuṣṭaḥ*. See Glossary.

9. 寂静 (JAKUJO), "tranquillity," represents the Sanskrit *śānta*. See Glossary.

10. 勤精進 (GON-SHOJIN). 精進 (SHOJIN), from the Sanskrit *vīrya*, is also the fourth of the six pāramitās. See Book 1, Glossary.

11. The Chinese compound 精進 (SHOJIN), "diligence," is explained character by character: 精 (SHO) means purified, refined, or devoted, and 進 (SHIN) means to progress, push forward, or make effort.

27] *5) Not to lose mindfulness.*[12] *(It is also called "to keep right mindfulness." To keep the Dharma and not to lose it is called "right mindfulness," and is also called "not to lose mindfulness.")*

The Buddha said, *"For you bhikṣus who seek good counselors and seek their good auspices, there is nothing like not losing mindfulness. If people possess [the ability] not to lose mindfulness, the bandits of affliction are unable to invade them. For this reason, you constantly should regulate thoughts and keep them in their place in the mind. Those who lose mindfulness lose all virtues. If your power of mindfulness is solid and strong, even if you go among the bandits of the five desires you will not be harmed by them—it is like entering a battlefield clad in armor and having nothing to fear. This is called 'not to lose mindfulness.'"*

28] *6) To practice the balanced state of dhyāna.*[13] *(To abide in the Dharma undisturbed is called "the balanced state of dhyāna.")*

The Buddha said, *"If you bhikṣus regulate the mind, the mind will then exist in the balanced state. Because the mind exists in the balanced state you will be able to know the Dharma-form of the arising and vanishing of the world. For this reason you constantly should be diligent in practicing all forms of balance. When a person gets the balanced state, the mind does not dissipate. It is like a household that values water attentively repairing a dike. Practitioners also are like that. For the sake of the water of wisdom, we attentively practice the balanced state of dhyāna and prevent [the water of wisdom] from leaking away. This is called 'the balanced state.'"*

29] *7) To practice wisdom.*[14] *(To engender hearing, thinking, practice, and experience is called "wisdom.")*

The Buddha said, *"If you bhikṣus have wisdom, then you will be without greed and attachment. By constantly reflecting on and observing yourself, you will prevent [wisdom] from being lost. This is just to be able, within my Dharma, to attain liberation. If you are not so, already you are different from people of the truth*[15] *and also different from those clothed in white;*[16] *there is nothing to call you. Truly, wisdom is a sturdy ship in which to cross the ocean of aging, sickness, and death. Again, it is a great bright torch for the darkness of ignorance; it is good medicine for all sick people; and it is a sharp ax to fell the trees of anguish. For this reason, you should hear, consider, and practice wisdom, and thereby develop yourself. If a human being possesses the light of wisdom, he or she is—although with eyes of flesh—a human being of clear vision. This is called 'wisdom.'"*

---

12. 不忘念 (FUMONEN). 念 (NEN) represents the Sanskrit *smṛti*. See Book 1, Glossary.

13. 修禅定 (SHU-ZENJO). 禅定 (ZENJO), representing both the sound and the meaning of the Sanskrit *dhyāna*, is the fifth of the six pāramitās.

14. 修智慧 (SHU-CHIE). 智慧 (CHIE) represents the Sanskrit *prajñā*, the sixth of the six pāramitās. See chap. 2, *Maka-hannya-haramitsu*, and Book 1, Glossary.

15. 道人 (DONIN), monks and nuns.

16. 白衣 (BYAKU-E), laymen and laywomen.

[130] *8) Not to engage in idle discussion.*[17] *(To experience, to go beyond discrimination, is called "not to engage in idle discussion." To perfectly realize real form is just not to engage in idle discussion.)*

The Buddha said, *"If you bhikṣus engage in all kinds of idle discussion your mind will be disturbed. Although you have left family life, still you will be unable to get free. For this reason, bhikṣus, you should immediately throw away disturbing idle discussion. If you wish to attain the joy of serenity*[18] *you should just inhibit well the fault of idle discussion. This is called 'not to engage in idle discussion.'"*

[131] These are the eight truths of a great human being. Each is equipped with the eight, and so there may be sixty-four. When we extend them, they may be countless. If we abridge them, they are sixty-four. *They are the last preaching of the great Master Śākyamuni; they are the instruction of the Great Vehicle; and they are the [Buddha's] supreme swan song, in the middle of the night of the 15th day of the second month.* After this, he does not preach the Dharma again, and finally he passes into pari-nirvāṇa.

[132] The Buddha said, *"You bhikṣus constantly should endeavor, with undivided mind, to pursue the truth of liberation. All the dharmas of the world, moving and unmoving, without exception are perishing and unstable forms. Let yourselves stop for a while, and talk no more. Time must pass, and I am going to die. This is my last instruction."*

Therefore, disciples of the Tathāgata unfailingly learn this [instruction]. Those who do not practice and learn it, and who do not know it, are not the Buddha's disciples. It is the Tathāgata's right-Dharma-eye treasury and fine mind of nirvāṇa. Nevertheless, today many do not know it and few have seen or heard it; it is due to the trickery of demons that they do not know. Again, those lacking in long-accumulated good roots neither hear nor see [this instruction]. During the bygone days of the right Dharma and the imitative Dharma, all disciples of the Buddha knew it. They practiced it and learned it in experience. Now there is not one or two among a thousand bhikṣus who knows the eight truths of a great human being. It is pitiful. There is nothing even to compare to the insidious degeneration of [these] decadent times. While the Tathāgata's right Dharma is now [still] permeating the great-thousandfold [world], while the immaculate Dharma has not yet disappeared, we should learn it without delay. Do not be slack or lazy. To meet the Buddha-Dharma, even in countless kalpas, is hard. To receive a human body also is hard. Even in receiving the human body, human bodies on the three continents[19] are better. Human bodies on the southern continent are

---

17. 戯論 (KERON), "idle discussion," represents the Sanskrit *prapañca*, which means prolixity or wordiness. See Glossary.

18. 寂滅 (JAKUMETSU), "serenity," represents the Sanskrit *nirvāṇa*. See Book 1, Glossary.

19. 三洲 (SANSHU), "the three continents," means Jambudvīpa (south; the transient human world in which it is easiest to feel the winds of impermanence), Pūrva-videha (east), and

best of all—because they meet Buddha, hear the Dharma, leave family life, and attain the truth. People who died prior to the Tathāgata's pari-nirvāṇa neither heard nor learnt these eight truths of a great human being. That now we are seeing and hearing them, and learning them, is due to long-accumulated good roots. In learning them now, in developing them life by life and arriving without fail at the supreme [truth of] bodhi, and in preaching them for living beings, may we become the same as Śākyamuni Buddha; may there be no differences.

Shobogenzo Hachi-dainingaku

Written at Eihei-ji temple, on the 6th day of the first lunar month in the 5th year of Kencho.[20]

Now, on the day before the end of the retreat in the 7th year of Kencho,[21] I have had the clerk-monk[22] Gi-en finish the copying; at the same time, I have checked it thoroughly against the original text. This was the last draft [written by] the late Master, in his sickness. I remember him saying that he would rewrite all of the *kana* Shobogenzo[23] and so on that he had completed before, and also include new drafts so as to be able to compile [Shobogenzo] in altogether one hundred chapters. This chapter, which was a fresh draft,[24] was to be the twelfth. After this, the Master's sickness grew more and more serious so that his work on original drafts and suchlike stopped. Therefore this draft is the last instruction of the late Master. That we unfortunately never saw the one hundred chapters is most regrettable. People who love and miss the late Master should unfailingly copy this chapter and preserve it. It is the final instruction of Śākyamuni, and it is the final bequeathed teaching of the late Master.

Ejo wrote this.

Apara-godāna (west). The fourth continent, Uttara-kuru (north), is an immortal realm inhabited by angels.

20. 1253, the year of Master Dogen's death. He is said to have died on 28 August.

21. 1255.

22. 書記 (SHOKI), clerk assisting the head monk, one of the six assistant officers.

23. 仮字正法眼蔵 (KAJI-SHOBOGENZO) means Master Dogen's Shobogenzo which he wrote using *kana*, the Japanese syllabary—as opposed to *Shinji-shobogenzo*, which is in Chinese characters only.

24. "A fresh draft" suggests that Master Dogen began the chapter afresh in the final years of his life. The 12-chapter edition of Shobogenzo not only includes such fresh chapters, which are generally dated 1255, but also includes earlier chapters such as *Kesa-kudoku* (chap. 12 in the 95-chapter edition; dated 1240).

Appendices

EDITIONS OF SHOBOGENZO

The original source text for this translation has been the 95-chapter edition of Shobogenzo published by the Iwanami publishing house as an Iwanami Bunko edition. When Iwanami first published their 95-chapter edition between 1935 and 1943, they also included, in a separate appendix, the following chapters: 1) ***Butsu-kojo-no-ji*** *from the 28-chapter "Secret Shobogenzo," which had only recently been made public; 2)* ***Ippyakuhachi-homyomon*** *which is included in the 12-chapter edition but not in the 95-chapter edition; 3)* ***Hensan*** *and 4)* ***Senmen****, both from the 60-chapter edition, and 5)* ***Sanji-no-go*** *from the 12-chapter edition. As the* ***Butsu-kojo-no-ji*** *chapter in the 28-chapter "Secret Shobogenzo" and the chapter of the same name in the 95-chapter edition are very different, it has been translated and included for reference in the Appendices.* ***Ippyaku-hachi-homyomon*** *is not included in the 95-chapter edition, and so has also been translated and included in the Appendices. However, the 60-chapter editions of* ***Hensan*** *and* ***Senmen*** *and the 12-chapter edition of* ***Sanji-no-go*** *are sufficiently similar to the chapters of the same names in the 95-chapter edition, and have not been translated again here.*

THE 95-CHAPTER EDITION

Also known as the Kozen Edition, because it was edited by Master Hangyo Kozen in about 1690

THE 75-CHAPTER EDITION

THE 60-CHAPTER EDITION

SECRET SHOBOGENZO:†

(28-chapters in three parts)

Part One:
1) Butsu-kojo-no-ji
2) Shoji
3) Shin-fukatoku (I)

† 秘密正法眼蔵 (HIMITSU-SHOBOGENZO), *The Secret Shobogenzo*, is so called because it was kept stored in secret at Eihei-ji temple. A book of the same name, but unrelated content, was also written by Master Keizan Jokin. Master Keizan Jokin was the third generation descendant of Master Dogen; he established Soji-ji temple.

4) Shin-fukatoku (II)
5) Shinjin-inga
6) Shoho-jisso
7) Butsudo[††]
8) Raihai-tokuzui
9) Butsudo[††]
10) Zanmai-o-zanmai
11) Sanjushichi-bon-bodai-bunpo

Part Two:

1) Den-e
2) Bukkyo *(The Buddha's Teaching)*
3) Sansuigyo
4) Mitsugo
5) Tenborin
6) Jisho-zanmai
7) Daishugyo
8) Shisho
9) Hachi-dainingaku
10) Jukai

Part Three:

1) Busso
2) Shizen-biku
3) Shukke
4) Bukkyo *(Buddhist sutras)*
5) Menju
6) Sesshin-sessho
7) Yui-butsu-yo-butsu

THE 12-CHAPTER EDITION

1) Shukke-kudoku
2) Jukai
3) Kesa-kudoku
4) Hotsu-bodaishin
5) Kuyo-shobutsu
6) Kie-bupposo-ho
7) Shinjin-inga
8) Sanji-no-go
9) Shime

[††]. Both chapters are titled 仏道 (BUTSUDO), *The Buddha's Truth*. One of them, however, corresponds to the chapter titled 道心 (DOSHIN), *The Will to the Truth*, in the 95-chapter edition.

10) Shizen-biku
11) Ippyakuhachi-homyomon
12) Hachi-dainingaku

THE BONSHIN EDITION

Edited by Master Bonshin—84 chapters

THE MANZAN EDITION

Edited by Master Manzan—89 chapters

[APPENDIX 1]

仏向上事

BUTSU-KOJO-NO-JI

The Matter of the Ascendant State of Buddha

*The words **butsu-kojo-no-ji** describe the fact that, even after realizing the truth, Buddhist masters continue their daily lives as they have always done; they do not attain some special state of "enlightenment" and become different. Comparing this chapter, which appears in the 28-chapter "Secret Shobogenzo," and the chapter with the same name that appears as Chapter 28 in the 95-chapter edition, we find many differences. The chapter in the 95-chapter edition is a collection of many stories relating to Buddhist masters in China, whereas this chapter contains a rather long philosophical explanation of **butsu-kojo-no-ji** and one or two related stories. It is thus helpful to read this chapter from the 28-chapter edition, which gives a more detailed explanation of **butsu-kojo-no-ji**, or "the matter of the ascendant state of buddha" than the earlier chapter.*

39] **Great Master Gohon of Tozan**[1] **said,** *"You should know that there is the matter of the ascendant state of buddha. When you know of the matter of the ascendant state of buddha, you will truly possess the means to speak."*[2] *"The means to speak"* is the means to turn the wheel of Dharma. In truth, if we do not know the matter of the ascendant state of buddha, we idly stagnate without penetrating to and getting free of the state beyond buddha. If we do not penetrate it and get free, we do not transcend the worlds of demons. Once we find the way that arrives at buddha, we leave the area of the common man immediately. The people who have mastered this way are few. Still, just because we are unable to know it, we should not, so saying, leave it at that. If, with a true will, we learn in practice under good counselors who have truly illuminated [the way], we will be able to attain it without fail. For this reason, Tozan teaches [us], *"You should know..."* The gist of his idea is [as follows: Consider,] for example, having arrived at buddha. It is hard for buddha to be realized as the buddha we were expecting yesterday having become the buddha of today.

1. Master Tozan Ryokai (807–869), successor of Master Ungan Donjo. Great Master Gohon is his posthumous title.
2. *Shinji-shobogenzo*, pt. 1, no. 12.

To continue making buddha aware that the buddha of today has existed not only today,[3] is called "the matter of the ascendant state of buddha." From [the attainment] of this state onwards, even explanation, being speaking of the truth, is said to be being preached: although until the present it has inevitably not ceased to be preached as speaking, and although yesterday's was yesterday's, it exists as the speaking [of the truth]. Further, when we know [this matter] as the matter of the ascendant state of buddha and hear it as the matter of the ascendant state of buddha, the wheel of Dharma that we have attained uses us as speech, to preach the great and the small, and causes us, as the wheel of Dharma, to possess the means to speak—such is the matter of the ascendant state of buddha.

[142] A buddha preached, *"Buddha turning the Dharma-wheel is beyond material particles of sound[4] and form."* The approximate meaning is that the Buddha-Dharma, in its teaching, practice, and experience, is originally not concerned with beginning or end.[5] Neither is it tainted by "now." That being so, we should know the voice of buddha and should learn the words of buddha. That is, [we should know and learn that] there is nowhere the voice of buddha does not reach and there is no matter that it does not reach. Again, [buddha] is beyond the level of the common man, the two-vehicles, non-Buddhists, and the like, who are concerned with beginning and end. It realizes the truth within its voice and radiates light within its voice. To raise the voice in the moment before the body, and to hear the voice in the moment after the body, also are [virtues] belonging only to buddha. So there are [instances of] living-and-dying and going-and-coming getting through to the voice of buddha; and there are [instances of] wind, rain, water, and fire raising the voice of buddha. The Kitchen Hall and the Temple Gates widely proclaim the voice, and the Monks' Hall and the Buddha Hall loudly redouble the voice. Not only that; all dharmas each let us hear a half of this voice of buddha, and none of the three worlds forgets a little bit of this voice of buddha: who need worry about it *"either disappearing or appearing."*[6] It is naturally without disorder and without mistakes. In general, when we hear the voice of buddha, we hear it through the ears and we hear it through the eyes; none of the six sense organs, even in sleep, or during wakefulness, fails to be able to hear the voice of buddha. Conversely, whether inside or outside the world of Dharma, whether in going-and-coming as every place or in

---

3. "The buddha of today has existed not only today" suggests that a person's normal life even before he or she realized the truth was the life of a buddha.

4. 声 (SHO, *koe*) means voice or sound. There follows a consideration of 仏の声 (*hotoke no koe*), the voice of buddha.

5. That is, they take place in the here and now.

6. 若退若出 (NYAKU-TAI-NYAKU-SHUTSU). Alludes to Lotus Sutra, *Nyorai-juryo* (LS 3.18): *"The Tathāgata knows and sees the form of the triple world as it really is, without life and death, or disappearance or appearance..."*

every place as going-and-coming, there can never be any place where the voice of buddha does not exist. It exists at a place and it exists at a time. Further, there is a principle that the voice of buddha preaches the voice with the voice, and hears the voice with the voice. Again, when we consider the concrete situation of the words of buddha, there is no case of them being preached separately from the voice. Being preached by the whole of the voice, one word or two phrases can exist; and in no case is it impossible to hear, in one word or two phrases, the whole of the voice. At the place of this voice, nothing fails to be penetrated or fails to be mastered. No person, nor even any thing, should ever have a voice that seeks to avoid [the voice of buddha], saying "I will not understand it, I will not be able to penetrate it." The words of buddha are not preached under such conditions, excited by thoughts. There is a voice that, while preached as a voice, is also thoughts. When it preaches a half or preaches the whole it is never unfamiliar and never obscure—not only are each of the hundred weeds clear; the will of the ancestral masters also is clear.[7] They never intend, from the standpoint of [abstract] matters, to define the edges of [concrete] things. Neither have they sought to patch matters up through the medium of doing, and [this state] is just the voice of buddha and the words of buddha. In learning the state of truth, we should, as the practice thereof, without fail diligently practice Zazen. This has been transmitted between buddhas without interruption from ancient times to the present. When we become buddha, we do not do so apart from this [practice]. Being transmitted by buddha, it is beyond human supposition. To endeavor to suppose it is not the traditional style in learning the truth. When practiced by us it is sometimes illuminated, but the peripheries of it that are supposed by us remain dark. Thus, there being no fathomable periphery, even if we think that, through exerting ourselves to the limit, we have fathomed it, we have not fathomed it; [our exertion] was only the restlessness of a frisky horse or a mischievous monkey. If, on the other hand, a true master bestows the teaching on us and leaves the traces of the Buddhist patriarchs, and if it is possible for training to be definitely realized, then it becomes apparent that day-to-day learning of the truth has not been in vain, and it becomes evident that action in the present has not been for nothing. At this time there is nothing to conceal the body-and-mind. With the intention of connecting this state with thinking, [however,] it is still hard for us to penetrate. Still less can people who count grains of sand[8] realize it, even in a dream. Only people who have experienced, in the mountain-still state,[9] the Zazen that is different from thinking, are able to grasp it.

---

7. Alludes to the traditional saying 明明百草頭、明明祖師意 (MEI-MEI *taru* HYAKU-SO-TO; MEI-MEI *taru* SOSHI-*no*-I), "Clear-clear are the hundred weeds; clear-clear is the will of the ancestral masters," quoted for example by the layman Ho-on in *Shinji-shobogenzo*, pt. 1, no. 88.

8. People who only read sutras.

9. 兀々として (GOTSU-GOTSU *toshite*), a phrase which also appears in *Fukan-zazengi*. The

[146] Briefly, there are two aspects to learning the Buddha's truth; namely, learning through the mind and learning through the body. "Learning through the body" describes, in sitting in Zazen pursuing the truth, the presence of acting buddha who does not seek to become buddha. When the Universe is realized, the body-buddha is, from the beginning, beyond "becoming buddha"; and because nets and cages have long been broken open, the sitting buddha does not obstruct at all the becoming buddha. When we learn through the body like this, we have the power eternally, for a thousand ages and ten thousand ages, to enter [the state of] buddha or to enter [the state of] demons. In forward steps and backward steps, we cause there to be light that fills ditches and fills valleys: who would not call this the features [we had] before [our] father and mother were born?

[148] "Learning through the mind" describes clarification of how the mind is. Clarifying the mind does not mean clarifying the mind of the common man, non-Buddhists, the two vehicles, and the like; it means illumination of the buddha-mind. In ancient times, a monk asked the National Master Echu,[10] *"What is the mind of eternal buddhas?"* The National Master said, *"Fences, walls, tiles, and pebbles."* Let us now listen to these words for a while, and let us quietly learn this mind. To resolve to learn the Buddha's truth, and to illuminate from the beginning the mind of eternal buddhas: this may be called "learning the truth through the mind." The selfish mind, though idly proud of knowledge and understanding, possesses only thinking and discrimination. The Old One Śākyamuni said, *"This Dharma cannot be understood by thinking and discrimination."*[11] Clearly we see that in ourselves there is no mind worth getting: in eternal buddhas there is the mind which we should learn. If we want to inquire into this mind, it is present in visible fences, walls, tiles, and pebbles, and if we want to experience this mind, it is present in the realization of fences, walls, tiles, and pebbles. Now, though these fences, walls, tiles, and pebbles are produced by human beings, at the same time they are words and deeds of Dharma. Who could hold sway over them? When we see them like this, it is evident that *fences, walls, tiles, and pebbles* are beyond substance before our eyes, and that substance before our eyes is not *fences, walls, tiles, and pebbles.* In sum, fences, walls, tiles, and pebbles on this side[12] are illuminating us as yonder objects; and we on this side are being illuminated by fences, walls, tiles, and pebbles as yonder objects. The fences, walls, tiles, and pebbles that exist like this as the mind of eternal buddhas are conspicuous in their brightness and in their merits, and so we can enumerate those

---

character 兀 (GOTSU) repeated for emphasis, lit. means "high and level," "lofty," or "motionless." The word originally suggests a table mountain, and hence something imposing and balanced.

10. Master Nan-yo Echu (d. 775), successor of Master Daikan Eno. See chap. 44, *Kobusshin.*

11. Lotus Sutra, *Hoben-bon.* LS 1.88–90. Also quoted in *Fukan-zazengi.*

12. 這辺 (SHAHEN), "this side," suggests the subject.

[merits] that are numerable and we can remember those that are knowable. In knowing things and also in discerning matters, we should not learn from common men, the two vehicles, non-Buddhists, and the like; we should learn from the mind of eternal buddhas. All through the twelve hours, night and day, of daily functioning, we should be single-mindedly learning from eternal buddhas. Where the mind of eternal buddhas is teaching, we are able to hear the mind of eternal buddhas. Having been able to meet the mind of eternal buddhas, we should learn it thoroughly. We should not think, even in a dream, that it may be like the mind with which the common man is equipped. Stupid people, however, who trifle with the knowledge of the common man, and who mistakenly believe that the buddha-mind also may be like that, discuss the knowing of a knower and the known, and talk about illumination as "serene illumination" or "spiritual illumination." We should totally throw away such false views. We should just learn the fences, walls, tiles, and pebbles that are the mind of eternal buddhas. It is not that we describe them thus because fences, walls, tiles, and pebbles are created from the mind of eternal buddhas and thus patterned after their creator: directly, without disturbing them, we call them "of eternal buddhas." We should learn that eternal buddhas, in every case, at the time of preaching the Dharma and doing training, at the time of nirvāṇa, and at the time of realizing the truth, have made this mind into [their own] mind. Thus our great Master Śākyamuni Buddha dwelt in and retained this as [his own] mind, and the ancestral Master also maintained and relied upon this as [his own] mind. Is it equivalent to or not equivalent to fences, walls, tiles, and pebbles? We must look into this thoroughly. Wherever Nature naturally possesses something familiar and direct, the mind of eternal buddhas is naturally preaching the mind of eternal buddhas—so we should get used to hearing that it is like this. When this mind is realized, it is unstoppable. Because it is unstoppable, both mastery of fundamentals and mastery of explanation are left utterly at the mercy of this mind, and there is no practice of the truth nor any way of moral discipline that is not left entirely at the mercy of this mind. Eternal buddhas, in all their preaching and teaching, may be like this. With this as [our own] mind, we learn the truth.

[52] Again, Great Master Shinsai of Joshu[13] once asked Nansen,[14] *"What is the truth?"*[15] Nansen taught, *"The normal mind is the truth."* In other words, the everyday[16] mind is the truth. To learn [the truth] as the normal mind may be

---

13. Master Joshu Jushin (778–897), successor of Master Nansen Fugan. Great Master Shinsai is his posthumous title.

14. Master Nansen Fugan (748–834), successor of Master Baso Do-itsu.

15. *Shinji-shobogenzo*, pt. 1, no. 19.

16. Master Dogen explained the Chinese characters 平常 (BYOJO or HEIJO), "normal," with the Japanese phonetic word *yonotsune*, which means usual, ordinary, common, or everyday.

extremely rare. It is to learn, both in regard to the body and in regard to the mind, that in time, they are normal. For instance there is not the slightest taintedness[17] nor any design. In the state of body-mind, we neither describe yesterday as today, nor describe nor practice today as tomorrow, nor make the body into the mind, nor proceed from the mind to the body.[18] The state like this is called *"the normal mind,"* but [people] are prone to misunderstand it to be a class of common miscellany.[19] While remaining in this [state of normal mind], we can intuit and affirm that the [miscellaneous] hundred weeds are normal. It is because this normal state of mind is the truth that the hundred weeds do not wither or rot. The Buddhist patriarchs, without being normal could never have got free from the world, forgotten themselves, and practiced the truth—for practice of the truth naturally is normal. We too, having thrown away former worldly emotions, are readily practicing, and moving forward in, the tracks of the Buddhist patriarchs, but if we are inclined to think that because the normal mind is the truth we might not need to practice, we may be purporting to misunderstand normality. Practice-and-experience is not nonexistent, [but] there is none that is not normal. There being none that is not normal, there can be none that is tainted. In ancient times the Old One Śākyamuni under the bodhi tree, on seeing the bright star, at once realized the truth. The principle here is the principle that not a single thing is fetched. Previously the Buddha had experienced the bright star, but from this time on the bright star was experiencing the Buddha. What is the basis [for saying that] he was experienced by the bright star and that he experienced the bright star? Namely: *"Practice-and-experience is not nonexistent, [but] it cannot be tainted."*[20]

[154] A [monk] named Chokei[21] asks Master Hofuku,[22] *"They say that to see form is to see the mind. But do you see the boat?"*

Hofuku says, *"I see it."*

Chokei says, *"Let us set aside the boat for the moment. Just what is the mind?"*

Hofuku points a finger at the boat.[23]

---

17. 染汚 (ZENNA), "taintedness," means separation of means and end, which stops us from being fully in the present moment.

18. Because in reality there is no past or future and no separation of body and mind.

19. 百草 (HYAKUSO), lit. "hundreds of weeds," symbolize miscellaneous trivial things. See note 7.

20. Master Nangaku Ejo's words to Master Daikan Eno. See, for example, chap. 7, *Senjo;* chap. 29, *Inmo;* chap. 62, *Hensan;* and *Shinji-shobogenzo,* pt. 2, no. 1.

21. Master Chokei Eryo (854–932). A successor of Master Seppo Gison. His posthumous title was Great Master Chokaku.

22. Master Hofuku Juten (died 928). Also a successor of Master Seppo Gison. There are many stories of conversations between him and Master Chokei, his elder brother in Master Seppo's order.

23. *Shinji-shobogenzo,* pt. 2, no. 92.

So, even in our learning of the truth in the present age, we should know that discussion of the mind of the Buddhist patriarchs is like this. Having recognized that it is so, we are not drawn by non-Buddhists, the two vehicles, and the like. When buddha-tathāgatas are always playing in samādhi, we call this the Buddha's truth. In this state, there is abandonment of the body for the Dharma. In order to illuminate and study that boat, we need to know what the Buddha-Dharma is. "The Buddha-Dharma," namely, is the myriad dharmas, the hundred weeds, all real dharmas, the triple world. No buddha has failed to perfectly realize this, and so there is nothing that is not perfectly realized as this by buddhas. That being so, when we inquire into life, there is none beyond real dharmas, and when we look for death, it is never separate from the myriad dharmas. Even to act in the interests of [life and death][24] also is this Dharma. For this reason, the principle of *abandoning the body for the Dharma* is clear. We have been abiding in and retaining this life and this death for a long time, [but] we have not received them from others; they do not depend on anyone else. As exhalation and inhalation at this concrete place, life is the body, and the body is the Dharma here and now. So the inevitable abandonment of life is, from the outset, for the Dharma. When we do not forget that death [also] is abandonment, we are experienced in the present by the Dharma; and even if we sought to abandon the body at a place beyond the Dharma, that could never be at all. As to the meaning of this *"abandonment,"* it is always incurred by *the body,* and just at the time of *abandonment of the body for the Dharma,* when we turn light around and reflect, it is also *abandonment of the Dharma for the body.* In other words, when the Dharma raises its own voice to proclaim itself, the expression *abandoning the Dharma for the body* is present; and when the body naturally raises its voice to announce itself, the expression *abandoning the body for the Dharma* is communicated: we should know that those to whom these buddha-actions, totally, have come, and those who have been learning them for long ages, are ourselves. Now and eternally, unable to regress or stray, we are put into practice by action in the present, and there is no instance in which action does not overflow from us. Since ancient times it has been said that a person who attains the truth entrusts life and death to the mind. Truly, it may be so; we should not doubt it. When this principle is apparent, we also know our own mind; and when we know our own mind *this principle* also is apparent. At the same time, we also know what our own body is, and we also clarify and learn the dignified behavior that belongs to our body. In learning this we illuminate the way life is and the way death is. To illuminate this is not to have deviously thrown light upon what [otherwise] might not have been illuminated. We should understand that this kind of illumination takes place

24. To act in the interests of life means, for example, to take care of one's own health. To act in the interests of death means, for example, to exert oneself in the pursuit of some end.

when we illuminate what is evident. To illuminate *this principle*, we should first know how the mind is and should learn how the mind is. To learn of its condition means, in other words, to know that *the myriad dharmas* are *the concrete mind*, and to understand that *the triple world* is *the mind alone*.[25] Even what is called "knowing" and what is called "understanding" are the myriad dharmas and are the triple world, and are their having been like this. Thereafter we must exactly investigate what life is entrusted to, and what death is entrusted to. As we continue investigating, an evident truth is present; it is, namely, the vigorous activity of *the mind alone*. It has not been produced by anything else; it is the real state of the mind alone itself—it has not been marshaled by objects. Thus, the real state of life and death is just the mind alone having been entrusted to itself. The reason, if asked, is that there is no mind alone that is not the myriad dharmas, and no myriad dharmas that are not the mind alone. Even if we purport to banish this life and death to a place beyond the mind alone, it will still be impossible for us to be hated by the mind alone. Truly, the two vehicles do not know, and non-Buddhists have no means [to comprehend], that to rely on the myriad dharmas is to rely on the mind alone; how much less could the common man realize it, even in a dream? Therefore, the matter of knowing our own body and the matter of knowing our own mind we should learn under the mind alone and we should learn under the myriad dharmas; and we should not do so in haste; we should do so in detail. This is called "the condition of entrusting life and death to the mind." To think of it as idle reliance on the mind of the common man is wrong. Even in the Buddha's vocal teaching we do not hear of entrusting life and death to the mind of the common man. At the same time, we should clearly know that our own mind also is not entrusted [to us] by life and death, and that we are beyond the common man.

[160] In the house of Buddha there is the bodhisattva Regarder of the Sounds of the World.[26] Few people have not seen her,[27] but very few people know her. We need not use coins to buy her elegant manner of being, and when we look into her faces, which is right and which is wrong? In order to speak she turns [our] body around and mounts the Zazen platform; in order to listen she takes [our] hand and stands on the ground. At places not hindered by even a single dharma, her compassionate eyes illuminate us. Her response and our being responded to[28] are a donkey looking at a well, and are the

---

25. 唯心 (YUISHIN), "only the mind" or "the mind alone," appears in the phrase 三界唯心 (SANGAI-YUISHIN), "the triple world is only the mind." See chap. 47, *Sangai-yuishin*.

26. 観世音 (KANZEON) represents the Sanskrit *Avalokiteśvara*. See Shobogenzo, chap. 33, *Kannon*, and Lotus Sutra, chap. 25, *Kanzeon Bosatsu Fumonbon*.

27. Images of Bodhisattva Avalokiteśvara, sometimes in female form and sometimes in male form, are commonly seen in China and Japan; e.g., in temple statues and in art works.

28. 応と応ぜらること (O *to oze raru koto*), "the response and being responded to," alludes to the belief, described in chap. 25 of the Lotus Sutra, that the Bodhisattva will respond to the

well looking at the donkey.[29] There may be no human being who clearly understands this state; *"it keenly avoids verbal expression."*[30] If we express it with words, horns will appear on the head. It is simply illumination of the mind in seeing forms, and realization of the truth in hearing sounds. The mind described as "the mind to be illuminated" may be the mind of Buddha. The truth to be illuminated may be the truth of Buddha. In the truth of Buddha and in the house of Buddha, we just illuminate the mind by seeing forms and realize the truth by hearing sounds; there is nothing else at all. A state that is like this, being already in the Buddha's truth, should preach, *"To those who must be saved through this body, I will manifest at once this body and preach the Dharma."*[31] Truly, there is no preaching of Dharma without manifestation of the body, and there can be no salvation that is not the preaching of Dharma. A man of old said, *"It is a long time since I sold you this paddy field. The four border-ridges, however, sometimes you leave unrecognized. Though I have always given the field unreservedly, I have not yet given the tree that has been in its center. From now on I will not begrudge the tree either."*[32] Studying this in experience, we should not forget that it has been a long time since this paddy field was given to us. Its ridges are kept level, and its four borders are evident. When we play in it, everywhere it produces good omens and produces happiness. Truly, we must conclude that a field like this has been with us all along.

---

cries of those in distress. See LS 3.242.

29. Alludes to *Shinji-shobogenzo*, pt. 2, no. 25: Master Sozan asks Ācārya Toku, *"It is said that the Buddha's true Dharma-body is just like space, and it manifests its form according to things, like the moon [reflected] in water. How do you preach this principle of mutual accordance?"* Toku says, *"It is like a donkey looking into a well."* The Master says, *"Your words are extremely nice words, but they only express eighty or ninety percent."* Toku says, *"What would the Master say?"* Master Sozan says, *"It is like the well looking at the donkey."* The story discusses the meaning of the character 応 (O, *o[jiru]*); "accord with" or "in response to," which suggests the mutual relation between subject and object.

30. The words of Master Dogo Enchi. See *Shinji-shobogenzo*, pt. 1, no. 57.

31. LS 3.252.

32. The quotation, which Master Dogen rendered into Japanese, has not been traced.

[APPENDIX 2]

一百八法明門

IPPYAKUHACHI-HOMYOMON

One Hundred and Eight Gates of Dharma-Illumination

__Ippyaku-hachi__ means "one hundred and eight." __Ho__ means Dharma; that is, the Buddha's teachings or the Universe. __Myo__ means "clarity," "brightness," or "illumination." __Mon__ means "gate"; that is, a means to something, or a partial aspect of something. So __ippyakuhachi-homyomon__ means "one hundred and eight gates of Dharma-illumination." In compiling this chapter, Master Dogen quoted two long paragraphs from the __Butsu-hongyo-jikkyo__, a biographical sutra about Gautama Buddha. This chapter forms the 11th chapter in the 12-chapter edition of Shobogenzo, but it is not included in either the 95-chapter edition or the 75-chapter edition.

[65] ***At that time*** *the bodhisattva Protector of Illumination finished contemplating upon the family into which he would be born. In Tuṣita Heaven*[1] *in that age there was a celestial palace, called Lofty Banner. Its height and width were exactly the same; sixty yojana. The Bodhisattva from time to time would go up into that palace to preach to the gods of Tuṣita Heaven the pivot of the Dharma. On this occasion, the Bodhisattva ascended to the palace and, after sitting in peacefulness,*[2] *he addressed all the celestial beings of Tuṣita, saying: "Ye gods! Come and gather round! My body before long will descend to the human world. I now would like to preach, in their entirety, the gates of Dharma-illumination, known as the gates of expedient means for penetrating all dharmas and forms. I will leave them as my last instruction to you, so that you will remember me. If you listen to these gates of Dharma,*[3] *you will experience joy." Then, after hearing these words of the Bodhisattva, the great assembly of the gods of Tuṣita, along with jeweled goddesses and all their entourage, all gathered together and ascended to that palace. Bodhisattva Protector of Illumination, after seeing that those celestial multitudes had convened, desired to preach to them the Dharma. Instantly, he produced by magic above that original celestial palace,*

---

1. Bodhisattvas who are about to become buddha in their next life are said to live in Tuṣita Heaven, the fourth of the six heavens in the world of desire. Gautama Buddha was imagined to have practiced there in the past, as the bodhisattva Protector of Illumination and as other bodhisattvas; and the bodhisattva Maitreya is imagined to be living there now.

2. 安座 (ANZA), or "peaceful sitting," is a synonym for Zazen.

3. 法門 (HOMON) represents the Sanskrit *dharma-paryāya*. The word *paryāya*, "going round," represented by 門 (MON), "gate," suggests regular progression through a series. See Glossary.

Lofty Banner, another celestial palace that was so high, grand, and wide that it covered the four continents. In its delightful exquisiteness and regularity, [the new palace] was without compare. Majestic and towering, it was embellished by masses of jewels. Among all the heavenly palaces in the world of desire there was nothing to which to liken it. When gods in the world of matter saw that magic palace, they had the stark realization that their own palaces were like burial mounds. Then Bodhisattva Protector of Illumination—having already in past ages performed valuable work, planted many good roots, accomplished much happiness, and become replete with virtue—mounted the decorated lion-throne[4] *that he had created, and there he sat. Bodhisattva Protector of Illumination, upon that lofty lion-seat, arrayed it intricately with countless treasures; he spread over that seat countless and infinite varieties of heavenly robes; he perfumed that seat with all kinds of wondrous incense; he burned incense in countless infinite jeweled censers; and he produced all kinds of finely-scented flowers and scattered them over the earth. Around the lofty seat there were many rare treasures, and a hundred thousand myriad koṭis of glittering ornaments lit up the palace. That palace, above and below, was covered by jeweled nets. From those nets hung many golden bells, and those golden bells tinkled delicately. That great jeweled palace itself sent forth countless varieties of light. Over that jeweled palace, a thousand myriad banners and canopies in all kinds of wonderful colors formed a resplendent mantle. From that great palace hung all sorts of tassels.*[5] *Countless infinite hundred thousand myriad koṭis of jewel-goddesses, each bearing miscellaneous varieties of the seven treasures, praised [the Bodhisattva], their voices making music, and told of the Bodhisattva's countless infinite past merits. World-protecting quarter-kings, in their hundred thousand myriads of koṭis, standing to the left and to the right, kept guard over that palace. Thousands of myriads of Śakra-devānām-indras prostrated themselves to that palace. Thousands of myriads of brahmadevas worshipped that palace. Again, hundreds of thousands of myriads of koṭis of nayutas of hosts of bodhisattvas protected that palace; and buddhas in the ten directions, numbering in myriad koṭis of nayutas, kept watch over that palace. Works practiced for a hundred thousand myriad koṭis of nayutas of kalpas, and all the pāramitās, accomplished their happy result; causes and conditions were fulfilled and were further promoted day and night so that countless virtues made everything splendid, and so on, and so on, indescribably, indescribably. Upon that great exquisite lion-throne, the Bodhisattva sat; he addressed all the celestial throngs, saying: "Ye gods! Now, the one hundred and eight gates of Dharma-illumination: When bodhisattva-mahāsattvas at the place of appointment in one life are in a Tuṣita palace and they are going to descend to be conceived and born in the human world, they must inevitably proclaim, and preach before the celestial multitudes, these one hundred and eight gates of Dharma-illumination, leaving them for the gods to memorize. After that,*

4. 師子高座 (SHISHI *[no]* KOZA), lit. "lion's high seat." The Buddha's preaching was compared to the roar of a lion. 師子座 (SHISHI-ZA), "a lion seat," is a common expression in sutras for a seat of Buddhist preaching.

5. 流蘇 (RYUSO). An ancient Indian ornament used to decorate carriages, horses, beds, curtains, banners, flags, et cetera. Each tassel was made of interwoven threads of the five primary colors.

they descend to be reborn. Ye gods! Now you must, with utmost sincerity, clearly listen and clearly accept [the one hundred and eight gates]. I now shall preach them. What are the one hundred and eight gates of Dharma-illumination?"

70] **[1]** *Right belief is a gate of Dharma-illumination; for [with it] the steadfast mind is not broken.*

[2] *Pure mind is a gate of Dharma-illumination; for [with it] there is no defilement.*

[3] *Delight is a gate of Dharma-illumination; for it is the mind of peace and tranquillity.*

[4] *Love and cheerfulness are a gate of Dharma-illumination; for they make the mind pure.*

[5] *Right conduct of the actions of the body is a gate of Dharma-illumination; for [with it] the three kinds of behavior*[6] *are pure.*

[6] *Pure conduct of the actions of the mouth is a gate of Dharma-illumination; for it eliminates the four evils.*[7]

[7] *Pure conduct of the actions of the mind is a gate of Dharma-illumination; for it eliminates the three poisons.*[8]

[8] *Mindfulness of Buddha is a gate of Dharma-illumination; for [with it] reflection of [the state of] Buddha is pure.*

[9] *Mindfulness of Dharma is a gate of Dharma-illumination; for [with it] reflection of the Dharma is pure.*

[10] *Mindfulness of Saṃgha is a gate of Dharma-illumination; for [with it] attainment of the truth is steadfast.*

[11] *Mindfulness of generosity is a gate of Dharma-illumination; for [with it] we do not expect reward.*

[12] *Mindfulness of precepts is a gate of Dharma-illumination; for [with it] we fulfill all vows.*

[13] *Mindfulness of the heavens is a gate of Dharma-illumination; for it gives rise to a wide and big mind.*

[14] *Benevolence is a gate of Dharma-illumination; for [with it] good roots prevail in all the situations of life.*

[15] *Compassion is a gate of Dharma-illumination; for [with it] we do not kill or harm living beings.*

[16] *Joy is a gate of Dharma-illumination; for [with it] we abandon all unpleasant things.*

---

6. 三業 (SANGO): behavior of body, speech, and mind.

7. 四悪 (SHI-AKU): 1) lying; 2) suppression of speech; 3) abusive speech; 4) two-faced speech.

8. 三毒 (SANDOKU): anger, greed, and ignorance.

[17] Abandonment is a gate of Dharma-illumination; for [with it] we turn away from the five desires.

[18] Reflection on inconstancy is a gate of Dharma-illumination; for [with it] we reflect upon the desires of the triple world.

[19] Reflection on suffering is a gate of Dharma-illumination; for [with it] we cease all aspirations.

[20] Reflection on there being no self is a gate of Dharma-illumination; for [with it] we do not taintedly attach to self.

[21] Reflection on stillness is a gate of Dharma-illumination; for [with it] we do not disturb the mind.

[22] Repentance is a gate of Dharma-illumination; for [with it] the mind within is stilled.

[23] Humility is a gate of Dharma-illumination; for [with it] eternal malevolence vanishes.

[24] Veracity is a gate of Dharma-illumination; for [with it] we do not deceive gods and human beings.

[25] Truth is a gate of Dharma-illumination; for [with it] we do not deceive ourselves.

[26] Dharma-conduct is a gate of Dharma-illumination; for [with it] we follow the conduct that is the Dharma.

[27] The Three Devotions[9] are a gate of Dharma-illumination; for they purify the three evil worlds.[10]

[28] Recognition of kindness is a gate of Dharma-illumination; for [with it] we do not throw away good roots.

[29] Repayment of kindness is a gate of Dharma-illumination; for [with it] we do not cheat and disregard others.

[30] No self-deception is a gate of Dharma-illumination; for [with it] we do not praise ourselves.

[31] To work for living beings is a gate of Dharma-illumination; for we do not blame others.

[32] To work for the Dharma is a gate of Dharma-illumination; for we act in conformity with the Dharma.

[33] Awareness of time is a gate of Dharma-illumination; for [with it] we do not treat spoken teaching lightly.

[34] Inhibition of self-conceit is a gate of Dharma-illumination; for [with it] wisdom is fulfilled.

---

9. 三帰 (SANKI): devotion to Buddha, Dharma, and Saṃgha.
10. 三悪道 (SAN-AKU-DO): hell, the world of hungry ghosts, and the world of animals.

[35] The non-arising of ill-will is a gate of Dharma-illumination; for [with it] we protect ourselves and protect others.

[36] Being without hindrances is a gate of Dharma-illumination; for [with it] the mind is free of doubt.

[37] Belief and understanding are a gate of Dharma-illumination; for [with them] we decisively comprehend the paramount [truth].[11]

[38] Reflection on impurity is a gate of Dharma-illumination; for [with it] we abandon the mind that is tainted by desire.

[39] Not to quarrel is a gate of Dharma-illumination; for it stops angry accusations.

[40] Not being foolish is a gate of Dharma-illumination; for it stops the killing of living things.

[41] Enjoyment of the meaning of Dharma is a gate of Dharma-illumination; for [with it] we seek the meaning of Dharma.

[42] Love of Dharma-illumination is a gate of Dharma-illumination; for [with it] we attain Dharma-illumination.

[43] Pursuit of abundant knowledge is a gate of Dharma-illumination; for [with it] we truly reflect on the form of the Dharma.

[44] Right means are a gate of Dharma-illumination; for they are accompanied by right conduct.

[45] Knowledge of names and forms is a gate of Dharma-illumination; for it clears away many obstacles.

[46] The view to expiate causes is a gate of Dharma-illumination; for [with it] we attain salvation.

[47] The mind without enmity and intimacy is a gate of Dharma-illumination; for [with it], when among enemies and intimates, we are impartial.

[48] Hidden expedient means are a gate of Dharma-illumination; for they are sensitive to many kinds of suffering.

[49] Equality of all elements is a gate of Dharma-illumination; for it obviates all rules for harmonious association.

[50] The sense-organs are a gate of Dharma-illumination; for [with them] we practice the right way.

[51] Realization of non-appearance[12] *is a gate of Dharma-illumination; for [with it] we*

---

11. 第一義 (DAI-ICHI-GI) is short for 第一義諦 (DAI-ICHI-GI-TAI), "the paramount truth."

12. 無生忍 (MUSHONIN) is short for 無生法忍 (MUSHO-HO-NIN). 忍 (NIN) can be interpreted as representing the character 認 (NIN), "recognition," or "realization." 無生 (MUSHO), "non-appearance" or "non-arising," is a synonym for nirvāṇa, the state in which interferences do not arise.

experience the truth of cessation.[13]

[52] The body as an abode of mindfulness[14] *is a gate of Dharma-illumination; for [with it] all dharmas are serene.*

[53] Feeling as an abode of mindfulness[15] *is a gate of Dharma-illumination; for [with it] we detach from all miscellaneous feelings.*

[54] Mind as an abode of mindfulness[16] *is a gate of Dharma-illumination; for [with it] we reflect that mind is like a phantom.*

[55] The Dharma as an abode of mindfulness[17] *is a gate of Dharma-illumination; for [with it] wisdom is free of blurs.*

[56] The four right exertions[18] *are a gate of Dharma-illumination; for they eliminate all evils and realize many kinds of good.*

[57] The four bases of mystical power[19] *are a gate of Dharma-illumination; for [with them] the body-and-mind is light.*

[58] The faculty of belief[20] *is a gate of Dharma-illumination; for [with it] we do not [blindly] follow the words of others.*

[59] The faculty of effort[21] *is a gate of Dharma-illumination; for [with it] we thoroughly attain many kinds of wisdom.*

---

13. 滅諦 (METTAI), the third of the Four Noble Truths.

14. 身念処 (SHIN-NEN-JO), from the Sanskrit *kāya-smṛtyupasthāna,* is the reflection that the body is not pure, which is the first of the thirty-seven elements of bodhi. See chap. 73, *Sanjushichi-bon-bodai-bunpo,* para. [4].

15. 受念処 (JU-NEN-JO), from the Sanskrit *vedanā-smṛtyupasthāna,* is the reflection that feeling is suffering.

16. 心念処 (SHIN-NEN-JO), from the Sanskrit *citta-smṛtyupasthāna,* is the reflection that mind is without constancy.

17. 法念処 (HO-NEN-JO), from the Sanskrit *dharma-smṛtyupasthāna,* is the reflection that the Dharma is without self. Nos. 52 to 55 are known as 四念処 (SHI-NEN-JO), "the four abodes of mindfulness," from the Sanskrit *catvāri smṛtyupasthānāni.* They are the first four of the thirty-seven elements of bodhi listed in chap. 73, *Sanjushichi-bon-bodai-bunpo.*

18. 四正懃 (SHI-SHO-GON), from the Sanskrit *catvāri samyakprahāṇāni.* In chap. 73, *Sanjushichi-bon-bodai-bunpo,* they are called 四正断 (SHI-SHO-DAN), or "the four kinds of right restraint." The Sanskrit *prahāṇa* covers both meanings, exertion and restraint (see Glossary). The four exertions are the fifth to the eighth of the thirty-seven elements of bodhi. They are, namely: 1) to prevent bad that has not yet occurred; 2) to cause bad that has already occurred to be extinguished; 3) to cause to occur good that has not yet occurred; and 4) to promote the good that has already occurred.

19. 四如意足 (SHI-NYOI-SOKU), lit. "the four bases of acting at will," from the Sanskrit *catur-ṛddhipāda.* See Clossary. In chap. 73, they are called 四神足 (SHI-JIN-SOKU), or "the four bases of mystical ability." They are the ninth to the twelfth of the thirty-seven elements of bodhi. In Sanskrit they are: 1) *chanda* (volition); 2) *vīrya* (effort); 3) *citta* (intelligence); and 4) *mīmāṃsā* (profound consideration).

20. 信根 (SHINKON), from the Sanskrit *śraddhendriya.*

21. 精進根 (SHOJINKON), from the Sanskrit *vīryendriya.*

[60] The faculty of mindfulness[22] *is a gate of Dharma-illumination; for [with it] we thoroughly perform many kinds of work.*

[61] The faculty of balance[23] *is a gate of Dharma-illumination; for [with it] the mind is pure.*

[62] The faculty of wisdom[24] *is a gate of Dharma-illumination; for [with it] we really see all dharmas.*

[63] The power of belief[25] *is a gate of Dharma-illumination; for it surpasses the power of demons.*

[64] The power of effort[26] *is a gate of Dharma-illumination; for [with it] we do not regress or stray.*

[65] The power of mindfulness[27] *is a gate of Dharma-illumination; for [with it] we do not [blindly] go along with others.*

[66] The power of balance[28] *is a gate of Dharma-illumination; for [with it] we discontinue all thoughts.*

[67] The power of wisdom[29] *is a gate of Dharma-illumination; for [with it] we depart from the two extremes.*

[68] Mindfulness, as a part of the state of truth,[30] *is a gate of Dharma-illumination; for it is wisdom that accords with real dharmas.*

[69] Examination of Dharma, as a part of the state of truth,[31] *is a gate of Dharma-illumination; for it illuminates all dharmas.*

[70] Effort, as a part of the state of truth,[32] *is a gate of Dharma-illumination; for [with it] we become proficient in realization.*

[71] Enjoyment, as a part of the state of truth,[33] *is a gate of Dharma-illumination; for [with it] we attain many kinds of balanced state.*

---

22. 念根 (NENKON), from the Sanskrit *smṛtindriya.*

23. 定根 (JOKON), from the Sanskrit *samādhindriya.*

24. 慧根 (EKON), from the Sanskrit *prajñendriya.* Nos. 58 to 62 are known as 五根 (GOKON), "five faculties" or "five roots," from the Sanskrit *pañcendriyāṇi.* See Glossary. They are the thirteenth to the seventeenth of the thirty-seven elements of bodhi.

25. 信力 (SHINRIKI), from the Sanskrit *śraddhā-bala.*

26. 精進力 (SHOJINRIKI), from the Sanskrit *vīrya-bala.*

27. 念力 (NENRIKI), from the Sanskrit *smṛti-bala.*

28. 定力 (JORIKI), from the Sanskrit *samādhi-bala.*

29. 慧力 (ERIKI), from the Sanskrit *prajñā-bala.* Nos. 63 to 67 are known as 五力 (GORIKI), from the Sanskrit *pañcā-balāni.* See Glossary. They are the five powers deriving from the five faculties and are the eighteenth to the twenty-second of the thirty-seven elements of bodhi.

30. 念覚分 (NEN-KAKUBUN), from the Sanskrit *smṛti bodhyaṅga.*

31. 択法覚分 (CHAKUHO-KAKUBUN), from the Sanskrit *dharmapravicaya bodhyaṅga.* 択 (CHAKU) is lit. "selection," but the Sanskrit *pravicaya* means examination or investigation.

32. 精進覚分 (SHOJIN-KAKUBUN), from the Sanskrit *vīrya bodhyaṅga.*

[72] Entrustment as a part of the state of truth,[34] *is a gate of Dharma-illumination; for [with it] conduct is already managed.*

[73] The balanced state, as a part of the state of truth,[35] *is a gate of Dharma-illumination; for [with it] we recognize that all dharmas are in equilibrium.*

[74] Abandonment, as a part of the state of truth,[36] *is a gate of Dharma-illumination; for [with it] we [can] turn away from all kinds of lives.*

[75] Right view[37] *is a gate of Dharma-illumination; for [with it] we attain the noble path on which the superfluous is exhausted.*

[76] Right discrimination[38] *is a gate of Dharma-illumination; for [with it] we eliminate all discrimination and lack of discrimination.*

[77] Right speech[39] *is a gate of Dharma-illumination; for [with it] concepts, voice, and words all are known as sound.*

[78] Right action[40] *is a gate of Dharma-illumination; for [with it] there is no karma and no retribution.*

[79] Right livelihood[41] *is a gate of Dharma-illumination; for [with it] we get rid of all evil ways.*

[80] Right practice[42] *is a gate of Dharma-illumination; for [with it] we arrive at the far shore.*

[81] Right mindfulness[43] *is a gate of Dharma-illumination; for [with it] we do not consider all dharmas intellectually.*

[82] Right balanced state[44] *is a gate of Dharma-illumination; for [with it] we attain undistracted samādhi.*

---

33. 喜覚分 (KI-KAKUBUN), from the Sanskrit *prīti bodhyaṅga.*

34. 除覚分 (JO-KAKUBUN), from the Sanskrit *praśrabdhi bodhyaṅga.*

35. 定覚分 (JO-KAKUBUN), from the Sanskrit *samādhi bodhyaṅga.*

36. 捨覚分 (SHA-KAKUBUN), from the Sanskrit *upekṣa bodhyaṅga.* Nos. 68 to 74 are 七覚分 (SHICHI-KAKUBUN), from the Sanskrit *sapta bodhyaṅgāni.* See Book 2, Glossary. In chap. 73 they are called 七等覚支 (SHICHI-TOKAKUSHI), "seven branches of the balanced truth," from the Sanskrit *sapta sambodhyaṅgāni,* and they are listed in a different order. They are the twenty-third to the twenty-ninth of the thirty-seven elements of bodhi.

37. 正見 (SHOKEN), from the Sanskrit *samyag-dṛṣṭi.*

38. 正分別 (SHOFUNBETSU), from the Sanskrit *samyag-saṃkalpa.* In chap. 73, it is rendered as 正思惟 (SHO-SHI-I), "right thinking."

39. 正語 (SHOGO), from the Sanskrit *samyag-vāc.*

40. 正業 (SHOGO), from the Sanskrit *samyak-karmānta.*

41. 正命 (SHOMYO), from the Sanskrit *samyag-ājīva.*

42. 正行 (SHOGYO), from the Sanskrit *samyag-vyāyāma.* In chap. 73, it is rendered as 正精進 (SHOSHOJIN), "right exertion."

43. 正念 (SHONEN), from the Sanskrit *samyak-smṛti.*

44. 正定 (SHOJO), from the Sanskrit *samyak-samādhi.* Nos. 75 to 82 are known as 八正道 (HASSHODO), "the eightfold path of rightness," or 八聖道 (HASSHODO), "the eightfold noble

[83] The bodhi-mind is a gate of Dharma-illumination; for [with it] we are not separated from the Three Treasures.

[84] Reliance is a gate of Dharma-illumination; for [with it] we do not incline towards small vehicles.

[85] Right belief[45] *is a gate of Dharma-illumination; for [with it] we attain the supreme Dharma.*

[86] Development is a gate of Dharma-illumination; for [with it] we realize all dharmas concerning the root of good.

[87] The dāna pāramitā[46] *is a gate of Dharma-illumination; for [with it], in every instance, we cause features to be pleasant, we adorn the Buddhist land, and we teach and guide stingy and greedy living beings.*

[88] The precepts pāramitā[47] *is a gate of Dharma-illumination; for [with it] we distantly depart from the hardships of evil worlds, and we teach and guide precept-breaking living beings.*

[89] The forbearance pāramitā[48] *is a gate of Dharma-illumination; for [with it] we abandon all anger, arrogance, flattery, and foolery, and we teach and guide living beings who have such vices.*

[90] The diligence pāramitā[49] *is a gate of Dharma-illumination; for [with it] we completely attain all good dharmas, and we teach and guide lazy living beings.*

[91] The dhyāna pāramitā[50] *is a gate of Dharma-illumination; for [with it] we accomplish all balanced states of dhyāna and mystical powers, and we teach and guide distracted living beings.*

[92] The wisdom pāramitā[51] *is a gate of Dharma-illumination; for [with it] we eradicate the darkness of ignorance, together with attachment to views, and we teach and guide foolish living beings.*

---

path," from the Sanskrit *āryāṣṭānga-mārga*. They are the last eight of the 37 elements of bodhi. See Glossary.

45. 正信 (SHOSHIN). Exactly the same term, 正信 (SHOSHIN), is listed as the first gate of Dharma-illumination. If the two gates of "right belief" are counted as one, then the sutra lists 108 gates. (Otherwise, there are 109.)

46. 檀度 (DANDO). 檀 (DAN) represents the sound of the Sanskrit *dāna*, "giving." 度 (DO) represents the meaning of the Sanskrit *pāramitā*, which means "accomplishment." See chap. 2, *Maka-hannya-haramitsu*, and Book 1, Glossary.

47. 戒度 (KAIDO), from the Sanskrit *śīla-pāramitā*.

48. 忍度 (NINDO), from the Sanskrit *kṣānti-pāramitā*.

49. 精進度 (SHOJINDO), from the Sanskrit *vīrya-pāramitā*.

50. 禅度 (ZENDO). The Sanskrit *dhyāna*, which means meditation or concentration, that is, the practice of Zazen, is sometimes represented as 静慮 (JO-RYO), lit. "quiet thought." See Book 1, Glossary.

51. 智度 (CHIDO), from the Sanskrit *prajñā-pāramitā*. Nos. 87 to 92 are the six pāramitās.

[93] Expedient means are a gate of Dharma-illumination; for [with them] we manifest ourselves according to the dignified forms that living beings admire, and we teach and guide [living beings], accomplishing the Dharma of all the buddhas.

[94] The four elements of sociability[52] are a gate of Dharma-illumination; for [with them] we accept all living beings and, after we have attained [the truth of] bodhi, we bestow upon all living beings the Dharma.

[95] To teach and guide living beings is a gate of Dharma-illumination; for we ourselves neither indulge pleasures nor become tired.

[96] Acceptance of the right Dharma is a gate of Dharma-illumination; for it eradicates the afflictions of all living beings.

[97] Accretion of happiness is a gate of Dharma-illumination; for it benefits all living beings.

[98] The practice of the balanced state of dhyāna is a gate of Dharma-illumination; for it fulfills the ten powers.

[99] Stillness is a gate of Dharma-illumination; for it realizes, and is replete with, the samādhi of the Tathāgata.

[100] The wisdom-view is a gate of Dharma-illumination; for [with it] wisdom is realized and fulfilled.

[101] Entry into the state of unrestricted speech is a gate of Dharma-illumination; for [with it] we attain realization of the Dharma-eye.

[102] Entry into all conduct is a gate of Dharma-illumination; for [with it] we attain realization of the Buddha-eye.

[103] Accomplishment of the state of dhāraṇī is a gate of Dharma-illumination; for [with it] we hear the Dharma of all the buddhas and are able to receive and retain it.

[104] Attainment of the state of unrestricted speech is a gate of Dharma-illumination; for [with it] we cause all living beings totally to rejoice.

[105] Endurance of obedient following[53] is a gate of Dharma-illumination; for [with it] we obey the Dharma of all the buddhas.

[106] Attainment of realization of the Dharma of non-appearance[54] is a gate of Dharma-illumination; for [with it] we attain affirmation.

[107] The state beyond regressing and straying is a gate of Dharma-illumination; for it is replete with the Dharma of past buddhas.

---

52. 四摂法 (SHISHOBO), from the Sanskrit *catvāri saṃgraha-vastūni.* The four in Sanskrit are 1) *dāna* (giving); 2) *priya-ākhyāna* (kind communication); 3) *artha-carya* (useful conduct); and 4) *samāna-arthatā* (sharing a common aim). See chap. 45, *Bodaisatta-shishobo,* and Glossary.

53. 順忍 (JUNNIN), one of the 五忍 (GONIN), five kinds of endurance.

54. 得無生法忍 (TOKU-MUSHO-HO-NIN). See no. 51, and accompanying footnote.

***[108]** The wisdom that leads us from one state to another state is a gate of Dharma-illumination; for [with it], having water sprinkled on the head,[55] we accomplish total wisdom.*

***[109]** The state in which water is sprinkled on the head is a gate of Dharma-illumination; for [with it], following birth in a family, we are at last able to realize anuttara-samyak-saṃbodhi.*

182] *Then Bodhisattva Protector of Illumination, having preached these words, addressed all those celestial multitudes, saying, "Gods, remember! These are the one hundred and eight gates of Dharma-illumination. I bequeath them to the gods. You should receive them and retain them, always keep them in mind, and never forget them."*

183] These are just the one hundred and eight gates of Dharma-illumination. That all bodhisattvas bound by a single life, when they are going to descend from Tuṣita Heaven to be born in Jambudvīpa, unfailingly proclaim to the multitudes of Tuṣita Heaven these one hundred and eight gates of Dharma-illumination, and thereby teach the gods, is the constant rule of the buddhas. "Bodhisattva Protector of Illumination" was the name of Śākyamuni Buddha when he was in the fourth heaven[56] as [a bodhisattva] at the place of appointment in one life. When Ri Fuma[57] compiled *Tensho-koto-roku*, he recorded the name of these one hundred and eight gates of Dharma-illumination. [But] the students who have known them clearly are few, and those who do not know them are as [common as] rice, flax, bamboo, and reeds. Now, for the benefit of beginners and senior students, I have compiled them. Those who would ascend the lion-seat and become the teachers of human beings and gods should painstakingly learn them in practice. Without having lived in this Tuṣita Heaven as [a bodhisattva] bound by one life, we are not buddhas at all. Practitioners, do not be proud of yourselves at random. For a bodhisattva bound by one life, there is no intermediate stage.[58]

---

55. 灌頂 (KANCHO), ceremonial sprinkling of water on a bodhisattva's head, is said to be done when a bodhisattva is about to enter the ultimate state and become buddha.

56. 第四天 (DAISHITEN), another name for Tuṣita, which was regarded as the fourth of the six heavens in the world of desire.

57. 李附馬 (RI-FUMA), or "Imperial Aide Lee," also known as Ri Junkyoku. 李 (RI), "Lee," was his surname. 附馬 (FUMA) was an official title. He first practiced in the order of Master Koku-on Unso and he became the successor of Master Koku-on. Later he maintained a close association with Master Jimyo So-en and the Buddhist layman Yo Dainen. He is also mentioned in chap. 73, *Sanjushichi-bon-bodai-bunpo*. He died in 1038.

58. 中叐 (CHUHATSU). The meaning of the character 叐 (HATSU) has not been traced, but 中叐 (CHUHATSU) may be a synonym for 中般, also pronounced CHUHATSU. 中般 (CHUHATSU) is explained as an intermediate stage between an anāgāmin's death in the world of desire and rebirth in the world of matter. The related concept 中有 (CHU-U), "intermediate existence" or "middle existence," represents the Sanskrit *antarā-bhava*. The point is that bodhisattvas must just

Shobogenzo Ippyakuhachi-homyomon, number 11.[59]

directly become buddha. See Book 1, Glossary.

59. This is the 11th chapter in the 12-chapter edition of Shobogenzo. A date is not recorded.

Chinese Masters

Japanese	Pinyin
Banzan Hoshaku	Panshan Baoji
Baso Do-itsu	Mazu Daoyi
Bussho Hotai	Foxing Fatai
Chokei Eryo	Changqing Huileng
Chosa Keishin	Changsha Jingcen
Dai-e Soko	Dahui Zonggao
Daikan Eno	Dajian Huineng
Engo Kokugon	Yuanwu Keqin
Fun-yo Zensho	Fenyang Shanzhao
Fuyo Dokai	Furong Daokai
Gensa Shibi	Xuansha Shibei
Godai Inpo	Wutai Yinfeng
Goso Ho-en	Wuzu Fayan
Gutei	Juzhi
Ho-on (layman)	Pangyun
Hofuku Juten	Baofu Congzhan
Hokken	Faxian
Hyakujo Ekai	Baizhang Huaihai
Joshu Jushin	Zhaozhou Congshen
Jozan Shin-ei	Dingshan Shenying
Kai-e (Haku-un) Shutan	Haihui (Baiyun) Shouduan
Kassan Zen-e	Jiashan Shanhui
Koboku Hojo	Kumu Facheng
Kozan Chien	Gushan Zhiyuan
Kyogen Chikan	Xiangyan Zhixian
Kyozan Ejaku	Yangshan Huiji
Myokyo Shori	Mingjiao Shaoli
Nan-yo Echu	Nanyang Huizhong
Nangaku Ejo	Nanyue Huairang
Nangaku Eshi	Nanyue Huisi
Nansen Fugan	Nanquan Puyuan
Obaku Ki-un	Huangbo Xiyun
Oryu Shishin (Goshin)	Huanglong Sixin (Wuxin)
Rai-an Shoju	Leian Zhengshou
Ri Fuma	Li Fuma
Rinzai Gigen	Linji Yixuan
Sakei Genro	Zuoxi Xuanlang
Seccho Juken	Xuedou Chongxian

Japanese	Pinyin
Seido Chizo	Xitang Zhizang
Seigen Gyoshi	Qingyuan Xingsi
Seizan Ryo	Xishan Liang
Shakkyo Ezo	Shigong Huicang
Sokei Reito	Caoxi Lingtao
Taiso Eka	Dazu Huike
Tando Bunjun	Zhantang Wenzhun
Tanka Shijun	Danxia Zichun
Tanka Ten-nen	Danxia Tianran
Tendo Nyojo	Tiantong Rujing
Tozan Dobi	Dongshan Daowei
Tozan Ryokai	Dongshan Liangjie
Unmon Bun-en	Yunmen Wenyan
Wanshi Shokaku	Hongzhi Zhengjue
Yakusan Igen	Yueshan Weiyan
Yakusan Ko (Śrāmaṇera)	Yueshan Gao
Yobunko	Yang Wengong
Yoka Genkaku	Yongjia Xuanjue

Glossary of Sanskrit Terms

This glossary contains Sanskrit terms appearing in Book 4 that are not already covered in the Sanskrit Glossaries of Book 1, Book 2, and Book 3. Definitions are drawn in general from *A Sanskrit-English Dictionary* by Sir Monier Monier-Williams [MW], (Oxford University Press, 1333pp.) Also used were *A Practical Sanskrit Dictionary* by A. A. Macdonell [MAC], (Oxford University Press, 382pp.), and *Japanese-English Buddhist Dictionary* [JEBD], (Daito Shuppansha, 456pp.).

Chapter references, unless otherwise stated, refer to chapters of Shobogenzo. Arrangement is according to the English alphabet.

abhimāna (self-conceit)
Represented by 増上慢 (ZOJOMAN), "self-conceit."
[MW] intention to injure, insidiousness; high opinion of one's self, self-conceit, pride, haughtiness.
See also Book 1, under **māna**.
Ref: ch. 90 [23].

alpecchuḥ (small desire)
Represented by 少欲 (SHOYOKU), "small desire."
[MW] *alpeccha:* having little or moderate wishes.
Ref: ch. 95 [122].

antagrāha-dṛṣṭi (holding extreme views)
Represented by 辺見 (HENKEN), "the extreme views."
[MW] *anta:* end, limit, boundary; end of life, death, destruction.
grāha: seizing, holding, catching, receiving; seizure, grasping, laying hold of.
dṛṣṭi: seeing, viewing, beholding; view, notion; (with Buddhists) a wrong view; theory, doctrine.
Ref: ch. 89 [11].

āryāṣṭānga-mārga (the holy eightfold path)
Represented by 八聖道 (HASSHODO), "the eightfold noble path."
[MW] 'the holy eightfold path' pointed out by Buddha for escape from the misery of existence: 1) right views, 2) right thoughts, 3) right words, 4) right actions, 5) right living, 6) right exertion, 7) right recollection, 8) right meditation.
Ref: Appendix 2.

catur-ṛddhipāda (four bases of mystical ability)
Represented by 四神足 (SHI-JIN-SOKU), "four mystical feet."
[MW] *catur:* four
ṛddhipāda: one of the constituent parts of supernatural power.
In Sanskrit they are: 1) *chanda* (will); 2) *citta* (thoughts); 3) *vīrya* (exertion); and 4) *mīmāṃsā* (investigation).
Ref: ch. 73 [21].

catvāri saṃgraha-vastūni (the four elements of popularity)
Represented by 四摂法 (SHISHOBO), "the four elements of sociability."
[JEBD] "the four ways of leading human beings to emancipation."
[MW] *catur:* four
saṃgraha-vastū: an element of popularity.
In Sanskrit the four are: 1) *dāna* (giving); 2) *priya-ākhyāna* (kind communication); 3) *artha-carya* (useful conduct); and 4) *samāna-arthatā* (sharing a common aim).
Ref: Appendix 2.

catvāri samyakprahāṇāni (four kinds of restraint)
Represented by 四正断 (SHI-SHO-DAN) and 四正勤 (SHI-SHO-GON).
[JEBD] Right exertion. Right effort of four kinds which are mentioned in a list of the thirty-seven bodhipaksa-dharmas. They are: To prevent demerit from arising, to abandon it when arisen, to produce merit, and to increase it when produced.

[MW] *catur:* four
samyañc: correct, accurate, proper, true, right.
prahāṇa: relinquishing, abandoning, avoiding; exertion, Dharmas.
[JEBD] Right exertion. Right effort of four kinds which are mentioned in a list of the thirty seven bodhipakṣa-dharmas. They are: to prevent demerit from arising, to abandon it when arisen, to produce merit, and to increase it when produced.
Ref: ch. 73 [15].

catvāro-dvīpāh (the four continents)
Represented by 四洲 (SHISHU), "the four continents."
[MW] *catur:* four
dvīpāh: an island, peninsula, sandbank; a division of the terrestrial world.
The four continents are Jambudvīpa (south), Pūrva-videha (east), Apara-godāna (west), and Uttara-kuru (north).
Ref: ch. 90 [56].

daśa-tathāgata-balāni (the ten tathāgata powers)
Represented by 如来具足十力 (NYORAI-GUSOKU-JURIKI), "the ten powers with which a tathāgata is equipped," or 十力 (JURIKI), "the ten powers."
[MW] *daśa-bala:* 'possessing 10 powers,' Name of a Buddha.
bala: power, strength, might, vigor, force; force or power of articulation; force considered as a sixth organ of action.
A traditional interpretation of the ten powers is as follows: 1) knowing right and wrong; 2) knowing which karmic effects follow from which causes; 3) knowing the various balanced states (four dhyānas, eight states of liberation, three samādhis, etc.); 4) knowing the superior or inferior makings of others; 5) knowing the desires of others; 6) knowing the states of others; 7) knowing the destinations of others (nirvāṇa, hell, etc.); 8) knowing the past; 9) knowing life and death; 10) knowing how to end excesses.
Ref: ch. 84 [114].

dharma-paryāya (succcession of dharmas)
Represented by 法門 (HOMON), "gate of dharma."
[JEBD] The teaching of the Buddha. The meaning is that the dharma is something like a gate, because through it sentient beings attain the enlightenment.
[MW] *dharma:* that which is established or firm, steadfast decree, statute, ordinance, law; the law or doctrine of Buddhism.
paryāya: going or turning or winding round, revolving, revolution; regular recurrence, repetition, succession, turn.
Ref: Appendix 2.

jana-kāya (community)
Represented by 聚落 (SHURAKU), "colony," or "community."
[MW] *jana:* creature, living being, man, person, race; people, subjects.
kāya: assemblage, collection, multitude.
Ref: ch. 85 [59].

pañca-śīlāni (the five precepts)
Represented by 五戒 (GOKAI), "five precepts."
[MW] *pañca-śīla:* the 5 chief rules of conduct for Buddhists.
śīla: good disposition or character, moral conduct, integrity, morality, piety, virtue; (with Buddhists, *śīla*, 'moral conduct,' is one of the 6 or 10 perfections or Pāramitās); a moral precept (with Buddh. There are 5 fundamental precepts or rules of moral conduct, cf. *pañca-śīla*).
The five precepts are: 1) not to kill, 2) not to steal, 3) not to commit adultery, 4) not to lie, 5) not to drink alcohol.
Ref: ch. 86 [75].

pañcāvīci-karmāṇi (the five actions leading to incessant hell)
Represented by 五無間業 (GO-MUGEN-GO)
[MW] *pañca:* five
avīci: waveless; a particular hell.
karman: act, action, performance, business.

[JEBD] The five deadly sins, the five cardinal sins: killing one's father, killing one's mother, killing a saint (*arhat*), injuring the body of a Buddha, and causing disunity in the community of monks.
Ref: ch. 84 [38].

pañcendriyāṇi (five roots)
Represented by 五根 (GOKON), "five roots."
[MW] *pañcendriya:* the 5 organs of sense (viz. the ear, eye, nose, tongue, and skin) or the 5 organs of action (viz. hands, feet, larynx, and organs of generation and excretion).
indriya: fit for or belonging to or agreeable to Indra; power force, the quality which belongs especially to the mighty Indra; faculty of sense, sense, organ of sense.
[JEBD] The five organs that lead man to good conduct—sense of belief (*śraddhendriya*), sense of endeavor (*vīryendriya*), sense of memory (*smṛtīndriya*), sense of meditation (*samādhīndriya*), sense of wisdom (*prajñendriya*).
Ref: ch. 86 [118]; Appendix 2.

piṇḍa-vana (forest ranks)
Represented by 叢林 (SORIN), "thicket-forest."
[JEBD] an assemblage of medicants or monks. Monks gathered at one place.
See also Book 1.
Ref: ch. 81 [248].

prahāṇa (restraint, exertion)
Represented by 断 (DAN), "restraint," or 勤 (GON), "exertion."
See **catvāri samyakprahāṇāni.**

prapañca (wordiness)
Represented by 戯論 (KERON), "idle discussion."
[MW] amplification, prolixity, diffuseness, copiousness (in style).
Note: In philosophical contexts, *prapañca* is used to mean the visible world, reality in front of us.
Ref: ch. 95 [130].

praśrabdhi-sambodhyaṅga
(confidence as an integrated requisite for attaining perfect wisdom)
Represented by 除等覚支 (JO-TOKAKUSHI), "elimination as a limb of the truth," 除覚分 (JO-KAKUBUN), "entrustment as a part of the state of truth."
[MW] *praśrabdhi:* trust, confidence
sam: with, together with, along with; conjuction, union, integration.
sambodhya: to be enlightened or instructed.
bodhyaṅga: a requisite for obtaining perfect knowledge.
One of the seven limbs of bodhi; represented by 七等覚支 (SHICHI-TOKAKUSHI), from the Sanskrit *sapta-sambodhyaṅga.* See also Book 2, under **sapta-bodhyaṅgāni.**
Ref: ch. 73 [37], [40]; Appendix 2.

pūjana (serving offerings)
Represented by 供養 (KUYO), "serve offerings."
[MW] reverencing, honoring, worship, respect, attention, hospitable reception.
Ref: ch. 87 [127].

saṃkalpa (thinking)
Represented by 思惟 (SHI-I).
[MW] conception or idea or notion formed in the mind or heart, (esp.) will, volition, desire, purpose, definite intention or determination or decision or wish for.
Ref: ch. 73 [44].

saṃnāha (suit of armor)
Represented phonetically.
[MW] equipment, harness; accoutrements, armor, mail, a coat of mail.
Ref: ch. 88 [184].

saṃtuṣṭaḥ (complete satisfaction)
Represented by 知足 (CHISOKU), "to know satisfaction."
[MW] *saṃtuṣṭi:* complete satisfaction, contentment with.
Ref: ch. 95 [123].

śānta (tranquillity)
Represented by 寂静 (JAKUJO), "tranquillity."
[MW] *śānti:* tranquillity, peace, quiet, peace or calmness of mind, absence of passion, averting of pain.
Ref: ch. 95 [124].

śaraṇa (refuge)
Represented by 帰依 (KIE), "returning to and depending upon."
[MAC] protecting, guarding; protection, refuge.
Ref: ch. 88 [181]

śūraṃgama-samādhi (powerful samadhi)
Represented by 首楞厳定 (SHURYOGON-JO) and 首楞厳三昧 (SHURYOGON-ZANMAI).
[JEBD] Powerful samādhi. The samadhi by which one can exterminate all illusions, just as a brave general destroys his enemies.
[MW] *śūraṃgama:* a particular samādhi; name of a Bodhi-sattva.
Ref: ch. 43; ch. 73 [5]; ch. 74; Bibliography.

upasthāna (abode)
Represented by 住 (JU), "abode," and by 処 (JO), "abode."
[MW] the act of placing one's self near to, going near, approach, access; staying upon or at, abiding, a place of abiding, abode.
Ref: ch. 73 [4].

veda (divine knowledge)
Represented phonetically.
[JEBD] The basic scriptures of Brahmanism, not recognized by Buddhists.
[MW] knowledge, true or sacred knowledge or lore; name of certain celebrated works which constitute the basis of the first period of the Hindu religion.
Ref: ch. 90 [46].

viparyāsa (inversion)
Represented by 顛倒 (TENDO), "inversion."
[MW] overturning, overthrow, upsetting; transposition, transportation; exchange, inversion, change, interchange.
[JEBD] Error, delusion.
Ref: ch. 90 [49].

Bibliographies

Bibliography One: Main Chinese Sources Quoted by Master Dogen in Shobogenzo

A. Sutras

Attempts at English translations of sutra titles are provisional, and provided only for reference.

Agon-kyo 阿含経 (Āgama Sutras).

In Chinese translation, there are four:

Cho-agon-kyo 長阿含経 (Long Āgama Sutra—in Pali, Digha-nikāya);
Chu-agon-kyo 中阿含経 (Middle Āgama Sutra—in Sanskrit, Madhyamāgama; in Pali, Majjhima-nikāya);
Zo-agon-kyo 雑阿含経 (Miscellaneous Āgama Sutra—in Sanskrit, Saṃyuktāgama; in Pali, Samyutta-nikāya);
Zo-itsu-agon-gyo 増一阿含経 (Āgama Sutras Increased by One—in Sanskrit, Ekottarāgama; in Pali, Aṅguttara-nikāya)
These are supplemented by the **Sho-agon-kyo** 小阿含経 (Small Āgama Sutras—in Sanskrit, Kṣudrakāgama; in Pali, Khuddaka-nikāya), a collection of all the Āgamas beside the four Āgamas. In the Pali canon, Khuddaka-Nikāya is the fifth of the five Nikāyas and comprises fifteen short books.

Aiku-o-kyo 阿育王経 (Aśoka Sutra)

Butsu-hongyo-jikkyo 佛本行集経 (Sutra of Collected Past Deeds of the Buddha)

Daibonten-o-monbutsu-ketsugi-kyo 大梵天王問佛決疑経 (Sutra of Questions and Answers between Mahābrahman and the Buddha)

Dai-hannya-kyo 大般若経 (Great Prajñā Sutra), short for
Dai-hannya-haramitta-kyo 大般若波羅密多経 (Sutra of the Great Prajñā-pāramitā—in Sanskrit, Mahā-prajñā-pāramitā-sūtra)

Daihatsu-nehan-kyo 大般涅槃経 (Sutra of the Great Demise—in Sanskrit, Mahāparinirvāṇa-sūtra)

Dai-hoko-hokyo-gyo 大方廣寶篋経 (The Mahāvaipulya Treasure Chest Sutra)

Dai-hoko-engaku-shutara-ryogi-kyo 大方廣円覚修多羅了義経 (The Mahāvaipulya Round Realization Sutra)

Dai-ho-shak-kyo 大寶積経 (Great Treasure Accumulation Sutra—in Sanskrit, Mahāratnakūta-sūtra)

Daijo-honsho-shinchi-kan-kyo 大乗本生心地観経 (The Mahāyāna Sutra of Reflection on the Mental State in Past Lives)

Daishu-kyo 大集経 (Great Collection Sutra—in Sanskrit, Mahā-saṃnipāta-sūtra)

Engaku-kyo 円覚経 (Sutra of Round Realization)

Fuyo-kyo 普曜経 (Sutra of Diffusion of Shining Artlessness—in Sanskrit, Lalita-vistara-sūtra)

Hige-kyo 悲華経 (Flower of Compassion Sutra—in Sanskrit, Karuṇā-puṇḍarīka-sūtra)

Hokke-kyo 法華経 (Lotus Sutra, Sutra of the Flower of Dharma), short for **Myoho-renge-kyo** (Sutra of the Lotus Flower of the Wonderful Dharma—in Sanskrit, Saddharma-puṇḍarika-sūtra)

Hoku-kyo 法句経 (Sutra of Dharma-phrases—in Pali, Dhammapada)

Honsho-kyo 本生経 (Past Lives Sutra—in Sanskrit, Jātaka)

Ju-o-kyo 十王経 (Ten Kings Sutra)

Kan-fugen-bosatsu-gyobo-kyo 観普賢菩薩行法経 (Sutra of Reflection on the Practice of Dharma by Bodhisattva Universal Virtue)

Kegon-kyo 華厳経 (Garland Sutra—in Sanskrit, Avataṇsaka-sūtra)

Kengu-kyo 賢愚経 (Sutra of the Wise and the Stupid)

Ke-u-koryo-kudoku-kyo 希有校量功徳経 (Sutra of Comparison of the Merits of Rare Occurrences)

Konkomyo-kyo 金光明経 (Golden Light Sutra), short for **Konkomyo-saisho-o-kyo** 金光明最勝王経 (Golden Light Sutra of the Supreme King—in Sanskrit, Suvarṇa-prabhāsottama-rāja-sūtra)

Kongo-kyo 金剛経 (Diamond Sutra), short for **Kongo-hannya-haramitsu-kyo** 金剛般若波羅密経 (Sutra of the Diamond-Prajñā-Pāramitā—in Sanskrit, Vajraccedikā-prajñā-pāramitā-sūtra)

Miroku-josho-kyo 弥勒上生経 (Sutra of Maitreya's Ascent and Birth [in Tuṣita Heaven])

Mizo-u-innen-kyo 未曾有因縁経 (Sutra of Unprecedented Episodes)

Ninno-gyo 仁王経 (Benevolent King Sutra), short for **Ninno-hannya-haramitsu-gyo** 仁王般若波羅密経 (Prajñā-pārapmitā Sutra of the Benevolent King)

Senju-hyaku-en-kyo 撰集百縁経 (Sutra of a Hundred Collected Stories)

Shobutsu-yoshu-kyo 諸佛要集経 (Sutra of the Collected Essentials of the Buddhas)

Shuryogon-kyo 首楞厳経 (Śūraṃgama Sutra—in Sanskrit, Śūraṃgama-samādhi-nirdeśa)

Shakubuku-rakan-kyo 折伏羅漢経 (Sutra of the Defeat of the Arhat)

Shugyo-hongi-kyo 修行本起経 (Sutra of Past Occurences of Practice)

Yoraku-hongyo-kyo 瓔珞本起経 (Sutra of Past Deeds as a String of Pearls)

Yuima-gyo 維摩経 (Vimalakīrti Sutra—in Sanskrit, Vimalakīrti-nīrdeśa)

Zuio-hongi-kyo 瑞應本起経 (Sutra of Auspicious Past Occurrences)

B. Precepts

Bonmo-kyo 梵網経 (Pure Net Sutra)

Daibiku-sanzen-yuigi-kyo 大比丘三千威儀経 (Sutra of Three Thousand Dignified Forms for Ordained Monks)

Juju-ritsu 十誦律 (Precepts in Ten Parts), a 61-fascicle translation of the vinaya of the Sarvāstivādin School

Konpon-setsu-issai-u-bu-hyaku-ichi-katsuma 根本説一切有部百一羯磨 (101 Customs of the Mūla-sarvāstivādin School)

Makasogi-ritsu 摩訶僧祇律 (Precepts for the Great Saṃgha), a 40-fascicle translation of the vinaya of the Mahāsaṃghika School of Hīnayāna Buddhism

Shibun-ritsu 四分律 (Precepts in Four Divisions), a 60-fascicle translation of the vinaya of the Dharmagupta School

Zen-en-shingi 禪苑清規 (Pure Criteria for Zen Monasteries)

C. Commentaries

Bosatsuchi-ji-kyo 菩薩地持経 (Sutra of Maintaining the Bodhisattva-State)

Daibibasha-ron 大毘婆沙論 (Abhidharma-mahāvibhāṣa-śāstra)

Daichido-ron 大智度論 (Commentary on the Accomplishment which is Great Wisdom—in Sanskrit, Mahā-prajñā-pāramitopadeśa)

Daijogi-sho 大乗義章 (Writings on the Mahāyāna Teachings)

Hokke-zanmai-sengi 法華三昧懺儀 (A Humble Expression of the Form of the Samādhi of the Flower of Dharma)

Kusha-ron 俱舎論 (Abhidharma-kośa-śāstra)

Maka-shikan 摩訶止観 (Great Quietness and Reflection), a record of the lectures of Master Tendai Chigi, founder of the Tendai Sect

Maka-shikan-hogyo-den-guketsu 摩訶止観輔行伝弘決 (Extensive Decisions Transmitted in Support of Great Quietness and Reflection), a Chinese commentary on *Maka-shikan* by Master Keikei Tannen

D. General Chinese Buddhist Records

Daito-sai-iki-ki 大唐西域記 (Great Tang Records of Western Lands)

Go-to-roku 五燈録 (The Five Records of the Torch), five independent but complimentary collections compiled during the Sung era (960–1279). They are represented in summary form in **Go-to-egen** 五燈会元 (Collection of the Fundamentals of the Five Torches). Namely, the five records are:

Keitoku-dento-roku 景徳伝燈録 (Keitoku Era Record of the Transmission of the Torch)

Tensho-koto-roku 天聖廣燈録 (Tensho Era Record of the Widely Extending Torch)

Zokuto-roku 続燈録 (Supplementary Record of the Torch)

Rento-eyo 聯燈會要 (Collection of Essentials for Continuation of the Torch)
Katai-futo-roku 嘉泰普燈録 (Katai Era Record of the Universal Torch)

Hekigan-roku 碧巌録 (Blue Cliff Record)

Ho-en-shu-rin 法苑珠林 (A Forest of Pearls in the Garden of Dharma), a kind of Buddhist encyclopedia in 100 volumes

Kaigen-shakkyo-roku 開元釈教録 (Kaigen-era Records of Śākyamuni's Teaching)

Kosonshuku-goroku 古尊宿語録 (Record of the Words of the Venerable Patriarchs of the Past)

Rinkan-roku 林間録 (Forest Record), short for **Sekimon-rinkan-roku** 石門林間録 (Sekimon's Forest Record)

So-koso-den 宋高僧伝 (Biographies of Noble Monks of the Sung-era)

Zenmon-shososhi-geju 禪門諸祖師偈頌 (Verses and Eulogies of Ancestral Masters of the Zen Lineages)

Zenrin-hokun 禪林寶訓 (Treasure-Instruction from the Zen Forest)

Zenshu-juko-renju-tsushu 禪宗頌古聯珠通集 (Complete String-of-Pearls Collection of Eulogies to Past Masters of the Zen Sect)

Zoku-dento-roku 続伝燈録 (Continuation of the Record of the Transmission of the Torch), published in China in 1635; sequel to *Keitoku-dento-roku*

Zokukan-kosonshuku-goyo 続刊古尊宿語要 (Summarized Collection of the Words of the Venerable Patriarchs of the Past)

E. Records and Independent Works of Chinese Masters

Baso-Do-itsu-zenji-goroku 馬祖道一禪師語録 (Record of the Words of Zen Master Baso Do-itsu)

Bukka-geki-setsu-roku 佛果撃節録 (Record of Bukka's Attacks on Knotty Problems); [Bukka is an alias of Master Seccho Juken]

Chorei-Shutaku-zenji-goroku 長霊守卓禪師語録 (Record of the Words of Zen Master Chorei Shutaku)

Dai-e-Fugaku-zenji-shumon-buko 大慧普覚禪師宗門武庫 (The War Chest of the School of Zen Master Dai-e Fugaku [Dai-e Soko])

Dai-e-goroku 大慧語録 (Record of the Words of Dai-e [Soko])

Dai-e-zenji-tomei 大慧禪師塔銘 (Inscriptions on the Stūpa of Zen Master Dai-e [Soko])

Engo-zenji-goroku 圜悟禪師語録 (Record of the Words of Zen Master Engo [Kokugon])

Joshu-roku 趙州録 (Records of Joshu [Jushin])

Jugendan 十玄談 (Discussion of the Ten Kinds of Profundity), by Master Do-an Josatsu

Ho-en-zenji-goroku 法演禪師語録 (Record of the Words of Zen Master [Yogi] Ho-en)

Hokyo-zanmai 寶鏡三昧 (Samadhi, the State of a Jewel-Mirror), by Master Tozan Ryokai

Honei-Nin-yu-zenji-goroku 法寧仁勇禪師語録 (Record of the Words of Zen Master Honei Nin-yu)

Hyakujo-roku 百丈録 (Record of Hyakujo), short for **Hyakujo-Ekai-zenji-goroku** 百丈懐海禪師語録 (Record of the Words of Zen Master Hyakujo Ekai)

Koke-zenji-goroku 興化禪師語録 (Record of the Words of Zen Master Koke [Sonsho])

Kido-shu 虚堂集 (The Kido Collection), a collection of the words of Master Tanka Shijun, compiled by Rinsen Jurin

Nyojo-osho-goroku 如浄和尚語録 (Record of the Words of Master [Tendo] Nyojo)

O-an-Donge-zenji-goroku 応菴曇華禪師語録 (Record of the Words of Zen Master O-an Donge)

Rinzai-zenji-goroku 臨済禪師語録 (Record of the Words of Zen Master Rinzai [Gigen])

Rokuso-dankyo 六祖壇経 (The Sixth Patriarch's Platform Sutra), attributed to Master Daikan Eno

Sandokai 参同契 (Experiencing the State), by Master Sekito Kisen

Seccho-Myokaku-zenji-goroku 雪竇明覚禪師語録 (Record of the Words of Zen Master Seccho Myokaku [Seccho Juken])

Sekito-so-an no Uta 石頭草庵歌 (Songs from Sekito's Thatched Hut), by Master Sekito Kisen

Shodoka 証道歌 (Song of Experiencing the Truth), by Master Yoka Genkaku

Shinjinmei 信心銘 (Inscription on Believing Mind), by Master Kanchi Sosan

Sotai-roku 奏対録 (Record of Answers to an Emperor), by Master Bussho Tokko

Tozan-goroku 洞山語録 (Record of the Words of Tozan [Ryokai])

Unmon-koroku 雲門廣録 (Broad Record of Unmon [Bun-en])

Wanshi-zenji-goroku 宏智禪師語録 (Record of the Words of Zen Master Wanshi [Shokaku])

Wanshi-koroku 宏智廣録 (Broad Record of Wanshi [Shokaku])

Wanshi-juko 宏智頌古 (Wanshi's Eulogies to Past Masters), also known as **Shoyo-roku** 従容録 (The Relaxation Record)

Yafu-Dosen-kongo-kyo 冶父道川金剛経 (Yafu Dosen's Diamond Sutra)

F. CHINESE SECULAR BOOKS ETC.

Confucianist:

Kokyo 孝経 (The Book of Filial Piety)

Rongo 論語 (The Discourses [of Confucius])

Taoist:

Bunshi 文子 from the Chinese *Wen-tzu*, the name of the author to whom the text is ascribed

Kanshi 管子 from the Chinese *Guan-tzu*, the name of the supposed author

Shishi 尸子 from the Chinese *Shi-tzu*, the name of the supposed author

Soji 荘子 from the Chinese *Chuang-tzu*, the name of a disciple of Lao-tzu (the ancient Chinese philosopher regarded as the founder of Taoism)

Inzui 韻瑞 (Rhymes of Good Fortune)

Rikuto 六韜 (Six Strategies)

Sango-ryaku-ki 三五暦記 (History of the Three [Elements] and Five [Elements])

Miscellaneous

Jirui-senshu 事類撰集 (Collection of Matters and Examples)

Jibutsu-gen-ki 事物原記 (Record of the Origin of Things)

Jokan-seiyo 貞観政要 (Jokan Era [Treatise] on the Essence of Government)

Mei-hoki 冥報記 (Chronicles of the Underworld)

Taihei-koki 太平弘記 (Widely Extending Record of the Taihei Era)

Bibliography Two: Other Works by Master Dogen

Fukan-zazengi 普勧坐禅儀 (Universal Guide to the Standard Method of Zazen)

Gakudo-yojin-shu 學道用心集 (Collection of Concerns in Learning the Truth)

Hogyo-ki 寶慶記 (Hogyo Era Record)

Shinji-shobogenzo 真字正法眼蔵 (Right-Dharma-Eye Treasury, in Original [Chinese] Characters); [also known as the **Sambyaku-soku** 三百則]

Eihei-koroku 永平廣録 (Broad Record of Eihei)

Eihei-shingi 永平清規 (Pure Criteria of Eihei):

- **Tenzo-kyokun** 典座教訓 (Instructions for the Cook)
- **Bendo-ho** 辨道法 (Methods of Pursuing the Truth)
- **Fu-shuku-han-ho** 赴粥飯法 (The Method of Taking Meals)
- **Shuryo-shingi** 衆寮清規 (Pure Criteria for the Monks' Dormitory)
- **Tai-taiko-gogejari-ho** 對大己五夏闍梨法 (The Method of Meeting with Veteran Practitioners of Five Summer Retreats)
- **Chiji-shingi** 知事清規 (Pure Criteria for the Temple Officers)

Bibliography Three: Main Japanese References

Bukkyo-jiten:	edited by Ui Hakuju
Bukkyogo-daijiten:	3 volumes edited by Hajime Nakamura
Dai-kanwa-jiten:	13 volumes by Tetsuji Morohashi
Dogen-no-kenkyu:	by Hanji Akiyama
Dogen-zenji-den-no-kenkyu:	by Doshu Ohkubo
Dogen-zenji-no-hanashi:	by Ton Satomi
Hokke-kyo:	published by Iwanami Shoten
Jikai:	edited by Kyosuke Kinta-ichi
Sawaki-Kodo-zenshu:	19 volumes by Master Kodo Sawaki
Shin-bukkyo-jiten:	edited by Hajime Nakamura
Shinshu-kanwa-daijiten:	by Shikita Koyanagi
Shinshu-taisho-daizokyo:	by Daizo Shuppansha
Shobogenzo-chukai-zensho:	10 volumes by Nyoten Jinbo & Bun-ei Ando
Shobogenzo-ji-i:	by Soku-o Eto
Shobogenzo-keiteki:	by Bokuzan Nishi-ari
Shobogenzo-shaku-i:	4 volumes by Kunihiko Hashida
Shobogenzo:	published by Iwanami Shoten, commentary by Nishi-o, Kagamishima, Sakai, and Mizuno
Shoten-zoku-cho:	by Master Osen Mujaku
Sogo-rekishi-nenpyo:	edited by Kenzo Nakajima
Tetsugaku-jiten:	published by Heibon Sha
Tetsugaku-shojiten:	published by Iwanami Shoten
Watsuji-tetsuro-zenshu (vols. 4, 5):	by Tetsuro Watsuji
Zengaku-daijiten:	edited by scholars of Komazawa University
Zengaku-jiten:	by Nyoten Jinbo & Bun-ei Ando

(Texts printed in Taiwan)

Keitoku-dento-roku:	Shin Zen Bi Shuppansha
Zoku-zokyo:	Collection of Buddhist Sutras not included in Shinshu-taisho-daizokyo

Shobogenzo in Modern Japanese:

Gendaigo-yaku-shobogenzo 現代語訳正法眼蔵 (Shobogenzo in Modern Japanese) by G. W. Nishijima, twelve volumes plus a one-volume appendix

Shobogenzo-teisho-roku 正法眼蔵提唱録 (Record of Lectures on Shobogenzo), by G. W. Nishijima, thirty-four volumes

These volumes are obtainable from the publisher:

Kanazawa Bunko Co. Ltd., Sumitomo Ichigaya Bldg., Honmura-cho 1-1, Ichigaya, Shinjuku-ku, Tokyo
Tel: (03) 3235-7060
Fax: (03) 3235-7135

Bibliography Four: Main English References:

A Practical Sanskrit Dictionary [MAC]: A. A. Macdonell, Oxford University Press

A Sanskrit–English Dictionary [MW]: Sir Monier Monier-Williams, Oxford University Press

Japanese Character Dictionary: Andrew Nelson, published by Charles Tuttle

Japanese Character Dictionary: Mark Spahn & Wolfgang Hadamitzky, published by Nichigai Asssociates

Japanese–English Buddhist Dictionary [JEBD]: published by Daito Shuppansha

Kenkyusha's New Japanese–English Dictionary: editor in chief, Koh Masuda

The Historical Buddha [HB]: H. W. Schumann, published by Arkana

The Threefold Lotus Sutra [LSW]: Kato and Soothill, published by Weatherhill

PRODUCTION NOTES:

This book was designed by Michael Luetchford and produced by Michael Luetchford and Jeremy Pearson. Typesetting was done entirely on an Apple Macintosh system using Microsoft Word, and output to a Fuji-Xerox Laserwind 1040PS laser printer.

New kanji Postscript characters were created using the Gaiji Edit Kit from Enfour Media Laboratory, Tokyo. Sanskrit fonts were created and supplied by Lew Mark-Andrews of Image Arts Inc., Tokyo.

The text and display typeface is Palatino.

Windbell Publications is the publishing arm of Dogen Sangha, an international group of people studying Buddhism in Tokyo with Nishijima Roshi.

For more information about the activities of Dogen Sangha and Windbell Publications, please visit our Web site at http://www.windbell.com. On the site you can also find a number of texts freely available for downloading.

Front cover: Portrait of Master Dogen Viewing the Moon, reproduced courtesy of Hokyo-ji, Fukui Prefecture.

Back cover: Portion of a scroll of *Fukan-zazengi*, believed to be in Master Dogen's own hand.